MW00593234

2002
Days & Nights
of SEX

2002
Days & Nights
of SEX

Richard Smith

BLACK DOG
& LEVENTHAL
PUBLISHERS
NEW YORK

Published by
Black Dog & Leventhal Publishers, Inc.
151 West 19th Street
New York, NY 10011

Distributed by
Workman Publishing Company
708 Broadway
New York, NY 10003

Designed by Tony Meisel

Library of Congress Cataloging-in-Publication Data
Smith, Richard, 1941–
      2002 days & nights of sex / by Richard Smith.
          p.   cm.
      Includes bibliographical references.
      ISBN   1-57912-045-8 (hardcover : alk. paper)
      1. Sex—Miscellanea.   2. Sex—Humor. I. Title.
  HQ23.S57   1998
306.7—dc21   98-28006
                                                CIP

Manufactured in the United States of America

ISBN: 1-57912-045-8

h   g   f   e   d   c   b   a

Contents

2002 Days and Nights of Sex

"Not tonight dear, I'm on the Internet."

We understand. The pressures of today's fast-paced world leave little time for sex. Even couples who want children, rather than waste time on frivolities like satin sheets, intercourse and wheezing, simply reach for the Yellow Pages and rely on the services of a fertility clinic.

Yet, satellite photos indicate that a growing number of people (besides those residing in trailer parks) are having more sex. Not only is frequent sex a stress-reliever, but, when supplemented by visits to Disneyland, can draw couples closer and revitalize a stale relationship. (You may actually find yourselves sneaking up to the bedroom for a quick romp before the guests arrive.)

2002 Days and Nights of Sex is a month-by-month sex management system, enabling time-pressed people—working couples, soccer moms, golfing pops, newlyweds, the newly divorced, even campaigning politicians—the opportunity to reap the rewards of a rich, abundant sex life. The book offers you two choices: Either enjoy 2,002 consecutive days and nights of sex (an approach that practically guarantees immunity to hemorrhoids); or space sexual activity out over a number of years, an alternate strategy that can increase longevity by up to 17 hours.

Remember, it is the quality rather than the quantity—studies have repeatedly shown that seven minutes of passionate sex is far more satisfying than two hours of S & M while watching The Weather Channel.

NOTE: As you work your way through the book, the benefits of regular sexual activity become manifest. Take special note of positive physical side effects such as:
- Hair: No more split ends
- Eyes: Noticeably fewer crow's feet
- Cheekbones: Much, much higher
- Abs: Tighter (or diminished beer belly, whichever comes first)
- Expression: Dreamy, far away stare (often mistaken for a Prozac "high")

JANUARY

Erotic goals for January:

1. Lose ten pounds
2. Lose virginity

Couples whose waistlines are "in recovery" from too much holiday spirit will want to spend the next few weeks following our exclusive Resolution to Lose 10 Pounds diet:

Romantic Activity	Burns Off
Flirting with each other	2 glasses of Champagne
Cuddling	6 ounces egg nog
Blowing in partner's ear	1 Godiva chocolate
Using a leaf blower	Entire box
Petting above the waist	1 small brownie
Petting below the waist	25 Hershey's® Kisses
Frantic groping	8 eclairs
Undressing partner	3 ounces caviar
Who's wearing a body stocking	Entire fish
Explaining what you really like	1 slice, cheesecake
If he's learning disabled	50 chocolate chip cookies
Intercourse – regular	1 scoop of ice cream
Intercourse – intense	1 pint of ice cream
(trailer falls off its foundation)	
Changing positions	4 french fries
While fending off a playful Akita	300 clam fritters
Regular orgasm (earth moves)	Medium slice, peach pie
Intense orgasm (bed slats break)	8 Buffalo chicken wings
Trying again	Tiramisu, huge helping
If he's watching the playoffs	2 pitchers, Miller Lite

Official aphrodisiac of the month:
Tic Tacs and alfalfa sprouts (you're dieting)

Five New Year's Resolutions

I resolve to be:

1. More optimistic (and buy a double bed).
2. Sexier (and burn those ratty slipper socks).
3. Less inhibited (no more covering my partner's ears when I moan).
4. More romantic (buy better, softer sheets for those special nights).
5. More considerate (snore after, instead of during, lovemaking).

Your Guaranteed Sexual Forecast

As a result of meeting a new and glorious love, you will:

• Discover (at last) an effective form of stress management.
• Cease taking phone calls during lovemaking.
• Be nice to your parents.
• Consider the purchase of a larger bed (or at least a new mattress—watch for sales).
• Achieve your target heart rate on a regular basis.
• Firm up.
• Slim down.
• Discover an astonishing ability to sleep till noon.

Suggested Goals

To find a lover who:

• Loves you for who you are.
• Belongs to the right club (optional).
• Always gets you in the mood.
• Finishes what you start.
• Doesn't know when to stop.
• Doesn't believe in portion control.
• Provides instant relief.
• Works the way a lover's supposed to.
• Can recommend a good mutual fund.

Seven More New Year's Resolutions

For variety and a year of incessant romance, resolve to make love at least once:

1. Spontaneously. (In your car, while waiting for the light to change.)
2. In a room other than your bedroom. (In the kitchen, while cooking a romantic dish like crab cakes.)

3. On an isolated beach. (Good: Aruba. Bad: Coney Island.)
4. On a canopied four-poster bed at a country inn. (Note: If bed is an heirloom, please go easy.)
5. In front of a roaring fire. (If no fireplace is available, in front of an oven heated to 450 degrees is nearly as good.)
6. Under a shady tree. (Good: in a deserted park. Not so good: in the middle of a yard sale.)
7. At a corporate headquarters (for the adventure).

The First Five Commandments of Sex

1. Thou shalt not deny thy mate's connubial rights because you want to watch (a) the playoffs and (b) the players.
2. During sex, thou shalt block out all distracting thoughts, such as traffic noise and the cost of the motel room.
3. Thou shalt not patronize a sex therapist who has not performed before a jury of his or her peers.
4. Thou shalt not discuss health reform during climax.
5. Thou shalt not check thy watch if thy partner is taking too much time to "finish" (unless thou hast a roast in the oven.)

Any Time of the Year Resolutions

1. Have more sex. (a) You'll walk around less angry and (b) It'll strengthen your marriage.
2. Meet a special someone who will (a) give you everything you want and (b) the one thing that you need.
3. Avoid partners who want you only for your (a) body, (b) trust fund, and (c) parenting potential.
4. Lose five pounds by spending less time in the kitchen and more time in the bedroom. (Tip: Use your lover as a free weight.)
5. Be less impulsive. (Wait until he gets in the door to jump him. You'll have fewer complaints from the Neighborhood Watch.)

The Dieter's Guide to Weight Loss During Sex

Four new positions for January.

Position	Calories Burned
Missionary (feminist): Man on top but woman doing most of the work	62
Missionary (masculist): Woman on top and doing *all* the work	185
Missionary (weary): Both lying down, facing each other	45
Missionary (wary): Both lying down, back to back	623

Pillow Talk

Sex Object. A pejorative term applied to people who are regarded less for their secretarial skills or philosophical outlook and more for their capacity to incite feelings of lust just by standing there (not always such a bad talent). Among sex scholars, controversy rages over whether "sex objects" can be valued also for their minds – a "stacked" systems, analyst, say, or a metaphysical hunk.

Note: Curiously, those who report never having been regarded as a sex object tend to express some regret.

Love Signs

One sign fits all. Our exclusive generic horoscope for lovers born under a billboard:

- *Ruling passion:* hands-on lovemaking and macaroons
- *Ruling sexual turnoff:* whisker burn
- *Chief sexual asset:* a libido the size of Greenland
- *Governing erogenous zones:* Cancun and the inside of your jeans
- *Aphrodisiac:* The four basic food groups, and tapas
- *Ruling sexual activity:* causing fireworks in lovers with a short fuse
- *Ideal times for sex:* day in, day out

Tip For the Environmentally Responsible

If great sex with your lover made the earth move, it's your responsibility to put it back.

Alternate Love Signs

Our exclusive horoscope for lovers who hate their own sign.
- *Ruling passion*: High-voltage sex without shorting out.
- *Sexual turnoff*: Lovers who dial 911 when you tell them what turns you on.
- *Sexual assets:* Good genes and a graphic imagination.
- *Favorite erogenous zones:* Your "Gee!" spot and Cuba.
- *Aphrodisiac:* Anything high in fiber (like a carrot or your lover's earlobe).
- *Ruling sexual activities:* Taking no prisoners.
- *Ideal time for sex:* The summer (when the kids are at camp).

Ecstasy: The Official Guide

Orgasm—the Five Levels
1. Sudden release of unreleased tension (and more indigestion).
2. Big smile.
3. The feeling you've been transported, nonstop, to Cloud Nine. (receive 100 bonus miles.)
4. The feeling you've been transported, nonstop, to Marlboro Country. (200 extra bonus miles).
5. Pelvis has achieved critical mass. Final climax can power Steubenville, Ohio, for a week.

January's Sexual Bill of Rights

You are entitled to a lover who:
- Can't get enough of you.
- Is always in the mood.
- Satisfies you totally and completely.
- Communicates sexual excitement by means other than a fax.
- Is in mint physical condition.
- Knows what you like (or at least has excellent learning skills).
- Doesn't keep asking, "How am I doing?"
- Cares.

Sexual Promises

Promise

1. To lose weight so I'll look terrific in my new cruisewear outfits.
2. To engage in cleaner living.
3. To perform community service.
4. To be kinder to my fellow man.

How to Implement

1. Have more sex. (Just one 8-hour sexual encounter can burn off the equivalent of two German chocolate cakes.)
2. Shower more with your lover.
3. Have an affair with a neighbor.
4. *You* sleep in the wet spot.

Heroic Moments in Sex

"While nibbling his ear, his earring got caught in my teeth. I didn't stop."

> – Paloma, corrections officer

"Her pearls broke in the middle of her climax. She kept right on going while I picked them up and restrung them. What a tigress!"

> – Orville, animal lover

"Our ankle bracelets got tangled up. Instead of admitting defeat we invented a new position and continued."

> – Arabella and Franz, farmers

Gem of the Month

Garnets to the lover whose lovemaking:

1. Replenishes your soul, especially when he or she uses both hands.
2. Gives new meaning to the concept of "overtime."
3. Often keeps you up all night.
4. Yet makes you wish the night would never end.
5. Brings you breakfast in bed (Belgian waffles, maple syrup and cocoa, to be precise).
6. And, afterward, does the dishes.

The Post-Holiday Emergency Diet
Our weight-loss guide for lovers who are over-indulged.

Lose	By
2 pounds.	Changing positions without (a) pausing and (b) informing your partner.
3 pounds.	Before sex, carrying your partner into the bedroom and gently lowering him onto the bed (add 2 pounds if he'd rather sit up).
17 pounds.	After sex, gently lifting your partner and carrying her into the bathroom so she can get ready for work (add 3 pounds if she hates her job).

Approved Condom Substitutes
- Abstinence
- Just hugging
- Just saying no
- Poison ivy
- Seeing her without makeup
- Seeing him in nothing but over-the-calf business socks
- Wet suits
- Keeping your seat belt fastened
- Your conscience
- Bootleg Viagra

Passion Scale (Level I)
A "bare bones" climax: not too loud, not too soft, just right if you don't want to disturb the neighbors. Partner may not even notice you had one.

How Manifested

Emission of little bleeps or, for those under 5'3", little blips. Gentle, knowing smile may decorate your lips. Fluttering of eyelids may cause partner some concern.

Suggested Positions for January
1. The Commuter position:

Man anxiously waiting.

Woman shouting "All aboard!"

2. The Energy-Saving position:
Both saying, "Not tonight, dear."

The Enlightened Lover
Make sure you find a lover who:
• Is ultra responsive.
• Is considerate (never answers the phone during sex unless it's her agent).
• After sex, always helps you clear the dishes.
• Never chews gum during sex.
• Makes house calls.
• Would rather fight about money than about sex.
• Waits until after sex to ask, "Was it good for you?"

The Recovering Lover

After steamy sex, a partner should be able to:	In:
Fall asleep	2.4 seconds
Walk unassisted to the bathroom	3 to 4 minutes
Operate heavy machinery –	
The toaster	7 minutes
A Q-tip	3 minutes
Tie sneaker laces	4.5 minutes
Flawlessly accessorize a wardrobe	1 hour
Competently sign a prenuptial agreement	1 week
Perform again (sorry, no hard data)	

Don't Forget . . .
The Intellectual Position
He: On top, having the time of his life.
She: Curled up with a good book.

The Enlightened Lover
Two hours of marvelous lovemaking once a week can help even the most fragile psyche withstand the rigors of:
• A sadistic boss.
• Trying to sell your house in a weak market.
• A volatile stock portfolio.
• Dieting.
• Psychoanalysis.
• A stale marriage.

Pizza and Sex: Part I

Don't order just any pizza when making love; it may not react favorably with your particular type of lovemaking. Some tips:

Type of Lovemaking
Frenetic, frantic, much perspiration, oodles of intercourse in all $16\frac{1}{2}$ positions, moaning in major *and* minor keys, a feeling that you can't get enough of each other.

Ideal Topping
Pepperoni (for energy), fresh mushrooms and onions (for luck) and green peppers (for roughage). (Candy corn also good).

What We Did for Sex

"Bought a sheer imported cotton nightdress with tiny bodice buttons and eyelet lace (midcalf length)."
      – Dee Dee, bus driver
"Helped her out of it."
      – Ben, Dee Dee's husband

Critics' Sexual Choice

Recommended position for the superior woman with a superior attitude:
Man: On bottom
Woman: Lowering herself

Advice from the Experts

The Problem
During sex, I often get the feeling that if I'm also talking to my ex on the phone, even if it's important, my partner feels excluded and sulks.

The Solution
Either:
1. Put your ex on hold and concentrate on your partner.
Or:
2. Let your partner say hello.

Lovers' Poll: #7

What was the wildest thing you ever did during a Level 8 climax?
"Revealed my middle name (Algernon)."
      – Matt, state trooper

"Went on to a Level 9. Still can't see straight."
　　　　– Claudia, bar maid
"Faked it."
　　　　– Millicent, cartographer
"Met her parents. Next time we lock the door."
　　　　– Harry, lawyer

Lovers' Seasonal Calendar

Ideal time to	Winter	Spring	Summer	Fall
Enjoy a second honeymoon in:				
Bermuda	X			
a Jacuzzi	X	X	X	X
Dine with your lover: al fresco		X	X	X
au naturel	X	X	X	X
Meet the perfect lover		X		
Make love: in your sleeping bag				
on your sleeping bag	X			X
Lose your innocence	X	X	X	X
Regain it	X		X	

> "Sex is the perfect Sunday morning activity– it's cheap, aerobic, and you don't have to reserve a court."
> – Googie Heimlich, dairy farmer

Climax: The Five Official Stages

1. *Honorable mention* – not too big, not too small, just right.

2. *Magical (more "feelable" than above)* – body is glowing and you don't care that you chipped a nail.

3. *Bed alert* – intense passion has somehow caused the bed to make its way into an adjoining community.

4. *Red alert (ultra-intense)* – you may actually experience a memory lapse in which you can't recall the name of our current vice president.

5. *Time release (rare)* – a series of aftershocks that may continue for up to one hour. Do not operate heavy machinery.

Words to the Wise Lover
• A night without sex is like a meal without wine.
• A meal without sex is like a night without wine.
• A meal without wine is like a night without sex.
• Sex without wine can still be pretty good.

Your Personal Sexual Forecast
• A naughtier, less puritanical you will call in sick more often so you can sleep late...with your lover.
• You will engage in cleaner sex by making sure to (a) vacuum cookie crumbs off the sheets before making love and (b) take more showers with your lover.
• You will finally begin to regard lovemaking as a contact sport (this will make your lover very happy).
• The flowering of your sex life will produce a significant decrease, by summer, of hay fever symptoms.
• There will be a major increase in sex between consenting adults. Happily, you'll be one of them.

10 Can't-Fail Excuses for Not Having Sex
1. Still waiting for the right one to come along.
2. Exhausted from having so much last month.
3. Compant policy,
4. Too depressed (found squirrels in the bird feeder).
5. All the good ones are taken.
6. Decided to lose weight the modern way (liposuction).
7. Switched to a less expensive sin (snuff).
8. Lover on loan (to U. S. Navy).
9. Lover on loan (to close friend).
10. My aunt keeps fixing me up.

Words of Wisdom
Cuddling in front of a glowing fire with a new lover is the perfect way to a) burn old bridges and b) forget an old flame.

The Ideal Male Sex Partner

A guide for discriminating women.

Assets:

1. Gorgeous face, yummy pecs, iron shoulders. A certified hunk.
2. Great sense of humor, sexual technique to burn, hands that could tune a Ferrari.
3. Stamina of Batman.
4. All action.

Will Compensate for:

1. I.Q. of 70. (Lip reads the "Help us improve our service" cards in motels.)
2. Poverty, unpromising future and has dinner with Mom every Wednesday night.
3. Teensy member (size of Robin's).
4. No talk.

A Lover's Seasonal Calendar

Ideal Time to:	Winter	Spring	Summer	Fall
Fall in love	X	X	X	X
Cuddle	X	X		X
Do it on a mountaintop		X		X
Skinny-dip with a lover			X	
Dump a lover with allergies		X	X	
Find a lover with body hair	X			
Date a voluptuous lover	X			X
Make love before a roaring fire				X
Make love	X	X	X	X

The Enlightened Lover

Some favorite after-sex pastimes:

1. Hungry? Feed each other ice cream.
2. Tired? Wait till it melts.
3. Want to improve? Study the videotape.
4. Contemplative? Observe an hour of silence.
5. Nothing to do? Help the kids with their homework.
6. Proud of your performance? Boast.
7. Curious? Hold a debriefing.
8. Still have lots of energy? Make the bed.
9. Still not satisfied? Try again.
10. Still restless? Check local movie listings.

Fitness Hint

You can't reduce stomach fat by exercising only the abdominal muscles. That's why we have:
- a personal trainer
- a personal lover
- sex

Note: If 1 and 2 are the same, double fat loss.

Not Sure How to React?

Recent ruling. He'll consider a sexual advance.

Welcome if:

You make him a counter offer.

Unwelcome if:

You make him a countertenor.

Nostalgia Tip

Seeing an old lover you never quite got over is a good way to:
- Realize why you broke up.
- See how he's aging.
- Compare him to your new lower.
- Get your dignity back.
- Get your keys back.

The Ideal Female Sex Partner
A guide for the fussy man.

Assets	Will Compensate for:
High cheekbones, perfect teeth, exquisitely sensual curve to small of back, wanton lips.	Flawed apartment, under-stocked refrigerator, a schnauzer that sheds.
Buxom, torrid eyes, great tan, leggy, and feet match perfectly.	Inability to bake a shepherd's pie, talks baby talk to her cat.
Terrific kisser, firm body, endlessly inventive.	Lack of career goals.
Trust fund.	Can't spend it till she's 60.

The Enlightened Lover
The 10 authorized stages of intercourse.
1. Togetherness.
2. Slow and easy.
3. Loss of control.
4. Elvis impersonation.*
5. Lift-off.
6. Enjoying the air rights above lover.
7. Moaning.
8. Groaning.
9. Silence.
10. Encore.
*Caution: Keys may fall out of pants.

The Dieter's Guide to Weight Loss
Just Moments Before Sex

Activity	Calories Burned
The jitters– caused by:	
Your first time with a new partner	26
Your first time, ever	100
Shyness	44
Guilt (it all feels much too good)	60
Anchovies	326
Coffee	35
Diouble latté	400

Question of the Day
An informal, unscientific shopping mall poll where we asked random individuals, "Why do you have sex?"*
• "It's one of the ten over-the-counter remedies I always keep on hand for migraines."
• "To repay her for carrying these four heavy bags of groceries."
• "For my ego. I was desperate until I discovered that having sex four times weekly could cure my impotence."
• "For beating the afternoon blahs. I find vigorous lovemaking with my husband perks me up far more pleasantly than twelve cups of coffee."
• "We want more children."
*All answers verbatim.

Quote of the Night
Things often said after:
• So-so sex with a new lover: *"I think I'm ready to settle."*
• Incredibly so-so sex with a new lover: *"I think I'm ready to settle down."*

Today's Sexual Forecast
Under mysterious circumstances (a blind date arranged by your florist), you will meet a perfect lover and partner either for life or for quite a long time. As a result you will:
• Cease calling friends to complain that a) there are no men out there or b) all the good women are taken.
• Finally understand why regular lovemaking is nature's remedy for a) stress and b) reading *Playboy*.
• Discharge your personal trainer.
• Change careers and get a job that pays more (two *can't* live as cheaply as one).
• Be sorry your tattoo says "butch".

Q. After sex, who pays for damaged furnishings?
A. The overturned night table, a shattered Ming vase—ardor takes its toll. According to a recent Supreme Court decision, the "instigator," that person who caused the other person to lose control and, say, fling the bedspread out the window, is responsible for all sex-related losses.

The Adventurous Lover: Part I
New places

For the Fun	For the Challenge
On grass	On Astroturf
Your laundry room	A laundromat
On newly fallen snow	On tightly packed snow
In the rear of a limo	In the rear of a New York City taxi
In a forest, on moss	In a forest, on something that appears to be breathing
In a bubble bath	On packing bubbles
On a Persian carpet	Still in its country of origin

Sexual Rules of Thumb
Assume there will be no sex tonight if:
1. After 30 minutes of foreplay, you still can't get her to put down her novel.
2. He puts on his sleeping mask as he's finishing dessert.
3. His bowling team lost.
4. His nightcap consists of three brandy flips.
5. She places a Help Wanted sign at the foot of the bed.
6. The dog is sleeping between you and your lover (and snoring).

From Our Lover's Glossary
"I'm so close." 1. The point, during sex, of no return. 2. That moment, during sex, when proper etiquette dictates that the partner of the person who utters this phrase must not:
• Run to the kitchen for a snack
• Make a phone call
• Presume sex is nearly over and begin to dress
• Gently inquire, "So close to what?"

Prediction
An ex-lover will call to ask if he or she can

See you again:	What to do:
For dinner.	Accept. Ex-lover will pay, so order surf 'n'turf.
To try to rekindle the flame.	If you're interested, accept. If not, hand ex a book of matches.
For sex.	Accept, if only to re-remind you why you dumped him in the first place.
To borrow $500.00.	Gently hang up.

Creative Lovemaking Tip

When you and your partner redecorate the bedroom remember:
•A queen-size bed leaves more room for lovemaking.
•A king-size bed leaves even more room for the imagination.

What I Did For Love

"Ignored my beeper."
> — Bennett M., emergency repairman

The Art of Romance

Four intimate things two lovers should share during sex:
1. Their innermost thoughts
2. Their innermost fantasies
3. The last taco
4. The channel clicker

Great Moments in Contact Visits

"She forgot to wax her legs; I got stubble burn. What a woman, what a night."
> — Craig, prisoner of love #855403

"He forgot to shave; I got a whisker burn. What a night, what a knight!"
> — Trish, Craig's visitor.

National Rapture Week

For the next seven days, improve your sex life by:
• Being more aggressive with your partner.
• Doing something sexy (don't wear socks to bed).
• Turning the TV to the wall and making love nightly.
• Violating company rules (thinking about sex after you punch in).
• Making love at least once (a) in the suburbs, (b) under the stars, (c) under a star.
• Throwing away that sex manual and being more inventive.
• Sharing your sexual fantasies with your lover (be gentle if partner curls up into a ball and starts to tremble).
• Getting a pet.

How Sex Helped

"My doctor told me that it was the only thing I could have the night before surgery. It worked better than the sedative."
— Barry, clam digger

"It makes the creative juices flow when I get writer's block."
— Sherry, romance novelist

"For two weeks before my twentieth high school reunion, my husband and I did it twice a night. I wanted to get in shape and look extra-good for ex-high school sweetheart."
— Kimberly, beautician

The Intuitive Lover: Part I

How do you hint to your spouse that you want to make love?
"Before we go to bed, I spend only three minutes in the bathroom, just enough time to remove my makeup, bathe and pray."
— Mira, time-management expert

"I pat her side of the bed, grin and say, 'Wish you were here.'"
— Craig, baggage handler

"I insert a special contact lens– it puts a glint in my eye."
— Suzanne, housewife

"That's easy, I push our beds together."
— Maurice, rocket scientist

The Two-Career Couple

Five reasons for a weak sex life:
1. She's sleeping when he gets home.
2. He's sleeping when she gets home.
3. Both are sleeping when both get home.
4. Both too tired to enjoy it.
5. Both not tired enough to enjoy it.

Thought for Tonight
Unspeakable sexual acts are best performed with a silent partner.

In Search of Romance

Eight best places to make love:
1. *For the atmosphere*: a hanson cab
2. *For the fresh air*: the Adirondacks

3. *For the tan*: Bermuda
4. *For the experience:* a restaurant booth
5. *For the wildlife:* any reputable zoo
6. *For the view*: the bathtub
7. *For your country*: the United States
8. *For the country*: Vermont

First Things First

For the busy, harried, two-career couple, making love in the morning:
1. Gets sex out of the way.
2. Keeps your evenings free for the important things.
3. Burns off the calories in your sticky bun.
4. Makes the commute more tolerable.

From Our Lover's Glossary

Casual Sex: *1.* Any sexual encounter that occurs (a) by chance (example: you and your lover suddenly pull off the highway and make love on a picnic table*); or (b) for pleasure, not for procreation; or (c) by accident (you both find yourselves in bed at the same time). 2. Any sexual encounter for which you don't put on makeup.
*Apologize if you crush the sandwiches of the people already sitting there.

Ethics Tip

A loyal spouse should never try to double his or her pleasure by having an affair with twins.

Love Poll #1

Percentage of 1,000 women polled in Tulsa, Oklahoma, who said that during lovemaking they prefer to be:

On top	26%
On the bottom	31%
Somewhere in the room	96%
With two men	28%
With one man who has the energy of two	37%
In control	24%
Out of control	100%

Sexual Rule of Thumb

Lovemaking– if it's worth doing at all, it's worth doing:
- In bed
- On the sofa
- In the jacuzzi
- In a meadow (check for farmers on patrol)
- In your car
- On the plane (for best results, place meal tray in upright position)
- Well

Sex Without Tears

The lover from:

Heaven	Hell
Is the person your mother warned you about (at last)	Is the person your friends warned you about (alas)
Brings flowers	To which you're allergic
Always calls	Only to break a date
Is always ready for sex	Leaves IOU's
Has no past.	Has no future.
Will make you see stars (Sirius)	Will make you see stars (Madonna)

A Lover's Horoscope

Our exclusive one-sign-fits-all predictions for lovers with the wrong birthdate.
- *Ruling passion*: unchecked sexuality no matter what the weather.
- *Chief sexual assets:* a new king-size bed and a great recipe for strudel.
- *Most responsive erogenous zones:* shell of your ear and London.
- *Favorite sexual activity:* wearing out your welcome.
- *Aphrodisiacs of choice:* peanut butter cookies and fan mail.
- *Sexual turnoffs*: whisker burn and lovers who want to do unnatural things with a pint of Ben & Jerry's
- *Compatible with:* any lusty lifeguard with a social conscience.

Phone Sex Advisory

If, during sex, your partner takes a phone call

You needn't stop if:

She rolls her eyes and mouths, "It's my husband, he wants me to bring home a loaf of bread."

You should stop if:

He holds the phone to your ear and says, "Say hi to my girlfriend."

How Sex Affects Longevity

Each time your lover	Add to life:	Subtract from life:
Nibbles on your ear lobes In front of your parents	20 minutes	18 minutes
Brings you flowers to which you are allergic	18 minutes	5 minutes
Wake you in the morning with his breath	25 minutes	1 hour
Whispers I'm leaving my fortune to my husband	5 hours	1 day

Communication Tip

A purring lover is the ultimate sign of contentment. (Unless it's the cat throwing its voice.)

The Dieter's Guide to Weight Loss During Sex

Critics' choice—two positions

Position	Calories Burned
Woman on bottom, man on his high horse	93
Man on bottom, woman on pedestal	157

The Inquisitive Lover

Questions most often asked by inquiring partners.

Before sex: "Is it me, or my trust fund?"

During sex: "Are we having fun yet?"

After sex: "Was that climax fact or friction?"

The Achievement-Oriented Lover—Goals:
To find a love who:
- Can raise your temperature.
- Can lower your cholesterol.
- Desires you fervently.
- Doesn't turn ashen when you suggest, after 4 hours of sex, "Let's try again."
- Is always on call to help you work off extra pounds so you'll look great in bicycle pants.
- Is recession-proof.
- Can help you with your resumé.
- Gets excited and calls out your name during sex...even if you aren't there.

Is It Getting Serious? Part 1
Met someone new? The warning signs that it just might be love. For him:
1. Sending sympathy cards to his old girlfriends.
2. Talking about her to his friends.
3. Buying
    - Another pot
    - Another towel
    - Another set of sheets
    - More hangers
    - Dishes that actually match

Tips for Cautious Lovers
Consider carefully before a) answering or b) asking these six loaded questions
1. "Do you like children?"
2. "What is the best sex you ever had?"
3. "Where were you last night?"
4. "Where have you been all my life?"
5. "What have you told your friends about me?"
6. "Where do we go from here?"

The Art of Romance
When driving your lover to ecstasy, be certain:
• Your wipers work.
• Your seat belt is fastened.
• You have enough gas.

The You-Thought-of-Everything-Bedroom
Five crucial extras.

Item	Purpose
Lie detector	To confirm that lovemaking is too good to be true.
Bible	To swear on in case partner says "you're the best."
Escape ladder	To toss over side of bed if sex gets too hot.
Sewing kit	To mend garments torn during fervid undressing.
Carrot on a stick	For lovers who do it like rabbits.

For Bold Lovers
Stolen sexual moments – where to do it:
• On an escalator – stand close to each other and smile at other, less fortunate shoppers.
• At a party – in the bathroom, behind the shower curtain. If you're quiet, no one will suspect.
• In the kitchen – while lover is slaving over a hot microwave, you slave over lover. (It works!)
• In a restaurant – on a leather banquette is best. Beware of table hoppers.
• At home – while the sitter's watching the kids.

Worksheet for Aggressive Lovers

After dinner check the appropriate box, detach this page and present it to your lover

----------detach here----------

Dearest, I'm still hungry for:

Just some dessert:

a Klondike Bar ___

Raisinets ___

Nibbling your fingertips ___

Knowledge ___

A nice glass of warm milk ____

A really good game of Scrabble

A cigar ___

Love:

Platonic ____

The other kind ____

A mixture of both ___

After Great Sex

To make a new lover feel extra-special:

• Pick up the phone and introduce her to your parents.
• Promote him from side dish to main dish.
• Exchange phone numbers.
• If there's no tree handy, carve her initials on the wall.
• Thank him for clearing your sinuses.
• Don't let him or her leave without:
  • Asking for a rematch.
  • Signing the bedsheet.
  • Name your car after her.

When You're in the Mood

Award-winning way to let her know.

"In the morning when the alarm goes off, I whisper, 'Let's mate,' then I press up against her, stroke her back and kiss her on the neck. This way, I get her before she gets to her garlic bagel."

– Otis, retired

The Enlightened Lover
There is nothing wrong with making love on an empty stomach, especially if it belongs to your partner.

Sex: What It Takes

To be better:	Best:
Energy	Synergy
Patience	A long shelf-life
Endurance	Stamina
Creativity	Originality
An interesting past	A dissolute past
Good luck	Good genes
A challenge	A rival
Talent	Artistry
A long time	Forever

The Art of Romance
In-bed etiquette:

To dab away tears of:	Use
Joy	A tissue
Laughter	A washcloth
Love	A paper towel
Passion	A napkin (paper)
Gratitude	A napkin (damask)
Relief	Edge of the pillowcase

Note: For tears caused by a lover who's eaten onions, use a cotton ball.

Beauty Tip
Dermatologists tell us that during wild lovemaking, the force of two frantic partners rubbing against each other can actually:
• Cleanse oily skin
• Moisturize dry skin
• Perk up lifeless skin
• Remove dead skin cells
• Erase even the most stubborn bikini line

Disappointing Moments in Lovemaking

"After two hours of magical sex she asked me for my hand but not, alas, in marriage."

> – Ward, high school

"I...I thought we'd made the earth move; turns out it was just a political upheaval."

> – Newlyweds honeymooning in the Middle East

"Because he'd taken a vacation day he insisted, during sex, that I do all the work."

> – Connie, newscaster

From Our Lover's Glossary

Snuggling. *1.* Intense cuddling. 2. A chilly-morning procedure* in which two lovers, reluctant to get out of bed, cling to each other and doze, hoping that, somehow, the morning will go away.

*It is not unheard of, especially if the thermometer has dropped to below 20 degrees, for one person, loath to emerge from beneath nice warm covers, to ask his or her partner, "Will you go to the bathroom for me?"

Bedside Manners

Should you be angry if your lover answers phone during sex?

No, if:	**Yes, if:**
It's a wrong number.	Lover keeps talking anyway.
There's a dial tone.	There's a moan.
Lover takes call in other room.	Lover takes call in other room—and closes the door.
Lover smiles and says, "Hi, Mom!"	Lover reddens and says, "I can't talk now!"

The Perfect Guest Lover

How to make sure you'll be invited back.

Do:

Bring a gift.

Pay for long-distance calls.

Leave something to the imagination.

Use the guest towel.

Ask for a souvenir.

Help clean up sex-related debris (bottles, pizza boxes, etc.)

Do not:
Neglect to wipe your feet.
Bring a guest.
Leave something to be desired.
Take it with you.
As for a reference.
Neglect to recycle.

Safety Tips for Ardent Lovers
After really steamy, exhausting, but totally satisfying sex:
• Never stand up too quickly.
• Don't worry if you can't quite walk a straight line.
• Always use the handrail when descending the stairs.
• Don't try to figure out how to set the timer on your VCR.
• Never attempt to read a Chinese take-out menu.
• Avoid hang gliding.
• Don't panic if you see only the whites of your partner's eyes.
• Panic, definitely, if you see the whites of your own.

Most Compulsive Sex Partners of All
"My husband the waiter. During oral sex he always tries to remove my plate before I'm finished."
> – Marlene, Astrologer

"My wife. Every night, out of habit, she wakes me at 1:30 A.M. and makes me take a pill. She's a nurse."
> – Anthony, golf pro

Cold-Weather Testimonial
The four best things about loving a chubby partner:
1. It shows you don't discriminate.
2. They appreciate your cooking.
3. There's so much more to have sex with.
4. On those cold winter nights– warmth without wait.

Turn-Ons
Seven things likely to arouse an especially sensitive lover.
1. Soft lighting, romantic music and poetry.
2. Neck kisses while muttering tender words of endearment.
3. The aroma of a toasting English muffin.

4. An all-leather sleeping bag.
5. Beating a speeding ticket.
6. Just enough cologne.
7. An insurance physical.

Sexual Ethics: Part I
Mercy sex is justified when:
• It's the only way to cure partner's a) flu or b) hangover.
• Partner craves exercise but her running shorts are in the laundry.
• Partner about to go on long, lonely business trip.
• Partner's VCR is broken.
• Partner is a virgin and hates it.

Helpful Hint to Improve Your Sex Life
Seven things it's better not to watch during lovemaking:
1. Television
2. The clock
3. The roast
4. The leaves change
5. The Dow Jones
6. Your language
7. Your weight

Compulsive Moment in Sex
"Because I wanted his full attention, I turned off the television. But while we made love, he watched the radio out of the corner of his eye."
                        – Ingrid, ornithologist

Abstinence Makes the Heart Grow Fonder
The ten official excuses for not having sex this year.
1. Guru said not to.
2. On a mission (peacekeeping).
3. Got a cat, instead.
4. Took early retirement.
5. Had plenty last year.
6. Stranded (can't find mall exit).
7. Teaching partner a lesson.

8. Live in L.A. – can't get to partner (freeway traffic).
9. Live in N.Y.C. – can't get to partner (can't cross picket lines).
10. Joined a health club.
(One unofficial reason: watching too many talk shows.)

Official Pleasure Guide

Orgasm Level	Signs and Symptoms
1	The smallest measurable orgasm. May show up as a "blip" on an air traffic controller's screen.
2	Enormous grin. Climaxee may miss his or her freeway exit on the way home.
3	Sudden spiritual insight: "Why don't I do this more often, instead of going to the mall?"
4	Instant replacement of vital nutrients lost while trying to balance a checkbook.

Remarkable Fact
Instead of being with two partners during sex, 93% of all women in Laramie, Kansas, preferred being with just one man who possesses the energy of two.

Pillow Talk
Arousal. Defined as any erotic action that causes one's interest in our trade imbalance with Norway to subside. The six accepted stages of arousal are:
1. Anticipation.
2. Dimming the lights.
3. Removing lover's headphones (be reassuring, this may cause some anxiety).
4. Nibbling lover's earlobe.
5. Kissing lover's neck.
6. Removing contact lenses.

The Inquisitive Lover
Q.
1. When is it appropriate to send a thank-you note?
2 Just how much love should we make?
3. What should one see during orgasm?

A.
1. When lovemaking leaves you tongue-tied.
2. Stop when your life begins to flash before your eyes.
3. With eyes open: the sky.
With eyes shut: heaven.

The Language of Flowers: Part I

To the lover who:	Send:
Frequently keeps you from getting a good night's rest	One dozen roses (short stem)
In the heat of passion, activated your home-security sensor.	Two dozen roses (long stem)

Tip for the Sexually Aggressive Woman

If, when undressing your lover, he begins to turn blue and his eyes started to bulge, it might be a good idea, before trying to slip it over his head, to loosen the knot in his tie.

About the "Stronger" Sex

With the right woman, a man in superb physical condition can have up to four climaxes within a three-hour period, but afterward don't count on him to help you:
• Make the bed.
• Empty the dishwasher.
• Floss.
• Fold laundry.
• With your term paper.
• Achieve climax.
• Fend off paparazzi.

Not So Innocent Signals: Lovers' Poll #9

How do you hint to someone you've just met that you're interested?

"Send a bottle of wine to her table with a note saying, 'Smile if you want the corkscrew."
        – Reggie, entrepreneur
"Flash her my high beams."
        – Barry, trucker
"Subtly, I invite him in for a nightcap, then open my hide-a-bed."
        – Denise, procurement supervisor

After-Sex Etiquette: The First Moments

Do	Do not
Cuddle	Leap out of bed and wash
Tell lover how marvelous it was	Whisper, "Better luck next time"
Return all compliments	Return phone calls
Exchange phone numbers	Exchange credit card numbers
Reward lover with M&Ms	Reward lover with S&M
Try again	Be greedy

Great Moments in Foreplay

"Winning the toss."
> – Leon, plumber

"Stopping the clock."
> – Leon's wife

"Going into overtime."
> – Both

Sex—Our Real National Pastime: Part I

Some facts concerning the 32,584,002 sexual encounters* that occur in the United States each night.

- Among married couples, only 24% are self-motivated.
- 67% occur in the bedroom.
- 33% do not.
- Only 9% involve a new position.
- 23% of all partners worry that the kids might hear.
- 5% worry about the neighbor's kids might hear.**

*Source: FBI.
**Source: Trailer Park Digest.

Great Lovers of Ancient History

Heavenly climactic moment:
"Oooh."
> – Vivian, Goddess, September, 693 B.C.

"Aaah."
> – Julius, Olympian, May, 487 B.C.

"Et ooooooh, Brutus?"
> – Unknown courtesan, August, 45 B.C.

About the "Weaker" Sex

With the right man, a woman in good physical condition can have up to six climaxes* within a three-hour period without:
• Losing consciousness.
• Breaking for lunch.
• Ruining her reputation.
*Figure doubles when she's with the wrong man.

You Know You Need a Lover: Part I

If:
• You don't mind working late.
• You cook for yourself, but eat directly from the pot.
• You toasted the New Year in by clinking your glass against the mirror.
• Even reading Trollope doesn't make you drowsy.
• You're living within your means.
• It's your doorman who tells you that you need a haircut.

Love Signs

Horoscope for an Avid Aquarius

• *Ruling passion:* committing unnatural acts
• *Ruling body lotion:* olive oil, extra virgin
• *Chief sexual asset:* aerodynamics hips
• *Governing erogenous zone:* shell of the ear
• *Aphrodisiac of choice:* thick shake, sipped from lover's loafer
• *Ruling sexual activity:* avoiding the wet spot
• *Ideal time for sex:* full moon

Is Your Sex Life Getting Monotonous?

Worry only if it meets three of the following five criteria.
Lover always:

	Yes	No
1. Sets the same goal – to finish before the playoffs start.	___	___
2. Engages in the same position even if you're in the other room.	___	___
3. Says "Ummmmmm" in the same key (G-flat).	___	___
4. During orgasm, mispronounces your name.	___	___

5. Thanks you the same way
(hands you a business card
and any loose change that may
have dropped on the floor.   ___   ___

Love Signs

Horoscope for an Alluring Aquarius.

- *Ruling passion:* achieving meltdown when touched
- *Ruling sexual turnoff:* doing it on wicker furniture.
- *Chief sexual asset:* a well-stocked refrigerator
- *Governing erogenous zone:* a wonderfully responsive mind
- *Aphrodisiac:* continental breakfast, in bed
- *Ruling sexual activity:* giving free (nearly) samples
- *Ideal time for sex:* the wonder years

Longevity and Sex

Our guide for 1994.

Each time you:	To your life, add:
Feel lustful	2 minutes
Call lover and do something about those feelings of lust	10 minutes
Touch each other in a new and exciting place (nape of the neck, or Santa Fe)	8 minutes
Have a sexual experience that:	
Makes you quiver with ecstasy	3 minutes
Causes your makeup to flake	13 minutes

Love Signs: Aquarius

(January 20 – February 19)

Opposite love sign: A loving (or, for noontime "quickies," a lascivious) Leo.

Outstanding sexual quality: Because you have a high I.Q., lovers go to bed with you for your mind. This means you never have to undress.

Most attractive physical feature: A libido the size of Holland.

Ruling sexual turnoff: Lovers who rub you the wrong way.

Ruling sexual turn-on: Hot tubs (the kind you bathe in and any severely overweight person in heat).
Ideal place for sex: From the waist down or, if it's busy, the turret of an old Irish castle.

More Love Signs: Aquarius
(January 20 – February 18)
Most attractive feature: You look luscious in a 3-way mirror.
Turn-on: A partner who wants it every night, especially from you.
Turn-off. Having sex in the middle of the night– and you're the only partner who's awake.
Ideal romantic adventure: A champagne-and-caviar picnic in a hot-air balloon that never leaves the ground (Aquarians are afraid of heights).
Favorite sexual fantasy: Having such wild sex that you know you'll never again be able to look your mother in the eye.

Thought for Tonight
When it comes to excessive sexual activity, falling asleep is nature's way of saying "enough."

Reminder
A climax a day keeps:
• the doctor
• flu
• depression
• the psychiatrist
• cellulite
• wrinkles
• the mumps
• boredom
• ambition
away.
           – French Medical Association

A Full-Service Lover

The criteria:
- *Courteous* – always wait for you to get into bed before starting to make love.
- *Patient* – never taps his or her foot while waiting for you to climax.
- *Fearless* – will try anything, twice.
- *Well-endowed* – always has extra postage stamps should you need to mail a letter.
- *Attentive* – during sex, flirts only with you and not with the researcher.

The Art of Romance

Intimate objects two equal opportunity lovers should share while making love:
- Their strengths
- A bialy (for stamina)
- A bagel (to clutch during a Level 5 climax*)
- A lottery number (this could be a fortuitous time)
- Lecture notes
- The blanket

*One in which the paint on the wall blisters.

Myth or Fact?

The Truth About Sex	Myth	Fact
It can remove the fat not susceptible to ordinary exercise.		X
"They're playing our song" may refer to your lover's moans.		X
It's possible to improve one's sexual performance by listening to motivational tapes.	X	
After an argument, it's a great way to kiss and make up.		X
If you don't have a partner, eating two pints of chocolate-chip ice cream can be just as satisfying.	X	
You should save yourself for your first lover.		X
It saps your energy (if you do it right).		X

The Inquiring Lover

Q. Instead of visiting a house of worship, is it ever proper, on Sunday morning, to stay in bed with my spouse and make love?
– Ernestine, tool and die maker

A. Yes, provided that:

1. The central purpose of your lovemaking is procreation.
2. You begin by saying "Grace."
3. Lovemaking lasts no more than three hours.
4. Your television is tuned to the Christian Broadcasting Network.
5. You call and make a donation.

The Dieter's Guide to Weight Loss During Sex

Activity	Calories Burned
Nibbling entire ear:	
Regular	21
Cauliflower	40
Blowing into lover's ear	6
If asthmatic	45
Blowing into both ears	12
Simultaneously	277

Communication Tip

Should you be angry if your lover answers the phone during sex?

No, if	Yes, if
It's for you	It's for your lover
It rings 6 or more times.	It isn't ringing.
It's a business call.	It's a personal call.
It's a car phone.	It's a pay phone.

Movies for Lovers: Part I

If your lover:	Rent
Has lots of moving parts	*RoboCop*
Knows exactly where to touch you in all the right places.	*Goldfinger*
Drives you up a wall.	*Fatal Attraction*
Sets off the sprinklers during torrid lovemaking.	*Singin' in the Rain*
Always leaves a wet spot.	*On Golden Pond*

It's Okay to Ask
During-sex request often addressed to a lover who is engrossed in constantly changing TV channels:
"Excuse me, but could you possibly use your free hand either to devote some attention to my erogenous zones or to hand me that magazine?"

Don't Panic
After sex, that "floaty," lightheaded, spacey, everything-is-right-with-the-world feeling of well-being is only your body saying thank you for rescuing it from another evening of watching *Wheel of Fortune*, reading *House Beautiful* and eating popcorn.

How to Keep a Lover From Leaving You
(Tips from our experts.)
"Give great back massages— she'll keep coming back for more."
        — Clyde, sales associate
"Never pitch story ideas during sex."
        — Mindy, screenwriter
"Hire him."
        — Carlotta, producer
"Hold him hostage by hiding his car keys."
        — Andrea, oboist
"Use your bike lock."
        — Cindy, pilot

A Guide to Vehicular Sex
Mercedes-Benz
Advantages
Tilt steering wheel enables both partners to fit. 100-way adjustable seat permits nearly unlimited positions, including "missionary overdrive" (both lovers revving their engines).
Disadvantages
Too much safety: moan-activated airbag may open and cause coitus interruptus (and resulting in a recall by the manufacturer).

The Art of Romance
Some obstacles to sublime lovemaking.
Not Serious
Partner just had hair done
Thin walls: afraid you might wake the children
Very little time
Had great sex an hour ago
Work night
Dinner guests waiting
Partner has cold feet
Serious
Partner wearing mudpack
Thin walls: afraid you might wake spouse
No appointment
Still recuperating
School night
Dinner guests watching
Partner has cold feet

Lover's Etiquette
When invited to your lover's house for dinner
Always:
• Show up.
• Bring a gift.
• Be on time.
• Ask for seconds.
Never:
• Ask who else will be there.
• Bring a date.
• Take a doggie bag into the bedroom.

Tip for Cautious Lovers
"Yes, we landed safely on the mattress, and we didn't cause too much damage to our ceiling, and it was...well...mind-boggling, especially during the free-fall. But we'll never again try to re-excite our sex life with a factory-second bungee cord."
– Ed and Martha, adventurers

Sexual Body Language

Expression	Can Mean
Grimace	"Get off my leg."
Glint in partner's eye	"How about an encore?"
Smile with eyes open	"I love the way you wake me in the morning."
Smile with eyes closed	"I love the way you wake me at night."
Eyes wide open	"Your hands are freezing."

A Lover Becomes A Partner

When he or she:
- Invites you to leave a toothbrush at his or her place.
- Gives you more closet space and your very own drawer.
- Wants to spend important holidays with you.
- Wants you to meet his or her.
- Parents.
  - "A"-list friends.
  - Presents you with keys to
  - His or her place.
  - His or her car.
  - The executive washroom.

What Do the Professionals Do?

Problem

1. During intercourse, my partner's cigarette ash keeps falling on my forehead – it ruins the mood.
2. In the heat of passion, I often call my lover Harris. His name is Lowell, and he gets very angry.
3. Loss of erection.

The Solution

1. You get on top.
2. Convince him that his name *is* Harris.
3. Check last place where used.

For the Public-Spirited Lover

Ten ways to make the world a sexier place.
1. Think more about sex.
2. Dim the lights.

3. Turn off the phones.
4. Wear underwear only when absolutely necessary.
5. Spend more time in bed.
6. Have more picnics.
7. Remain calm.
8. Don't eat garlic.
9. Be kind to strangers (gently blow in their ears).
10. Pair off.

Trade Secret

During sex, the three best ways to let a man know that you're irresistibly attracted to him, that he's needed and wanted, that you desire him and that he really turns you on is to:
1. Allow him to participate.
2. Call him by his first name.
3. Stay until the end.

Good News

New federal rules governing lust permit sex in the workplace provided that:
1. It doesn't occur on company time.
2. It's in addition to, and not instead of, a Christmas bonus.
3. It takes place either in your, or your lover's, home office.
4. It's not part of a severance package.

Your Guaranteed Sexual Forecast

As a result of meeting the person your mother warned you about:
• You'll work out regularly (but not at a fitness studio).
• You'll finally streak your hair.
• The "secret" parts of your body will no longer be such a secret.
• Your cholesterol level will decrease (love nibbles contain no fat).
• Friends will wonder why you haven't been calling as much.
• So will your parents.

Bizarre Moment in Sex

"The first time I got undressed he looked at my navel ring and asked me why I wear my ankle bracelet so high."
  – *Veronica, groupie*

The Enlightened Lover

What to do with your first orgasm:
- Of the morning: *poach it*
- Of the day: *photograph it*
- Of the night: *relish it*
- Of the week: *freeze it*
- Of the year: *frame it*
- Ever: *bronze it*

Life Part I

With Sex	Without Sex
Satin sheets	Cotton/Dacron blend
Whisker burn	Heartburn
"Happy Hour" in bedroom	"Happy Hour" in bar
Moon is for lovers	Moon is merely Earth's satellite
Contented sighs caused by lovemaking	Contented sighs caused by Ben & Jerry's
Increased craving	For sweets
Cuddling with your lover	Cuddling with the cat
Dinner by candlelight	Only when you blow a fuse

A Lover's Night Table

Items to assist the professional and the amateur.

Basic	Advanced
Blender	Cocktail shaker
Hot plate	Waffle iron
Pad and pencil	Word processor
Washcloth	Pastry brush
Aspirin	Acupuncturist
Candle	Flashlight
Photo of Mom	Photo of therapist
A book of poetry	Jumper cables

Sexual Demerits

Violation by Host	Demerits Earned
Inferior aphrodisiacs (too much fiber, no junk food)	6
Distractions	
Jingling bracelet	3
Squeaks	
Bedsprings	2
Mouse	10
Making bedroom eyes in the foyer	1/4
Giggling in the right places	4
Giggling in the wrong places	16

The Bitter Truth

How do you hint to a new lover that he needs to improve?

"I send him a 'Get Better' pop-up card."

    – Bernadine, costume designer

"By example: I invite an old lover over (for demonstration purposes only) and show my lover how it's done."

    – Michelle, publicist

"I ask for my apartment key back."

    – Karen, aerobics professor

"Diplomatically. I dial his number and play 'I Got Plenty of Nothing' on his answering machine."

    – Beverly, optician

Tonight's Tip for Working-Class Lovers

Feel free to call in sick and stay in bed with your lover tomorrow morning if:

1. You hate your job.
2. You worked extra-hard yesterday.
3. It's part of your union benefits.
4. Your lover owns the company.

The Dieter's Guide to Weight Loss During Sex

Each position has its own, unique calorie count. The Kama Sutra, for instance (Kama on top, Sutra on bottom), can consume nearly 400 calories provided both partners are in the mood. Because we scarcely have space to mention the 15,000 positions recently approved by the FDA, we present the two most effective.

Position	Calories Burned
Regular missionary (man on top; woman wishing the headboard were padded)	146
Irregular missionary (woman on top, wishing he were padded)	500

The Well-Informed Lover

What you should hear at the precise moment of orgasm.

Right	Wrong
Choir of angels	Mormon Tabernacle
Lover asking, "Am I too early?"	Guests asking, "Are we too late?"
Pounding surf	Jackhammer
Silence	Snores
Voice of lover	Voice from beyond
Bells	Door chimes
Ding	Dong

The Reluctant Lover: Part I

Popular excuses for not having sex.

Excuse Should you believe it?	Yes	No	Maybe
• Headache		X	
• Cluster headache			X
• Butterflies in stomach (have the jitters)			X
• Butterfly in stomach (ate one)		X	
• We just did it last night	X		
• Might wake the kids			X
• Might wake the watchdog	X		

Sexual Rule of Thumb

Uncertain about your lovemaking abilities? You can be sure you're doing it right if your leg falls asleep before your partner does.

Pre-Sex Warm-Up Tip

Stretching before lovemaking will enable a lover, without straining, to:

1. Reach up and shut off the light.
2. Reach out and touch his or her
   - Partner
   - Lucky rabbit's foot.
3. Reach for more Hershey Kisses (an aphrodisiac of choice, but only if they've been unwrapped).
4. See the time.
5. Wave to passersby.

Negative Ambience

Eight worst discoveries on a new lover's nightstand.

1. A guest book.
2. A talking photo of his mother.
3. *Soap Opera Digest* (It could mean you'll have to value your new lover pretty much for the body.)
4. A well-thumbed sex manual.
5. A glass containing teeth.
6. An ashtray.
7. A *Barney* cassette.
8. A stopwatch.

How Chinese Food Complements Sexual Activity
The Inscrutable Orient deciphered.

Eating:	Goes best with:
Cold noodles with sesame sauce	Undressing each other
Fried (or boiled) dumplings	French kissing
Hot-and-sour soup	Nibbling lover's neck
Assorted seafood delight	Oral sex
Aromatic Chinese eggplant	Oral sex with chopsticks
House crispy duck	Intercourse
General Tseng's historic chicken	Intercourse (in the General Tseng position– no MSG)
Sizzling steak with scallops	Orgasm
Ice cream with fortune cookies	Sleep

Pillow Talk
Cloud nine. That period of dozy, post-orgasmic bliss during which satisfied lovers yield to temptation and abandon their plans to:
• Visit the health club
• Clean out the garage
• Dress and go out for dinner
• Not fall asleep
Remarkably, in mentally healthy lovers, there are only minimal feelings of guilt.

The Typical Lover's Brain

Left Hemisphere	Right Hemisphere
Worrying about sexual performance	Confidence
Orgasms	Keeping track of them
Low sex drive	Elevating it
Blushing	Deciding which shade
Fantasies	Implementing them
Bringing out the best in you	Bringing out the best in your lover
Turning a bad day	Into a good night

Fitness Counts

How often do American lovers have sex? On a yearly basis, studies show that if they're:

In Shape
7 times, weekly
Out of Shape
7 times (gasp), weakly

Breaking the Ice

Tongue-tied after sex? Some favorite conversation starters.

If:	What to say:
Sex was great.	"I'm glad I skipped volleyball practice."
Sex was phenomenal.	"Are you still breathing?"
You feel satisfied.	"You make me feel like such a man."
You want to see him or her again.	"I'm in the phone book."

What Happened When I Met the Perfect Lover

"Stopped jogging 80 miles a week and cut my Prozac bill in half."
  – Gordon, member, Generation X
"At first we made love seven, eight times a week. Now, the initial attraction's worn off. We're down to six times a week."
  – Malcolm, surgeon
"Discovered he had a communicable disease– I, too, became a sports fanatic."
  – Shirley, department-store buyer
"Gave up cigars."
  – Louise, blacksmith

Should You Leave the Lights On? Part I

The value of visual stimulation cannot be overestimated, especially if your partner has majestic thighs. However:

If You	Turn the light off	Leave them on
Lied about your weight	X	
Height	X	
Age	X	
Are tan from the neck up	X	
All over		X
Smile at the sight of frontal nudity		X
Can't get your wedding ring off	X	

The Enlightened Lover

Choice positions

Good:

Woman on bottom

Man at the height of his powers

Better:

Man on bottom

Woman at the height of her powers

Best:

Man on bottom

Woman at the height of his powers

The Dieter's Guide to Weight Loss During Sex

Recommended positions for the year 2000:

Activity	Calories Burned
Standard positions:	
She on top, he on bottom (double bed)	59
He on top, she on bottom (queen-size bed)	81
Unusual position (male partner showing off):	
He on top, she on bottom (bunk beds)	730

Those Special Touches
Five ways to make the shy lover feel wanted:
1. *In your appointment book* – his name.
2. *On the nightstand* – his photo.
3. *On the bed* – you, with a smile.
4. *At the foot of the bed* – an "All Aboard" sign.
5. *Beside the bed* – a welcome mat.

Rude Awakening
Feminist phrase most often uttered the morning after a disappointing night before:
"Have I got a girl for you."

Morning Romance Tip
That person sitting across from you at the breakfast table (possibly your husband or your wife), face buried in a newspaper, muttering little more than "Mmmmm" when spoken to, is just waiting for you to tear off your robe and pajamas, toss the editorial page to the floor and do something sinful all over the Granola.

Great Moments in Afterplay: Part I
"I light a cigarette."
> – Craig, lutenist

"I put one out."
> – Yvonne, his accompanist

Etiquette for the Sexually Correct: Part I

What to do	For Formal Lovemaking	For Informal Lovemaking
Lighting:	Moonlight	Sunlight
Fuel:	Caviar	Pretzels
Crystal:	Baccarat	Juice glass
Libation:	Champagne	Wine cooler
Ambience:	Dozen roses	Plastic flowers
Poetry:	Wordsworth	*The Star*
Personal:	Brush teeth	Gargle
Greeting:	Hugs and kisses	Hearty handshake

Sexual Demerits: Part I

Moving violations *while* driving your lover to ecstasy.

Violation	Number of Demerits
Sticker shock	6
Failure to signal when changing positions	3
Passing on a curve	4
Passing out on a curve	7
Making a U-turn:	
During foreplay	3
During intercourse	10
Stalling	7

Critic's Choice: Position
- **Man:** Lying there, worried about his potency.
- **Woman:** Rising above it.

Thought for Today

According to the experts, the perfect lover is one who:
- Worships you.
- Pampers you.
- Yearns for you.
- Adores you.
- Grows on you.

Perfect Lovemaking – Some Ingredients

- Flowers by the bedside (doesn't apply to partners with allergies).
- An energizing bedside snack (our expert suggests oatmeal-raisin cookies or occasional sips of pasta e fagioli soup).
- Candlelight (starlight acceptable if you're a) economizing or b) astronomers).
- A roomy bed (queen-size or larger for best results).
- That warm glow (known as lust) when he or she calls.
- Attention to detail.
- Lots of practice.

Something Different for Tonight

Try your video camera. The advantages:
1. The ultimate teaching aid (instant replay enables you to see

what you're doing wrong).

2. The ultimate ego-booster (instant replay enables you to see what you're doing right).

3. Entertainment (9 out of 10 guests will find this more diverting than your wedding album).

4. Proof you did it (in case the IRS asks).

5. Fond memories.

Mixed Messages

What Lover Says	What Lover May Mean
"Let's try something different."	My leg's falling asleep.
"Yes, yes, yes, yes, yes, yes."	Yes.
"Are you nearly finished?"	"I've got such a headache.
"You make me so happy."	I can't stop laughing.
"I never felt this way before."	In this particular city.
"I can't hold out any longer."	Have to catch a plane.
"I didn't know it could be this good."	But can he hang a door?
"I'm your slave."	This is your captain speaking.

During-Sex Reminder

In the heat of passion, never try to:

• Open a bottle of Champagne
• Balance your checkbook
• Proofread galleys
• Make smart buying decisions
• Recall a recipe
• Update your diary
• Think "snow"

What Every Lover Should Know

During sizzling sex, nonstick sheets make it a breeze to get out of bed to:

• Receive guests.
• Get a snack.
• Tidy up.
• Retrieve a lost pillow.
• Frighten a prowler.
• Check the mailbox.

- Get more vitamins.
- Confer with your coach.

The Thinking Person's Guide to Sex

- Knowledge is power. Ask, "Where'd you learn that?"
- Travel broadens. Know how to say, "I'm very close," in at least three romance languages.
- You are your brother's keeper, so let him sleep with your girlfriend. (It's also a good way to get a second opinion.)
- Partner too sexy? Intellectuals prevent premature you-know-what by thinking about Karl Marx.
- Always go to bed with someone for their mind. (Don't worry, the body will automatically come along– it's attached.)

The Reluctant Lover

Four reasons why people didn't have sex on the first date.
1. "He didn't buy me enough dinner."
        – Velma, hypnotherapist
2. "I was too awed by her beauty to make a pass."
        – Calvin, bartender
3. "My nails hadn't dried."
        – Theresa, producer
4. "I didn't trust myself to be alone with him."
        – Ellen, nurse

What Kind of Lover Is Your Partner?

Low-Maintenance	High-Maintenance
Moans when excited	Uses flash cards
Loves fresh air	Always feels a draft
Knows when	Has to be told
Lets mind wander	Pays strict attention
Takes instructions	Gives instructions
Enjoys hard work	Is hard work
Likes to be undressed	Has to be undressed
Has to be held back	Has to be held up

Perk Up Your Love Life Tonight
• Sprinkle Romano cheese on your lover– it's an ideal low-calorie snack.
• Lend your lover to a needy person – such as friend who's between lovers.
• Put a big bowl of fruit on the corner of the bed – it will provide ballast and prevent the bed from capsizing.
• Hang a string of garlic from the bed – it will ward off the kids.
• For tender lovemaking– marinate your lover in a milk bath.

From Our Lover's Glossary
"I'll call you." A purposely vague phrase uttered by a new lover as he or she is leaving your apartment after a night of lovemaking. If such night was extra-glorious, the temptation of your part to ask "When?" will be overwhelming, but Lover's Etiquette dictates that you remain "cool" lest such person think you over-anxious and head for the hills. (*Note:* If this person does not call within 10 days, it is legally permissible to sell any item of apparel or the watch that he or she may have left behind.)

Ambiance Tip for Quarrelsome Lovers
It's more fun to fight over money while you're both lying in bed than it is to argue about sex while you're both standing on a bank line.

Are You Growing Addicted to Sex?
The signs:
• Doing it in inappropriate places (like an elevator, or while going through a car wash with the top down).
• Using sex as a crutch (to relieve tension).
• Thinking about last night's juicy details at your work station.
• Wearing less underwear so that when you meet your lover you can have sex faster.
• Forgetting to call your mother.
• Using the pages of this book.

Time Out

Tonight, take a five-minute break between foreplay and whatever comes next to:

- Finish the rest of the Oreos (for energy).
- Take another shower (for stamina).
- Neaten up the bed.
- Pick up your messages (for a change of pace).
- Decide whether to continue (in case you have to rise early).
- Set the alarm.

MONTHLY QUALITY OF LIFE® CHECKUP

How good a lover is he?
•He takes his time: Yes___ No___
Only if his carpool isn't honking___
•He locates your G-spot without a:
Map: Yes___   No___
Laser pointer: Yes___   No___
•He removes non-essential items that
hinder lovemaking like his:
Socks___
Garters___
Pacemaker___
•He makes sure you achieve ecstacy: Always___
 Sometimes____   Only when he wants to borrow money___
•He doesn't freak if your animal sounds wake:
The neighbors___
His roommates___
•After sex he:
Stays awake long enough to make dinner reservations___
Lets you use the bathroom first___
Tells you how wonderful you are___
Reaches for:
   a) You___
   b) The TV Guide___
   c) The rest of his Hershey® Bar___

                              Signed_____

                              Witnessed_____

FEBRUARY

•Erotic goals for February:

1. Work up courage to tell lover about shoe fetish
2. Have sedative ready if lover flips out

The perfect month to rekindle romance. On Lincoln's birthday, snuggle in bed and read the Gettyeburg Address to each other. On Washington's birthday, when your lover asks, "Am I the best you've ever been with?," reply, "I cannot tell a lie." As for Valentine's Day, it's not too early to start thinking about the perfect gift.

For the woman of your dreams, why not an emerald tennis bracelet, or, if the time is right, a diamond engagement ring? (Etiquette tip: It is insensitive to base the number of carats on her bust size).

For the man who loves the outdoors, a new set of golf clubs or, if you've already maxed out your credit card, something less expensive, like new mudflaps for his van. For the man who's always broke, there's a low-interest loan. And for the man who's wonderful in bed**, a Cartier watch.

**Clinical definition of "wonderful in bed" includes:
•Able to last at least 30 minutes before needing a Snapple®
•Is exquisitely sensitive to your needs (i.e. Doesn't reach for a footstool when you say, "A little higher."
•Doesn't panic when you get aggressive (even if your spurs are makig welts on his love handles)
•Gives you the kind of climaxes other women can only dream about (Cause your bicycle pants to melt).

•Official aphrodisiac of the Month:

Black bean vegetable chili

Reminder
A day without sex is like a night without sex.

Lovemaking: The Luxuries
• Battery-powered portable fan—so lover doesn't overheat
• Indoor thermometer—to make certain room doesn't overheat
• Mini-heater—for when lover cools off
• Magazines—to thumb through while lover recuperates
• Sheepskin slippers—for warmth on midnight snack runs to kitchen
• Takeout menus—for ordering in
• Bathrobe—to slip into when your order arrives
• Hand-held vacuum—for instant crumb removal

Sexual Monotony: The Causes
Making love each week.
• At the same time.
• In the same way.
• In the same car.
• On the same bed.
• On the same sheet.
• With the same technique.

Gem of the Month
Amethysts set in gold (or just a big informal handful) to the lover who:
1. Isn't fussy about where the two of you make love . . . the kitchen, the dining room, in a château or on Cloud 9 (only your laundry room's off limits).
2. Isn't fussy about when you make love (fervently believes that 4 P.M. is an appropriate time for a nooner).
3. Isn't fussy about how you make love (any chiropractor-approved position is fine).
4. Is always up for something new.

Sex Secrets of the Great Lovers
Three romance tips for gourmets.
1. On a cold winter night, instead of foreplay, warm your partner up by serving a steaming bowl of split pea-and-ham soup.

2. During sex, keep your cookies moist and chewy by popping them in a hungry partner's mouth.
3. Never moan with your mouth full.

Met That Special Someone?: Part 1

Preferred Assets	Nice to Have	Important	Crucial
Source of income: trust fund	X		
Great job		X	
Compatible astrological signs			X
Sane parents			X
Good nesting instincts		X	
Has own house	X		
With fireplace in bedroom		X	
Can be trained to: dress better		X	
Heed a mating call			X

The Enlightened Lover

You are having too much sex at one time if:
• You have an irrational craving for rhubarb.
• The bed has achieved meltdown.
• Your life is flashing before your eyes.
• You've somehow undergone a change of
a) Season
b) Nationality
c) Life

Groundhog Day

If you can see your lover's shadow, stay in bed for another six weeks—make sure your lover stays there with you.

The Inquisitive Lover

Q. Should I lend my lover to someone less fortunate than I?
A. Yes, but only to someone who:
• Has an inferior lover.
• Happens to be between lovers.
• Needs their sofa moved.
• Once did the same for you.
• Wants a second opinion.
• May make improvements.

72

How the Other Half Loves
Sex styles of:
The Rich and Famous:
Thing often said after sex in a limo: "You may go back to the front seat now, James."
The Poor and Unknown:
Thing often said after sex in a limo: "Thank you, madam."

The Joys of Frequent Sex: Part I
Five benefits according to our reader survey.
1. "It keeps my prostate humming right along."
2. "Never a worry about sun damage . . . we do it at twilight."
3. "In the back-to-back position, it actually reverses negative thinking."
4. "I . . . I think it's really helping my hernia."
5. "The constant nudity helps me achieve outer peace."

Alert!
This is National Sexual Dysfunction Month. Be extra understanding of the partner who:
• Wears a mask when he's sent to rent an X-rated video.
• Is over 40 and still lives with his mother.
• Thinks about money more than sex.
• Thinks about sports more than sex.
• Is always a) too tired or b) obsessed with his back.
• Would rather hold the TV clicker than your hand.
• When you say, "I could lie here in your arms forever," replies, "Sorry, my dog expects me home."

> "Sex makes you alert, confident, and ready to face the world—it's *the* ideal substitute for a hot breakfast."
> – Delilah Kissoff, nurse

Pillow Talk
No-fault sex. A learned borrowing from casualty insurance, involving the following conditions:
a. Each partner takes responsibility for his or her own orgasm;
b. Both partners chip in and pay for furniture damaged by a nuclear climax

c. Equal custody of edible leftovers;

d. One lover does not blame the other if

• Air bag opens (vehicular sex only)

• Either lover falls asleep from exhaustion

• Really torrid sex causes the piñata to break

Sexual Demerits: Part II

Moving violations *after* driving your lover to ecstasy.

Violation	Number of Demerits
Failure to sound horn when finished	7
Leaving the scene of an accident that's:	
Unforeseen (two or more climaxes)	$2^1/_2$
A calamity (climax activates smoke alarm)	3
A catastrophe (climax activates sprinklers)	4
Unexpected (prowler says, "Hi," and leaves)	7
A mishap (popped contact lens)	1
An act of God (makes bed move)	6
An act of Goddess (makes earth move)	8

Tip for Exhibitionist Lovers

For better during-sex concentration and to get the most pleasure out of lovemaking, make sure, before you begin that you:

• Lock the door

• Draw the shades

• Lower the lights

• Ask the audience to hold their applause until afterward

A Lover's Wish List

The ideal partner:

• Is considerate (uses hand signals when changing positions).

• Gives great back rubs (even when you're standing up).

• Believes in equal rights (sex at night and in the morning).

• Causes Level 5 climaxes (instant disappearance of those telltale wrinkles around the eyes).

• Peaks sexually (at least 3 times a night).

• Never panics when you behave scandalously (and set off the burglar alarm).

• Doesn't sulk when it's his turn to do the housework.

When a New Lover Stays Over

The gallant partner shows he has her best interests at heart by having:

1. A flashlight to illuminate her way when she uses the bathroom at 3:22 A.M.
2. The ingredients on hand for a healthy but lavish breakfast (she'll be impressed).
3. A spotless bathroom and shower curtain, plus lots of fluffy towels.
4. A soothing bedtime story (in case of first-night jitters).
5. An ashtray (in case she smokes).
6. Chewing gum (in case she's trying not to).

Thought for Tonight

If, during sex, you can read your mail, balance your checkbook or carry on a conversation, you may be doing it wrong.

Reminder for the Weekend

Get ready: Sex is an ideal Friday morning activity—it's fun, it's dietetic and, best of all, it lets you start the weekend early.

From Our Lover's Glossary

Nooner. A working lunch. One in which sex serves as a nutritional substitute for a hamburger with french fries, a chef's salad or a kosher salami on rye, hold the mayo. Those who enjoy lunchtime sex and actually make it back to the office, may or may not note an increase in job performance, depending on whether they are able to:

- Sit upright
- Think rationally*

* One woman, a vice president in charge of third world loans at (*deleted*), after 95 minutes of sex on a vibrating bed, lent a South American country $40,000,000, accepting, as collateral, the president's stamp collection. She did not get a bonus.

The Moment I Knew It Was Love

"When he made me experience those two most elusive of all orgasms:
1. Loud.
2. Soft."

— Velma, auto mechanic

"When she spent four hours going through the entire alphabet with my body before she finally discovered my G-spot."*

— Hans, real-estate appraiser

*"I gave her no hints."

Great Moment in Marital Relations

"The night I was lying there like I always do, my body tense, gritting my teeth and waiting for her to get it over with when I suddenly realized, hey! I, too, can participate."

— Freddy, state trooper

Q. What is the secret of making one's partner feel needed and wanted during lovemaking?
A. Removing your ankle weights.

Communication Tip

Suggested "Thinking of you" fax to send to your lover.
Thinking of what we did last night is making me:
(*Check appropriate space*)

- Hot ___
- Experience a meltdown ___
- Blush ___
- Hungry for: ___
    More ___
    Less ___
    An encore ___
- Purr ___
- Creative ___
- Warm all over ___
- Think positive ___
- Think bridal shower ___

Secret of the Great Lovers

Sex: Never leave your bed without it.

Sex Poll #4

What do you do immediately after having sex in your car?
(Asked of several panting couples.)

• "Cease revving the engine."
• "Pull over."
• "Climb out of the air bag."
• "We get a wild craving for Pepsi and Ritz Crackers—that's why we do it in a convenience store parking lot."
• "Fall asleep on each other's shoulder—that's why it's so neat to have a chauffeur."

Common Sexual Afflictions

Complaint	Cause
Gas	Either: 1. Nerves
	2. Watching too many cooking shows
Complexion not what it should be	
	Either: 1. Too much chocolate
	2. Too much light

Nourishment for Lovers

Tonight's Menu	Purpose
Caviar	Facilitates location of partner's erogenous zones, even in fog
Burritos	Releases the "Lust Response" in men who've had a religious up-bringing
Kasha varnishkas	Inspires hope when partner begins foreplay by saying Grace
Buffalo wings	The perfect bedside energizer for lovers who don't know when to stop
Belgian waffles	Transforms repressed women

After-Sex Etiquette: The Thank-You Note*

Send a thank-you note to anyone who made lovemaking extra-special. It should:
• Be mailed, never faxed.
• Be handwritten and *never* dictated to your secretary.
• Mention the specific a) position, b) orgasm and c) love bite that gave you so much pleasure (if you forgot, simply call it "all that good stuff")
• Never be *too* specific (lover may be under surveillance).
* For best results, sign it.

Reminder for the Prudent Lover

Unless you issue a disclaimer, undressing, getting into bed with your lover, then snuggling, kissing, fondling, blowing gently into each other's ear, whispering endearments in a quivering voice and administering feverish love bites will almost always lead to sex.

Sex—Our Real National Pastime: Part II

More facts concerning the 32,584,002 sexual encounters* that occur in the United States each night.
• 19% of all couples turn the television on after sex.
• 34% turn the television on during sex.
• 11% have sex only because it's easier than arguing about money.
• 16% of all partners wish they were with someone else.
• 13% of all partners are with someone else.
• 14% of all partners wish they were with someone.
* *Source:* FBI.

Alert For Really Senior Lovers

Your partner may have long-term memory loss when, after having sex for the third time that day, he or she says, "Gosh, I forgot what a good lover you are."

Is It Getting Serious? Part II

Met someone new? The warning signs that it just might be love. For her:
1. Buying cards that begin, "Times with you are unforgettable."
2. Making room:
   • In her closet for his clothes

- On her desk for his picture
- In her life for him

3. Exchanging:
  - Gifts
  - Love letters
  - Keys

Magic Numbers: Part I

$1^1/_4$ **minutes:** How long it takes for the average lover to fall asleep after sex if you've done your job correctly.

15 feet: The romantic range of the typical men's aftershave if it's been applied too generously.

5 seconds: How long it takes the average make to undress completely once she gives her consent.

8: The number of times a woman must utter the phrase, "A tad more to the right," if she's with a learning disadvantaged partner.

20%: The usual discount given by a woman who sells appliances to a partner who really pleases her.

Love Poll #43

Based on responses by 1,000 males, it is appropriate to don a condom:

When it's chilly out	10%
Right after dinner (to save time)	9%
When we get in bed	12%
When certain that foreplay is going reasonably well	18%
10 minutes before intercourse	50%
10 minutes after intercourse (respondent a moron)	0.1%

The Inquisitive Lover

Q. Is it ever acceptable to see two different lovers on the same day?

A. Yes, when:
- They're teammates.
- Or twins (Siamese).
- You're honoring a raincheck.
- A physician has declared you clinically oversexed.
- You truly believe that three heads are better than one.
- You need a second opinion.

Profile of a Great Lover

• Knows exactly where to touch you, even if the room is dark.
• Has fitted sheets (so they don't bunch up during those torrid sexual moments).
• Can function under adverse circumstances (even while enduring heartburn from your ginger custard).
• Can make you laugh in bed.
• Is considerate (during sex, won't change to a new position just as you're really starting to like the present one).
• Is thoughtful (waits until after sex to take you home).

Apologies for Last Night

If lovemaking was not as majestic as usual, check the appropriate reason why and send to your lover:

----------detach here----------

___ Forgetfulness (couldn't think of any more positions).
___ Conscience was bothering me (but I can't tell you why).
___ Distracted (busy counting the moments till the next time).
___ Upset stomach (never again deli for a midnight snack).
___ Headache (real, this time).
___ Finals.
___ Allergies.
___ Labor pains.

What Do Men Really Want From A Lover?

Based on a telephone survey of 1,500,000 men:
• 60% liked it when a woman opened her front door and was standing there in nothing but a black negligee.
• 55% felt they should pick up the check on their first date.
• 99% felt she should pick up the check on their last date.
• 90% liked it when a woman flirted with them unless she was (a) an aunt or (b) their commanding officer.
• 49% wanted a woman to be kind when, while tousling his hair, she discovered it's a weave.
• 98% said that in an emergency they'd go to bed with a woman just for her body.

Reminder For the Ardent Couple

Not to worry. An above-the-national-average frequency rate (5 to 9 times a week) may simply mean:
• You're unemployed.
• You're both addicted to each other.
• Your social circle's limited.
• You take your marriage vows seriously.
• The TV's out for repairs.

Cold-Weather Tip for a Dieting Sex Partner

Did you know that snuggling against a hairy lover can provide warmth without weight?

The Bedside Eater

Aphrodisiac of the Evening
Meat loaf (vegetarians may substitute tofu).

Erotic Effect
Independence: enables indecisive lovers to decide how much sex to have without calling a psychic.

Aphrodisiac of the Night
Mousse (vanilla or chocolate will do just fine).

Erotic Effect
Suppresses audible panting common to lovers where foreplay includes a piggyback ride around the bed.

Thought for Tonight

A smaller bed will make your lover seem bigger.

Advice for High-Chemistry Lovers

If you think you're doing it too much:
• Ration your contact visits.
• Make love with your body stocking on.
• Have the decency to express remorse if you make love more than nine times in one week.
• Perhaps you aren't—consult your clergyman.

What Do Women Really Want From a Lover?

Based on a telephone survey of 1,500,000 women:

• 78% think a man should carry her into the bedroom as part of foreplay, even if he doesn't happen to be going that way.

• 86% like it when a man opens a door for her, especially if he doesn't hold out his hand for a tip.

• 69% think the man should pay his share of the dinner check on the first date (if the sex was really good).

• 95% think the man should pick up the entire dinner check, but give her the receipt (if the sex was really great).

• 41% thought making love under the stars was romantic and sexy, unless it occurred in the bed of a pickup truck.

Signs That You May Be With the Right Partner

• Although you've just celebrated your 20th wedding anniversary, he still, each time after lovemaking, announces, "That was the best sex I've ever had."

• He never mixes business with pleasure—unless you happen to show up at his office in a diaphanous black dress.

• Neither of you can remember where the laptop is.

• You needn't show him what makes you feel good—he already knows.

• Your favorite sexual gadgets are your partner's hands.

A Guide To Vehicular Sex

Jaguar

Advantages

Sumptuous leather seats lend added dimension of sensuality. Erotic design of car considered form of foreplay. Hood ornament a sex symbol.

Disadvantages

Between-seat shift console may cause over-ardent male to experience his first hernia. Also difficult to find parts.

The Grateful Lover: Part I

How to send a thank-you note if lovemaking was extra-special.

If you're	Then:
Shy (but a bit daffy)	Put it into a bottle; float in lover's bathtub.
Romantic	Write it on the mirror in lipstick.
Not sure it will be seen	Write it on lover's glasses.
Silly	Spell it out in pretzels.
Afraid to wake lover	Leave on pillow.
Afraid the room is bugged	Whisper it.

From Our Book of Sexual Records

Fastest lover (unscheduled sex): Gaylord R., of Toledo, Ohio, managed to undress, fold his clothing neatly, open the hide-a-bed, plump up the pillows and "satisfy" both himself and Gloria, his lover, in 61 seconds. He had theater tickets.

Communication Tip

Thing often said to a frightened lover by a totally uninhibited partner who has spent two hours uttering indecipherable shrieks of pleasure:

If the lights are off
"It's okay, sweetie, you can come back to bed now."
If the lights are on
"Don't look at me like that."

The Second Five Commandments of Sex

6. Thou shalt not attempt to seduce thy mate when her water's about to burst.
7. Thou mayest feel free to consider orgasm a religious experience.
8. Thou mayest feel free to consider simultaneous orgasm two religious experiences.
9. Thou shalt not use a worklight to find thy partner's erogenous zones. (A magnet's okay.)
10. Thou mayest not interrupt sex because you hear the chimes of (a) the front door or (b) the ice-cream truck.

Too Little Sex?: The Symptoms
• Tension
• Wrinkles (reversible when your sex life improves)
• Anxiety
• Overweight
• Community activism
• Bar hopping
• Apathy, even when there's a sale at your favorite boutique
• Golf more than once a week
• Sex less than once a month

Sex and the Basic Food Groups
Chinese: Considered "arousal friendly" by unregistered dietitians, especially those dishes (beef with cashews, $7.95) containing the recommended dosage of MSG. Additional examples:

Dish	Application
Spicy, Crispy Sea Bass	Emboldens timid lovers, eases bran-related performance anxiety.
Paradise Chicken in Szechuan Sauce	Relieves trembling in male virgins; makes orgasm-related facial expressions more scrutable.
Sliced Pork with Scallions	Anti-jitters agent; makes female virgins less modest; transforms heartburn into an erotic experience.

Test Yourself: Are You A Slave To Sex?
Do you:
1. Find it impossible to stop after the first climax? _____
Lover? _____
2. Think about sex more than twice an hour? _____
3. Do it more than five times a week (well above federal standards)? _____
4. Make house calls? _____
5. Find yourself sneaking an orgasm when no one's looking? _____
6. Often find yourself using sex as an excuse not to play golf? _____
7. Feel flattered when you're referred to as a sex object? _____
8. Ignore public opinion? _____

The Enlightened Lover
What every lover should know about orgasm:
1. You can't have too many.
2. You can have too few.
3. There's no such thing as a bad one.
4. The ability to receive them is a natural skill.
5. The ability to give them is a marketable skill.

Good News For Extra-Passionate Lovers
Your are flirting correctly if:
• You make eye contact with your victim
• Your eyelids flutter
• Your contacts pop
• Your ski goggles fog up

Why I Gave Up Celibacy
"It was our wedding night; I figured, what the heck."
– Angela, nice girl
"My Prozac bill was astronomical."
– Oscar, air controller
"Peer pressure."
– Irving, retired
"To cut down on my craving for sweets."
– Selma, law enforcement
"Who wants to sit in a hot tub alone?"
– Roberto, director

From Our Lover's Glossary
Phone Sex.
1. Taking a phone call during any portion of lovemaking.
2. The ultimate form of safe sex, unless the person to whom you are speaking has caller ID.
3. Sex with someone just for their mind.

What Do the Professionals Do?

Problem	The Solution	
	A Professional	An Amatuer
The bed collapses during vigourous intercourse (10-14 mph).		
	Keeps going.	Stops.
You break your longest nail on his back.		
	Keeps going.	Tries to find it.
Your partner's silicone implants suddenly shift.		
	Keeps going.	Screams.

The Dieter's Guide To Weight Loss During Sex

Activity	Calories Burned
Getting to the point of "no return":	
If you're with a good lover	12
If you're not	95
Arriving at point of "no return":	
Holding back	170
Just letting go	2

What Do the Professionals Do?

The Problem	The Solution
Sudden increase in sex drive	Contact a dating service
Tension, acid stomach, that headachy feeling	Avoid shellfish out of season
Hiccups	Breathe into the pillowcase
Not sure, just feel kind of restless	Orgasm (1 or 2)
Must fit into bathing suit by this weekend	Orgasm (4 to 6)

You Are Not Alone

Some common responses to an extraordinary climax:

Typical

Out of body, "floaty" feeling (you regain your senses in the kitchen)

Feeling relaxed in all the right places (head, neck, shoulders)

Earth moves (just enough to upset the pitcher of sangria beside the bed)

Unusual

Out of body, "floaty" feeling (you regain your senses in June)

Feeling relaxed in all the right places (Maui, Bali, Indianapolis)

Earth moves (a bit too much: astronauts can't find their way back)

Cold-Weather Romance Tip

Morning frost on your lover's windshield? Scratch a personalized "Let's make love tonight" message (be as naughty as space and your religion permits) and hope that:

- No one else sees it.
- It doesn't violate community standards.
- It doesn't melt until he does.

From My Wife's Little Instruction Book

Hold my hand more often. It'll:

1. Make us feel closer.
2. Remind you that I still don't have an engagement ring.

Sexual Ethics

Further justifications for mercy sex:

- Compassion (last night before Lent)
- Debt of honor (partner paid for dinner and/or motel room)
- Gratitude (partner hooked up stereo or moved couch)
- Patriotism (soldier home on leave)
- Sympathy (partner just had root canal)
- Kindness (partner has no one else)
- Charity (you forgot to give at the office)

The Considerate Lover

- Never rushes (exception: early checkout time).
- Is never distracted (exception: prowlers or reporters).
- Is confident (can continue even if bed splinters).
- Is creative (uses positions that work all the muscles)
- Never denies encores.
- Sends warm thank-you notes.
- Gives at the office.

Ten Things To Be Happy About After Sex

1. Finally getting your breath back.
2. Ski season is just around the corner.
3. The little bubbles.
4. You can finally switch off the television.
5. You can sleep late.
6. It was worth the wait.
7. It's Miller time.
8. The nonstop service.
9. A moonlight stroll.
10. The sequel.

False Alarm

"I experienced a great deal of chest pain during lovemaking until I finally got up the courage to ask her to be a bit more gentle when tugging on my heartstrings."
— Michael, poet

From Our Lover's Glossary

Guest Lover. A substitute lover whose services you avail yourself of if your current lover:

- Is indisposed.
- Has put you on hold.
- Hates your cooking.
- Has the flu.
- Is ignoring you.
- Has a substitute lover.
- Has gotten too fat.
- Is having a nice day…without you.

Note: Follow the rules—sex with a guest lover must take place in the guest room.

You Know You Need a Lover

When:

- You figure, what the hell, and join the Bible Studies Singles Weekend.
- You buy *New York Review of Books* for the personals instead of "The Mythic Significance of Chess" monograph.
- You've bought an infant carrier for your Yorkie.

- You're always free for lunch, dinner and helping friends move.
- You sent yourself a Valentine card signed "Guess Who?"
- Your favorite movie is *Marty*.
- The order takers at the local Chinese, Italian and Mexican take-out places know your voice.

Communication Tip

The worst thing about telephone sex is that you can't reach out and touch someone.

F.Y.I.

Achieving a healthy, satisfying climax. (On a scale of 1 to 10.)

Circumstance	Level of Difficulty
Very attracted to partner	2
Very attracted to partner but distracted by:	
• Car alarm	4
• And it's your car	8
• Walkman earphones keep slipping off head	7
• Partner chewing gum	5
• And cracking it	9
• Fax coming in	5
• Caring in-law asking how things are going	10

Tip For Active Lovers

During sex, when changing positions, for best results:
- Follow the diagram.
- Do it smoothly.
- Don't show off (stop if you have to).
- If you're not sure, ask directions.
- Don't forget to take your partner along.
- Always use hand signals.

Harmonious Lovers

No stereo? It's easy to make music if

She moans in:	He groans in:
C sharp	F natural

Virtuous Sex: Part I

Event	Permissible	Sin
Level I climax	X	
Multiple climaxes		X
Simultaneous		X
Bathing alone	X	
With your partner	X	
Peeking		X
Moaning from sex		X
Moaning because you missed your freeway exit	X	
Lust		X

Aprés-Lovemaking Ritual #1

While lying there in post-orgasmic bliss:

Serve	If You Plan To
Expensive champagne	Celebrate your love
Bargain champagne	Propose a modest toast
Ten-year-old Cognac	Just relax and enjoy the afterglow
Twenty-year-old Cognac	Also have a conversation
Iced tea	Get dressed and drive to your favorite restaurant
Herbal tea	Get rid of him

The 7 Official Stages of Afterglow

I. Levitation (body rises slightly off the bed—careful of the mirror on the ceiling)

II. Rapture (sudden indifference to Gothic architecture)

III. High rapture (and Roman architecture)

IV. Nirvana (same feeling as when you find something great at a crafts fair)

V. Heaven (double vision, terrific view)

VI. Seventh Heaven (don't care that your lover made several technical errors)

VII. Cloud Nine (not a good time to make a career decision)

Gift Certificate No. 1720

---------Detach here, send to lover---------

GIFT CERTIFICATE

Bearer entitled to:

• One dinner for two
• Kiss me all over
• Unlimited back rubs
• Nibble on my earlobe
• Make me gasp with pleasure
• Stay the night
• One hot session (in the morning)
• One hot breakfast
• Cab fare

Expires: (not applicable)

Lover Appreciation Day

To the lover who:	Give
Makes you sweat.	Swimming lessons
Keeps you thin.	His or her weight in gold, or sex.
Keeps you busy.	A rest.
Always wants more.	A rematch.
Gives you whisker burn.	A better razor.
Keeps you warm on cold nights.	A sweater.
Keeps you hot on any night.	Praise.

The Sentimental Lover

Reserve a special place in your heart for the lover who:

• Notices your first gray hair (but doesn't tell you).
• Whispers naughty things in your ear.
• Writes a billet-doux that's non-computer generated.
• Lets you decide the water temperature when you shower to-gether.
• Pampers you by serving breakfast in bed (even cuts your French toast into delicate bite-size pieces).
• Believes it's the thought that counts but pearl earrings are nice, too.
• After lovemaking, reads Shakespeare sonnets by the light of either:
  • The silvery moon.
  • Your afterglow.

Floral Thought for Today

A bouquet of roses to the lover who:
• Can ad-lib in bed.
• Thinks your vaccination mark is cute.
• Has beachfront property.
• After sex, cheerfully presses your pants (removed in haste) so you can go back to work looking well-groomed.
• Makes you feel welcome by asking, "Must you go so soon?"
• Always lets you leave feeling better than when you arrived.

Loving Thought for Today

Send your sweetheart one rose for each time he or she:
1. Although it was your turn, walked the dog in a pouring rain.
2. Went to see what that strange noise downstairs was at 4:12 A.M.
3. Called you at work and said things that made you a) blush and b) hot (two roses if you were in the middle of an important sales conference).
4. Resisted temptation and didn't a) answer the pager during sex, b) ask, as you got undressed, "Why'd you stop working out?" or c) cheat.
5. Took you to the south of France.
6. Without leaving the bedroom.

What I Did For Sex

"Missed an appointment with my hairdresser, twice!"
       – Gladys Pipp, ornithologist

Lover Appreciation Day: Phase I

To the lover who keeps you:	Give:
Warm	A blow dryer for his or her chest hair
Happy	A testimonial dinner
In shape	His or her weight in gold or (better) massage oil
Aroused	A blood pressure monitor
Perspiring	A smoke detector
Radiant	Sunglasses
Walking on air	A pair of comfortable shoes

Sexual Ethics

You may read a lover's diary only if:
• You're curious.
• You're in it.
• You're sure you won't get caught.
• It's already in the bookstores.

For Lovers Who Are Parents-To-Be

Researchers tell us that a baby conceived in or within five miles of a Disneyland has a 72% chance of being extra cute.

Sexual Etiquette 101

Q. Who gets to control the TV clicker after sex?
A. The partner who:
1. Worked the hardest.
2. Can still wiggle his or her thumb.
3. Needs the exercise.
4. Can't sleep.
5. Most fears intimacy.

Checklist For Lovers

Last things done before sex.
Make sure:
___ The doors are locked.
___ The answering machine is on.
___ The champagne's chilled.
___ Place your jewelry in a neat pile so you don't panic should

you, after sex, have to dress quickly.

___ Compliment your partner ("Hod do you stay so svelte?" is the compliment of choice)

___ Read him his rights (ritual for extra-aggressive women only).

How Often Do You Make Love?

Frequency Rate

___ times weekly

What It Means

Sex still fun, but also a duty. You do it:

1. For reproduction
2. To keep warm
3. To get even

The Art of Romance

Ideal gift for the lover who has nothing: Lessons

Ideal gift for the lover who has everything: More of it.

The Art of Romance

Moans alone cannot convey the ecstasy of a perfect sexual experience. That's why we

When out of Bed:	When in Bed:
Read poetry.	Listen to Frank Sinatra
Buy gifts.	Cuddle.
Go dancing.	Snuggle.
Tell our friends.	Take photos.
Smile a lot.	Hold hands.
Prepare a breakfast tray.	Enjoy it.
Whisper sweet nothings.	Use a Post-it.

Tip for Lovers With a Hearty Appetite

Provided that you're gentle and loving, it's okay to bite* the hand that feeds you:

• Breakfast in bed
• Those great during- sex snacks (Fig Newtons)
• Vitamins

*Or munch on.

Count Your Blessings

If you have a partner who:
• Gently wakes you and makes sure you get to work after a wondrous night of sex and little sleep.
• Is faithful (even on business trips).
• Waits until after sex to roll over and fall asleep.
• Thinks your love handles are neat (and uses them to flip you over when you're done on one side).
• Is the perfect size (you both fit so nicely in your bathtub).
• Loves a challenge (like finding a new erogenous zone).
• Has incredible stamina (makes you wish the night and the morning would never end).

The Inquiring Lover

Q. What should I do when, before we go to bed, I spend twenty minutes in the bathroom making myself sexy (slink nightgown, no mudpack) and then I come out and my husband's in bed, fast asleep. He says he's not tired of me, just tired.
A. Have sex anyway. It's your right. Just be sure you don't:
1. Disturb him.
2. Tell him.

Pizza and Sex: Part II

Better sex requires tastier pizza.
Type of Lovemaking
Slow, languid, much non-intercoursal activity—licking, kissing, reviewing stock portfolio, snuggling, flicking of tongue at those areas most vulnerable to flicks.
Ideal Topping
Extra cheese (bulk and strength), garlic (provokes the arousal glands), sausage (provides thiamin) and meatballs (improved concentration). (Tic-Tacs optional.)

One Sign Fits All

A generic horoscope for those without a birthdate but who still believe that sex is a gift from heaven.
• *Ruling passion:* unnatural acts that cause gooseflesh
• *Ruling turnoffs:* phone sex or a ring in the bathtub
• *Chief sexual asset:* insomnia

- *Favorite erogenous zone:* your zip code
- *Ruling sexual activity:* using both hands
- *Aphrodisiacs of choice:* fast cars and fried foods
- *Ideal times for lovemaking:* Eastern Standard, Central Pacific and Western Electric
- *Most compatible with:* any partner who's breathing (but you're actually not that fussy)

Enlightening Moments in Sexual History
When friends suddenly become lovers:
"The evening I realized Kim was good for more than just a shoulder to cry on and her tuna melt casserole."
– Elroy, construction worker
"The night I realized Elroy was good for more than just picking lottery numbers and putting up sheetrock."
– Kim, flight attendant

Philosophy Of A Happy Working Couple
"We make more time for sex by mixing business with pleasure. Of course, when things get really slow, we do it the other way around."
– Edna and Wayne, owners,
mom-and-pop copy center

Sexual Rule of Thumb
When confronted by an annoyed host, couples who arrive late for a party because they just couldn't stop having sex should have the decency to:
- Look sheepish.
- Express remorse.
- Stammer.
- Blush.
- Not bring a bottle of wine that's already been opened.
- Not leave early so they can go home and have more sex.
- Mingle.

The Resourceful Lover

How do you pass the time when your lover's on a business trip?"
"Comparison shop. I want to make sure I really am with the right one."

          — Laurie, graphic designer

"Perfect my lovemaking technique by reading sexy novels, kneading kreplach and using the blow-up doll my wife gave me for Christmas."

          — Dwayne, banking executive

"Feel sorry for myself, clutch my teddy bear, pine away and count the moments until she returns, hopefully with a gift."

          — Walter, attorney

Love Signs

Ruling For a Passionate Pisces

- *Ruling passion:* any sexual act that's labor-intensive
- *Ruling body lotion:* baby oil
- *Chief sexual asset:* perfect love handles
- *Governing erogenous zone:* back of the knee
- *Aphrodisiac of choice:* foot-long hot dog and refried beans
- *Ruling sexual activity:* cooperating
- *Ideal time for sex:* you're loose

The Candid Lover: Part I

Should you keep your new partner guessing?

If you are:	Tell partner	Let partner find out
Great in bed		X
A bit rusty	X	
Married		X
Not as tall as you said you were		X
Desperate		X
Getting carried away	X	
No longer in the same room		X

97

Love Signs

Horoscope for a Passionate Pisces.
- *Ruling passion:* lovers who are politically erect
- *Ruling sexual turnoff:* being loved for your body only
- *Chief sexual asset:* talent
- *Governing erogenous zone:* a quite corner of your bedroom
- *Aphrodisiac:* potato skins
- *Ruling sexual activity:* staying in touch
- *Ideal time for sex:* morning, noon or night (not fussy)

Cold Weather Advice

If you make love for three or more hours at a time:

1. Wear a hat. 25% to 26% of the body's heat is dissipated through the hair follicles.

2. Don't wear earmuffs. A poll of lovers indicates that, next to mittens, they are considered the least sexy item of during-sex apparel.

3. During periods of inactivity, use a quilt or warm blanket. You'll need the heat.

4. Prevent frostbite. Have a neighbor, relative or friend come in and check your toes regularly.

Love Signs: Pisces

Opposite love sign: A virginal (or reasonably pure) Virgo.

Outstanding sexual qualities: Great legs and an uncanny ability to pick the best mutual growth funds.

Most attractive physical feature: You're a certified hunk.

Ruling sexual turnoff: Lovers who check the silverware drawer after you leave.

Ruling sexual turn-on: Your driver's license photo.

Ideal place for sex: A revolving bed (known, if you giggle in the right places, as a merry-go round).

Five During-Sex Breaches of Etiquette

(So you don't commit them.)

1. Intrusive close-ups with the camcorder.

2. Forgetting to say, "Excuse me," if you step on his foot during sex in the vertical position.

3. Tricking your partner into lying in the wet spot.

4. Asking, "Was it good for you?" while you're still undressing.
5. Running to the bathroom to sneak a cigarette.

Terms of Endearment

Use	If You
"Darling"	Forget your lover's name
"Honey"	Recall your lover's name but hate it (say it's Mandrake or Penelope)
"Baby cakes"	Are not on a first-name basis with your lover

Ten Things To Be Happy About After Sex

- You're not in the wet spot.
- Spooning.
- Your tan's still intact.
- Those post-orgasmic shock waves (they aid digestion).
- A back rub.
- You did nothing to harm the ozone layer.
- It's not your turn to walk the dog.
- That deliciously wicked feeling.
- You can start all over again.
- For once, your fortune cookie was right.

Lover's Etiquette

Some guidelines should you arrive home unexpectedly to find your lover in bed with another person.

Do Not	Do
Forget to act surprised	Ask if now's convenient
Forget the other person's still a guest in your home	Be polite and offer refreshments
Unless invited, join in	Wait until they finish
Interrupt	Say good-bye if person leaves abruptly

When Pleasure Becomes Unbearable

Seven items to gnaw on during a Level 9 climax.*

If you:	Chew:
Are nervous	Gum
Can barely see	A carrot
Feel protein deprived	A lambchop
Hope for even more	A wishbone
Have no teeth	Minestrone
Are teething	A bagel (a best bet)
Are dieting	Your partner's thumb

*(You spill your drink all over yourself).

Great Moments in Sex

"The day my boss made a welcome sexual advance...finally!"
— Leo, secretary

"The day she made an unwelcome sexual advance, but I figured...hey, I'm flexible."
— Seymour, bartender

Love Signs: Pisces

Most attractive features: Lovely legs and an uncanny ability to time the stock market.

Turn-on: A lover who believes in world peace, respecting the environment and gifts from Neiman Marcus.

Turnoffs: Small dogs, hamsters and listening to a partner, after deliciously dreamy sex, eat celery.

Ideal romantic adventure: Making love in the wine cellar of a 5-star restaurant and watching the corks pop.

Favorite sexual fantasy: Watching a fabulously aroused lover struggling to remove your cowboy boots while you're still standing in them (Pisces can be sadists).

Bedroom Manners

If, while kissing her eyelid, your front cap comes off in your mouth, do not:
1. Swallow it.
2. Attempt to reinstall it.
3. Allow the cat to play with it.

Great Moments in Afterplay

"Helping each other climb back on the bed."
> – Bill 'n' Bobbie, owners,
> mom-and-pop insurance company

"I pat her until she burps."
> – Egbert, gynecologist-in-waiting

"He rocks me in his arms until I fall asleep."
> – Lena, greengrocer

"He rocks me in his arms until he falls asleep."
> – Judy, gardener

Advice For The Novice

If you're not yet very good at sex, it's okay to just lie there and watch until you get better.

Tip For Fastidious Lovers

When sex gets really hot, experts advise using a mattress pad to protect your precious mattress from unsightly stains should:
• You knock over the Snapple
• Your mascara starts to run
• Your hot-water bottle springs a leak

Random Stress Points

(Scale: 0 to 50.)

New lover turns out to be:	Stress points:
Better than you thought	10
Worse than you thought	25
And you paid for dinner	33
You just left the tip	14
Weird	
Foreplay consists of swinging a golf club	40
Carbohydrate loads by asking you to get on top	50
An old lover in disguise	75

The Intuitive Lover: Part II

How do you suggest to your spouse that you want to make love?
"I look him straight in the eye and tell him 'Horace, we need another kid.'"
> – Gwendolyn, rebirther

"I tussle his hair and stop talking shop talk."
> – Eloise, museum curator

"I put a special note in his lunch pail. He gets a sandwich, a slice of pie and coffee only if I get him."
> – Amy, housewife

"I strip down to nothing but boxer shorts, then ask our guests to leave."
> – Arnie, mason

Frigid Day Survival Guide

If inclement weather prevents you from going out.

Recommended Indoor Activity
1. 25 minutes of gently munching on shell of lover's ear.
2. 5 minutes deciding who lies in the wet spot while the other goes for help.
3. 2 hours of writhing.
4. Praising your lover.

Comparable Outdoor Activity
1. Power walking to nearest convenience store for seltzer.
2. Shoveling driveway (for best results, be sure there's snow).
3. Jogging.
4. Schmoozing with mailman.

Etiquette For The Sexually Correct: Part II

For Formal Lovemaking	**For Informal Lovemaking**
The bath: Luxurious towels	Drip-dry
Hygiene: Jacuzzi	Deodorant stick
For clothing: Quilted hangers	Back of chair
For lover's body: Rare oils	Tapioca
Arousal: Sweet nothings	Brief lecture
Ideal lover: Has pedigree	Has law degree

Spicing Up Your Sex Life: Part I

A gourmet's guide:
Condiment/Application
Allspice: All-purpose passion enhancer—makes a "blah" lover more appealing.
Cayenne: Stimulates sexual creativity—induces more imaginative couplings.

Chili powder: Gives courage to utter louder, more quotable moans (use sparingly).

The Typical American Sex Partner: Part I
A statistical portrait.

Age. Between 21 and 68. (Exception: Hardy farmers perform well into their 80s.)

Pastime. Thinks about sex at least 14 times daily but will admit to only twice daily (once while commuting, once during sex).

Beliefs. When it comes to sex:
• Less is less.
• More is plenty.

Inquiring Lovers Want To Know
What most concerns you with a new partner?

"Can he make a commitment...and love my plants?"
> – Audrey, computer consultant

"Will my mother like her?"
> – Bruce, carpet installer

"How to tell him that during my orgasm, when I totally lose control and grab the sheets and bite my knuckles and scream and kick and writhe and moan and roll my eyes and foam at the mouth, that I'm just having fun and not to panic and call an exorcist."
> – Mabel, teamster

"First knight jitters."
> – Giselle, damsel

First Day Of Lent
No sex today. Instead:
• Only think about it.
• Learn to roller blade.
• Change your hairstyle.
• Put a message in a bottle and float it in the cute guy's soup at the next table.
• Eat a pint of ice cream for breakfast (it'll compensate for sexual deprival).
• Prepare for tomorrow—read the *Kama Sutra*.
• Just shower together.

The Adventurous Lover: Part II

More new places (so the maid can clean your bedroom).
• The kitchen (for gourmets)
• A McDonald's drive-up window (for gourmands)
• The front porch (if you're impatient)
• The den (for intimacy)
• The bathroom (for privacy)
• The elevator (for spontaneity)
• In a Jaguar (for the bold)
• On a Jaguar (for the daring)

From Our Lover's Glossary

The Quickie. Defined as any act of sex that takes more than one minute and less than five. Pioneering efforts by volunteers at truck stops and historical sights throughout the nation have shown that it is possible to enjoy a complete and satisfying sexual experience (one in which both partners finish) without benefit of bed or pillows. The Quickie is now considered to be an acceptable form of sex when it occurs on an elevator, in the rear of a speeding taxi or on a ski lift.

Seven Pretty Good Reasons To Make Love Tonight

1. To burn off your 5 P.M. martini.
2. To discover yet another undiscovered erogenous zone.
3. To make you smile (especially if you fall asleep first).
4. To see your partner only partially clad (assuming this is a good thing)
5. To honor that rain check.
6. To ease that migraine.
7. It'll give you a head start on tomorrow night.

Just Desserts

After-sex rewards for a deserving lover.

Serve:	To a lover who:
Cupcakes	Told you what a cute chest you have.
Cherry cheesecake	Compared you with the bathing suit issue of *The Wall Street Journal*.
Sponge cake	Needs to firm up.
A strawberry fool	Can't tell when you're faking it.

True Love Is...

"Letting my girlfriend borrow my new Porsche to visit her girl-friend who lives 100 miles away...before she got back I swallowed a mere 17 Valiums."
> – Brad, electrician

"Being considerate and also eating only rice and vegetables when my boyfriend's on a diet (and having the decency to eat the pizza that I sneak home in the bathroom).
> – Veronica, mortgage broker

"My wife offering to get up, in the middle of sex, to close the window when she feels a draft."
> – Benjamin, test pilot

Wine And Your Lover: Part I

Disregard all previous rules. Simply remember: the more ardent the lover, the darker the wine.

If your lover is:
Meaty, vigorous, leaves no corner of your body unmassaged
A slow starter but, when warmed up, a real "pistol"
Sexually stingy: Wham-bam-thank-you whomever you are
Serve:
A bold Cabernet or a courageous Gamay
Pinot noir or a vintage Chianti
Catawba pink, a tawny port or an off-year Florsheim

What I Did For Love

"Refused to have sex-bypass surgery."
  – Winny, social worker
"Had my sex-change operation reversed."
  – Enrique, assistant sous-chef, lumber camp

To Perk Up A Blah Sex Life

Seven unusual lovemaking locations, all field-tested by volunteer couples.

1. *For spiritual fulfillment*: a flotation tank
2. *For the view*: a limousine (instruct the driver to take a scenic route)
3. *For the variety*: while house hunting (use the bedroom and ask your realtor to wait in another room)
4. *For the breeze*: on the fire escape
5. *For the danger*: the dressing room of a boutique
6. *For that "outdoor" feeling*: a park bench
7. *For the novelty*: the suburbs

Tip For A Totally Satisfied Lover

After an especially powerful sexual experience, feel free to use either:

• a broom
• a hand-held vacuum
• a little shovel
• a small dish

to collect your senses.

Making Your Sex Life Easier

During-Sex Problem	Solution
Garlic for lunch.	Either chew a sprig of parsley or don't yawn.
Partner taking too long to finish.	Hint by drumming your fingertips on the night table.
Sagging mattress.	Excessive intimacy—order Saint Bernard to lie on the floor until you're finished.
Partner getting too hot.	Lower your flame.
Poor service.	Complain to the manager.

The Inscrutable Lover

Five things never to tell a susceptible partner when he or she asks about your sexual past.

1. That you have one.
2. That you've been equally turned on by other people.
3. That you occasionally see past lovers (a no-no unless you have joint custody of the cat).
4. The juicy details.
5. That it keeps coming back to haunt you in the way of:
• Flashbacks.
• Child support.

Great Moments In Afterplay: Part II

"We order room service."
> – Carly, receptionist

"We start all over again."
> – Buck, wrestler and gemologist

"We bathe together. Then, while we're still wet, we go out to eat."
> – Mike and Mimi, co-manicurists

Pillow Talk

Calling in Sick.* The act of calling one's place of employment, usually in a "weak" voice, for the express purpose of not going to work and, instead, staying in bed for the day with one's lover. Ethically, such act is justifiable provided that one *only* makes love and does not engage in related activities such as tennis or shopping.
*Sometimes referred to as "calling in well."

The Language of Flowers: Part II

To the lover who:	Send:
Provides long-lasting relief from Stress	Daisies
Anxiety	An orchid
Sexual frustration	Lots of orchids
Aging	Azaleas
The greenhouse effect	The greenhouse

A Lover's Seasonal Planner

The Ideal Time To	Winter	Spring	Summer	Fall
Plan a romantic ski trip	X			
Light a fire:				
In the fireplace	X			
Under your lover	X	X	X	X
Make love on:				
Flannel sheets	X			X
Satin sheets	X	X	X	X
A pile of leaves				X
Hunt for dear	X	X	X	X

Lovers' Poll: #10

Why do you leave the lights on when you make love?

"So I can tell if my partner's sweating."

> – Leslie, body builder

"I wanted to see if he had a cute butt. You know how kilts can lie."

> – Olivia, electrician

"So I can see my fingers when I'm counting her orgasms."

> – Theodore, weatherperson

"It assures me of an honest answer when I ask him, 'Do you like what you see?'"

> – Winifred, delegate, United Nations

The Dieter's Guide To Weight Loss During Sex

Activity	Calories Burned
Deciding position:	
By discussion	11
By Ouija board	55
Using labor negotiator	90
Arguing over position	22
Winning	100
Changing positions	38
Without stopping	494

The Dieter's Guide To Weight Loss During Sex

The major components of intercourse.

Activity	Calories Burned
Breathing:	
Normal	9
Heavy	22
Getting crazy	81
Losing control	274
Returning to Earth:	
Regular way	13
Floating	–

The Dieter's Guide To Weight Loss During Sex

Coping with an evasive partner.

Activity	Calories Burned
Chasing your lover:	
Around the bed	24
Around the room	47
Around the house	70
Across 3 continents	15,937

The Well-Appointed Bedroom
Contains:

Door mat. So your lover can wipe her feet before you kiss them.

Soda siphon. Just one squirt cools off and quenches the ardor of even the most over-heated lover.

Wind chimes: Position near the bed and enjoy the lovely tones created by your lover's heavy breathing

Hammock: To lie in when you're playing hard to get.

Step stool: To help a tired lover rise to the occasion.

The Considerate Lover
Thing often said by one partner to another during sex in the bathroom at a crowded cocktail party:
"Let 'em knock."

Quality Sex Advisory
Phrase often uttered after the kind of lovemaking that leaves a partner feeling a) totally relaxed and b) utterly devoid of stress and c) too sleepy to get up and fix dinner and d) certain life doesn't get any better than this:
"I may just never leave this bed."

Passion Scale
Level II
Slightly more intense than Level I. Beginning, perhaps, to feel all the hard work and practice are paying off, but not quite—multiple orgasms still elusive.

How Manifested
Perceptible mussing of hairdo as well as devastating but not life-threatening cracks in your mud-pack. Vital signs normal; minimal memory loss (test: can you still quote the recipe for frutti di mare?).

A Lover's Brain: Part I
Responsibilities of left and right hemispheres.

Left	Right
Attraction to partners mind	Attraction to partner's body
Selection of titillating nightwear	Converting sight of nude partner into erotic bliss
Deciding when	Deciding how
Detecting drafts	Gooseflesh
Savoring partner's right breast	Savoring partner's left breast
That "floaty" feeling	Getting carried away
Stores past sexual experiences	Retrieval of highlights

Ways To Impress A New Lover: Part I
Make brilliant suggestions.
• "Let's do it in the kitchen."
• "Shall we try it while rollerblading?"
• "Why not have your legs waxed?"
Help your lover lose weight in all the right places.
• Aspen.
• Cannes.
• Acapulco.
Be helpful.
• Give your lover a note of explanation if you make him or her late for work.

Sexual Etiquette
No matter how anxious he or she may be, it is not considered in the best of taste for an inexperienced lover to station a prompter at the foot of the bed, unless he refrains from (a) offering a second opinion, (b) singing along and (c) participating.

Tip For Childless Couples
Trying to have children? Our consulting fertility expert tells us that having sex three or more times weekly* in the family room of your home can increase, by nearly 22%, your chances of conceiving.
*At least five times weekly if you want twins.

The Caring Lover
Five ways to practice cruelty-free sex.
1. Never snicker should he experience impotence.
2. After sex, never say, "Is that all it does?"
3. Never stop in the middle of lovemaking to:
• Meditate.
• Straighten a picture.
4. During particularly torrid moments, avoid statements like:
• "I'm just going through the motions."
• "How are we on time?"
• "I think we should date other people."
5. Be patient: Don't make the bed while she's still in it.

Pre-Sexual Rituals
Why is your lover spending so much time in the bathroom? Some answers.

Lover claims to be:	But is really:
Brushing teeth	Checking breath by exhaling into medicine cabinet
Combing hair	Eating extra oysters
Removing makeup	Studying sex manual
Singing	Weeping
Flossing	Flexing
Showering	Calling therapist on cellular phone

The Enlightened Lover
You may omit foreplay *only* if:
1. You have too little time.
2. You have too little energy.
3. It wouldn't be cost-effective.
4. It would be too distracting.
5. You're already warmed up.

Arousal Tip #1

To get partners excited if you go to bed with them for their

Mind:

Read to each other.

Ask them the capital of Haiti.

Watch *Jeopardy!*

Whisper in their ear.

Body:

Play with each other.

Ask them to flex.

Admire their "pecs."

Just blow in it.

Senior Lovers

During-sex questions indicating:

Short-term memory loss

"Are you my first?"

Long-term memory loss

"Were you my last?"

Ruining the Mood

Eight things never to say to a partner during lovemaking.

1. "My feet are getting cold."
2. "Could you possibly do any better?"*
3. "Cut it out."
4. "For this I broke curfew?"
5. "Who was that on the phone?"
6. "Who's wearing the condom?"
7. "You're ruining my makeup."
8. "You're ruining my career."

*Especially unwise to say to a partner with low self-esteem.

Happy Endings

How would you describe an indescribable climax?

"Like winning the lottery without leaving the bedroom."

— Harold, auto mechanic

"I always get confused and think I'm being abducted by aliens."

— Julie, cocktail waitress

"It makes me swallow my chewing gum."

— Larry, carpenter

"Like I was just granted a no-interest car loan."

— Sonya, court stenographer

Embarrassing Moments
"I was on top wearing my new toupee, when it slid off my head and into her mouth. She couldn't stop coughing for nearly an hour. It was kinky but sure destroyed the mood."
— Jerry R., lingerie salesman

When The Unthinkable Happens

Event	What to Do
Lover bursts in and catches you in bed with your wife.	Nothing. You lead a charmed life.
Partner on top too virile—is knocked unconscious by chandelier.	Don't stop—this is not your problem.
While counting orgasms on your fingers, you break your best and dearest nail.	Stop. Call manicurist. Make an appointment. (Lover obliged to pay.)

Love Poll #3
The official results of an official government sex-survey:
• 31% of all Americans felt that it was impossible to concentrate on sex while clutching an unopened letter from the IRS.
• 44% of all Americans felt that as a contact sport, sex was preferable to shaking hands with a politician.
• Only 16% of all Americans abide by the official North American mating hour (11:30 P.M., rain or shine).
• After-sex statement most uttered by 41% of all Americans: "Have a nice day."

The Inquiring Lover
When people argue over sex, what do they actually argue about?
A Good Sign
1. Whether to have it 5 or 7 times a week.
2. "Not again! Refers to the third time this night.
3. "It's your turn to be on top, I want to watch us in the ceiling mirror."
4. "I can't tonight, I'm still exhausted from last night."
A Bad Sign
1. Whether to have it.
2. "Not again!" refers to tuna casserole.

3. "It's your turn to be on top, I have to see the clock so I'm not late for the hairdresser."
4. "I can't tonight, I'm still exhausted from last month."

Poor Bed Manners
Among 10,000 lovers surveyed, the top turnoffs were:
• Failure, before sex, to remove decorative objects (bracelets, earrings, spurs, tattoos) that might jingle.
• Rushing sex—commencing lovemaking before the other partner (a) arrives and (b) gets into bed.
• Asking, just as it's getting good, "Did you hear anything about tomorrow's weather?"
• A partner who refers to the bed as a "work station."
• A partner who leaves too much to the imagination.
• After sex, saying the wrong thing ("I'd ask you in, but the postman's waiting").

Wellness Tip For Women
Women who experience at least two orgasms a week:
• Often smile at inappropriate moments (while they're being asked by their boss to get coffee, for example).
• Complain less about fatigue.
• Shop less.
• Are more certain of their (and their lover's) sexuality.
• Prepare better, healthier meals for the man responsible for at least one of those orgasms.

Lover Appreciation Day: Phase II

To the lover who:	Send:
Is shy	A free introductory offer
Knows six great positions	A back brace
Knows one incredible positions	Vitamins
Makes you crazy	Your therapist's bill
Has a good sex drive	A Hyundai
Has a great sex drive	A Mercedes
Takes a long time	A watch
You can barely keep up with	A friend

Romance Advisory for Today

Cherish the lover who:

• Never laughs at your dreams (and gets really excited over some of your fantasies).

• By the light of the silvery moon

a) Reads you love sonnets.

b) Taught you to balance your checkbook.

• Knows that when it comes to gifts it's the thought that counts, but a quilted robe with a Piaget watch in the pocket is also nice.

• Loves you for what you are (especially when you've slipped into your Venetian lace push-up bra and thong bikini).

• Gives you gooseflesh when she a) blows in your ear or b) tells you she's late this month.

MONTHLY QUALITY OF LIFE® CHECKUP

•**We did it:** 7 times___ 12 times___ 20 times___ Not at all (I punished him for forgetting Valentine's Day)___

•**Usual duration of sexual activity:**

10 minutes___

17 minutes___

30 minutes___

As long as it takes___

•**In addition to sex I use my lover for:**

Emotional support___

Walking the dog when its freezing outside___

Shiatsu massage___

Companionship___

Moving heavy furniture___

•**Biggest obstacle to perfect sex:**

Partner's ego___

Partner's hernia___

Partner always afraid it might muss her hairdo___

Partner always worried it will injure his bowling hand___

Traffic noise___

We need a larger bed___

Partner thinks sex should be self-service___

Unclipped toenails___

Signed_____

Witnessed_____

MARCH

•Erotic goals for March:
1. Make bedroom more sensual (or at least change the sheets)
2. Empty the litter box more often
3. Shave legs

A perilous month for those susceptible to that most dreaded of all maladies: Spring Fever. Do you have it? Is it contagious? Perhaps the following facts will prove helpful.

•**Symptoms and signs:** Onset of Spring Fever is marked by acute inflammation of the libido, daydreaming and, in severe cases, installation of a kissing booth at your work station. Itchy, watery eyes and persistent sneezing may be present if a secret admirer sends you roses. In rare cases, the aroused male partner, especially one whose hormones are bubbling, will experience what the Surgeon General refers to as a "premature climax" (occurs while he's asking you for a date.)

•**Treatment:** Spring Fever requires immediate and vigorous treatment lest the sufferer go mad. Intense lovemaking, as well as antibiotics (e.g. Champagne, caviar and Milky Ways®) should be started early and continued until the beginning of April, at which time you'll have to switch focus and decide whether to take a share in a summer house.

•**Prognosis:** Happily, mortality is low, particularly among couples who indulge in public displays of affection such as holding hands, sharing sushi and, when the flight attendant isn't looking, joining the "Mile High" club on a flight from Tampa to Seattle. (See *"The In-Flight Sex Manual,"* Part V: "Earning Bonus Miles—Sex With Your Meal Tray Down." TWA Press.)

•Official aphrodisiac of the Month:
Roast loin of pork with sausage stuffing
(Roast loin of tofu for vegetarians)

Traveler's Advisory #1

A brief guide to in-flight sex.

1. If the serving area's busy, use the lavatory.
2. Suggested in-lavatory positions:
   Both standing (best)
   Both sitting (worst)
(If turbulence occurs, switch.)
3. Recommended position if lavatory occupied: heavier passenger in seat, lighter passenger on meal tray.

Most common reason for failure to achieve orgasm: "This is the captain speaking."

Great Moments in Afterplay

"Pulling my knee-highs back up."
            – Charlotte, model
"Studying the Polaroids."
            – Herman, our technical adviser

Things Often Said

• *Before great lovemaking:* "Lock the door."
• *During great lovemaking:* "Wow, I could really get used to this!"
• *After great lovemaking:* "Please, sir, can I have some more?"
• *Way after great lovemaking:* "Zzzzzzz."

Gem of the Month

His or her weight in aquamarines to the lover who never stops in the middle of sex to:
• Offer criticism.
• Go through the day's mail.
• Listen for tomorrow's weather.
• Take a quick nap.
• Reach for another cookie.
• Thumb through a magazine.
• Make a diary entry (even if it's brief).
• Ask your sign (or try to change it to one more compatible).
• Tell his teammates he'll be right down.
Note: Several bonus gems, however, to the lover who stops in the middle of sex to toss another log on the fire.

Roll Models: What I Did for Love

"At harvest time went out in the fields and, along with his lunch, gave him a roll in the hay."
> – Muffy, 4-H club president

Verrrrry slowly undressed him, then, to keep his strength up, gave him a roll* instead of a bialy."
> – Amanda, baker

"Loved her 8" x 10" glossies so I interviewed her, then gave her a role in the hay."
> – Jack, movie producer

*Seeded with butter.

From Our Lover's Glossary

Spontaneous combustion: The bursting into flame of two vigorous lovers because of heat produced while they're a) on their honeymoon or b) making love after not having seen each other for several weeks or c) saying delightfully filthy things to each other on the phone or d) snacking on chili containing an injudicious number of habañeros. Etiquette tip: It is the partner who is least exhausted who gets up to deactivate the smoke alarm.

Pillow Talk

Neck kisses. Very much like back kisses except they're higher and, with properly puckered lips, can cause the ears of the kissee to flutter most charmingly. Neck kisses from an ardent lover have been found to reduce the monotony of:

• Stirring soup
• Proofreading a diary
• Waiting on line to use a cash machine
• A dinner party

Sex: The Four Basic Exercises

Exercise	Purpose
Pushups	Enable lover, after sex, to lift self off partner unassisted.
Situps	Tighten stomach muscles, permitting lover to support a) partner and b) a laden breakfast tray.
Jogging	Enables lover to run to a neutral corner should sex get too hot.
Stretching	Flexibility. Permits lover to reach over sleeping partner to shut off alarm.

Sexual Stress

Five ways to control sexually stressful situations:

1. Set realistic goals (have sex no more than seven times a week).
2. Organize time (spend no more than two hours on foreplay).
3. Just say "No" when asked to do it for the third time that night.
4. Don't be afraid to ask questions during sex ("How am I doing?" or "What's our ETA?").
5. Take early retirement.

The Diplomatic Lover

The Question: "Where'd you learn that?"
When asked: During a particularly serious sexual moment, when you've taken your partner's breath away.
By whom: Your enchanted and very satisfied partner.
Your choice of answers:

1. *Innocent:* "Learn what?"
2. *Romantic:* "I don't know, I was a virgin till I met you."
3. *Honest:* "From you—you talk in your sleep."

March Music
Melodies to help lovers cope with incipient Spring Fever:

Activity	Music
Sex with a small but vigorous lover	"Little Things Mean a Lot"
Necking on a park bench or in a movie theater	"People Will Say We're in Love"
When making love in the "Hollywood" position (you on top, famous person on bottom)	"When You Wish Upon a Star"
Convincing a shy lover to make the first move	"Onward Christian Soldier"

One Way to Meet
"This really dreamy guy was walking down the street, not looking where he was going, and just in time I pointed out the huge pile of dog doo his Gucci loafers were about to step in. He showed his gratitude by marrying me."

– Penny, pretty good samaritan

Reminder
When you lover dozes off during sex in the missionary position, it can get lonely at the top.

Advice for Busy Lovers
To steal those sexual moments—a few suggestions.
- *On the elevator*—press "Stop." Time limit: one minute
- *Before a party*—while waiting for you host to answer the door.
- *At a party*—in your host's bedroom, under the coats.
- *In the kitchen*—while lover is cooking.
- *At home*—while lover is talking on the phone.
- *At the museum*—in an under-visited gallery (try Etruscan pottery).
- *In your car*—during an oil change or while driving the baby-sitter home.

The First Time

Frequent reactions by novice lovers to their first sexual experience.

- *If sex was good:* "Where have you been all my life?"
- *If sex was great:* "Where have I been all my life?"
- *If sex was only so-so:* "Is that all it does?"

Sex Poll #6

What happened when you experienced your first simultaneous orgasm? (Asked of three married couples whose children had gone off to college.)

"Intense hunger. We both had to leap out of bed, run to the deli and satisfy our craving for a knish."

> — Elroy and Cyndi, together 19 years

"Awe. We couldn't believe we still had that many moving parts!"

> — Dagmar and Gomer, together 22 years

"Special effects. At our next door neighbor's birthday party, all the balloons popped."

> — Greta and Clark, together 26 years

A Lover's Night Table: Part I

Preparing for a new partner? Five items to keep beside the bed.

1. A sewing kit. To suture the seams of garments removed in haste.
2. Shoe horn. For putting shoes on quickly should you hear (a) a prowler or (b) a mating call.
3. Emery board. Women pausing during sex to file a broken nail is the sixth leading cause of sexual dysfunction in males.
4. Condoms. (The exceptional hostess offers a choice of colors and sizes, including S M L and Petite.)
5. Milk and cookies. For the partner who needs mothering.

A Lover's Medicine Cabinet: Part I

Item	Application
Anti-oxidant tablets	Prevents lovers from getting rusty
Megavitamins	Obvious
Geritol	Increases shelf life of partners over 40
Tums	For lovers who ignore a partner's warning about eating fried food

A Day in the Life of a Lover
Good Day
The phone rings: it's your partner, telling you how wonderful you were last night.

The doorbell rings: it's flowers from your lover.

The earth moved.

Your lover made the bed.

You did it three times.

Bad Day
The phone rings: it's your partner, asking what's for dinner.

The doorbell rings: it's the tax assessor.

Because you're on a fault line.

With you still in it.

Has to last until May.

Guilt Alert
Five sex-related causes of guilt:
1. Inflicting too much pleasure on a vulnerable lover.
2. Thinking about a past lover during present sex.
3. Staying in bed after the alarm goes off because your lover's body feels so good.
4. Failure to change sheets between lovers.
5. Enjoying sex with the person your mother warned you about.

Breaking the Ice
A long, passionate glance is one way. If you prefer to rely on verbal skills, however, we suggest you ask:
Before sex
• "How much did that negligee cost?"
• "What time should I set the alarm for?"
• "Do nice girls do this?" (May be said by either partner.)
During sex
• "What are you trying to prove?" (Most effective when said during the fourth hour of sex.)
After sex
• "Any good stock tips?"

The Inquiring Lover

Q. My question is one of a romantic nature: During sex, is it ever permissible to excuse myself to heed the call of nature?

A. Only if the call comes from:
- Greenpeace
- The World Wildlife Federation
- The Sierra Club

Lovers Never Forget

After conducting an uncontrolled experiment, researchers tell us that 91% of all people who refrained from sex for six months or more report regaining full sexual function within ten minutes of going to bed with an attractive partner.*

*Exception: Divorcées who tried to make up for lost time.

You Know You Need a Lover: Part III

If:
- You haven't had one since Woodstock (the original).
- You've redone your bathroom more than twice in one year.
- You fantasize about the telemarketer who called you about buying a juicer.
- You're always the first to arrive.
- And the last one to leave.

A Night in the Life of a Lover

Good Night	Bad Night
One hour of sex, seven hours of sleep	Eight hours of sleep
Three hours of sex, six hours of sleep	Nine hours of sleep
Partner acting frisky	Partner acting
Tossing and turning from steamy sex	Tossing and turning from steamed mussels
Moaning	Groaning
Sweet dreams	Nightmares
Wet dreams	Roof leaking

The Dieter's Guide to Weight Loss During Sex

First-Night Jitters	Calories Burned
If caused by having sex with a new lover	83
If caused by having sex with an old lover	19
Who you thought was new	278

Movies for Lovers: Part II

If your lover:	Rent
Helped you experience your first orgasm.	Deliverance
Falls asleep moments after getting into bed.	Night of the Living Dead
Has a weight problem.	Giant
Has difficulty maintaining an erection.	Bye Bye Birdie

After-Sex Etiquette

You need never apologize to your partner for taking so long unless he or she has:
- Patients waiting.
- Theater tickets.
- Restaurant reservations.
- An appointment.
- A date.
- Visibly aged.

Inside a Lover's Fortune Cookie

Stop searching forever. Happiness is just next to you—if only you could:
1. Wake him up.
2. Get her attention.

The Well-Equipped Lover

Four indispensable bedside items.

1. **Floss.** For use after ingestion of aphrodisiacs such as: a) brownies, b) hazelnut ice cream, and c) edible underwear.

2. **A camcorder.** If you're insecure about your lovemaking abilities and need a third opinion.

3. **A compass.** Vital for lovers who want to explore their own sexuality.

4. **A pencil.** For:
• Indicating that you want to perform an unspeakable act.
• Grading him.

In the Beginning
Things to change when you start a new relationship.

Item	Why
The sheets	The old ones contain memories.
The pillowcases	The old ones contain your ex's mousse.
The mattress	Breaking in a new one will strengthen the relationship.
Your phone number	If your old lover gets lonely late at night.
Your parrot	The old one may reveal past secrets.
Your birth date	If your astrological signs conflict.

Hearts and Flowers: Part I

Give:	To the lover who:
Petunias.	Always makes you feel sexy (even if you've just given birth).
Delphiniums.	Makes your toes tingle just by thinking about last night's session.
Gardenias.	Never begins lovemaking without you.
Daisies	Loves you for your body.
Gladioli.	Loves you for your libido.

Earth Tip for Lovers Against Pollution
Sex is the environmentally safe way to drive your lover to ecstasy without using a car.

Great Moment in Lovemaking

"After trying for several days, I got through to my local Sex Addict's Hot Line, which furnished me with 26 names—I finally found compatibility!"

— Ivana, parapsychologist (all major credit cards)

When the Unthinkable Happens

Event	What to Do
Leg cramp:	
In calf	Warm up sufficiently—10 deep knee bends should be adequate.
In thigh	Avoid positions that defy the laws of gravity.
Lower back pain	Cease bending over backward just to learn a new position.

The Dieter's Guide to Weight Loss During Sex

A woman's responsibilities.

Activity	Calories Burned
Before intercourse: Helping her eager partner on	3
After intercourse: Getting her dozing partner off	126

How Often Do You Make Love? Part II

Frequency Rate

1-2 times weekly (dual-career couples)

What It Means

Sex now much more "spiritual" (i.e., not quite so much fun). Arousal consists of flossing, then on to foreplay (10 minutes of passionate kissing) and, to maintain excitement level, uttering sweet nothings ("You're on my leg").

Sexual Etiquette

Bedroom guide for the hospitable lover. Always remember:

1. You come last.
2. Guests come first.

The Inquisitive Lover

Q. I was wondering, when used in a conscientiously applied program, can sex straighten my teeth?

A. No.

Q. Will it remove plaque?

A. Yes.

Are You Too Lustful?: Part I

(Answering yes to even one question means your soul may be in jeopardy.)

1. You sometimes wake up early just so you can gaze over at your still-sleeping spouse and think about how lovely it would be to make love just once more before going off to work.

___ No   ___ Yes, especially if it's my turn to drive.

2. Have you ever done more than just think about it?

___ No   ___ Yes, and I'm so embarrassed.

3. In addition to bringing home flowers, you've been known, on occasion, to express affection for your spouse with sex.

___ Never   ___ Yes, as often as possible, in fact.

Virtuous Sex: Part II

Event	Permissible	Sin
Reasons for sex:		
Pleasure		X
Biological clock ticking	X	
Obligation (he helped you move)	X	
Remedial fondling:		
Regular		X
Therapeutic massage	X	
Après-sex aphrodisiac:		
Black Forest chocolate cake		X
Carrot sticks	X	
More sex		X

Rewarding Your Love: Poll #29

After sex, how do you reward your lover for a job well done?
"I make him his favorite dishes: Spanish rice with herring and rugelach."

> – Marita, flight attendant

"I give her free tax advice."
                    – Elliot, accountant
"I put a hundred-dollar bill in his hand, then gently usher him and his room service cart out the door."
                    – Paula, hotel guest
"Kinkily—I massage her back with the ball of my roll-on deodorant bottle."
                    – Hans, ski instructor

Official Rain Check

When last night's lovemaking wasn't what it should have been, check where appropriate and fax to partner.

                    ----------Fold here----------

___ Next time, I won't invite our new puppy to bed.

___ I realize I'm impossibly demanding, but don't you think sex is better without your laptop on your lap?

___ I promise no more recreational positions (you on top, me practicing my golf swing).

___ I don't think foreplay is the right time to discuss your mother coming to live with us.

___ Gosh, honey, you forgot to make a pass at me.

Fitting It All In

How loving (but busy) couples make more time for sex:

"We do our weekly food shopping but once a month."
                    – Carl and Nancy

"We always arrive late at the movies and hope that some kind soul in the audience will tell us what's already happened."
                    – Millie and Dan

"While making love, we also water the houseplants and feed our tropical fish. They don't mind."
                    – Beth and Horace

"We do it faster."
                    – Elaine and Ed

The Enlightened Lover

What to do after:

Good sex	Great sex
Stretch	Call a chiropractor
Dress	Try to find your clothes
Wonder about your future	Wonder about your lover's past
Do nothing till your mind clears	Do nothing till the smoke clears
Nap	Dream

The Well-Bred Lover

Always	Never
Arrives on time	Undresses until the door's completely closed
Brings a gift	Tracks in mud
Removes his or her lucky baseball cap	Has sex while wearing a Walkman
Keeps partner warm	Lets partner cool off
Knows when it's time to go	Forgets to (a) sign the guest book and (b) send a thank-you note

The Seven Wonders of the Sexual World

Natural	Unnatural
Orgasm	Exorcism
Afterglow	Fireworks
An enthusiastic lover	A Sphinx (never moves)
During orgasm: achieving lift-off	After orgasm: going into orbit
Multiple orgasms	All at one time
Erogenous zones	"Ohhhhh" zones
Moaning	Chirping

"It is after the first two hours of sex that I get a feeling of sublime mental clarity and can finally remember where I parked the car."
  – Jerome Fish, merchant

Q. He's a wonderful lover, kind considerate, incredible in bed, and gives me orgasms that make my mascara run, but he's always out of town when I have to hang a picture. What can I do?
A. Make him feel that he's more than just a sex object. Show an interest in his life: ask him his last name, or, more personal, why he sleeps in his car. If this doesn't work, avoid art galleries.

The Inquisitive Lover
Q. Is it ever immoral to see two lovers on the same day?
A. Only if:
• One shows up without an appointment (walk-in applicant).
• It wasn't a bona fide emergency.
• They're related.
• One is not your spouse.
• Your reach doesn't exceed your grasp.
• You're getting double time.

Are You a True Romantic?
You are if, while making love, you don't stop although you:
• Sustain external injury (a broken fingernail).
• Suddenly recall your vow of abstinence (your eighth).
• Hear footsteps.
• Suffer internal injury (anxiety).
• Overdoes on pleasure.
• Are still bidding guests good-bye.
• Had a bad day at work.
• Feel paranoid (think you smell gas).
• Feel psychotic (think you smell electricity).

Wondrous Moments in Afterplay
"Deciding whether to continue making love. I examine my partner's pulse. If he's still ticking, off we go."
— Irma, lawyer
"Letting the dog back into the house. I miss him so."
— Phil, fax machine technician
"Checking in with my answering machine, you never know."
— Gloria, starlet
"Wondering if I faked it."
— Yvonne, psychic friend

Five Things to Do When the Right Lover Comes Along: Part I

1. Rejoice.
2. Dump the wrong one (and change your locks).
3. Report to the nearest house of worship, fall to your knees and give thanks (tip generously on your way out).
4. Carefully check for the Ghost of Lovers Past:
   - By the bathroom sink—the "extra" toothbrush.
   - Between the couch cushions—a hoop earring (not yours).
   - On your night stand—incriminating photos.
   - On your arm—the "I'll always love Alan" tattoo.
5. Get an extra closet.

The Enlightened Lover

Six reasons to leave the lights on during lovemaking.
1. Better photos.
2. Makes searching for obscure erogenous zones less of a chore.
3. You can see the dimples in all four of your partner's cheeks.
4. Easier to sign an autograph if you're a celebrity and your partner is not.
5. It'll be easier to find your head when he wants to run his fingers through your hair.
6. You can tell if it's love at first sight.

Love Poll #3

In a random poll of 500 couch potatoes, 62% said they refuse to make love for two hours before a big nap, insisting it would make them too tired to sleep.

The Guest Lover: Part I

It's appropriate to invite a guest lover if your regular lover is:
- Busy making breakfast.
- Watching the playoffs.
- Sleeping (again).
- Insatiable.
- Snowbound.
- On sabbatical.
- Making a house call.

The Dieter's Guide to Weight Loss During Sex

Being sociable during sex does not, alas, induce significant weight loss. However, these numbers might be of interest to finicky lovers.

Activity	Calories Burned
Whispering an endearment	5
Distinctly	7
Praising your lover (examples):	
"Gosh, that feels good."	11
"Wow!"	3
"Those latkes were perfect."	20
Imparting vital information:	
"We're on the floor."	8
"The baby's crying."	14

From Our Lover's Glossary

Silent partner. 1. A lover who just lies there passively and lets his or her partner do all the work. 2. A lover who, during sex, makes no sound whatsoever, not even a standard "Oooh," or "Ohhh!" for fear that:

• The children will hear; or
• The neighbors will hear; or
• He'll give himself away.

Sexy Signals: Poll #23

How do you let someone you've just met know you're interested?
• "I invite her to spend a weekend in Rome, all expenses paid except transportation and meals."
• "Ask if I can feel her muscles (I do get slapped a lot)."
• "I cross my legs, my cuffs ride up and she sees my incredibly sexy shins."
• "Gaze straight into his eyes, run my finger up and down his wrist and ask him if he could possibly help me out with the rent."

Phone Sex
How they met the love of their life.

"I was standing around, waiting to use the pay phone he was monopolizing. He kept borrowing quarters from me which, because he was so good-looking, I happily lent him interest free. The rest is history."

> – Marsha, court stenographer

"She dialed a wrong number and heard my answering machine tape: 'If you're not a gorgeous woman, ages thirty-five to forty-eight, with a great body, nifty legs and financially secure, don't bother leaving a message.' She left her name and number."

> – Claude, chemist

Tips for Lovers with High Blood Pressure
A perspiring partner's upper lip can contain up to one teaspoon of salt.

Show or Tell
Eight ways to inform a new lover about your sexuality.
1. *Most attention-getting:* flash cards
2. *Most fun:* charades
3. *Most graphic:* guiding lover's hands
4. *Most entertaining:* slide show
5. *Most direct:* pointing
6. *Most unusual:* semaphore
7. *Most enlightening:* demonstrating with an old lover
8. *Most impressive:* an affidavit

Sexual Rule of Thumb
When getting into bed with your lover, if one or both of you sink nine or more inches below the surface and disappear, it's time to get a new mattress or add water.

Intensive Care
Until the drugstore opens, generic sex with someone you love is an inexpensive and safe alternative* to:
• Tranquilizers
• Antidepressants
• Diet pills

- Antipsychotic pills (especially)
- Aspirin
- Sleep medication
- Biofeedback
- High blood pressure remedies
- Chicken soup
- Rice pudding

*Not, however, an inexpensive and safe alternative to birth control pills.

Nonverbal Communication Tip
The happiest lovers claim that their best heart-to-heart talks occur during sex, with their chests firmly pressed against each other.

Après-Lovemaking Ritual #2
Things heard from our test couples after a wondrous climax.

Intensity Level Utterance
1 "Thank you, I needed that."
2 "It must have been those oysters."
3 "There is a God."
4 "Don't you think we should climb back on the bed?"
5 "You just lie there and look beautiful, I'll shovel the driveway."

A Guide to Vehicular Sex
Chrysler Imperial

Advantages
Anti-lock brakes prevent skidding during extra special orgasm. Spacious seats invite lust.

Disadvantages
Inconvenient shift lever almost guarantees headache in awkward positions (any position in which either partner's head makes contact with the gas pedal).

Should You Leave the Lights On? Part I

If you live in a glass house next to:

	Turn the lights off	Leave them on
Woods		X
Curious neighbors	X	
Envious neighbors		X
Deer		X
Prudish deer	X	
Astronomers		X
A Little League field	X	

Rest Advisory for Marathon Lovers

When you feel overwhelmed by too much sex, take a 10-minute break and:

- Compose your thoughts.
- Leaf through your favorite cookbook.
- Rearrange your closets.
- Make that phone call to a shut-in aunt.
- Catch up on your sleep.
- Do the laundry.
- Finish your needlepoint.

My Most Memorable Sexual Moment

"After eight months I finally met Mr. Right and broke my vow of chastity. It felt really good."
— Wayne, rear admiral, U.S. Navy, ret.

"After seven years of trying, we were finally able to make love without our sex therapist watching on closed circuit TV."
— Victoria and Ed, tag team

"Simultaneous orgasm and we were in different rooms!"
— Gwen and Percival, antique dealers

Magic Words

What to Say	When
"May I help you?"	Your new lover can't get your belt undone.
"So, what's up?"	During sex—breaks the tension should the male partner suddenly find himself impotent.
"This never happened before."	What a male partner says who finds himself suddenly impotent.
"Please keep trying."	What the female partner says to put the male partner at ease.

Therapeutic Lovemaking

More things to expect from an extra-satisfying sex life.
1. Spring fervor (out goes the bad air, in comes the good air).
2. A smile that enrages preachers.
3. A sunnier disposition.
4. Reduced risk of:
    • Insomnia.
    • Heart disease.
    • Divorce.
5. Upper body workouts that cause you to giggle.
6. A sense of well-being (even if you IRA's underfunded).
7. A higher sperm count.

Reawaken Your Sex Life: Part I

Give your bed a rest. Some alternate lovemaking locations:

Basic	Advanced
The rear deck of your house	The front porch
In a jacuzzi	On a dental chair
Under the stars	Under the stairs
In your bedroom	On the balcony
In front of your fireplace	In front of your in-laws

The Art of Romance
Seven necessities that honeymooners:

Can do without	Can't do without
Phone calls	Calls of nature
Fresh air	Fresh water
Sunlight	Moonlight
Food	Room service
The mail	A male
A change of position	A change of linen
A sign from above	A do-not-disturb sign

The Cautious Lover
Seven things to check for in a new lover's bedroom.
1. A hidden microphone
2. A one-way mirror
3. The house detective
4. A poster of his or her therapist
5. Fingerprints
6. The nearest exit
7. An old, leftover lover.

Rewarding a Perfect Lover
When extra good in bed, allow your lover to return your empty bottles and keep the deposit money. (And it's good for the environment, too.)

From Our Lover's Glossary
Sexual Misconduct. Improper behavior during lovemaking, such behavior to include:
• Using a metronome to have sex by the rhythm method.
• Failure to express remorse for not satisfying partner.
• Failure, before sex, to ask all nonessential personnel to leave the room.
• Promising to replace a partner's virginity with something much better.

What I Did for Sex

"Borrowed a best-selling sex manual from the library. The librarian followed me home."
– Georgina, scholar
"Bought her a drink, then dinner, then a winter coat, then a new car, then an engagement ring, then, finally, a house."
– Carl, appliance salesman
"Smooth-talked a new client into going away with me for the weekend. He's no longer my client."
– Donna, agent
"Got my eyebrow pierced. Ouch!"
– Sidney, astrologer

The Enlightened Lover

The best way to watch your favorite films is snuggled up in the bedroom. Here's why.

In the Bedroom	In a Movie Theater
Sweet and gracious partner	Rude usher
Sipping champagne	Carrying drinks to seat prohibited
Sprawled out on a comfy bed	Scrunched up in a lumpy seat
No clothes necessary	Rigid dress code
Nothing to stop you from making love	Armrest

A Guide to Restaurant Flirting: Part I

Activity	Purpose
Playing footsies:	
Shoes on	Eases boredom while listening to the waiter announce the "specials"
Shoes off	More legroom
Holding hands	Gives each other the courage to: a) Ask for a larger table b) Ask if the sole is fresh
Rubbing knees	An appetizer substitute for those on a budget

Wellness Tips for Lovers
How much sex do you need to keep healthy?

To Prevent

Shopping	Twice a week
Plaque buildup	Twice a day
Stress buildup	Once a week
Colds and flu	Once a day
Weight gain	Once each time you go to sleep
Insomnia	Five times a week
Wrinkles	Four times a week

Getting Away from It All: Part I
Stolen sexual moments—a guide for adventurous lovers.

Where	**Why**
A booth in a diner	If sex is bad, there's the jukebox.
Scenic overlook	Fresh air and cloud formations.
At a party, in the bathroom	Kitchen's too crowded.
At the bank	It's Teller Appreciation Week.
On the golf course	*The* way to improve your putts.

Met That Special Someone?: Part II
Preferred Assets (Specific)

	Nice to Have	Important	Crucial
Lover-friendly hands	X		
Non-vegetarian		X	
Tall, dark and looks great in a dinner jacket (if looks are important)	X		
Short, light and grotesque (if intellect is important)		X	
An easy laugh			X
Thinks "politically correct" means using a voting booth properly."			X

What Do the Professionals Do?
Problem
1. You have an overwhelming urge to go to the bathroom but worry your partner will lose interest if you stop.
2. Your partner is beginning to o.d. on gooseflesh caused by nibbling on and blowing into his or her ear.
3. You're starting to tire.
Solution

A Professional	An Amateur
1. Grits teeth.	1. Stops.
2. Keeps going.	2. Switches ears.
3. Doesn't.	3. Does.

Pillow Talk
A hopelessly vain lover. One who, during frantic, passionate lovemaking, uses the ceiling mirror only to study his bald spot.

Tip for Suburbanites
How does great sex really feel? The results of our on-site, while-they're-actually-doing-it sex survey.

"As though I'm rapidly losing IQ points."
> – Lil, chemist

"Too weak to wiggle my toes."
> – Kate, talent scout

"Please, I'm only human."
> – Melissa, accountant

"Read my lips."
> – Zsa Zsa, dental assistant

The Considerate Lover
Mood-upsetting questions never to ask.
Moments before sex:
- "May I make just one last phone call?"
- "Have you gone off your diet?"

During sex:
- "Did you remember to mail in the car payment?"
- "Could you possibly make a little less noise?"

Moments after sex:
- "Could I have my love letters back?"

The Joys of Frequent Sex: Part II

Five more benefits according to our reader survey.

1. "Lowered my triglycerides . . . they're now down around my knees."
2. "Moaning keeps my breath fresh (and blasts away plaque)."
3. "Less time to shop and spend my wife's hard-earned money."
4. "I'll take love bites over insect bites any time."
5. "My bosom just adores the workouts."

After-Sex Etiquette

Say something complimentary like:
- "Was it good for you, too?" or
- "What's a nice person like you doing in a bed like this?"

Offer to do something special for your partner like:
- Make coffee.
- Take out the garbage.
- Feel around on the floor for her contact lens.
- Ring for the nurse.

Volunteer to make:
- The bed.
- Dinner reservations.

Communication Tip
Words alone cannot convey the extraordinary ecstasy of the sexual experience. That's why we moan.

The Art of Romance

Common reasons for not making love.

The Excuse	The Reply
Too tired.	I'll do all the work.
Headache.	We'll do it from the neck down.
The kids will hear.	They're away at college.
I just had a manicure.	It will help your nails dry.
We just did it last night.	Don't be cynical.
Our guests will be here soon.	Here's an hors d'oeurvre.
Our signs clash.	Be flexible.
You need an appointment.	My secretary called

The Bliss Report

If you've had a difficult day at work, tonight, when you get into bed try the Commuter's Position:
Park and Ride

The Four Exceptions

It's permissible to use a phone during sex only to:
1. Place a bet.
2. Order food.
3. Check your messages.
4. Report a lost or stolen credit card.
For extra-energetic lovers: A cellular phone provides nearly twice the freedom as a conventional phone.

Female Frigidity

The leading causes.
1. Male impotence.
2. Disillusionment. Partner turns out to have (a) narrow shoulders and (b) disappointing buns.
3. Negative aromatherapy. (He's OD'd on Aqua-Velva.)
4. Partner doing two things at once (foreplay while customizing his truck).
5. Partner pleading for another chance (but hasn't yet had his first one).
6. Negative ambiance. (He's wearing a dress-for-success athletic supporter.)

Finally!

You may have found the right partner when you meet someone who:
• You can sit with in silence for hours at a time without feeling a) uncomfortable or b) neglected.*
• Really enjoys your salmon croquettes.
• Rubs you the right way.
• Can help you with the crossword puzzle.
• Makes you forget what went wrong with your first marriage.
*Unless, of course,
    1. You've been married 20 or more years or
    2. There's a language barrier.

What I Did for Sex

"Gave up abstinence."

> – B.J. Klopman, therapist

The Colorful Lover

Today, turn your lover green with envy by learning how to:
1. Give a massage.
2. Make the earth move.
3. Get your Irish up.

The Reluctant Lover: Part II

More excuses for not having sex.

Excuse	Should you believe it?		
	Yes	No	Maybe
• We're too old			
• I'm already asleep			
• I'm not asleep, yet			
• Back acting up			
• Can't pry my sleeping mask off			
• Already did it before dinner			
• I'm Irish			

The Enchantment of Afterglow

What do you do immediately after a perfect climax?

"Realize I'd been driving on the wrong side of the road."

> – Neil, sales manager

"Keep going, why stop?"

> – Heidi, marine

"Smile at the neighbors, bow, then pull the shades down—there's nothing more to see."

> – Barry, TV personality

"Knock on wood, what else?"

> – Sadie, reader of Tarot cards

Sex with Your Ex

Four pros:
1. No break-in period (knows exactly what you mean when you say, "Move up a little").
2. No more complaints if dinner is late.

3. It's a good way to find out what the kids are up to.
4. It'll remind you of why you remarried.
One con: Your ex will know you're lying if you say, "I've never done this before."

The Transformed Lover
If a Level 15 climax changes your blood type from:

	It means:
Red to blue.	You're with a first-rate lover—he turned you into a princess.
Red to clear.	Rapture has drained you of iron—you need calve's liver.
Red to fluorescent orange.	You're afterglowing.
Red to green.	"Fondle me, I'm Irish."

After-Sex Etiquette
Who gets to use the bathroom first? Courteous men always allow the woman this right. For those, however, who disagree, the right to use the facilities first is accorded the person who is:
1. Stickiest
2. Leakiest
3. Fastest
Note: For lovers who belong to a union, it goes by seniority.

A Lover's Brain: Part II
Responsibilities of left and right hemispheres

Left	**Right**
Anguish over cellulite	Anguish over love handles
Suppressing sexual fantasies	Releasing them
Afterglow	Deciding how many watts
Blissful thoughts	Recalling where car is parked
Determining what women really want	Giving it to them
Determining what men really want	Talking them out of it

Arousal Tip #2

How to stay excited if you go to bed with someone *only* for their
Mind:
Try not to look at their body.
Body:
Try not to speak.

A Lost (Then Found) Weekend

Everything you wanted to know about staying in bed and making love from Friday night to Sunday afternoon:

1. Beware of malnutrition. *Fact:* Lovers in heat find it's all but impossible to read a takeout menu with crossed eyes.

2. Be responsible, let someone know where you are. *Fact:* For every 10,000 couples who devote two or more days in a row to wild, lustful sexual activity, three are never heard from again.

3. Consider the consequences. *Fact:* Our of every 50,000 couples who indulge in a weekend sex marathon, four feel naughty on Monday morning. (The rest wait until the middle of the week.)

First Things Done After Sex

By the:

Rich and Famous	Poor and Unknown
1. Dismiss the servant	1. Leave the room
2. Call a lawyer	2. Call *The Star*

Positive Reinforcement

Sweet nothings to express your appreciation.

To a lover who:	Appropriate phrase:
On the first try, found your erogenous zones.	"What a guy!"
Lingered over every part of your body.	"You really do try harder."
Made you see stars.	"Nice job."
(With your eyes closed.)	"Here's my credit card, buy something expensive."
Didn't leave until you were satisfied.	"I'll make the bed."

When to Think About Sex
(To make those "down" moments pass more agreeably.)
1. During a job interview.
2. While waiting on a bank line (a Critics' Choice).
3. In bumper-to-bumper traffic.
4. During any television commercial for room freshener.
5. On the elevator, during any ride longer than 10 floors.
6. During your therapy session.
7. On the phone, while waiting for the next available customer service representative.

The Enlightened Lover
Tips to keep the flames of passion from fizzling:
• *Make love in a new location*—instead of the bedroom, try it at midnight in your car (keep the windows closed if your neighbors are light sleepers).
• *Be more spontaneous*— ravish your lover when he or she least expects it (during, instead of after Oprah).
• *Set goals*—at least seven climaxes a week (choose either one nightly or all seven on Saturday night).
• *Use a camcorder*—learn from your mistakes and improve performance (a zoom lens really helps).

To Make Lovemaking More Affordable
For romance: Use generic massage oil.
For ambiance: One 40-watt light bulb.
For nourishment: Drink domestic Champagne.
For efficiency: Cut out the middleman.

The Bedside Eater
A survey of nutritional habits when:

Not in Love	In Love
Vitamin C from frozen juice or a tablet	Vitamin C from sunshine in the Caribbean
Canned ravioli	Lamb osso buco
Garlic	Tic Tacs
Calcium from milk and alfalfa	Calcium from jumping lover's bones
Whine	Wine

The Enlightened Lover

Most of the things you need to know about your orgasms.

1. They're good to have.
2. They make your partner feel useful.
3. Sometimes they make a mess.
4. 94% of them occur when you yield to temptation.
5. You can't have too many.
6. You can have too few.
7. A real one can't be faked.

Love Signs

Horoscope for an Ardent Aries

- *Ruling passion:* piggyback rides around the bed
- *Ruling body lotion:* polyunsaturated vaseline
- *Chief sexual asset:* animal magnetism (you sometimes attract teamsters)
- *Governing erogenous zone:* any freckle below your chin
- *Aphrodisiac of choice:* salmon croquettes
- *Ruling sexual activity:* flossing lover's teeth (shows you care)
- *Ideal time for sex:* just before the 11 o'clock news

Lover's Health Check

Feel your forehead. Do you have spring fever?

The Symptoms	The Signs
Absentmindedness	Forgetting to remove socks during lovemaking
Nutritional disorder	Going on a radical, fit-into-bathing-suit juice fast
Idiocy	Smiling at other, happy couples
Unsteady gait	Walking on air
Increased sexual drive	Shopping for a convertible
Finally waking up and smelling the roses	Eyes watering

Love Signs

Horoscope for an Amorous Aries.

- *Ruling passion:* making our planet move
- *Ruling sexual turnoff:* the bar exam
- *Chief sexual asset:* intuitive fingertips

- *Governing erogenous zone*: any warm room
- *Aphrodisiac*: reading *Forbes*
- *Ruling sexual activity*: making a dull lover glow
- *Ideal time for sex*: 11:36 P.M.

Romantic Tip for the Vocally Gifted

During sex, moaning with pleasure is the ideal way to sing the praises of a perfect lover, especially if you accompany yourself on a mandolin.

Love Signs: Aries

Opposite love sign: A lusty Libra or a passionate Pisces.

Outstanding sexual qualities: Head of a lover, hands of a surgeon, adequate malpractice insurance.

Most attractive physical feature: A chest against which many a weary lover has snuggled into a deep, post-lovemaking sleep.

Ruling sexual turnoff: a partner who doesn't appreciate the finer things in life—love, commitment, trust, caring, closeness.

Ruling sexual turn-on: Flowers, candy, jewelry, a Porsche, Cancun.

Ideal place for sex: Under a huge, downy quilt (or, in warm weather, under a huge, downy lover).

Wellness Tips for Lovers

Heart-healthy acts to improve fitness.

1. Instead of push-ups, gain upper body strength by carrying your partner into the bedroom.
2. Improve manual dexterity by undressing each other.
3. Firm stomach muscles by moaning from your diaphragm.
4. Tighten a sagging jawline by pulling champagne corks with your teeth.
5. Bit your lover's arm when ecstasy grows intense (with an in-shape lover, it's a low-fat snack).
6. Giggle. It will help you reach your target heart rate.

Spring Fever, More Symptoms of

Symptom	Cause
Fidgeting, restlessness, indifference to work.	Picnic deficiency. Need to frolic with significant other while fighting off ants.
Social withdrawal, staring into space.	No lover, or one unable to quench spring fever fires.
Kopellman's Syndrome (despising happy couples).	Need to meet someone special.
Smiling, perpetual state of world-love. Studying cookbooks and decorating magazines.	New lover.

What I Did for Love

"Gave him bed 'n' breakfast."
            – Daphne, not an innkeeper
"Became a natural blonde."
            – Louise, psychic
"Put her on a pedestal."
            – Jack, crane operator
"Put him on a place mat."
            – Audrey, waitress

Thought for Today

To the unbelievably considerate but slightly anxious lover who, after sex,

Always asks:	Send:
"Have I forgotten anything?"	A pad and pencil.
"Have you forgotten anything?"	Your lawyer.
"Have we forgotten anything?"	A make-up test.

Are You Too Sexually Gifted?

You are if:

1. Your spouse never complains if dinner is late.
2. You argue only about money, never sex.
3. The phrase "Rest Stop" applies only to long vacation trips.
4. Old lovers occasionally call for a "consultation," especially on the first day of spring.

5. You've been known to cancel a tennis date for sex.
6. You're often in treatment for back problems.
7. When making love, your partner is most likely to utter the following phrase (check only one):
___ "I never knew it could feel this way."
___ "You're the best I've ever been with."
___ "Move down a little."

The Enlightened Lover
Six things couples with a great sex life avoid.
1. Meaningful conversation during foreplay.
2. Fighting over money during intercourse.
3. Worrying about world peace during climax.
4. A full-time job.
5. Publicity.
6. The neighbors.

Alternate Love Signs: Aries
Most attractive features: A perfect nose, two beautiful shoulders, four gorgeous cheeks (two with dimples).
Turn-on: A lover who, when you're not home, leaves wicked messages on your answering machine that make the butler blush.
Turn-off: A significant other who asks, when you arrange to meet at your favorite restaurant, "What will you be wearing?"
Ideal romantic adventure: Putting the top down on your convertible and going on safari in downtown Los Angeles.
Favorite sexual fantasy: Getting a baby-sitter for the evening and then, with your spouse, visiting a motel with hourly rates.

Lovemaking Tips for the Two-Career Couple
Okay to Skip
1. Rubbing each other with exotic oils from the mysterious East
2. Removing beeper—you're only going to put it on again in the morning
3. Caressing those hard-to-get-at erogenous zones
4. Simultaneous orgasm
5. Praising lover

Not Okay to Skip
1. Shaking hands—always a great icebreaker
2. Removing shoes—indicates that you plan to stay awhile
3. Caressing the easy-to-get-at erogenous zones
4. The other kind of orgasm
5. Suggestions for improvement

Thought for Tonight
The biggest obstacle to simultaneous orgasm is a stale mate.

Lover's Ritual #1
Feeling overwhelmed by too much lovemaking? Take a breather by locking your lover in the other room, then relax by:
• Reorganizing your closet
• Thumbing through *Time*
• Finally writing that letter you owe Mom
• Planning dinner
• Opening your mail
• Taking a warm bath
• Considering what you'll do when you resume making love

The Bedside Eater

Aphrodisiac of the Evening	Erotic Effect
Grappa (choose one of the "lite" varieties if you're watching your weight).	Provides the timid male with sufficient courage to finally tell his partner what he really likes during lovemaking.
Champagne (Taittinger if watching your weight, Cold Duck if watching your pocketbook).	Provides the female partner with sufficient courage to try his suggestion . . . or at least think about it without calling her lawyer.

How a Wonderful Lover Changed My Life
"Got call waiting. He phones me a lot."
> – Della, sportscaster

"Made a commitment—got rid of the 'Ladies Welcome' sign in my window."
> – Carl, car salesman

"Went to bed a short, dumpy 'mouse,' and woke up a leggy blonde."
— Pia, librarian

It's Getting Serious
When someone:
• Gives you a pet name (especially if it ends in "kins," as in "Lambikins" or "ums" as in "Sweetums").
• Sews a button on your shirt.
• Gently starts trying to mend your fashion ways ("Do you really want to wear a Hawaiian shirt with a dinner jacket?").
• Stops insisting that his or her intentions are honorable.
• Has the Yellow Pages open to "Caterers."
• Can say the word "commitment" without choking.

After-Sex Etiquette
How to remove a hair.

Location	Method
Tip of tongue	Thumb and index finger (or discreetly lick partner's shoulder)
Back of tongue	Gentle coughing while flailing tongue
Roof of mouth	Teaspoon
Soft palate (very tricky, especially if hair is elusive)	Chopsticks, tweezers or (very intimate) lover's finger.
Throat	Mop.

Pillow Talk
Static cling. The inability, during searing sexual moments, to tell where you leave off and your lover begins because of:
a. Intense chemistry; or
b. A narrow bed; or
c. Science friction.

Words to the Wise Lover
After disappointing lovemaking, it is important to remember not to:
• Ask for your flowers back.
• Hiss at a partner with a weak ego.
• Breathe an audible sigh of relief.

- Call in reinforcements.
- Say, "Better luck next time," unless you really mean it.

When the Right One Comes Along
What will you do for love?
"Tell him about my torrid past, he'll love it."
> – Victoria, country and western singer

"You name it."
> – Claude, poet and care giver

"Get my teeth cleaned."
> – Frankie, beer delivery person

"Break curfew."
> –Heather, flight attendant-in-training

Sex Secrets of the Great Lovers
How to make her wish the evening would never end.
1. Take her to a romantic restaurant (soft lighting, cozy booths, waiters who speak little English).
2. Show her you're emotionally stable. Don't keep asking the waiter to come back because you can't decide what to order.
3. Don't talk about yourself unless (a) you're marvelously interesting and (b) her mouth is full.
4. Compliment her. Tell her how cute she looks with that napkin tucked under her chin.
5. When the check arrives, even if she earns more than you, be gallant—offer to leave the tip.

How Do You Get Your Partner in the Mood?
"Tell him how deeply and unconditionally I love him, serve him five piña coladas and let him wear his lucky baseball cap."
> – Debbie, electrician

"In the middle of the night, I kiss him all over while he's sleeping. He's fine as long as he thinks it's a dream."
> – Meg, jazz flutist

"I stand beneath her window and serenade her. Unfortunately, she lives on the thirty-second floor so I'm pretty hoarse by the time she invites me up."
> – Ashley, photojournalist

Sex and the Basic Food Groups: Part II

Italian: A high-energy food enabling the impossible-to-satisfy partner to plead for more in a high, clear voice. Also prevents fading due to flagging strength.

Dish
1. Scungilli Fra Diavolo with Clams
2. Pasta Primavera
3. Boneless Chicken Breast Bolognese

Application
1. Provides the "armchair" lover with a nonerotic form of self-pleasuring.
2. Enables bumbling lovers to administer postcoital back rubs like licensed professionals.
3. Activates the fondling reflex; prevents that "empty" feeling in pit of stomach if sex is not quite perfect.

The Dieter's Guide to Weight Loss During Sex

Air traveler's advisory.

Activity	Calories Burned
Sex aloft:	
One lover on bottom, the other earning bonus miles	120
A round trip	240
A seat upgrade	45
Sudden turbulence	87
Unscheduled stop	50
Preferred status:	
One lover on bottom, the other flying standby	353

Hot Numbers

6: The number of climaxes a woman can have within a one-hour period before her mascara starts to run.

4: The most orgasms a man can have within a three-hour period without losing his ability to metabolize strudel.

2: The number of buttered croissants burned off during three hours of lovemaking.

1.6: The hours of sleep the average couple gets the first time they make love.

Source: Union of Concerned Sex Partners, Maine chapter.

Mental Health Tip

To reduce stress: Researchers tell us that it's much better to think about sex while you're at work than it is to think about work while you're having sex.

Thought for Today

Last night was wonderful? Before he or she leaves for work, hide a billet-doux in your lover's:
- Brief case (under the tuna sandwich)
- Laptop computer
- Wallet
- Car (taped to the visor)
- Gym bag
- Water bottle

The Eight Least-Suspected Locations for Sex

1. Self-service elevators (for best results, press "Stop").
2. Nursing homes (the attendants are too busy dozing to notice).
3. Secluded scenic overlooks.
4. Supermarkets (that's why the manager's never around when the cashier screams, "I need a price").
5. Sleeping cars on the Trans-Siberian Railroad.
6. The apartment-complex pool at midnight.
7. The Senate cloakroom.
8. The rear of a limo (consider it a social call).

Passion Scale

Level III

An intermediate-level climax which, if authentic, should register in the "red" zone on your turbo gauge. A good climax, but not yet a great one.

How Manifested

Slurred moans, rigidity of extremities and popping out of contact lenses. Desire to shower lover with compliments may be impeded by your tongue's inability to function.

The Enlightened Lover

A spirited climax can:
Start a forest fire.
Crack a mirror or ruin a floral arrangement.
Power either a Cuisinart or a PC for 45 minutes.
Raise property values.
Burn off one brownie.
Panic your partner.

An out-of-control climax can:
Put it out.
Ruin a hairdo (beehives the exception).
Power Rhode Island for 6 minutes.
Scare of tax assessors.
Burn up one lover.
Panic your neighbors.

The Art of Passion

When driving your lover up a wall, be certain that:
• You have enough gas.
• Your seatbelt is fastened.
• Your blinkers are on.
• You don't strain your power plant.
• You have anti-lock brakes (for those sudden stops).
• You shift seamlessly

From Our Treasury of Sexual Wisdom: Part I

Sex should never be used as a form of escape unless:
• You've read all the magazines.
• You're lonely (spouse is on a business trip).
• Your experimental eggplant wrapped moussaka with minted yogurt sauce has been condemned by the FDA and you need a substitute.
• There's nothing on prime time TV.

The Sexual Halftime

How marathon lovers spend their rest period:
"I inspect my bed for damage, it's an antique."
            – Rhoda, decorator
"I inspect my partner for damage, he's an antique."
            – Selma, home-care nurse
"Check my lover's pulse rate. We're into heart-smart sex."
            – Randolph, private investigator
"We never stop, why lose momentum?"
            – Karen and Bruno, tag team

Oscar Night

A gold statuette to the lover who:
• Kept smiling when you told her that you don't want children.
• Didn't make a face when he ate your tofu manicotti.
• Said, "No problem, let us pray," when you were unable to achieve an erection.
• Smiled and said, "That's okay," when you told him that your mother was coming for two weeks.
• Sometimes has to fake it but you can't tell when.
• Kept smiling when you told him, "Those photos were taken by a reputable photographer."

Approved Excuses: Part I

It is permissible to leave a sexual I.O.U. if you:
• Have a bad sunburn.
• Are temporarily attracted to lover's mind but not lover's body.
• Are unable to locate partner's erogenous zones.
• Can't decide what not to wear.
• Have to leave suddenly (partner's spouse arrives home unexpectedly).
• Doze off.
• Just had your hair done.

Reminder

A few ways to show your gratitude. In your lover's name, endow a:
• Bed at your favorite motel.
• Water bed at your favorite seedy motel.
• Booth at your favorite restaurant.
• Glider on your favorite porch.
• Chair at your local beauty parlor.

Ways to Impress a New Lover: Part II

Solve problems instantly.
• If your lover's cholesterol is high, use palm oil only for massages.
• If there's a height difference of 15 inches or more, stand on a phone book.
Know when not to talk.
• When you're moaning.
• When your lover's listening to the weather report.
Always use the correct utensil.

What to Do Until Your Lover Arrives

1. Prepare bedside snacks.
    - If you're eating wisely: wheat toast and broccoli.
    - If you're eating: scones, ice cream and pretzels.
2. Prepare an ice bucket. Necessary for chilling Champagne and easing sex-induced sprains.
3. Scour the bathtub. You never know.
4. Pace.
5. Count the moments.
6. Calm yourself.

Sexual Rule of Thumb
During lovemaking, you know you're doing it right if:
- Your partner gets completely undressed.
- You start to perspire.
- You see stars.
- You hear trumpets (or, in Nashville, Dolly).
- Your hair extension comes off.

Spring Cleaning Advisory
The eight approved ways to take a shower with your lover.
1. Turn on the water (woman always decides temperature).
2. Wear shower caps if you're modest.
3. Slowly soap each other.
4. Use a loofah to scrub each other's back.
5. Avoid sexual arousal—this is a rite of purification.
6. Intimacy tip: Swab each other's ears with a Q-tip.
7. Buff your partner to a high gloss with a bath towel.
8. Remove your shower caps.

Pizza and Sex: Part III
Good sex requires great pizza.
Type of Lovemaking
Slow and languid (arousal alone may take up to three hours) and no stopping except to rest and feed the goldfish. Particular attention is paid to each erogenous zone, especially those that jingle.
Ideal Topping
Sausage (to achieve momentum), extra cheese (for endurance and whiter teeth), broccoli (for peripheral vision) and anchovies (for the climax).

Pillow Talk

The Miracle Comeback (rare). An after-sex event in which one partner, seemingly exhausted by lovemaking, is suddenly and inexplicably energized by either rekindled lust or perfect whitefish salad and is able to engage in additional lovemaking (up to 2 hours, 20 minutes) without turning ashen.

The Art of Romance

During sex, a truly versatile lover should be able to:
1. Cover your body with feathery kisses while listening to his or her phone messages.
2. Re-affix false eyelashes correctly without a mirror.
3. Moan in any romance language.
4. Whisper sweet nothings into both ears at once.
5. Wave at visitors.

Thought for the Night

All the world loves a lover—unless he neglects to call her the next day.

More Timesaving Tips for Busy Lovers

"During sex, my partner and I divide the chores. While I'm blowing in her ear, she listens for the kids."
    – Clyde, roofer
"I read the day's mail while waiting for my husband to climax."
    – Penelope, bridal consultant
"I flip through the New England Journal of Medicine while waiting for my wife to climax."
    – Brad, M.D. and Penelope's mate
"During sex, instead of closing my eyes, I leave my closet door open and plan my next day's wardrobe."
    – Joyce, copywriter

What I'd Do for Sex

(Asked of forlorn singles who'd been without it for six or more months.)
"Place a personal ad in a reputable trade journal if I thought it would find me a soulmate."
    – Edgar, cowboy

"Go back with my boyfriend if he promised to stop using so much aftershave."
> – Bonnie, cashier

"Give my orderly a weekend pass. He's such a doll."
> – Heather, staff sergeant

"Anything."
> – Hillary, trailer park manager

The Dieter's Guide to Weight Loss During Sex

Spring training: determining what turns your lover on.

Activity	Calories Burned
Asking:	
Lover	22
Lover's former lover	100
Guessing:	
Using language	31
Using body language	127
Using hands (a Best Bet!)	150
Discussing	3
Experimenting	200

Fashion Tip for the Curious Lover

What to wear when you explore your own sexuality:
1. White
2. A compass
3. Your favorite scent
4. A smile
5. Loose clothing
6. A floatation vest

The Three Biggest Pre-Sex Lies

1. "I don't usually do this so quickly."
2. "I'm legally separated."
3. "This could be the start of a beautiful friendship."

The Enlightened Lover

Six things likely to annoy a sensitive partner during sex:
1. Using a kitchen timer.
2. Off-putting expressions of affection (a clammy handshake, for instance).

3. Goal-setting. Example: "We have to finish by 11:33 P.M., that's when my roommate gets home."
4. Refusing to share your umbrella if steamy sex sets off the sprinklers.
5. Talking in your sleep.
6. Calluses.

Weak Moments
Eight things never to do in those first all-is-right-with-the-world moments after mood-altering sex.
1. Propose.
2. Change the beneficiary in your will.
3. Buy penny stocks from a broker named Slim.
4. Toss out your Valium, Thorazine and diet pills.
5. Comply with any request to "Sign here."
6. Shop for a new wardrobe.
7. Respond generously to pledge week on PBS.
8. Kiss and tell.

Go Ahead, Make My Night
• Call me at the office and tell me all the wicked things we're going to do tonight (if my calls are monitored, better just send a telegram).
• Bring home our favorite aphrodisiac (a box of chocolate truffles or, as a backup, triple fudge ice cream).
• Don't forget a salad, I like to eat healthy.
• Meet me in the Jacuzzi.
• Do several laps.
• Towel me dry, carry me into the bedroom and make me see stars.

Sexual Ethics: Part III
Should you hate yourself in the morning if you did it:

For love	yes	no
For a part in a movie	yes	no
To help you make it through the night	yes	no
Because he was a hunk	yes	no
Because she was a doll	yes	no
For a promotion	yes	no
For the experience (your first gypsy)	yes	no

Breaking the Ice

The first thing I do with a new lover:

"Make him sign in."
        – Ellen, receptionist

"Make him sign a waiver."
        – Angie, paralegal

"Invite her to initial my guestbook."
        – Todd, investment banker

"Read her her rights."
        – Ellsworth, wrestler

The Language of Flowers: Part III

To the lover who:	Send:
Is supportive (keeps saying positive things over and over again throughout your orgasm)	Violets
Is a tiger (and makes you purr)	Tulips
Really stimulates you	A cactus
Is a sexual acrobat	Tumbleweeds

From Our Book of Sexual Leasts

Least romantic, but most to-the-point sexual invitation ever uttered by a harried housewife (car pool, shopping, bake sale, kids, tanning salon) to her husband as he walks in the door:
"Got a minute?"

A Guide for the Stong Silent Type

Speechless during sex? No need to be.

What to Say	When to Say It
"Ooooooh!"	Partner located (finally) your G spot.
"Aaaaaaah!"	Partner located your ultra spot.
"Ooof!"	Partner heavier than you thought.
"Gee!"	Nothing else comes to mind.
"Heavens!"	You experience lift-off
"My goodness!"	Partner getting warmed up.
"Oh, goodness."	You noticed.

From Our Love-Management Seminars

Pressed for time? Busy couples tell how to enjoy twice as much sex in half the time.

• *Minimize interruptions:* Send your in-laws to Europe.
• *Get right to the main course:* Skip foreplay.
• *Focus on what you're doing:* During lovemaking, never think about career advancement (unless you're a starlet and your partner is a) a producer or b) a star).
• *Don't be a perfectionist:* One orgasm is enough (as long as it's yours).

Bed Manners

Call in a stunt lover only of your real lover:
• Might get hurt
• Has the jitters
• Is out of town
• Calls in sick
• Needs a second opinion
• Wants to watch
• Leaves

Early Spring Training for Lovers: Part I

3 Basic Exercises

1. Just lying there
2. Thinking positive
3. Arm curls

The Benefits

1. Teaches patience while waiting for lover to a) remove makeup and b) remove contacts.
2. Enables you to give timid lovers rousing pep talks.
3. During torrid sex, a) to better cling to partner if you feel self sliding off the bed; b) uncorking Italian wine bottles.

From Our Lover's Glossary

Bisexual. 1. *Adj.* Able to do two mental things at once, such as have sex while thinking about it. **2.** *n.* A person who, while making love, can also perform an additional nonsexual task like shave, dust bric-a-brac or phone in and order from Home Shopping Network. (*Technical point:* Daydreaming or thinking about what to make for supper while your mate is kissing your neck does not constitute true bisexuality.)

Tips for Unsure Lovers
How to tell when the best part of sex is over: symptoms and signs.
• One of you stops moving.
• The other doesn't notice.
• One, or both, of you puts on a robe.
• One partner is reading the back of a cereal box.
• You're back to worrying about the mortgage payment.
• Your heart rate's back to normal.
• So are you.

When Seconds Count
Timesaving tips for the busy lover.
1. During lovemaking, wear your ignition key around your neck. Then you won't have to hunt for it if you're rushing to get back to the office.
2. Combine romance with practicality: while showering with your lover, rinse out your socks.
3. During sex, to speed thing up, use both hands.
4. Improve yourself: during sex, instead of romantic music, listen to a meditation tape.

The Nicest Thing About Your Lover: Poll #39
"After sex, if I'm tired, she gently carries me back over the threshold into the kitchen and tells me what she wants for dinner."
     – David, furrier
"He takes our relationship seriously. During lovemaking, he never a) watches the clock or b) makes personal phone calls."
     – Anne, prison guard

More Great Moments in Afterplay: Part III
"He covers my body with feathery kisses until I fall asleep."
     – Martha, wrangler
"We call my parents and tell them, in detail, what we just did. It really makes them proud."
     – Rapunzel, actress and psychic

The Enlightened Lover

Thing often said before having sex: *"Your place or mine?"*

Thing often said before trying a new position: *"Your back or mine?"*

Thing often said after trying a new position: *"Was that your back or mine?"*

MONTHLY QUALITY OF LIFE® CHECKUP

•Sex in March was: Average___ Good___   Terrific (we gave her a few extra bucks and our sex therapist actively participated___
•Best source of lovers:
Friends' recommendations___
Personal ads___
Singles bars___
Church socials___
Mass transit___
Parents without Partners___
Partners without Parents___
Sperm banks___
•What do you find most annoying about your lover?
Nothing, I'm perfect___
Keeps looking at his watch___
Brings me Champagne with a screw-off top___
Loses interest when he hears Good Humor man's bells___
Keeps running to the bathroom to sneak a puff of his cigar___
Always looks puzzled when I say, "A little to the left."___
•How do you hint that your lover needs improvement?
Tell him diplomatically___
Begin with sex flash cards___
Leave a message on the office bulletin board___
E-mail___
Make him lie in the wet spot___
Start sleeping with her twin___

Signed_____

Witnessed_____

APRIL

•Erotic goal for April:
1. Connect to every aspect of sexuality????
2. Improve networking skills
3. Learn to Play "Feelings" on ukulele

For many lovers, April *is* the cruelest month. Warm weather beckons and suddenly we must think about fitting into a bathing suit. Happily, increasing sexual activity by a mere 22% can help you and your partner lose up to 10 pounds by May (15 pounds if you indulge in "high-impact" erotic exercises like moaning, writhing and attending Spring Break Tequila Bash.) As you progress through the month, the diligent couple will note not only significant weight loss, but a decreased craving for knishes—a sure sign that things are going well. The following is a chart listing some additional calorie burners:

Things Often Uttered During Sex	Calories Burned
"Slower"	6
"Faster!"	11
"Shhhhh, the kids might hear."	8
"Not yet, not yet, oh, please, not yet."	77
"Any General Ching's chicken left?"	12
"Your pearls are hitting my teeth."	9
"Your wife wants you to bring home a pumpernickel."	25

Tip: Aerobic instructors suggest that holding extra tight to one's partner during a #7 climax (in a burst of mental clarity you realize how you can suddenly open your own laundromat) can firn the upper arms of women over 60 years of age.

Official aphrodisiac of the Month: Blueberry cobbler

Should You Sleep with Him or Just Nap a Little?

Sleep if he has:
• A well-stocked refrigerator
• A working shower
• Lots of clean, fluffy towels
• The seasonal amenities—air conditioning in summer, a fireplace in winter

Just nap if he has:
• None of the above

April Fools' Day

Today, without moral consequences, you may fake:
• A headache
• An orgasm
• The appropriate moans
• The appropriate groans
• Matching facial expressions
• Sleep
• And an unquenchable passion for your lover's meat loaf

From Our Book of Sexual Records

Slowest lover: Byron H., the "Lingering Lover of Nottingham," using only his lips, took 14 hours, 12 minutes and 31 seconds to travel from his partner's ear to her knees via her neck, shoulders and torso. She napped throughout.

April Fools' Day

Today is the only day of the year that you may:*
• Fake a climax (or have a real but teensy one and enhance it with moans and the appropriate facial expressions).
• Feign sexual pleasure (by biting down on your index finger).
• Engage in simulated sex (over the phone, by fax or with a not over-alert partner).
• Tell your partner, when he looks beseechingly into your eyes, "Yes, Elvis, you're the best I've ever been with."
*Without a guilty conscience.

The Deserving Lover: Part I

A cash bonus for that extra-special partner.

To the Lover Who	Suggested Gratuity
Made you finally forget your ex	$3.00
And helped you remember how great sex is	$7.50
Taught you a new position	50¢
That didn't throw your back out	$5.25
Has bedroom eyes	$1.70
That are just as seductive:	
In the kitchen	$2.00
When they're shut	$10.00

A Lover's Medicine Cabinet: Part II

Item	Application
Hydrocortisone cream	An anti-bedsore fighter
Depend pads (regular absorbency)	For lovers who laugh while making love (provides superior bladder control)
Aspirin	Relieves muscle pain caused by too much missionary position
Throat lozenges	A must for deep throats

Sex and the Basic Food Groups: Part III

French: Permits ultra-sophisticated lovemaking that allows lovers, during foreplay, to take incoming calls. (The secret is the sauces, the lighter the sauce, the more feathery the kiss.)

Dish
1. Coquilles Saint-Jacques
2. Boeuf en Daube
3. Crêpe Fromage

Application
1. Heightens passion, lowers cholesterol and erections that are too high (the Eiffel effect).
2. Enhances side effects of orgasm (deeper sleep, indifference to German unification).
3. Reinforces climax-related religious beliefs.

The Dieter's Guide to Weight Loss During Sex

Activity	Calories Burned
If at the precise moment of climax:	
The earth moves	158
Just your street moves	77
Only you move	41
You twitch	9
You startle your cat	4

Fighting Temptation

The seven approved ways to prevent premature climax during steamy lovemaking.

1. Use a stopwatch.
2. think about something else. (Have you ever thought about starting your own business?)
3. Study yourself in the mirror.
4. Call a friend.
5. Call your support group.
6. Eat a pickle (a Best Bet).
7. Hope that's only the dog who's nibbling on your toe.

In Case You Can't Decide: Part I

Lovers on the:

A list

1. Believe that a night without sex is like a day without sunshine.
2. Caress your erogenous zones.
3. Like to watch you squirm with pleasure.
4. Moan.
5. Are always ready to try again.

B list

1. Believe that a night without sex lets him get more sleep.
2. Just stare at them.
3. May panic and call 911.
4. Chant.
5. But not that week.

From Our Lover's Glossary

"Better luck next time." The phrase used by a sensitive lover to comfort a troubled partner who, because of

- Stress
- Anxiety
- Higher interest rates
- Traffic noise
- A naughty invitation
- An indecent proposal

is unable to perform.

The Art of Romance

How do you take the sexual initiative?

"I put on our favorite song ('Can't Help Lovin' That Man of Mine'), then wrap my arms around her and hope she wakes up."

> – Melvin, interior decorator

"I apply big wet drippy kisses to every nook and cranny of his body. He says I ruin his best business suits, but I don't care."

> – Donna, fund-raiser

"By falling to my knees and begging. I have absolutely no pride."

> – Henry, psychiatrist

The Dieter's Guide to Weight Loss After Sex

Activity	Calories Burned
Trying again:	
If woman is ready	11
If man is not	200

Late Spring Training for Lovers: Part II

4 Vital Exercises

1. Deep breathing
2. Shallow knee bends
3. Weight training
4. Aerobics

The Benefits

1. Endurance (to better survive sensual overload, i.e., orgasms that leave you breathless)
2. Stealth (changing positions without your partner knowing)
3. Moving a very heavy lover when he or she snores
4. Leaping tall lovers at a single bound

Not-So-Great Moments in First-Time Sex
"Gee, she looked better with her clothes on."
            – Luke, data processing
"Gee, he looked better with his clothes on."
            – Brittany, mortician

Gem of the Month
A diamond (zirconia is okay if you're on a budget) to the lover who knows:
- When all the good showroom sales are.
- That during hot lovemaking, it's much more fun to try something new than to try on something new.
- How to revive you when you're overcome by sex (a chocolate Easter bunny, administered orally).
- How to find undervalued stocks.
- That you don't quite mean it when you say, "I can't take anymore."
- The zipper code for all your erogenous zones.

Our Lovers Tell All
These are a few of their favorite things.
"Comparing our sexual frequency rate to that of our neighbors. It really boosts our ego."
            – Ginny Mae, homemaker
"An impromptu weekend at a sleazy motel where we do nothing but live on love . . . and Popeye fried chicken."
            – Clyde, attorney
"Having sex all night, then hating each other in the morning because we didn't get any sleep. It's so great."
            – Pauline, heavy equipment operator
"Waking up and smelling coffee, baking bread and sizzling bacon, then instantly going back to sleep. I'm on a diet."
            – Dee Dee, real estate broker

Eight Ways to Improve Your Sex Life
1. Brush regularly.
2. Stop leaving so much to the imagination.
3. Stop leaving so much to legislation.
4. If you're not in the mood but your partner is, be honest—she'll love the challenge.

5. Consider a heated argument with your partner as foreplay (unless it's over child support).
6. Wear sexier underwear.
7. Always respond when your partner makes a welcome sexual advance.
8. Shave your legs.

A Few Sexual Atrocities
1. Talking to lover #1 on the phone while you're in bed with lover #2
2. And thinking about lover #3
3. Chewing gum during arousal (permissible, however, if it relieves nervous tension)
4. Cracking it during foreplay
5. Avoiding sex by:
• Faking sleep
• Faking headache
• Faking orgasm

A Lover's 1040 (The Short Form: Part 27)
Dependents: For the past year you may take an exemption for any lover who meets all four of the following tests.
1. Satisfaction: Lover depended on you for over half of his or her gross orgasms (blockbusters) for the fiscal year.
2. Home office: Lover did it in your bedroom *most* of the time during the year (a pullout sofa in parlor disallowed).
3. Necessary uniforms: For lover you purchased at least one support garment such as silk briefs or push-up bra.
4. Education: Fee for attendance at approved educational institution (Cancún or Paris) to improve in-bed skills.

The Prudent Lover
Our technical adviser cautions strongly against using a meat thermometer when trying to determine whether one's lover has spring fever.
Tip: Feel his or her forehead instead. It's more romantic.

It's a Lover's Question

Q. Sometimes, during sex, when I make a lot of noise, I get so embarrassed that I actually crawl underneath the bed. Is it okay if my companion joins me and we continue making love?
                                                    – Sigrid

A. Yes if:

1. The floor is carpeted.
2. The dust balls don't make you sneeze.

New Tax Law Tips

You may consider your lover an exemption if he or she

1. After a long, hard day, needs you to run a hot bath.
2. On romantic rides in the country, gets hopelessly lost unless you're there to read the map.
3. Relies on you for over half of his or her (a) moral support, (b) wardrobe advice or (c) tuition.
4. Obtains at least 75% of the MADRS (minimal adult daily requirement of sex) from you.
5. Can't get along without:
• Your coconut-raisin macaroons
• You.

Après-Lovemaking Ritual #3

What to say to a departing lover if first-time sex was
Good: "Parting is such sweet sorrow."*
Very good: "Don't be a stranger, I'm in the book."
Great: "I'd like to see you again, leave your Rolex here."
Beyond anything you've ever experienced: "Here are my house keys. What would you like for dinner?"
So-so: "That was really special. I'll call you when I get back from the Ukraine."
Yccch: "Please close the door behind you."
* "Go in peace" if you're a New Age lover.

Pillow Talk

Back kisses. For best results, partner should be lying on stomach. Lips of kisser should be light and moist, much like angel cake. When administered by skilled lips, back kisses provide nearly total and immediate relief from:

- Lower back pain
- First-time jitters
- Cares of the day
- Spring fever

Great Moments in Sex
"The day we canceled our health club membership and bought a new bed instead."
> — Tom and Tammy, tag team

Ethical Considerations for Great Lovers
By what means is it proper to promote one's sexual prowess?

Ethical	Unethical
Word of mouth	Television (paid programming)
Fax	Billboard
Calling card	Handbills (on windshields)
Public notice (newspaper ads)	Public notice (restroom walls)
Spot announcements (radio)	Spot announcements (street corner)
Chain letter	Direct mail
Yellow Pages	Magazine insert

Inside a Lover's Fortune Cookie: Part I
You have an active mind and a keen imagination. Don't forget to use them when you're:
- Writing a personal ad
- With a new lover
- With an old lover who's getting stale
- Working on your income tax deductions

Getting Away from It All: Part II
Three ultimate stolen sexual moments.

Where	Why
In a BMW.	You're a baby boomer.
A sunlit meadow.	You're the farmer's daughter.
A maternity ward.	A woman's work is never done.

Four Ways to Prolong Tonight's Foreplay

1. Be optimistic. Perhaps this will be the night the baby doesn't wake up.
2. Focus on the task at hand. Don't also try to browse through a magazine, select new fabric or consider whether to shift investments from stocks to bonds. It's distracting.
3. Begin early. Kiss your partner long and deeply when you leave for work in the morning. He'll stay aroused until you get home.
4. Hand a "Do Not Disturb" sign on your front door.

What to Do Until Your Lover Arrives

• Inspect the bed. If mattress is lumpy, noisy or soggy, replace it.
• Look under the bed. Remove dustballs, maiden aunt and previous lover's sweatsocks.
• Inspect sheets. If unclean, flip them over.
• Place champagne in ice bucket.
• Create the proper ambiance. (Rule of thumb: first date, 75-watt bulb; second date, 50-watt; third date, two beeswax candles.)
• Check pillows: Did you remember place cards?

Pillow Talk

Lust handles. Anatomically similar to love handles, only slightly more developed.* Used to grasp firmly and hold on to a slippery partner during moments of extreme ecstasy, when there is a clear and present danger of sliding either off the bed or off one's partner.

*Usually due to an inability to forgo the blueberry muffin while on one's morning coffee break.

Thought for Tonight

Sex is one of the few treatments that can cure a problem overnight.

Family Values Tip: Part I

No matter how intense the peer pressure, no matter how great the temptation, the woman who is pure of heart believes that she should save herself for her first lover.

Can Animals Think?

"Absolutely. After sex, my husband grunts pensively, then falls asleep."

— Rhoda, scholar

"He may look like an ape, but whenever he climaxes, my boyfriend roars in Latin."

— Cynthia, TV shadow traffic

"Sure. My wife may be a tigress, but she's thoughtful. After sex, she always says, 'Thank you, my pet.'"

— David, pilot

"I guess so. If my boyfriend meditates before sex, he always turns out to be a lion in bed."

— Mary Lou, math teacher

"We think so. After making love, we look into each other's eyes and coo sweet endearments to each other."

— Harry* and Heidi,** lovebirds

*Robin

**Nuthatch.

The Ultimate Aphrodisiac: Part I

Good news: Calories don't count when chocolate is consumed for romantic purposes only.

Type of Chocolate	Application
Layer cake, huge slice	Extra strength. Enables lovers to prolong sex until the wee small hours of the *Tonight* show.
Chocolate-chip cookies	Foreplay enhancer. Alternate bites of cookie with bites of partner until either cookie or partner is all gone.

Nothing in Common?

You may still have sex if it's for:
• Pleasure
• A weekend in the Bahamas
• Ski instruction
• Dinner
• A recipe
• The exercise

- Charity
- Tension relief
- Tax advice

Advice to Women

When making love, it's a good idea to remove all jewelry—it adds unnecessary weight. Also:
- During fiery sexual moments, your locket may soften and, if pure gold, melt.
- Those without cable may find that silver bracelets affect television reception.
- Oversexed men, when nibbling on a woman's earlobes, tend to get carried away and gag on the hoops (you can be sued).
- During dull sexual moments, you'll be tempted to extend your hand and admire your rings (not good for his ego).

Is Your Interest Waning?

It's time to look for a new lover when, during The Act, you:
- Find yourself, during foreplay, watching TV over your lover's shoulder.
- Refuse to let go of the clicker.
- Try to get in at least 10 reps during intercourse.
- Manage to finish two chapters of a Russian novel.
- Neglect to ask all non-essential personnel to leave the room.
- Find yourself doing a pretty fair job of balancing your checkbook.

Family Values Tip: Part II

No matter how intense the peer pressure, no matter how great the temptation, the man who is pure of heart hopes that he will be the one she saves herself for.

Male Impotence

The leading causes.
1. She earns more than he does (and won't file a joint return).
2. Feeling rushed ("Please hurry, my handsome personal trainer's at the door").
3. Inappropriate device on the headboard (surveillance camera).
4. Inappropriate aphrodisiac (noodle pudding).

5. Republican peering through bedroom window, holding up a sign saying, "Repent!"
6. Pressure to perform (167 pounds of woman on top of him).

The Ultimate Aphrodisiac: Part II
The bad news: Calories do count when a chocolate-induced climax is faked.

Type of Chocolate	Application
Hot chocolate	Will seduce a reluctant partner who doesn't think you earn enough.
Truffles	Mental stimulant. Causes during-sex creative juices to flow, a bad thing unless you have a mattress pad.

Q. Is it ever ethical to send two different lovers the same poem?
A. Yes, if you:
1. Composed it yourself, and
2. It's just too good to use on only one lover, and
3. The recipients live in different time zones.

A Lover's 1040 (The Long Form: Part 98)
Romance-related deductions and the IRS.

Deduction	Allowed	No Way
A dozen magnolias	X	
One modest shrub	X	
Purchase of Lover Helper (vitamins)		X
Breakfast in bed		X
Day-care expenses so you and lover can:		
Go to work	X	
Be alone		X
Penalty for early withdrawal	X	
Of savings		X

What Do the Professionals Do?
The Problem
"There is too much chemistry between us. We can't keep our hands off each other. We do it first thing in the morning, then at noon and sometimes twice at night. We haven't done a laundry in four months, our parents are getting worried and our houseplants are dead."
The Solution
1. Make sure your life insurance is paid up.
2. Lie back and enjoy it.

The Typical American Sex Partner: Part II
A statistical portrait.

New Age Thinking. Believes that Days Inn motel sheets store up sexual energy.

Morality. Believes in Family Values (considers non-wholesome i.e., lustful thoughts to be the work of his or her spouse).

Environment. Is Earth-kind (always recycles old lovers).

Social Conscience. Believes in helping those who are sexually challenged (into bed).

Lovers and UFOs
The ultimate out-of-body orgasm:
Missing and presumed happy.

Haven't Had Sex in a Long Time?
Things to be grateful for when you finally have it.
- You weren't disappointed.
- The earth still moves.
- There's leftover moo shoo pork in the fridge.
- Your partner's too sleepy to eat it.
- You unplugged the phone.
- You remembered what to do.
- It still works.
- So does your lover's.

*9 or more months.

The Emergency Sex Kit

Don't leave home without:

For Him

Razor (for face)
I.D. (in case of accident)
Change of socks
Vitamin tablets
Mom's phone number
Photo of dog (for courage)
Nitro pills (for position-related angina)
Condoms (regular)

For Her

Razor (for legs)
I.U.D. (in case of accident)
Change of panty hose
Calcium tablets
Therapist's phone number
Photo of cat (for security)
Aspirin (for position-related backache)
Condoms (one size fits all)

The Morning After a Wonderful Night

The lover who is:	Will wake up and smell:
Happy	The roses
Content	The coffee
Sensitive	Room freshener
Hungry	Bacon frying
Pessimistic	Trouble
Compulsive	Gas

Reminder

Lovers who like to stay up late will find the best way to burn the midnight oil is with an old flame.

Official Tax Table for Lovers

Five possible deductions.

Item Allowable?	Yes	No
Scale: To check weight after sex to see if exercise really helped.		X
Sunglasses: To diminish effect of ultraviolet rays caused by comet sightings during great sex.	X	
Potato latkes: To use as a partner substitute should your lover break the date.		X
50¢: To place under lover's pillow should he or she lose a tooth during robust sexual activity.		X
Slippers with a built-in compass: To help lover find the way back from the bathroom if you have a large home.	X	

Disappointing Moment in Sex

"After three sumptuous hours of lovemaking (kissing me all over, nibbling me in places I didn't know I had, covering me with love bites, plus a to-die baby oil massage that had me moaning in Arabic), he never even noticed that just for him, I'd:
• Lost 10 pounds
• Changed my fragrance.
• Had my legs waxed.
• Gotten implants.
• Left my husband."

Survival Advisory: What to Do When a Lover Walks Out

1. Change the locks.
2. Close the joint checking account.
3. Call in sick and take to your bed for several days with only your cat and a pail of Chardonnay.
4. Listen to Frank Sinatra tapes (a cathartic).
5. Gather everything he or she left at your place and hold a tag sale.
6. Use the proceeds to "clear your head" and visit a) Venice or b) a shrink.

7. Call an old flame to tide you over.
8. Find a new tenant.

No Sex Today
Rest. Contemplate nature. Regain your strength and select one or all of these just-as-much-fun-as-sex alternatives:
1. Finally balance your checkbook.
2. Finish your income tax.
3. Go to work.
4. Test-drive a car you can't afford.
5. Cook a wonderful dinner.
6. Buy a new compact disk.
7. Think about having sex tomorrow.

Some Last-Minute Tax Advice
Donating an old but still usable lover to a needy friend or favorite charity is considered a deductible contribution by the IRS. (Don't forget to get a receipt.)
Note: Value of lover assessed according to lover's remaining serviceability. (See IRS form 1040x)

Sex and Taxes
In general, expenses related to sex for the express purpose of experiencing pleasure are not deductible. The purchase of a "Lover Helper" (much like Hamburger Helper, except taller and better built) was disallowed by the IRS. (*United States* v. *Bambi*, 55 Ohio App. 471.) Remedial sex, however, is usually regarded favorably by the IRS. Your deduction will seldom be questioned if the purpose of sex was:
1. Reproduction
2. Sounder, more restful sleep
3. To relieve job-related stress
4. To further your career
5. Inspiration

The Best Tax Shelter?
Lying snuggled up against your lover under a down quilt on a queen-size bed with the fireplace roaring in a cabin on a very private acre of land in the middle of a Maine forest. The IRS will never find you.

Official Tax Deductions for Lovers

Item Deductible?	Yes	No
Cost of driving to meet your lover		X
If lover also a client	X	
Flowers		X
Vase		X
Purchase of sex manual		X
If written by an M.D.	X	
Making love in:		
Your bedroom		X
A legitimate home office	X	

Today's Reconciliation Tip

Caught by your spouse with another partner?
The one thing to do:
• Deny everything.
The one thing to say:
• "It's not what you think it is."
The one thing not to say:
• "You don't know what you've been missing."

Level IV

Also known as Le Petit Mort, possibly due to the climaxee's tendency to just lie there, responsive only to the thrusting of little tea cakes into his or her mouth and whispered reassurance that it's going to be all right.

How Manifested

Nearly immediate relief, perhaps for the first time in months, of job-related stress and a feeling that you're lying in a field of alfalfa. You show your gratitude by covering lover's head with a cool compress

Love Poll #3

To the during-sex question "Why did you stop?" 100 men responded (to the same woman) as follows:

• "I did?"	3%
• "Eager to get back to my book."	21%
• "Middle-age spread."	25%

- "Threatened—you're too good in bed."   9%
- Shouldn't have eaten herring salad."   2%
- "Saving my strength for my girlfriend."   15%
- "Thought it was a quickie."   18%
- "Have to drive the baby-sitter home."   7%

Advice for Modest Lovers
The best way to avoid public displays of affection is to keep your window shades down.

Unofficial Tax Tips for Lovers
Unusual sex-related deductions (check with your accountant):
- Any wine costing over $15.00 prescribed by either your lover or a reasonably reputable physician to help you relax in bed.
- Nightlight to help you find your partner in the dark.
- A car phone so you can be immediately contacted should your lover succumb to a passion attack.
- Medical care for lust-related injuries such as love bites and bed sores. (Note: IRS considers this a gray area.)
- Cost of sending your child to day camp (or a very long movie) so you and your spouse can have some time for yourselves.

Hearts and Flowers: Part II

Give:	To the lover who:
Marigolds.	Doesn't wait until feeding time to turn you into an animal.
Roses.	After two hours of sex, makes you beg for mercy.
Orchids.	Ignores your pleas for mercy.
A Bonsai tree.	Knows the six secret sexual uses for a salad spinner (sorry, no hints).
Daffodils.	When you're away, feeds your cat.
A hanging plant.	When you're home, feeds your ego.

Frequently Overlooked Tax Deductions: Part I

Item Deductible	Yes	No
Sex:		
For pleasure		X
To alleviate depression (attach therapist's note)	X	
Patriotic duty	X	
Birth control pills:		
To prevent pregnancy:	X	
As a snack		X

Try Something Different Tonight

You be the one to initiate sex.
• Leave an erotic note on your lover's windshield. State in 500 words or more what you plan to be. Be explicit.
• Hope it doesn't rain.
• Make sure you leave the note on the right car.

The Art of Romance

Worst excuse ever for not having sex with one's spouse:
"You've looked so perfect lying there, I just couldn't bear to disturb you."

      – Name and address withheld

The First Thing I Do After Terrific Sex

"Write down my dreams."
      – Barbara, reporter
"Thank my lover for the ride."
      – Brandy, machinist
"Reach for the phone—I have to tell someone!"
      – Brendan, clergy
"Get his phone number."
      – Gretchen, tax attorney

Sex's Not-So-Well-Kept Secrets

• There's no such thing as a wasted motion.
• In cold weather, it's the preferred treatment for cabin fervor.
• For achieving that healthy indoor look, honeymooners swear by it.

- It's a considerate way to wake a lover without using a buzzer.
- For the highly polished lover, rubbing against a partner will remove wax buildup.
- It keeps the birth rate up.
- It's a lovely way to keep in touch.

Lover Appreciation Day
For a partner who:

For a partner who:	Send:
Writes intimate love notes.	More office supplies.
Can't get enough of you.	Snapshots.
Makes your skin glow.	Ray Bans.
Makes house calls.	In-line skates.
Keeps you warm on cold nights.	Flannel pajamas.
Is fun to be with.	An invitation.
Is heaven to be with.	A halo.

Frequently Overlooked Tax Deductions: Part II

Item Deductible	Yes	No
Vasectomy:		
For birth control	X	
Fore care-free sex		X
Bust enhancement:		
To make your lover want you more		X
To get a better job	X	
Bust reduction:		
To relieve back pain	X	
To teach partner a lesson		X

Wine and Your Lover: Part II
You can use *any* wine to toast your lover's erogenous zones.
If your lover is:
1. Very gentle, kind of "strums" you, knows exactly which buttons to press.
2. Enthusiastic, but doesn't always get it quite right unless you communicate with a megaphone.
3. Comatose, just goes through the motions—all three of them.
Serve:
1. Riesling, chilled, or a chalky California Chardonnay.
2. Any inexpensive blush wine—move up to a hearty burgundy if lover improves.
3. Ripple and a straw.

Ten Things to Be Happy About Before Sex
- All the good lovers aren't married.
- The delicious anticipation.
- You've been dieting.
- This week, your ex has the kids.
- The fantasies that might come true (God help you).
- The next two hours.
- You won't have to wear a tie.
- The arrival of your lover.
- The audition.
- The warmup.

Tax Deductions for Lovers

Item Deductible?	Yes	No
For writing love notes:		
Ballpoint pen	X	
Mont Blanc fountain pen		X
To make one more attractive:		
Black garters	X	
Face-lift		X
Oceanfront condo		X
Depilatory	X	
Gatorade to calm first-time jitters	X	
Depreciation of one's pillow (but on appeal)		X

On-The-Job Training
The benefits of sex in the workplace:

"It's a smart career move."
> – Donald, secretary

"It's a terrific career movement (a little to the left)."
> – Nancy, Donald's supervisor

"Afterwards, he can't immediately roll over and fall asleep—I'm his boss."
> – Charlene, sales manager

A Lover's Night Table: Part II
More items to keep beside the bed.
1. At least three pieces of fruit. (Rare is the lover capable of performing all night without fiber.)
2. Glue. To repair knickknacks knocked over during extra-fervent sexual activity.
3. Dirt Devil. To remove cookie crumbs from the sheet.
4. New toothbrushes. (One for your lover and one for you—your old one may still contain the spirits of lovers past.)
5. Flashlight. (Vital if you have sex in the dark but believe in love at first sight.)

Sin Taxes: Part I
The Treasury Department's official guide.

Sin	Tax
Celibacy because:	
Saving yourself for the right one	none
Even though you're 54 years old	$2.00
It's fashionable	$3.50
Sex education class said to "Just say no."	none
But you're the teacher.	$3.75
But you're on your honeymoon	$5.50
You're waiting for a ring:	
On the phone	$4.25
On your finger	none

Sorry About Last Night
When an apology for less than perfect sex is needed, check the appropriate box and send to your lover.

___ Kids kept knocking on bedroom door
___ You kept letting them in
___ Worried about the roast burning
___ Martinis: Too many
___ Too few
___ Bad day at work
___ Worried about the extra 10 pounds I put on
___ Let's try again on ___

The Guest Lover: Part II

It's appropriate to insist on a guest lover when you need:
- Variety.
- A third opinion.
- Company.
- Assistance (either for sexual reasons or to help you move a sofa).
- A cheering section.
- Someone to hold the camera.
- It more often.
- The deduction.

The Enlightened Lover

The warning signs of:

Too much sex

Smiling at the world

Feeling just a bit guilty

Puffy eyes (too much sleep)

Neglecting your friends

Morbid interest in chocolate

Too little sex

Snarling at the world

Making others feel guilty

Puffy eyes (insomnia)

Annoying your friends

Morbid interest in politics

From Our Treasury of Sexual Wisdom: Part II

Sex should never be used as a form of escape unless:
- You're seriously dieting.
- Your hairdresser had to cancel.
- The mall is closed.
- Your golf date's rained out.
- It's the only way the warden will give you a pass.

The New Tax Law—IRS Bulletin 7945

"Uniforms your lover said you must have to arouse him or her and which you may not usually wear away from the bedroom:
- A frilly, see-through chemise
- Bikini briefs

• Any lace-up thong bodysuit
• A padded push-up demi bra that (a) provides maximum décolleté and (b) is unsuitable for sales presentations
• A motorcycle jacket
are considered a deductible expense."

Sin Taxes: Part II

The Attorney General's official guide.

Sin	Tax
Lying:	
About your age	$1.25
About your height	$1.80
About where you go on Tuesday nights	$10.00
About wearing a push-up bra	$2.30
When a new partner asks:	
"Are you interested in commitment?"	$6.50
"Do you like children?"	$7.00
"Are you married?"	$9.25

The Itemized Sheet

Sex-related drug and medical expenses and the IRS.

Deductible	Usually Disallowed
Smelling salts	Flowers
Dehumidifier	Air conditioner
Heating Pad	Loofah
Ben-Gay (for aching muscles)	Whipped cream
Vitamin E	Steroids
Blister cream	Vaseline
Lavoris	Gatorade
Champagne (if used as a calmative)	Champagne (if used for toasting)

How Long Should You Wait to Have Sex?

Suggested waiting periods after stressful events.

After:

Breaking up with a lover:	**Wait:**
If lover initiated breakup	1 month
If you initiated breakup	1 hour
Filing your income tax:	
If you owe the government money	1 week
If the government owes you money	1 second
Your in-laws leave	1 nanosecond

The Inquisitive Lover

Q. At what age should I cut back on my sex life?

Happily, there is no age limit. Researchers have shown that an active sex life, right up to the moment your pension kicks in, can prevent:
• Hardening of the arteries
• Irregularity
• Wheat-germ madness
• Short-term memory loss
• Loss of sexual function
• Migrating to Florida

A Lover's Guide to Affordable Sex

1. Don't overtip your partner (20% of the check is plenty).
2. Recycle flowers: After dinner, take the tulips from the dinner table and place them beside the bed.
3. Charge admission when you leave the shades up.
4. Instead of candles, use moonlight; it's free, and won't drip on the carpet.
5. Take advantage of early-bird specials: make love before noon.

Recovery Foods for the Exhausted Lover

Nutritionists recommend the brownie, an all-purpose edible which, if made properly (lots of chocolate) and served in the correct portion size (5" x 5"), provides 98% of the nutrients needed to give the typical partner enough strength to say, "Let's do this again." Additional suggestions:

Food

Belgian endive salad

Jelly doughnut

Application

Replenishes testosterone levels. Enables the partner who experienced a Level 7 climax to uncross his or her eyes.

Mood-Wreckers

During sex with your spouse, it's considered inappropriate to mention:

• How you'd kill for a tuna melt
• What you're missing on TV while making love
• How cute the cat looks perched on the bureau
• Politics*
• Re-doing the family room
• That your parents are coming next week
• Past arguments
• Past loves

*Unless you're a candidate for office

Love Poll #4

To the question "How do you last so long?" 500 lusty men replied:

• "Thinking positive": 16%
• "Lucky charm": Rabbit's foot, 23%; chai, 10%
• "Good genes": 16%
• "Secret aphrodisiac": Oat bran, 56%; smelts, 9%
• "Insomnia": 4%
• "Encouraged by great cheering section:" 62%
• "Feel I'm finally doing something with my life": 11%
• "She gives me no choice": 72%

Thought for Today

A healthy sex life is nature's antidote for:

• A long commute
• Shopping
• A poor job attitude
• Dry skin
• Lack of sex

- Too much golf
- A short temper
- Paying income tax

From Our Lover's Glossary

The G spot. An eponymous erogenous zone found only on those persons who think they have one. Touching such zone in an appropriate manner will cause its owner to:
- Do three things at once (smile, purr and writhe)
- Re-fall in love with the toucher
- Discern the true meaning of life
- Utter "Gee!"

A Lover's Jukebox

Our exclusive guide to romantic music.

If:	Play:
You're delicate	"Love Me Tender"
You like to fool around	"It's All in the Game"
You sometimes have trouble finding a lover's erogenous zones	"Sixteen Candles"
Your bed's too small	"He'll Have to Go"
You prefer sex in the great outdoors	"Earth Angel"
You practice extremely safe sex	"It's Only Make-Believe"

Count Your Blessings

If your lover is not only good in bed but:
- Knows where to get one wholesale.
- Always recommends great stock picks.
- Is a match for your tennis game.
- Cooks, cleans and sews, but almost never during sex.
- Makes house calls when (a) you're lonely and (b) it's raining.
- Can fix a traffic ticket.
- Likes you for your mind.
- Loves you for your body.

Loving Couples Tell All
Great moments in afterplay:
"We exchange vows . . . to do it again as soon as he regains feeling there."
> – Selma, fitness instructor

"We hold each other close and whisper words of endearment to our guru."
> – Nancy, aromatherapist

"We hold each other close and make dinner reservations."
> – Milton, plumber

"We rush to the scale to see how much weight we lost."
> – Rupert, financial planner

Great Moments in Afterplay: Part IV
"I talk, he falls asleep. What fun."
> – Rhonda, army brat

"I write sexy words on the soles of her feet with my finger. She tries to guess what I'm saying."
> – Pablo, all-around good fellow

"We take the rest of our clothes off."
> – Babe, waitress

"We swap recipes."
> – Dick and Jane

The Inquisitive Lover
Three frequently asked questions.
Q.
1. *Re incompetence:* On what should one put a lover who is not quite up to the task?
2. *Re quality:* What are the differences between a superior and a brilliant performance?
3. *Re courtesy:* After lovemaking, which lover gets to use the bathroom first?

A.
1. Probation.
2. The size of the wet spot.
3. The one who is stickiest.

The Language of Flowers: Part IV

To the lover who:	Send:
Turns your living room into the ultimate day-care center	Gardenias
Turns your bedroom into the ultimate night-care center	Daffodils
Turns your bed into the ultimate learning center.	Buttercups

The Sounds of Love

If, during sex, you hear:	It could mean:
Your heart	You're doing it right
A heavenly voice	An out-of-body climax
"Fasten your seat belt"	You're about to land
A knock on the door	Someone wants to use the bathroom
Bubbling	The chemistry's wonderful
The television	He's done
The baby crying	You're done
Screams	Your deodorant's fading

The (Pleasantly) Surprised Lover

Nonsexual events that may induce a certified:

Minor Climax

1. Your team won
2. A promotion
3. The state owes you money
4. Religious experience #1—Your child got into college
5. Lost weight
6. Playing hooky by calling in sick

Major Climax

1. You were in the office pool
2. With a salary increase
3. The IRS owes you money
4. Religious experience #2—On full scholarship
5. Without suffering
6. They believe you

The Enlightened Lover

During sex, assume you are a great lover if your partner replies "Absolutely not" when you ask:
1. "Am I keeping you?"
2. "Would you rather go back to just being friends?"
3. "Would you rather watch *Sleepless in Seattle*?"
4. "Are you going back to your first wife?"
5. "Are you still going to cash your alimony check?"

How Often Do You Make Love? Part III

Frequency Rate
3-5 times weekly (typical married couple except those with 4 or more children)

What It Means
Love life still good: sight of each other in non-flannel underwear continues to thrill, but he no longer playfully puts his tongue in her ear while she's mixing the salad, sending endives and arugula all over the new puppy.

Reminder

For the shy lover:
It's easier to laugh with all your clothes off.
For the shy but serious lover:
It's easier to lighten up in a darkened room.

Sexually Related Stress

(On a scale of 1 to 100)*
• Discovering girlfriend in bed with:

A woman	29
(Who invites you to join in)	41
Another man	68
Two men	83
One of them is you	100

*Source: *Journal of Suburban Sex,* Vol. II.

Tip for the Lonely Lover

When, for some strange reason you don't quite feel like yourself, it's perfectly okay, instead, to go out and have sex with a friend.

Seniors in Love: Part I

"For our 50th anniversary we finally got an unlisted number. Now we don't worry about our grandchildren calling during sex to find out how we are. It's none of their business."

– Ben and Yetta, Century Village, Florida

"I love it when he puts on his reading glasses so he can better find my erogenous zones."

– Virginia, Daytona Pines, Florida

"Every afternoon we enjoy two 'Early-Bird Specials'—the first in our bedroom, the second at a marvelous fish restaurant."

– Claire and Eugene, Ocala Palms, Florida

During-Sex Technical Difficulties

Some leading causes:

• No sense of direction (both partners facing away from each other).
• Partner grinding, instead of gritting, her teeth.
• Chipping a nail while opening the condom package.
• It's the first time.
• One partner being fashionably chaste.
• High armrest between movie theater seats.
• One partner has a higher sex drive (and neither can figure out who it is).

A Guide to Vehicular Sex

Oldsmobile Cutlass

Advantages

Excellent cruise control permits nonstop lovemaking, even while going through toll booths. Strategic placement of windshield washer control makes it easy to rinse each other off after fervent passion.

Disadvantages

Automatic safety belts may offend those not into bondage.

The Enlightened Lover

A guide for the slow learner.

Erotic	Less Erotic
Love bites	Tax bites

Sexually Induced Longevity: Part I
Each time

Your lover:	To your life, add
Sends you flowers	5 minutes
Brings you flowers	11 minutes
You try something new	8 minutes
And it actually feels good	15 minutes
You do something naughty but nice	9 minutes
You do something nice but naughty	1 hour

The Morning After: Part I
Six love notes to send to a blush-prone lover.

If you write:	Lover's face will be:
"Why did you stop?"	Magenta.
"When did you stop?"	Ashen.
"Loved the way you woke me up—twice!"	Vermilion.
"Now I know how to make you stop snoring."	Roseate.
"Instead of lunch, how about a nooner?"	Plaid.
"I faked the first four."	Pink.

The Weary Lover
Feeling faint? After two hours of sex with a tireless partner, it's permissible to encourage a rest period by faking:
• Orgasm
• Sleep
• Cramps
• The call of nature

The Moment I Knew It Was Love
"She was the first woman who didn't get upset when I checked my E-mail while she undressed me."
— Geraldo, columnist

"After sex, he held my hand instead of the TV clicker."
> – Maggie, environmentalist

"The first time we petted below the waist—I couldn't resist his southern charm."
> – Delia, hair colorist

Love Signs
Horoscope for a Torrid Taurus
- *Ruling passion:* temptation
- *Ruling body lotion:* seltzer (the little bubbles make your skin tingle)
- *Chief sexual asset:* you make house calls
- *Governing erogenous zone:* that mysterious corner of your soul
- *Aphrodisiac of choice:* knockwurst
- *Ruling sexual activity:* slipping in and out of consciousness
- *Ideal time for sex:* harvest time

Sexual Etiquette
When showering together, who decides on the water temperature?
If it's before sex: the lover who wins the toss.
If it's during sex: the lover with the most sensitive skin.
If it's after sex: the lover who did the most work.

Love Signs
Horoscope for a Tempestuous Taurus.
- *Ruling passion:* doing the unthinkable
- *Ruling sexual turnoff:* portion control
- *Chief sexual asset:* a total lack of discipline
- *Governing erogenous zone:* the finish line
- *Aphrodisiac:* all-you-can-eat buffets
- *Ruling sexual activity:* showing no mercy
- *Ideal time for sex:* happy hour

Why I Love Sex
"I'm so darn good at it."
> – Krista, bowling champ

"It makes the commute more tolerable—I just think about what I have waiting for me at my homes."
> – Donald, developer

"A climax a day keeps the psychiatrist away."
> — Tammy, exterior decorator (parade floats)

"It improves my job attitude."
> — Sharon, engineer

More Love Signs: Taurus

Opposite love sign: A sizzling Scorpio or an "All-You-Can-Eat" notice.

Outstanding sexual quality: Get wild on just one glass of wine.

Most attractive physical feature: Eyes so seductive (thanks to tinted contact lenses) they're registered with the police.

Ruling sexual turnoff: Partners who fidget when you ask about (1) their past and (2) your future.

Ruling sexual turn-on: Any activity that involves leather.

Ideal place for sex: Under a starlit sky, or, when it rains, an umbrella.

Extra Love Signs: Taurus

Most attractive features: You're a low-calorie feast for the eyes and cost only pennies a day to operate.

Turn-on: A fearless lover who, after eating a garlic-pepperoni pizza, spurns a breath-freshener.

Turnoffs: Lovers who don't come when you call them.

Ideal romantic adventure: Duty-free shopping at Kennedy Airport with my foreign lover's charge card.

Favorite sexual fantasy: Doing it for the first time after a very long time (two years, four months) and not being disappointed.

Pizza and Sex: Part IV

Great sex requires, no, demands terrific pizza.

Type of Lovemaking

Stunningly inventive, even kinky; during foreplay, both partners my actually be in separate rooms. Favorite position during fourth hour of sex: one partner clinging desperately to one side of the bed while the other partner bails.

Idea Topping

Onions (to heighten passion and keep away onlookers), meatballs (for self-confidence), calamari (optional—the link between this substance and better lovemaking is still hazy) and garlic (for self-awareness and to help blow out the candles).

The Grateful Lover: Part II
How to send a thank-you note if lovemaking left you tongue-tied.

If you're:	What to do:
Musical	Gift-rap it.
Bashful	Fed Ex it.
In shape	Deliver it yourself.
Flamboyant	Send a singing telegram.
Impatient	Fax it.
Patient	Use a carrier pigeon.
Very patient	Mail it.

What I Did for Love
"Trusted him. (I left my purse in the other room yet had only minimal anxiety.)"

— Darlene, psychiatrist

"Trusted her. (I left my medication in the other room. She was very supportive.)"

— Boyd, Darlene's patient

The Supportive Lover
Six ways to praise a partner for a job well done.
1. "Good lover."
2. "Gee, you make the inner child in me want to come out and play."
3. "Take anything you want from the refrigerator."
4. "Everything I have is yours—except the stuff that's in my safety deposit box."
5. "I'd like you to be my guest . . . at the mall."
6. "I couldn't have done it without you."

When You Finally Meet the Right Lover
Possible drawbacks:
"I wasted money. She made me toss out the rest of the responses I got to my personal ad."

— Larry, photographer

"I'm neglecting my reading, my friends, my parents, my volunteer work and my bridge game. I feel so liberated."

— Diane, sales assistant

"It's cut heavily into my job search."
                    — Jason, ski instructor
"I can tell my therapist's getting jealous. He hardly says a word to me."
                    — Brittany, in Freudian analysis

Common During-Sex Fibs
- "Of course these sheets are fresh."
- "I can stop at any time."
- "Wow! I've never tried that before."
- "They were taken before I met you."*
- "I didn't think we were going to do this tonight."
- "These aren't silicone."

*Or: "They were taken while I was drunk."

Sex Without Guilt
Observe environmentally safe sex.
Outdoors:
- Don't crush the moss
- Don't annoy the animals
- Save the wails

Indoors:
- Use cotton instead of polyester sheets
- Avoid baby oil spills
- Contain the wet spot

The Enlightened Lover
You can tell that your partner's had:

Enough when:	Too much when:
Circles appear under eyes.	Circles become squares.
He or she begs for ice water.	He or she begs for jury duty.
Pulse rate's in the low 50s.	Pulse rate's undetectable.
Sleep occurs and partner is snoring.	Sleep occurs and partner doesn't know it.
A rash appears.	An orderly appears.

The Bedside Eater: Part I
Spaghetti with Italian sausage (aphrodisiac for the pasta lover):
Erotic Claim
Transforms mild lovers into movers and shakers, especially during a grade-6 climax; low-energy lovers no longer panic if, after two hours of marathon lovemaking, partner says, "Let's try again."
Scientific Evidence
Users report high success rate; formerly insecure lovers now have enough confidence to offer money-back guarantee, especially if pasta is done *al dente*.

From Our Lover's Glossary
Post-Lovemaking Stress Syndrome. An after-sex state of mental confusion in an overwhelmed male partner, the chief sign of which will be his efforts, when he tries to get dressed, to insert both feet into the same trouser leg. Scientific studies suggest such condition is caused either by:
1. Sex so awesome that he neglects his hernia;
2. His partner's standing ovation; or
3. His partner's demand for an encore.
Tip: Revive him by administering a gentle, come-to-your-senses smack with a buttermilk pancake.

Great Moments in Afterplay
"Looking for my other sock."
> – Alan, lawyer

"Watching my lover float back to earth."
> – Kiki, balloonist

"Feeling ever so used."
> – Portia, V.P., marketing

"Feeling ever so used up."
> – Rocco, Portia's personal trainer

After-Sex Etiquette
You may dress immediately after sex only if:
• You're the next model down the runway.
• You're asking yourself, "What am I doing here?" and can't come up with an answer.
• You hear footsteps (forest ranger approaching—applies to hikers only).

215

• You hear the front door opening (your spouse's business trip ended early).
• You have customers waiting.
• You've been gently asked to respect the "No Loitering" sign above the bed.

Communication Tip
If you find it difficult to ask your love for sex, beg.

Tip for the Environmentally Aware
So long as your breath contains no chlorofluoro-carbons, moaning, shouting and calling out your lover's name during sex does absolutely no harm to the earth's ozone layer.

The Dieter's Guide to Weight Loss During Sex

Making the First Move	Calories Burned
Before sex:	
If you're bold	9
If you're shy	68
After sex:	
If lovemaking was wonderful	23
If lovemaking was exhausting	350

Environmental Lovers
• Carry home the food for their intimate candlelit dinner in a paper bag instead of a plastic one.
• Practice safe outdoor sex—no matter how romantic the spot, they avoid making love near a hazardous waste site.
• Reduce during-sex energy consumption by getting a tune-up every 100 nights.
• Save forests with love notes written on recycled paper only.
• Protect the ozone layer by covering each other's mouth after those extravagant, after-sex yawns.
• Save the wails.

Shakespeare for Lovers
Movies to rent after sex that was:
• Good: Romeo and Juliet
• Great: A Midsummer Night's Dream

- Mediocre: Much Ado About Nothing
- Lascivious: King Leer

Message from Earth-Friendly Lovers

"We write our love notes only on recycled paper, never use massage oil that's been tested on animals, shun furniture made from trees cut down in the rain forest, never kill those miserable biting, stinging insects that make sex so uncomfortable when we're on a picnic, read only sex manuals printed on acid-free paper, consider orgasm a cleansing experience, take our champagne bottle to a redemption center immediately after sex, and do it only on (ugh) recycled sheets."*

> – Durward and Muffy, regression therapists

*They have an arrangement with a nearby motel.

What I Did for Love

"Gave her a passing grade."

> – J.D., Professor of Economics, Mel's College

"His income taxes."

> – Evelyn D., CPA

The Dieter's Guide to Weight Loss During Sex

Activity	Calories Burned
While at work, thinking about seeing your lover tonight:	
Anticipation	45
Thinking how good it's going to be	77
Thinking how to make it even better	100
Racking your brain	458
Trying to concentrate on work	163
Wishing 5 o'clock would come	58
If it's only 10:45 A.M.	200

Spicing Up Your Sex Life: Part II

An epicure's guide.

Condiment	Application
Cumin	Eases hoarseness caused by climax-related shouting.
Curry	Increases sensitivity of those difficult-to-reach erogenous zones.
Ginger	Prevents premature peaking during unbridled sex in lovers over 30.
Juniper	None, but tastes good.

Advice for Marathon Lovemakers

How to make love:

When the Chemistry's Good

Day in, day out

When the Chemistry's Great

Day in, night out

Five Things to Do When the Right Lover Comes Along: Part II

1. Learn to make lentil salad, beef Wellington, corn bread, French fries and cocoa (the breakfast of champion lovers).
2. Buy (a) a new shower curtain, (b) satin sheets and (c) fluffier towels.
3. Promise friends you'll keep in touch (just not as often).
4. Buy sexy, diaphanous underwear—to enable your new lover to better see your inner beauty.
5. Always leave a number where you can be reached.
Note: When the wrong lover comes along, get an unlisted number.

The Enlightened Lover

Life after:

Super sex: *"Changed my outlook—there is a God!?*
        – Sheila, flight attendant
Great sex: *"Changed my outlook—there is a Goddess!"*
        – Paul, pilot

Good sex: *"Changed my attitude—I'm no longer depressed and anxious."*

> — Webster, parson

So-so sex: *"Changed astrologers. We must have been doing something wrong."*

> — Noreen, nail technician

The Enlightened Lover: Too Much Sex?

After two hours of lovemaking, you are wearing:

Him out if he's:
Pleading for Spam
Biting his nails
Speaking in tongues

Her out if she's:
Pleading for herbal tea
Biting his nails
Unable to speak

Sex's Best-Kept Secrets

What millions of satisfied users say.

1. It makes spring cleaning a lot more fun.
2. Next to television, it's the evening activity preferred by nearly 62% of all American adults.
3. In experiments with volunteer gorillas, sex has been known to increase intelligence by three IQ points.
4. Whether one needs it or not, a level 5 orgasm* can actually realign one's vertebrae.
5. Corn chowder is not the aphrodisiac most experts claim it to be.

*Sudden change of religious belief.

Lover's Etiquette

After sex, it is not considered good form to calculate the number of orgasms you had by counting them on your fingers. (And . . . there's always the danger that you might run out of fingers.)

Daytime Love Making

The advantages:

1. You can see if your complexion really is clearing.
2. Not having to grope around for your partner.
3. If pressed for time, you can keep your eye on the clock.
4. It's much easier to identify your partner's points of interest.
5. If sex is exhausting, you can watch as your partner grows pale.
6. It's much easier to find the partner who gets swept away.

Sex Secrets of the Great Lovers

How to make him wish the night would never end.

Pre-play: Warm him up by kissing him where it will do the most good (either in the restaurant or as he's pulling into the driveway).
Foreplay: Sizzle. Undress him while you're still in the elevator. If he trips because his pants are around his ankles, help him up.
During-play: Relax him. Rub his back with rare oils while singing Renaissance love songs.
After-play: Tuck him in.

The Art of Romance

Seven ways to show your lover you care.

1. Give up smoking.
2. Learn a new position.
3. Occasionally use cloth instead of paper napkins.
4. Undress completely when you make love (including your headphones).
5. Make a housecall at her office. Arrive wearing nothing under your raincoat.
6. When he asks, "When can we see each other again," don't reach for your Filofax.
7. Cut his meat.

What Do the Professionals Do?

The Problem	The Solution
Morning mouth	Brownies.
Difficulty arousing a dozing lover who's eaten too much.	Don't bother—make love anyway.
Nearsighted lover can't find erogenous zones.	Make lover guess—it could be more fun.

What I Did for Sex

"Discovered the perfect complex carbohydrate—my lover!"
> – Bambi, dietitian

"Missed my stop."
> – Henry, commuter

"Moved to a larger city."
> – Brock, salesman

Movies for Lovers: Part III

If your lover:	Rent
Likes to do it outdoors.	Field of Dreams
Gives you out-of-body orgasms.	The Exorcist
Is difficult to satisfy.	48 Hours
Is insatiable.	Another 48 Hours
Is really insatiable.	9¹/₂ Weeks

The Inquiring Lover

What do you most like about afterplay?

"The feeling of togetherness. In a warm, sexy voice he reads his '75 Dodge Dart shop manual to me."
> – Shanna, potter

"The sense of adventure. We play gin rummy, for money!"
> – Adam, poet

"The challenge. I read my lover's palm while he's wearing mittens."
> – Ross, analyst

The Enlightened Lover

The five nice things about making love in a darkened room:

1. You finally get to light those bayberry candles (the lighting removes years from your face).
2. The intimacy.
3. During those extra-special moments, your partner can't tell that you're blushing.
4. Your "problem" areas don't show.
5. You don't have to worry about a power failure.

Breaking the Ice
The first thing I do with a new lover:
"Make her a client."
> – Roy, stockbroker

"I have sex with him just for his mind, then I have sex with him just for his body, then I decide which is better."
> – April, heavy-equipment operator

Sexual Demerits: Part I

Violation	Demerits Earned
Inadequate foreplay (four caresses and some begging)	16
Failure to remove all jewelry	19
Especially wedding ring	25
Malingering	20
Watching TV out of corner of eye	33
Taking a phone call	40
Yawning	11
Failure to cover mouth	15
Parking in a non-erogenous zone	50

Love Poll #5
More official results of an official government sex-survey:
• During sex, 12% of all Americans improve their in-bed performance by listening to motivational tapes.
• Only 9% of all Americans don't see what all the fuss is about.
• When sex with a person is not available, 11% of all Americans use their home-shopping channel as a viable substitute.
• After sex, 26% of all Americans approve of their in-bed performance when watching the video tapes.

During-Sex Etiquette
A lady never pours her own Champagne unless (a) there's no gentleman present, or (b) a gentleman is present but his hands are engaged.

A gentleman gets into bed first and warms it up for his partner. (Exception: A lady who outweighs her partner by 30 or more pounds is obliged to warm the bed.)

A gentleman demonstrates especially good breeding if he rises each time his partner gets out of or into the bed.

It is distracting and inappropriate to applaud between movements.

Hot Numbers

25: Number of days of lovemaking required by an insecure partner to get over first-night jitters.

4.6 miles: Average distance a meticulous groom's lips travel on his wedding night before he realizes his bride's still in the bathroom.

586: Average number of times the bride's toes curl back and forth while her erogenous zones are being explored.

2: Number of weeks a cautious person goes back in history when a new lover asks about his or her past.

7: Number of names dropped by the average starlet during orgasm.

Signs of a Successful First Date

• You don't notice what you're eating.
• You keep staring into each other's eyes.
• You make each other laugh.
• You don't mind if your date keeps tasting your food.
• You don't care that you have little in common.
• You fight over the check.
• You kiss goodnight well into the morning . . .
• . . . and go to work in the same clothes you wore yesterday.

Reminder

The latest research indicates that long-terms sexual deprival (fewer than 26 times a month) may cause blurred vision.

When the Unthinkable Happens

Event

1. Appearance of constable demanding to know why you and your lover are making so much noise.
2. While gently blowing into lover's ear, lover's head begins to enlarge.

What to Do

1. Just go along quietly.
2. Quickly get out of there.

Common Reactions to the Extraordinary Climax
A guide for the novice lover.

Typical Response	Unusual
Loss of composure	Loss of pocket change
A knowing smile	A wince
Fogging of one's glasses	Fogging of the window
Unable to find pulse	Unable to find partner
Earth moved	Bed moved
Heart pounding	Neighbors pounding
Rockets	Applause

Sex Poll #8: What Turns You Off?
"Crumbs in bed, especially if they were from her last lover."
> – Joe, plasterer

"A lover who, during sex, wipes sweat from my hot, gyrating brow with a squeegee."
> – Ramona, nail consultant

"Impatience. Being asked to make love in the Jacuzzi while the plumber's still working on it."
> – Donna, florist

"Lovers who mumble when they moan."
> – Barbara, news anchor

How to Keep Sex Exciting
Our checklist:

___ Make love where you might be caught (at a party in a bathroom with a broken door lock, or in a greenhouse).

___ Dirty words at the right moment ("Where's my alimony check?").

___ Lots of creativity—never wear the same color underwear (or condom) twice in a row.

___ Do it at an unusual time (like in late spring).

___ Save up—instead of having sex every night, wait until the last night of the month and do it 30 times.

___ Don't marry an actress.

Weight-Control Tip for Ex-Smokers
Instead of reaching for
- 10 Oreos
- 1 Hostess fruit pie
- A McDonald's Quarter Pounder
- 4 Kentucky Fried Chicken Drumsticks
- 3 Taco Bell tacos
- 6 fried dumplings
- A bowl of Häagen-Dazs chocolate-chocolate chip inlayed with Reese's Pieces

simply reach for your partner.

> "We constantly fought about sex until we began to have it."
> – Happily married couple

Pillow Talk
Crash sex. An extreme form of lovemaking in which both partners, on their lunch hour, try to a) eat lunch, then b) enjoy the full sexual spectrum (arousal, foreplay, intercourse, orgasm, debriefing*) and c) attempt to get back to work on time. Such form of sex is usually ill-advised since it may cause heartburn.
*E.g., "Was it good for you?" or "Would you like my business card?"

What I Did for Love*
"Improved my on-time performance"
               – Milton, pilot
"Helped him get the nose down."
               – Gloria, co-pilot
"Didn't stand until my partner came to a complete stop."
               – Rapunzel, flight attendant
*From an airport poll of smiling crew members arriving on flight #874.

Schedule of Gratuities

To the Lover Who	Suggested Tip:
Is always ready	25¢
Keeps your tummy flat	50¢
Showed you the best facial scrub of all	$2.00
Is also your best friend	10¢
Feels great in a bathing suit	$5.00
Lends you his or her fingers so you can count the moments till next time	$3.25

Sex Over 85

Three problems:

1. "I have to shout into the phone when I call my girlfriend to tell her how great it was. (She's an older woman.)"
    — Gustav, retired county clerk

2. "I hate commitment and after three or four dates, if things are going well, they always want children."
    — Rafael, writer

3. "During lovemaking, we keep forgetting where we are and have to keep starting over and over again. It's quite tiring."
    — Elsie, graphic designer

Life-Extension Tip

Great sex with a loving spouse on a regular basis (or irregular if he or she works odd hours) can take years off your face but add years to your life.

The Dieter's Guide to Weight Loss During Sex

Overcoming various intercourse-related obstacles.

Activity	Calories Burned
Looking for legroom (footboard in way)	66
Pulling partner back from edge of bed	109
If partner's head already touching floor	140
Maneuvering partner into better position	81
Partner not cooperating	200

Tip for Marathoners
If in the middle of vigorous sex you "hit the wall," be happy. It means you've actually moved the bed across the room.

Amazing Sexual Facts
How extraordinary lovemaking affects lovers.
Physical agility: After the third climax within a two-hour period, even a lover in peak condition may not be able to bend over and touch his partner's toes.
Mental agility: When asked, only 14% of all lovers were able to recall their credit card number during a grade-7 climax (both partners hydroplane into another zip code).
Spiritual agility: After a night of very steamy lovemaking, 71% of all agnostic lovers were willing to concede there might be such a thing as a Higher Power.

From Our Surveillance Tapes
Things said by amazed partners after certifiably hot sex:
• "Mens sana in corpore sano."
• "My rash is gone!"
• "I need gefilte fish."
• "You forgot to remind me to breathe."
• "You shout the sweetest things."
• "Ready for more?"*
*Should not be uttered until a 30-minute cooling-off period has transpired.

Inside a Lover's Fortune Cookie
Your lover will never wish to leave you:
• For another man.
• For another woman.
• Unhappy.
• Unsatisfied.
• Waiting at the altar.

From Our Book of Wondrous Climaxes

"We were so proud. The moans made our neighbors call 911."
— Fidel and Maria, Miami

"It blew out the tires of the car next to us."
— Ellen and Dean, Chicago

"We think it caused the earthquake."
— Iris and Marvin, Los Angeles

"Our tent collapsed."
— Ted and Estelle, Grand Canyon

MONTHLY QUALITY OF LIFE® CHECKUP

•We had sex _____times this month.
•**I answered the above question honestly:**
True_____   False___
•**I love sex because:**
We get to go to a motel (and I'm low on towels)___
It consumes calories—I don't have to go on that crummy grape-fruit diet___
We can do it anywhere (except the rear of my Corvette)___
It's inexpensive (no greens fees)___
It puts a non-contact-lens-assisted twinkle in my eye___
After a tiff we always make up in bed___
It makes a great birthday gift to the lover who has nothing___
It calms my nerves___
It's an outlet for creativity___
•**Our favorite way to prolong lovemaking is:**
Not set the alarm clock___
Send the kids to camp___
Take the curves really slow___
Lip read our sex manual___
Stop in the middle to baste the roast___
•**After sex my lover usually asks:**
"Was it good for you?"___
"Was it good for me?"___

Signed_____

Witnessed_____

MAY

•Erotic goals for May:
1. Be more sexually aggressive in bed
2. Learn CPR, just in case

The ideal month to prepare for warm-weather sex. Some tips:
1. Check bedroom air conditioner. Sex in a non-airconditioned space often leads to something known as "sweating," a situation in which both partners, after, say two hours of vigorous lovemaking, produce a wet spot the size of Capri.
2. When creating a romantic atmosphere, use Christmas lights instead of lighted candles, which will raise the bedroom temperature by several degrees and cause the ceiling mirror to fog.
3. Keep no fewer than three pints of ice cream in the freezer. Medical researchers tell us that a massive ingestion of either chocolate chocolate chip or butternut crunch is the fastest way to revive a partner felled by heat exhaustion.
4. To compensate for energy lost during sex in the popular "Missionary" position (woman on top, missionary on bottom), keep a bowl of chilled fruit beside the bed. Our unregistered dietician recommends plums, necterines, kiwis, or any fruit in season.
5. Drink lots of fluids. Warm-weather lovemaking is dehydrating. Particulary rejuvenating is a piña colada. Lovers not partial to rum may substitute a large tureen of sangria.
6. Avoid shedding—If your lover has a hairy chest, shave it.

•Official aphrodisiac of the Month:
Low-fat cherry muffins

Reminder

After a really special night, always send your lover a note or a drawing expressing how truly wonderful it was. (If lover actually put you on cloud nine, use skywriting.)

Life: Part II

With Sex	Without Sex
Champagne	Cold Duck
Burning off that lunchtime cheeseburger in bed	Must visit health club
Lots of phone calls	To parents and friends
Moaning and writhing	From something you ate
Sweating	Over a hot stove
Working late, but not overtime	Working late, getting overtime
Closing your eyes	Only to sleep

"I thought I was drowning in a sea of love until I realized I was lying in a wet spot."
— Kiki, recovering model

Sex—Our Real National Pastime: Part I

Statistics show that one in six American adults has no desire for sexual intimacy. Instead this sixth American goes into either:
• Law
• Politics
• A monastery
• A deep depression

The Enlightened Lover

You know you're a great lover if your partner:
1. Keeps coming back for more and doesn't ask for travel expenses.
2. Is too winded to reply when you ask, "How was it?"
3. Thinks it's neat that you have a teeny potbelly.
4. Always brings you a treat like
• Flowers
• A snack (Dad's apple pie)
• Something to read
5. Is totally monogamous (and not out of loyalty).

Marathon Advisory

Sports physiologists tell us that it's better to make love once a night than to try and make up for lost time by doing it 31 times on the last day of the month.*

*But do what's most comfortable for you.

What Do the Professionals Do?

Problem

While kissing your lover's face, her false eyelashes come off in your month.

Solution

Don't panic. Pretend nothing's happened and try not to swallow them. When her attention's diverted, press them back on to her lid (she'll never know what happened).

Thought for Today

It is entirely possible that Mother Nature gave us sex specifically to take the drudgery out of reproduction.

Reminder for Divorced Lovers

If you have a really understanding ex: Sex, rather than money, is considered in some states to be an acceptable way to make your alimony payment. Check with local authorities.

Gem of the Month

An emerald friendship ring to the thoughtful, kind, sensitive, terribly passionate lover who:

1. Is always ready to help you work out even your most complicated fantasies with the aid of nothing but
- A queen-size bed
- A satin sheet (high-quality percale is okay)
- A bottle of chilled Taittinger
- A computer

2. Doesn't think of you as a sex object.

3. But happily, when in bed, treats you like one.

Sexual Statistics

10: The typical number of feet covered when two lovers throw themselves at each other.

629: The number of tears shed by a lover named Darryl when his new partner has "Sergio" tattooed on her chest.

3.416: The number of seconds it takes for the typical male to regain his composure and respond to a welcome sexual advance.

17 out of 20: The number of women who do not mind being regarded as a sex object, as long as it isn't by their gynecologist.

7 minutes, 26 seconds: The time it takes a partner to recover from a level 20 orgasm (one that can be seen by the Hubble Telescope).

Substitutions?

Assumption	Myth	Fact
Sex isn't everything, there's always:		
Just showering together		X
TV	X	
Tabloid TV		X
A good cigar		X
Literature		X
Gothic romances	X	
Politics	X	
Shopping:		
For a new spring wardrobe		X
For a new spring lover		X

Three Ways to Burn Off Last Night's Martini

Good: Discover a new erogenous zone.

Very Good: Discover two new erogenous zones.

Better: During moans, correct your lover's grammar.

Best: Make love in the nautical position (woman on her back, man going overboard).

Pillow Talk

Stage fright. Reluctance to undress completely in the presence of one's lover by any light stronger than that shed by an open refrigerator due to real or imagined bodily imperfections.

A Common Female Fear
My thighs may be larger than his.
A Common Male Fear
I'll like it.

More Hot Numbers

146: The number of lovemaking sessions it takes for an unusually dense lover to finally grasp the meaning of "a little more to the left."

15: The minimal number of minutes sex must last before it can be considered live entertainment.

19: The age at which the average male peaks sexually.

76: The age at which the above-average male peaks sexually.

82: The age at which the typical female peaks sexually, unless she's with a younger man.

*Source: Union of Concerned Sex Partners, Miami chapter.

The Inquiring Lover

Asked of couples married 25 years or more—what do you do immediately after sex if it was:

Great:
"Up his weekly allowance."
— Trish

Terrific:
"Have a good nap."
— Rhoda

The usual:
"Have a good cry."
— Colleen

Glorious:
"Hold a mirror to my mouth to see if I'm still breathing."
— Jean-Claude

Mid-Love Crises

- "Am I making too much noise?"
- "You want me to do what?"
- "Oh God, my leg fell asleep before he did."
- "Am I satisfying her?"
- "Can I get away with wearing the same outfit to work tomorrow?"

- "Did I shut the iron off?"
- "Can I sue the matchmaker?"
- "How do I tell her I'm not the man I thought I was?"
- "How do I tell him he's not the man I thought he was?"

Between Relationships?

Six uses for a boy-toy.*
1. To help you survive a difficult divorce.
2. As a jogging partner.
3. To run errands and walk the dog.
4. For non-Nordic Track workouts.
5. As a fashion accessory.
6. To prepare you for the real thing.
*Also known as an impersonal trainer.

A Guide To Vehicular Sex

Chevrolet
Advantages
Convenient display indicates when you're out of gas.
Disadvantages
Weird electrical system: writhing during orgasm may activate flashers.

How Long Can a Lover Go Without Sex? Part I

The first three weeks.
Week 1. Only slight sense of deprivation. Transient feelings of depression and uneasiness compensated by plunging self into work.
Week 2. Elevation of anxiety level plus onset of free-floating boredom. Find self actually reading last-page essay in *Time* magazine.
Week 3. Perceptible weight gain. Hungry for love, but ice cream no longer seems the ideal sex partner. Decide to work off excess sexual energy by joining a health club. (Favorite exercise machine—the Jacuzzi.)

Tips for the Committed Recycler

How to use an old but still faithful lover.
Lover still has some energy left:
For an emergency substitute.
To answer the door.

To answer the phone.
To help you with your income tax.
As a decoy.
To help you find a new lover.
Lover completely worn out:
For compost.
As a doorstop.
To tell you it's ringing.
As a deduction.
As a trophy.
As the trade-in.

From Our Lover's Glossary
Animal. Any lover who likes to pet and
• Before sex: eats like a horse.
• During sex: makes love like a tiger.
• After sex: sleeps like a lamb.

After-Play Tips
Was sex fabulous? Reward your partner by:
• For once, staying awake until he finishes telling you about his day at the office.
• Bringing her a marvelous midnight snack.
• Giving him a pedicure while he's sleeping.
• Letting him have the TV clicker (render it harmless by removing the batteries).
• Letting her use the bathroom first.
• Lighting his cigarette.
• Taking her on a tour of the studio.

What I Changed For Love
"My act. Now I fake orgasms instead of headaches."
　　　　　– Clarissa, hairdresser
"I'm a much more open person. I'm so proud of my new lover that, when we make love, I leave the window blinds up."
　　　　　– Bruce, auditor
"Zip Codes. We moved in together."
　　　　　– Tabitha, acupuncturist

The Dieter's Guide to Weight Loss During Sex

Some common during-sex movements.

Activity	Calories Burned
Switching positions	31
While both partners are still connected	126
If both partners are woefully uncoordinated	402
Orgasm:	
The first shock wave	85
The last	2

The Dieter's Guide To Weight Loss During Sex

For musical partners.

Making Love To	Calories Burned
Rock	53
Heavy Metal	140
FM "lite"	9
Classical	41
Blues	39
Rhythm and blues	100
Rap	65
If you try to catch the words	294

During-Sex Etiquette

The only six acceptable reasons for abruptly stopping and leaping out of bed in the middle of lovemaking:

1. Leg cramp.
2. You smell something burning.
3. You're a volunteer fireman.
4. Your guests are leaving.
5. The plumber has finally shown up.
6. Your lover's in the next room, calling your name.

Hearts and Flowers: Part III

Give:	To the lover who:
An amaryllis.	Believes that no time spent cuddling is wasted.
A yellow narcissus.	Has a swelled head.
Violets.	Without medication, helped you effect a complete recovery from abstinence.
Irises.	Makes you smile just by thinking about (a) what you did this morning and (b) what you're going to do tonight.

From Our Treasury of Sexual Knowledge

1. During lovemaking, hanging a braid of garlic from the bedpost will ward off a) evil spirits, b) aggressive insurance salesmen and c) dandruff.*

2. Researchers report that 71% of all cases of first-night jitters respond favorably to Manhattan clam chowder.

3. Instantly warm up a lover who gives you the cold shoulder with a trip to Bermuda.

*Courtesy: *The Italian Sex Manual*

Everything You Need To Know About Orgasm

• There's no such thing as a bad one.
• Some are noisy.
• Others are silent.
• A few are faked.
• It transforms timid people into movers and shakers.

Love Poll #7

To the during-sex question "Why did you stop?" 100 women responded (to the same man) as follows:

• "My life began to flash before my eyes."	5%
• "Stop nagging."	7%
• "Had to, we were done."	17%
• "Lost my place."	12%
• "Lost my voice."	23%
• "There's more?"	3%

- "Guess I'm old-fashioned."   10%
- "Ran out of film."   6%
- "I didn't."   1%

Moments In Sex
Great
"Had sex with someone just for their body."
> – Rodney W., unemployed

Not-So-Great
"Had sex with someone in spite of their body."
> – Melody, ordained beautician

Grounds For Annulment
As they're getting into bed, a wedding night question asked by:
The bride who always feels a chill:
"Is there also room for my hot water bottle?"
The groom who's led a sheltered life:
"I'm not very good at sex, do you mind if I just watch?"

From Our Lover's Glossary
Chivalry. *1.* An act of consideration in which the male partner, after sex, rolls you over and then goes to sleep. *2.* An act of valor in which the male partner says, "You stay here, I'll go see what that noise is downstairs." *3.* An act of courtesy in which the male partner (usually at 3:45 A.M.) leaves a soft, warm bed to comfort a wailing baby.

Was It Good for You?
Post-orgasmic questions to assist you in assessing the quality of sex.
Question
1. "Do you always make that much noise?"
2. "Where have you been all my life?"
Learned Commentary
1. Rule of thumb: Moans that make you wish you'd removed your Miracle Ear are a good sign.
2. Often asked on a second honeymoon, when husband and wife rediscover why they married each other.

Outdoor Position for the Unpretentious
Man on top
Woman down to earth

Sexual Etiquette
When should you answer your lover's phone?
1. When your lover can't reach it.
2. When you're curious.
3. When it's for you.

Sexually Induced Longevity: Part II
Our exclusive guide continued.

Each time	To your life, add
You grow sexually aroused	7 minutes
Even if it's inappropriate (while taking your driving test)	19 minutes
Your lover gives you a back rub:	
After sex	4 minutes
During sex	20 minutes

How the Other Half Loves: Part II
Sex styles of:
The Rich and Famous
Stimulant: Champagne
Live string quartet provides inspiration during lovemaking
Caviar
Lovemaking under an umbrella at Cannes
A Personal Shopper buys the finest in sexy lingerie
After sex: count money
The Poor and Unknown
Stimulant: wine cooler
Musical partner hums a Bach chorale during climax
Rice pudding
Lovemaking in a tanning salon at the mall
Order from Victoria's Secret sale catalog
After sex: count blessings.

Inside A Lover's Fortune Cookie

You have a keen mind and a vivid imagination. Make sure you use them when
1. Your partner asks:
- "Do you think the Minoxidil is working?"
- "Is my diet working?"
- "Am I the best you've ever been with?"
- "Whose cuff link is this?"
2. Typing up your resumé.

No Bedroom Should Be Without

A digital scale: To determine whether sex is making your weight creep up. . .or creep down.

Pliers: To help a nerdy partner pull off those short, black business socks.

Software (a flight simulator): To perfect in-bed maneuvering skills after you've cleared your lover for take-off.

A leaf blower:* To quickly clear the bed of during-sex munchies such as cracker crumbs, bread crusts and popcorn salt.

*Lover's choice.

Signs of Love

The 10 recognized stages:
1. Nerves
2. Stagefright
3. Blushing
4. Another sip of champagne
5. Much less blushing
6. Eye contact
7. Thigh contact
8. Fireworks
9. Sleep
10. Guilt

A Guide to Restaurant Flirting: Part II

Activity	Purpose
Blowing on each other's soup	Intimacy
Flipping dinner rolls at the waiter	Privacy (repels compulsive waiters who fuss incessantly with the table)
Kissing	Digestive aid and non-caloric dessert
Staring into each other's eyes	To guess who will reach for the dinner check first

Thought for Tonight
You are only half responsible for your own orgasm.

The Enlightened Spouse
Appropriate times to ask:
Him for sex
If his team won
As he's walking in the door
Mother's Day
Her for sex
If her candidate won
As she's walking out the door
Father's Day

Just as It Was Getting Good: Part I
Frequently heard answers to "Why'd you stop?"

If your partner:	You'll hear:
Forgot to stop.	"We're out of whipped cream."
Isn't imaginative.	"I'm out of positions."
Is a couch potato.	"We're sliding off the sofa."
Is compulsive.	"Must throw another log on the fire."
Is conscientious.	"There's a customer waiting."

Unsuccessful Moment in Lovemaking

How do you let your partner know "tonight's the night?"

"I cut out paper footsteps and make a path leading from the front door to the bedroom where my wife, when she gets home from work, finds me lying seductively on the bed."

— Irv, househusband

"I get home from a rough day at work and wonder who made this mess all over the floor. I wish he'd just greet me at the door with a martini."

— Connie, Irv's wife

The Dieter's Guide to Weight Loss after Sex

Financial Bonus

Activity	Calories Burned
Rolling over:	
A lover	31
A Treasury bill	93

Advice for the Sexual Animal

To prolong lovemaking:
• Take frequent cat naps.
• Don't eat like a bird.
• Be playful as a kitten.
• Be a tiger in bed.

Lover's Ritual #8

To the lover who	Send
Makes you happy	Flowers
Makes your day	A bottle of wine
Makes your night	A bottle of Champagne
Makes you wish the night would never end	A case of Champagne
Sends you sexy thank-you notes	Your private fax number
Sends you	Your private PIN number

Sex Poll #9: How Do You Feel After Great Sex?

"A teensy bit repentant."

— Enoch, recovering preacher

"Unrepentant."

— Dodie, Enoch's gal Friday (and also on Saturday)

"Ever so pampered."

— Barbie, playmate

Six Things to be Happy About

After sex with a new lover:

1. No disappointment (it was better than you thought it would be).
2. No sweat (the air conditioner worked).
3. No anxiety (you remembered to get your house key back from your old lover).
4. No embarrassment (you began your diet months ago).
5. No worrying about seeing him again (he forgot his Rolex).
6. No worrying about seeing her again (she left her Filofax).

The Enlightened Lover

Six reasons to leave the lights off during sex.

1. You won't be distracted by glare if your lover's bald.
2. Fewer problems if your tattoo says "Burton" and your new lover's name is Hank.
3. No staring neighbors if you're newlyweds and can't yet afford curtains.
4. No embarrassment if you lied about your vital statistics.
5. He can't see those sexual fantasies that don't include him.
6. During the supreme moment, it's easier to watch her light up the room.

A Lover's List of Worsts

- Worst fad: *impotence*
- Worst position: *both on top*
- Worst place to have sex: *water slide*
- Worst time to have sex: *rush hour*
- Worst token of love: *preowned roses*
- Worst reason to have sex: *resolving conflicts*
- Worst way to show how much you care: *stifling a yawn*
- Second worst way to show how much you care: *nodding off*

When the Unthinkable Happens

The Problem

In the middle of lovemaking, your partner asks a strange question: "Who's that staring at us?"

Why It Happened

Carelessness. You left the door unlocked, allowing entrance of determined activist with petition to sign.

Are You Addicted to Sex?

Symptoms	Probably addicted	Just like it
You sometimes set the alarm early so you can make love before leaving for work	X	
You find that sex helps you relax.		X
Sex is affecting your reputation:		
For the better.		X
For the best.	X	
More than once, a sexual encounter has run into overtime.	X	
After sex, you want more immediately.		
The next hour.	X	
The next day.		X

The Morning After: Part II

Four faxes to send to a bashful lover.

If you send:	Lover's face will be:
"Don't worry, I still respect you."	Red.
"I'd tell you how I really feel, but this is a family fax machine."	Beet red.
"Don't ever do to me again what you did to me last night. . . unless you know what's good for you."	Scarlet.
"Wow, no more plaque!"	Crimson.

The Inquiring Lover
Why did you give your phone number to
Him:
"He said he was a talent scout."
"Gratitude—he kept bringing me cocktail franks."
"Everyone else was. I didn't want to feel left out."
"I'm moving."
Her:
"I was grateful. She said I had a lovely smile."
"I felt obligated—she bought me three margaritas."
"She had a great line—'Would you like to sleep with me?'"
"She wouldn't give me hers."

The Inquiring Lover
Q. After sex, who makes the bed?
A. The partner who's:
1. Done the least work.
2. Idea it was to have sex.
3. Got the steadiest hands.
4. Not in it.

The Well-Dressed Man
What to wear to turn your lover on.

Sexy	Not Sexy
Wellingtons	Sandals with socks
Baseball cap	Porkpie hat
Suspenders	White patent-leather belt
Motorcycle jacket	Car coat
Tank top	Dickie
Ascot	Gold chains (four or more)
Jeans	Waders (unpleated)
Uniform (armed forces)	Uniform (security guard)

Tip for the Environmentally Responsible
When recycling lovers, remember to keep all plastic partners from those who are down-to-earth.

Trade Secret
The best way to tickle your lover's fancy:
• Get a map
• Locate the correct erogenous zone
• Use a feather

The Versatile Lover
Eight sought after out-of-bed assets:
1. Willingly makes morning coffee while you're still dozing.
2. Can wake you without disturbing you.
3. Is a good influence on your children.
4. Makes housecalls when you're lonely, even if it's raining.
5. Has a car with a passenger-side air bag.
6. Looks divine in a bathing suit.
7. Gives superb decorating advice.
8. $5,000,000.

The Morning After a Perfect Night Before
Know the five dreaded symptoms of too much pleasure:
1. Guilt (but not enough to prevent you from making another assignation for tonight).
2. Waking up and smelling the coffee (very bad if this occurs at work).
3. Displaying a naughty grin at the slightest provocation (like when a co-worker asks what you did last night).
4. A more cheerful outlook even if (a) you still have 47 car payments left and (b) your checking account is overdrawn.
5. Seriously considering the purchase of:
• New decorator sheets.
• A larger bed.

Thought For Tonight
Setting the alarm early will give Dad ample time, tomorrow morning, to:
1. Send the kids out to play.
2. Cook her favorite breakfast.
3. Serve it to her in bed (even if she protests).
4. Help her digest the meal by making love until the wee hours of the morning (11:45 A.M.).

The Well-Dressed Woman
What to wear to turn your lover on.

Sexy	Not Sexy
High heels	Flip-flops
Tight sweater	Cardigan
Tight leather pants	Sweatpants
Bunny slippers	Slipper socks
Driving gloves	Mittens
Leg warmers	Knee-highs
T-shirt	Smock
Sunglasses	Ski mask

Should You Leave the Lights On? Part II

If you:	Turn the lights off	Leave them on
Are modest	X	
But want to change		X
Have a tattoo of:		
A previous lover's name	X	
A recipe for great Beef Stroganoff		X
Have to read:		
The clock		X
Your lover's lips		X

A Lover's Bedroom: Part I
The basics.

Item	Function
Smelling salts	Revive a partner overcome by sex so you can make the bed.
Lemon juice	Remove mildew from a lover who's been in the same position too long.
Dustbuster	Vacuum sheet made crunchy by crumbs.
Bottled water	Avoid dehydration.
Aspirin (placebo)	Cure faked headache.

Things Often Said After Sex
If lover is
Absent-minded: "When do we start?"
Demanding: "Why did you stop?"
Compulsive: "I thought I told you not to muss my hair!"
Disoriented: "Help me. I can't remember my PIN number."
On an air shuttle: "I think we missed our stop."
Completely and totally satisfied: "Mmmm."
Perceptive: "Who paid for your acting lessons?"

Loving Couples Advisory
The right way to start the weekend:
7 A.M.: Shut off the alarm.
7:20: Shut off the other alarm.
7:40: Makelove.
8:25: Call in sick (you call for him, he calls for you; this is known as "teamwork").
10:00 Enjoy an intimate candlelight breakfast.
11:00 To aid digestion, go back to bed and nap.
Noon: Enjoy a nooner.
1 P.M.: Plan your weekend.

Lovemaking—The Technical Aspects: Part I
Change positions when:
• The sun is directly in your face (outdoor sex only).
• Either partner's head is touching the floor.
• Either partner's head is bouncing off the headboard.
• You're being strangled by the blanket.
• One more thrust and you slide into the next county.

What I Did for Love
"Stopped hating myself in the morning and, instead, waited until late in the afternoon."
– Sid Rooney, junior copywriter

Emergency Sex: Part I
Is called for:
• To turn a bad day into a good night.
• When regular sex isn't fast enough.

- On an elevator.
- To relieve pre-job interview stress.
- To calm first-night jitters.
- When there's no time for a regular honeymoon.
- When lover has insomnia.

East Coast vs. West Coast Sex
During the perfect orgasm:
The Atlantic Motion
Earth moves
The Pacific Motion
Earth quakes

In Case You Can't Decide: Part II
Lovers on the:

A List	B List
Bring you flowers	That are pre-owned
Always make you feel like a million	Then ask to borrow it till payday
Know precisely how and where to touch you	Are not great when it comes to contact sports
May linger after sex	Malinger during sex
Make the nights longer	Just make them seem longer

Overhead After Sex
Proof positive that lovemaking clears the arteries.
Him: "I feel ten years younger."
Her: "And look, the sheet's covered with plaque!"

The First Time
Four criteria for judging a potential lover.
1. *Passion potential:* When dancing together, does he make the wool on your business suit stand up?
2. *On the first date:* If she picks you up, does she open the car door for you?
3. *In the restaurant:* Does she eat everything on her plate? If not, she'll probably leave a ring in your bathtub.
4. *Leaving the theater:* Does he hold the door open for you? If so, he'll get into bed first and warm it up.

Pillow Talk

Motion sickness. A disorder caused by up-and-down, "bouncy-bouncy" movements performed on a bed with inferior suspension. People who prolong sexual activity beyond what is reasonable (beginning, say, at 9 P.M. and ending in June) are particularly susceptible and should seek medical attention if they begin to turn indigo or experience:
• The bends
• Bedsores
• Shinsplint

Reminders

For the under-endowed lover: Less is more.
For the insecure lover: More is less.
For the lusty lover: More is more.
For the procrastination lover: Do it now.

Performance Anxiety

The leading causes among extra-sensitive lovers:
• Fear of being too good in bed
• Conscientious objector
• Cabin pressure too high (business-class only)
• Tainted potato salad (summer picnics particularly)
• Oil painting of partner's last eight lovers on nightstand
• Might make the soufflé fall
• Partner enters bedroom doing the goosestep

If You're Considering Abstention

Be warned. The person who doesn't get enough sex may:
• Watch (and order from) a local televised home shopping network. (Beware of anybody wearing a one-size-fits-all paisley pullover.)
• Become an activist.
• Go into politics.
• Lose their sexual desire.
• Gain weight.
• Turn back into a frog.

Today, Ask Yourself
Is your partner:
- **Sponge trained:** After dinner did he wipe the dinner table and do the dishes while you prepared for lovemaking?
- **Paper trained:** Will he go out and fetch the Sunday paper while you're still dozing?
- **Spatula trained:** Is he making your favorite raspberry pancakes while you loll in bed?
- **Electric trained:** Did he give you several high-voltage, or at least high-tension, climaxes?
- **Toilet trained:** Did he finally remember to put the seat back down?

Tip for the Law-Abiding Lover
Sex becomes illegal when:
- You finally see what all the fuss is about.
- Your writhing violates your chiropractor's orders.
- You violate the laws of nature (you're doing it in a position that defies gravity).
- Sounds you didn't know you could make emerge from your throat.
- You're neglecting your a) friends and b) studies.
- It feels too good to be true.
- But it is.

The Art of Romance
Gentle taps on your lover's forehead can convey a world of meaning. Paste this page on your headboard for easy reference.

Number of Taps	What They Mean
1	Please, don't fall asleep yet
2	You were great
3	Either: Need, fudge, or the kids are home from school
4	More of everything
5	That was so nice
6	You're on my leg
7 (very rapid)	Can I use the bathroom first?

The Art of Communication

When lovemaking leaves you speechless, use gentle taps on the top of your lover's head to communicate.

Number of Taps	What They Mean
10	Satisfaction guaranteed.
3	Faster.
1 big one	Don't stop now.
7	Hurry, or we'll be late for work.
4	Stop, I'm seeing double.
2	Who knew?
6	Who's counting?

From Our Book of Sexual Records

Most tears of joy ever shed: Sybil T., of Yonkers, New York, wept a total of 4.7 fluid ounces of tears of ecstasy during one 34-minute climax. Her lover showed his devotion by lying in the wet spots.

New Hope for the Oversexed

Researchers suggest that after $2^1/_2$ to 3 hours of glorious sex (or 4 to $5^1/_2$ hours of pretty good sex) you are essentially immune to feelings of lust for up to 45 minutes.*
*Nymphomaniacal cheerleaders excepted.

Sexual Etiquette

After sex, a woman need never apologize for making too much noise (high-pitched squeals, repeating the phrase, "Oh yeah, oh, yeah," eighteen or more times, etc.) unless a) her partner is visibly shaken or b) sex occurred in:

• A bird sanctuary.
• His dorm.
• Her hospital room.
• The library.
• The airplane lavatory.
• The dining room (of a church supper).

Q. Does rolling over and nudging your spouse at 2:32 A.M. and expressing, either by word or deed, a desire to "fool around" count as both a day *and* a night of sex?

A. Yes, if:

1. Sex lasts until dawn or breakfast, whichever happens first.

2. At least one partner remains alert throughout.

Sex's Worst-Kept Secrets

What millions of satisfied users say.

1. Between two strangers, it's a great way to melt the ice.

2. It's not addictive, but it can be habit-forming.

3. It's the weight-loss activity preferred by 89% of all registered dietitians.

4. Of those polled in retirement communities:

• 85% preferred it over bingo

• 61% preferred it

5. When used in a conscientiously applied program of oral hygiene and regular professional care, it can reduce plaque buildup.

Sexual Rule of Thumb

The lover who says, "I'd really like to go to bed with you," just moments after orgasm almost certainly possesses either a low IQ or a faulty memory.

National Chastity Awareness Day

No sex for the next 24 hours if:

• You need the rest.

• You have the willpower.

• You took a vow of silence.

• You need time to recover from bad news (the IRS disallowed your home office).

• You're on a mission.

• You need all your strength (it's exam week).

• You just got back from your honeymoon.

The Ethics of Sex

Our morals adviser suggests that a partner who insists his or her intentions are honorable should be:

1. Given the benefit of the doubt.

2. Invited in for a nightcap.

3. Placed upon a queen-size (or larger) bed.

4. The recipient of your undivided attention.

5. Given all night to prove it.

From Our Lover's Glossary

"**Lover's high.**" A sexually-induced euphoria, usually experienced in the second to third hour of lovemaking, during which time both partners, instead of succumbing to exhaustion, get a "second wind," start all over again and forget:

1. The dog has to be let in.
2. There's popcorn in the microwave.
3. Which son has to be picked up from little League.
4. Where the field is.
5. Their vows of abstinence.

The Working Lover's Lunch Hour

A Great 60 Minutes

Drive to motel	10 minutes
Get undressed	12 seconds
Arousal	48 seconds
Foreplay	1 minute
Intercourse	30 minutes
Orgasm	5 minutes
Cuddle	2 minutes
Roll over and nap	3 minutes
Roll over and drive back to work	8 minutes

Not So Great 60 Minutes

Bank line	11 minutes
Refund line	15 minutes
Sandwich line	25 minutes
Elevator line	4 minutes
Think about sex	5 minutes

Great Moments in Afterplay

"Figuring out what we did wrong."
    – Ellen, systems analyst
"Figuring out what we did right."
    – John, Ellen's husband
"Then trying again."
    – John and Ellen

Seven Steps to Recovery from Sublime Lovemaking

The ideal cool-down:

1. 10 push-ups
2. Stretch
3. Lots of bran
4. Check your messages
5. Check your partner's pulse
6. Adjust boutonniere
7. Try again

Intimacy Tip

"We realize that according to the President's Energy Council, there are over 1,583 approved sexual positions but, for us, the nice thing about making love in the standard missionary position is that we're both at see level."

> — Alice and Roland, cellmates

Post-Sexual Relaxation Techniques

Some favorites:

"While taking a long, hot bath, we gently caress each other with a special medicated loofah. It opens the pores."

> — Eloise, soup therapist

"You can take the girl out of the seminary, but you can't take the seminary out of the woman. Even though we've been married fifteen years and have five children, I have to whisper in her ear, 'Wilma, I'll still respect you in the morning.' Then she sleeps like a baby."

> — Stuart, tea trader

Time-Management Advisory: Part I

How soon after	Should you have sex
Starting your honeymoon:	
In a luxurious resort	2 hours
In a motel with hourly rates	1 minute
A triple	
Martini	2 hours
Bypass	2 weeks
Talking him into coming up to your place	2 minutes (before the nightcap wears off)
Your attractive neighbor's husband leaves her	10 minutes (move quickly she'll be in demand)

Advice for Ardent Lovers

Five warning signs of sexual enfeeblement:
1. Running stop signs
2. Cheating at pinochle (rare)
3. Thumb sucking (yours)
4. Thumb sucking (your lover's)
5. Overtipping

The Enlightened Lover

What to do if your lover can't get enough of you.
Good: Send a friend who looks like you.
Very good: Call more often.
Better: Send photos.
Best: Increase your contact visits.
Ultimate: Gain weight.

The Inquisitive Lover

Q. Because I'm such a tigress, my husband, a well-known baseball player, refuses to have sex for at least one week before a big game. He says he needs all of his strength to autograph balls for adoring fans. I'm suspicious—his signature isn't that complicated.
— Distrustful

A. Hmmmm. Writing with a ballpoint pen doesn't require that much effort—it kind of glides over the ball. If he's stylish and uses a fountain pen, however, he should be given the benefit of the doubt.

Myth or Fact?: Part I

Conventional Wisdom Suggests	Myth	Fact
First night jitters can often be caused by a look at your lover's passport photo.		X
It almost always takes longer to travel from your lover's chin to your lover's ankles if you take the scenic route.		X
Any climax that makes you forget your outstanding credit card balance is a good one.		X
It's impossible to reach one's sexual peak while making love at sea level.	X	

Signs of a Considerate Partner

Before sex. Allows you to prepare for lovemaking at your own pace. Doesn't slip notes under the bathroom door asking, "Are you ever coming out of there?"

During sex. Calms first-night jitters by offering you either:
• A Valium.
• A rain check.

After sex. Makes you feel wanted by asking, "Did you bring a toothbrush?"

Reminder for a Meek Lover

A leading sex therapist cautions that the formerly passive woman who finally decides to take the sexual initiative should warn her partner first, lest he faint from the shock.*

*FDA-approved warning devices include a) bathing the eyelids and b) rubbing the inside of his wrist and hauling him by his tie into the bathroom.

"It's easier to laugh with your clothes off."
                    —California proverb

For Speedier Sexual Service: Part I
Standard during-sex abbreviations.

Use:	When you mean:
"M.T.T.L."	More to the left.
"P.D.S."	Please don't stop.
"J.A.L.M.	Just a little more.
"F!"	Faster!
"J.T.T.B.S."	Just the teensiest bit slower.
"T.R."	Turn right.
"N.S.W."	Need some water.
"T.G.T.V."	There goes that vase.
"F.C.I."	Fax coming in.

The Enlightened Lover
Six legitimate reasons to make love tonight.
- **Good:** your guests canceled.
- **Better:** to burn off today's lunch.
- **Best:** you need the practice.
- **Great:** you need the sleep.
- **Terrific:** doctor's orders.
- **Sensational:** nurse's orders.

A Guide for Lapsed Lovers
Some official recovery times:

If you go without sex for	To make a full comeback will take
2 to 3 years	1 hours, 46 minutes
12 to 15 months	1 hours, 10 minutes
9 to 11 months	51 minutes
4 to 7 months	30 minutes
1 to 3 months	15 minutes
2 to 3 weeks	4 minutes
1 week	16.8 seconds

The Deserving Lover: Part II

A tipping guide for that extra-special partner.

To the Lover Who	Suggested Gratuity
After sex: Spoon-feeds you ice cream	75¢
And makes you melt	$1.25
Feeds your cat when you're away	$1.00
Doesn't pout when you can't have sex because:	
You're working late	$1.50
You have a headache	75¢
Your husband's in town	$7.50

Warning Signs of Insufficient Sex

• Ennui
• Being seen leaving cheap motel rooms—alone
• Constantly baring your soul, but with your clothes on
• You're back to taking aspirin for pain
• And pills to fall asleep

Before-Sex Etiquette

In addition to removing makeup and *both* socks, responsibilities include:

He	She
Turns on the stereo	Selects the music
Sets the alarm	Sets the timer
Turns down the bed	Turns off the phone
Opens the sex manual	Gets the reading glasses
Waters the plants	Places little mints on the pillow
Warms the bed	Gets into it
Gets on his knees	Prays
Keeps doing it	Keeps count

Pillow Talk

Ear nibbles: A handy way to a) gently awaken a dozing lover or b) express great fondness for one's lover should one's hands be otherwise occupied. Ear nibbles, especially if one has perfect teeth, are distracting and should never be administered while lover is:

• Landing an aircraft
• Removing contacts
• Donating an organ

- Making a career decision
- Shaving

Sensitivity Training 101

It is not considered insensitive to make love to someone while they talk on the phone as long as (1) they clearly motion for you to continue when they pick up the receiver and (2) the person to whom they are speaking is not:
- Their spouse
- Your spouse
- A recording

Hot Numbers

27 minutes, 45 seconds: The minimum time it takes for a really popular woman to go from the last time with an old lover to the first time with a new lover. (Add 7 minutes if her cab gets stuck in traffic.)

3.5 mph: The average rate of intercourse for American couples.

27 mph: The average rate of intercourse for American couples who have theater tickets.

7: The number of days it takes for the swelling to go down if, while trying something new during sex, your partner hits your nose with the zoom lens.

Quote of the Night

Least romantic thing ever said after two hours of glorious sex: "Mission accomplished!"

Lover's Poll #45

Percentage of happy couples who experienced love at first:
- Sight   10%
- Kiss   17%
- Sexual experience:
  - Petting   5%
  - Going all the way   50%
  - Horseback riding   17%
- Taste of
  - Her Spanish rice with sausage   15%
  - Her minestrone   13%
  - His rhubarb-beet compote   1/2%

265

Love Signs
Horoscope For A Juicy Gemini
- *Ruling passion:* making love on unusual surfaces (Astroturf)
- *Ruling body lotion:* maple syrup, direct from the tree
- *Chief sexual asset:* your cheeks
- *Governing erogenous zone:* birthmark shaped like Paris
- *Aphrodisiac of choice:* melon in season
- *Ruling sexual activity:* ordering in
- *Ideal time for sex:* lunch hour

Lovemaking: The Extra Touches
- Electronic translator—for the international business traveler (instantly translates "Don't stop" into French, Italian, Spanish and Yiddish.)
- Shredder—to destroy incriminating love notes
- Pedometer—for long-distance sex (tells how far you've gone)
- Sunglasses—for surviving floral print underwear
- Folding guest bed—for you to sleep on when your lover has a) a headache or b) a guest

Love Signs
Horoscope for a Generous Gemini.
Ruling passion: superior customer service
Ruling sexual turnoff: felons
Chief sexual asset: a muffler-repair franchise
Governing erogenous zone: any politically stable isle
Aphrodisiac: the latest gossip
Ruling sexual activity: riding out turbulence
Ideal time for sex: whenever your Filofax says you're free

Guidelines For Marathoners
What to expect during five hours of sex.
First Hour: Feels wonderful, pleasantly surprised you both have this much stamina. (Love those vitamin pills.)
Second Hour: Pleasure more intense, beginning to recall why you were attracted to each other.
Third Hour: Still capable of pleasure, but memory failing.
Fourth Hour: You're hoarse from saying, "I can't take any more." Emergency throat lozenge makes you feel better.
Fifth Hour: At least one more hour.

Love Signs: Regular Gemini

(May 21-June 21)

Opposite love sign: A succulent Sagittarius.

Outstanding sexual quality: Can moan ever so persuasively because your erogenous zones and vocal cords are well connected.

Most attractive physical feature: Love handles which, when not being grasped by a passionate partner, retract.

Ruling sexual turnoff: Partners who have sex only to relieve stress (unless, of course, it's yours).

Ruling sexual turn-on: Lovers who ask, "How do you stay so thin?"

Ideal place for sex: The floor of a pine-scented forest.

Love Signs: Irregular Gemini

(May 21-June 21)

Most attractive feature: A melodious giggle that kicks into high during the good parts of sex.

Turn-ons: Truth, beauty, literature and the gift of love, preferably in 24K gold.

Turnoff: A compulsive lover who, immediately after sex, makes the bed while you're still in it.

Ideal romantic adventure: Bribing the guard and making love on top of Stonehenge at twilight.

Favorite sexual fantasy: Being invited, for the opening of the 1996 baseball season, to throw out the first fan.

Passion Scale

Level V

The most fun you can have without reserving a court; also considered by the Morals Division of the IRS to be "a sudden and unexpected act of great destructive force" and therefore tax-deductible. There may also be a temporary inability to metabolize chicken salad.

How Manifested

Delirium. Calling out to your houseplants using their Latin names (inexplicably, as you've never studied the language) and a need for chocolate ice cream (a class A calmative). Climaxee may also experience a sudden change of political attitude.

The Enlightened Lover
Is your partner really enjoying it? The indicators:

Reliable	Very Reliable
"Mmmmmmmmmm"	"Ahhhhhhhhhhhh"
Blanket rumpled	Blanket on floor
Laughter	Applause
Perspiring	Salivating
Partner waving "Hi"	Partner waving white flag
Partner saying your name	Partner shouting your name
Partner begging for mercy	Partner begging for a knish
Eye contact with you	Eye contact with ceiling mirror

National Space Center Sex Poll*
• 16% of all lovers report the sighting of UFOs during a grade-4 climax (ignition).
• 9% of all lovers reports seeing UFOs land during a grade-6 climax (blast-off).
• 2% of all lovers report seeing little green couples disembark from a UFO during a grade-10 climax (in orbit).
Note: In nearly all cases, UFO turned out to be their partner.

Quote of the Night
"The best thing about my lover? He's so reliable. During sex, he never lets me down, especially when I'm on top."
— Mimi, train conductor

Seniors in Love: Part II
Statement from a rather naive senior lover:
"My boyfriend has such good genes (his parents thrived on Big Macs, Hormel chili and bourbon and still lived to be 97) that I asked him to be the grandfather of my children."
—Monica, retired administrator

Magic Numbers: Part II
185 pounds: The weight limit for brides who insist on being carried over the threshold.
5: The number of times a woman must make a sexual advance to a dimwitted male before he gets the hint.

7,491: The minimum number of chest hairs a man should have if she expects him to keep her warm.

55: The number of knocks before you and your partner are required to open the bathroom door at a party.

2: The number of hands to use if you want to speed things up.

Terms of Endearment
Use
1. "Sweetie"
2. "Dear"
"3. Dearest"
If You
1. Are not quite sure how you feel about your lover and need a general, all-purpose endearment
2. Want your lover to do you a favor (such as close the drapes, bring you a glass of water, feed the cat)
3. Need a big favor (such as more sex or walking the dog)

The Art of Romance
"It is at the point when sex really begins to get interesting (usually between arousal and her braid coming undone) that the female partner, to prevent her lover from becoming black and blue, may wish to sacrifice aesthetics and consider removing heavy objects, such as her necklace, earrings and wrist weights."

     – Ellen, experienced

The Art of Romance
Those who feel guilty about staying in bed on Sunday morning, sipping Orange Blossoms, eating French toast, making love, giving and getting a massage, ignoring the phone, cuddling and occasionally dozing off may alleviate their discomfort by watching a televised sermon.

Good News for the Guilt-Ridden
Our new, relaxed rules suggest you should hate yourself in the morning only if you did it:
• For discount bowling lessons.
• Because she looked great in a uniform.
• For old time's sake (you've been married 35 or more years).

- For free orthodontic work.
- Out of pity (he spent all that money on the honeymoon).
- Because you're on an athletic scholarship.
- For the aerobic benefits only.
- Just to see what all the fuss is about.

The Enlightened Lover
Assumption
1. The more sex you have, the more you want.
2. The more sex you want, the more sex you have.
3. Sex saps energy.
4. A man doesn't need to climax each time he has sex.
5. A great sex life makes you vice-proof.
Fact
1. With the right partner, sex is addictive. With the wrong partner, even more addictive.
2. If you're lucky.
3. It makes you weak in the knees.
4. It's the thought that counts.
5. It's helped millions quit smoking and renounce abstention.

Seeking Greener Pastures
It may be time to consider a new relationship if your current lover:
- Calls you only when he needs something (such as decorating advice or sex).
- Has, at age 47, been "between careers" for the past five years.
- Is about to be "born again." (Once is enough.)
- When you ask, "Do you want to fool around?" suggests "charades."
- Despite promising to, still hasn't gotten a divorce.

The Dieter's Guide to Weight Loss During Sex
Telling lover what turns you on:

If you:	Calories Burned
Are you in touch with inner self	4
Just outer self	25
Are shy	19
Don't know	66
Know but don't dare utter the words aloud	131
Just point	10

The Ideal Lover
- Is multifaceted (does both you and floors).
- Is dishwasher safe.
- Has children, but only on alternate weekends.
- Wakes up first and brews a perfect cup of coffee.
- Doesn't fog up during steamy sex.
- Is fun to sleep *and* nap with.
- Is flexible (can make love on a circular staircase).
- Has an identical twin (for emergencies).

The Traveling Lover's Care Package
- *Vitamins*—making love in a different bed may cause stress
- *An extra toothbrush*—for your guide
- *Book of Shakespeare*
- *Chocolate*—for emergency energy
- *Baby oil*—in case olive oil's unavailable
- *Cellular phone*—should you need roadside assistance
- *Travel alarm*—for morning sex, in case of early checkout time
- *Passport*—should your lover ask for ID

Great Moments in Lovemaking
May 9, 1992, 10:34 A.M: The discovery on a gorgeous Saturday morning by two avid gardeners that despite the joys of crop rotation, the bedroom was a far better place to make the earth move.

Hot Numbers
24: The number of minutes it takes to coax the average male lover out of a fetal position when told by his partner what really turns her on (add 7 minutes if she's flicking a riding crop).
$25.00: The amount of hush money to give your doorman so he doesn't say anything about the person who left your apartment at 6 A.M. when your spouse was out of town.
5: If you're playing hard-to-get with a new lover, the number of times to let your phone ring before answering it.

True or False?
1. Sex drains your energy.
2. The more sex you have, the more sex you want.
3. Sex can help you lose weight.

4. There are three different kinds of orgasm.
5. Sex can help induce sleep.
Answers: (over)

Pizza and Sex: Part V
Ultimate sex requires ultimate sustenance.
Type of Lovemaking
Labor-intensive
Ideal Topping
Everything (no extra cheese for those with a lactose intolerance).

The Beneficial Energies of Sex: Part I

Activity	Benefit
Undressing each other	Improved manual dexterity
Seeing each other unclothed	Enthusiasm
Smiling	Higher cheekbones
Bubble bath with lover	Secretion of hormone that causes younger, firmer skin
Climbing into bed	More defined calf muscles
Writhing with passion	Flexibility
Caressing lover all over	Spot shaping

Sad Moments in Sexual Fitness
"Had to give her up. Turned out my heart's desire was much too high in cholesterol."
> – Jerome, ghost writer

Why I Hate Sex
"I can look forward to nothing else. It distracts me from my work."
> – Sylvia, grief counselor

"It cuts rather heavily into my TV watching time. Who needs it?"
> – Henry, husband

"It always leads to other things."
> – Randy, parson

The Potential Lover

Our exclusive guide when to accept a blind date.

Friend's Description	Should You Go?
"He has his own business."	Yes. But make sure it's legit.
"He's nice, and still lives with his mother. He's a devoted son."	No (too much competition).
"She just broke off with a Leo."	No, she's still on the rebound.
"She's very perky, lots of fun, a real high-energy person."	Yes, but she'll need a sedative.
"A great personality."	Get a photo first.

Three Points Of View

"All the good ones are, alas, married."
> – Cheryl, single, biological clock chugging away

"The good one is married, thank goodness."
> – Kate, happy housewife

"All the good ones are married, but that never stopped me."
> – Lorraine, happy optimist

Love Poll #5

According to our survey of 500 sex partners in New England:
• Only 1% believe that oral sex is the work of the devil.
• 96% believe that oral sex is the work of the partner.
• The other 3% insisted that oral sex involves parts of speech.

The Dieter's Guide to Weight Loss During Sex

Activity	Calories Burned
Any frenzied orgasm. Typical results:	
Destruction of private property	350
Itemized:	
Splintering the headboard	40
Shattering the wine goblets	25
Capsizing the bed	80
Upsetting the nightstand	35
Removing candlewax from carpet	20
General loss of composure	90
Swallowing chewing gum	10
While blowing a bubble	50

Advice for the Recovering Celibate
1. Be patient—it may take time to remember how.
2. Don't do too much at once.
3. Try to take it one night at a time.
4. Admit you are powerless over passion.
5. Consult a physician if you intend to recover vigorously.
6. Take responsibility for lustful thoughts (they're fun).
7. Avoid temptation—resist that first night alone.
8. Don't skip meetings.

Advice for the Recovering Celibate
Has it been a long time? Five things to remember during lovemaking:
1. Not too much at once. Initially, keep sex to under 4 hours lest you do permanent damage to your elbows.
2. If sex gets so good that your partner asks "Where have you been all my life?" hold up your passport.
3. It is impolite to stop unless (a) you're getting exhausted or (b) your Amway rep shows up.
4. Not to mumble when you moan—you'll diminish the sensual effect.
5. Don't try anything too advanced. Whispering sweet nothings into both ears at once takes years of practice.

How Did You Meet? Part I
"Purely by chance. He was standing on the corner, distributing 'Seeking Ms. Right' handbills. I took one only because I needed something to wipe my nose with (hay fever)."
              – Claudia, waitress
"A TV infomercial—she was demonstrating juicers and wearing a bathing suit. She kept smiling right at me, how could I resist?"
              – Dork, clairvoyant
"A chain letter. I broke the chain—she came to arrest me."
              – Ludwig, bus driver

Romance Tip #55
Lover giving you a hard time? When bathing together, get even by:
• Instead of a loofah, use steel wool (a proven tattoo-removal technique).

- Hiding his rubber duck.
- Making him bob for the soap.
- Using the wrong end of the bath brush when scrubbing his back.

The Novice Lover

Not knowing where to begin and when to stop is a common problem. Suggestions:

1. Put on negligee or remove it, whichever is appropriate.
2. Control jitters by discussing your day at work.
3. Omit foreplay if sleepy or pressed for time.
4. Lower volume on hockey game.
5. Commence intercourse (no need to make a grand entrance).
6. Experience orgasm, or polish off the Chinese food.
7. Turn up volume on hockey game.

When Is Lovemaking Over? Part I

Unofficially	Officially
Both partners out of new ideas.	Both partners out of new positions.
Alarm goes off.	Partner goes off.
Both partners just lying there, staring.	Both partners just lying there, snoring.
Either partner lights a cigarette.	Either partner puts one out.
Appearance of rust.	Appearance of mildew.

(Etiquette tip: Let your partner make the final decision. . .unless you're alone.)

From Our Lover's Glossary

Ultra spot. 1. The "Gee!" spot. 2. That area on an aroused lover which, when stroked, kissed, gently blown upon or, in rare instances, stared at, activates that portion of the brain (the cerebellum) which causes gooseflesh, thus rendering such person temporarily incapable of (a) naming the capital of Norway or (b) worrying about the US economy.

Inside a Lover's Fortune Cookie: Part II

"Stop searching forever. Depending on your position, happiness is either just (a) next to you or (b) above you."

"Better a little sex with a great partner than a lot of sex with a mediocre partner. But both are good for the circulation."

"Sex comes first. You can always do the sales reports later."

"You should not return to the past to revive an old relationship—unless you're having trouble getting a date."

Health Tip for Lovers

After sex, a mere 20 minutes of rubbing against a partner with an extra-yummy body can replace nearly all the vital nutrients lost while trying to:

• Remove your partner's cowboys boots.
• Glance at the time.
• Achieve climax.
• Balance your checkbook without a calculator.
• Improvise.

Substitutions Permitted

It is ethical to use the services of a guest lover* when your present lover:

• Plays you like an instrument (the tuba) during sex.
• Is getting increasingly difficult to reach on the phone.
• Cannot account for certain suspicious absences.
• Seldom wants to do it, even with you.
• Is having an affair. (Suddenly showering you with gifts means he or she is trying to ease his or her conscience so a) take the gifts and b) dump the lover).
• Took two Sudafeds.

*Such as a selfless neighbor, a caring co-worker or an understanding ex.

The Traveling Lover

When making love in the car, always come to a complete stop:

• To pay the toll.
• At crosswalks.
• At any McDonald's or Burger King drive-up window.
• If the windows fog up.

Tip Regarding Marathon Lovemaking

It is the fourth to fifth hour of sex that you may begin to see spots before your eyes. Not to worry. . .it may only be your partner disintegrating.

The Gourmand Lover
An etiquette guide for the bedside eater.

If you have:	It's acceptable, after sex, to:
Spare ribs	
Plain	Lick your fingers
Lots of sauce	Also lick lover's fingers
Texas style	Shower
Chinese food	
Fried dumplings	Use a napkin
Spring roll	Use a fingerbowl

Optimistic Fact About Sex In America

Percentage of 10,000 lovers throughout the United States who believe the American Dream is:

Wet	82%
Dry	7%
Just a little moist	11%

Communication Tip

During sex phrase often uttered by one lover into the other's ear when

• The bay starts to cry
• One partner (usually the male) experiences impotence
• One partner (usually the female) won't accept his explanation ("Sorry, dear, too many soft drinks.")
• There's a knock on the door (activist with a petition)
• The snooze alarm goes off
• His knee goes out
• Her chignon comes undone
• Their fans show up

"Dear, we are experiencing technical difficulties."

Sex Without Love

When it's permissible.

If You Do It:	Yes	No
For a promotion at work	X	
In the army		X
To celebrate your divorce	X	
With your ex	X	
As a last fling before marriage		X
If it's not with your fiancée	X	
For medical reasons:		
Doctor's orders		X
Nurse's orders	X	

The Language of Flowers: Part I

To the lover who:	Send:
Located all three of your G-spots.	Jack-in-the-pulpits.
Prefers you to golf.	Violets.
Pointed out the aerobic benefits of painting audibly.	Daisies.

The Language of Botany: Part I

To a lover who:	Send:
Discovered a G-spot you had long given up for:	
Inactive	A nice houseplant
Broken	Tulips
Lost	Roses
Helped you break into:	
Show business	Gardenias
Commercials	Orchids

The Six Biggest During-Sex Lies

1. "I'm not thinking about anyone else."
2. "I learned that position from a book."
3. "I was only resting my eyes."
4. "I never knew it could be this good."
5. "Love handles are such a turn-on."
6. "That scarf looks better on you."

The Enlightened Lover
Did you know that during sex, when they're repeatedly dug into a muscular partner's back, your fingernails can get up to 50% stronger?

Professional Lovers Tell All
First things done after sex:
• Make the bed.
• Check the clock—to see where the time went.
• Check the scale—to see where the weight went.
• Help her find her sock.
• Help him find his car keys.
• Ask, "What's next?"

Banishing the Blahs
Present your love life from growing stale by:
• Seizing the day.
• Spending more time on foreplay (at least one hour).
• Changing position at least three times (twice if you're being timed).
• Setting goals (doing it whether you want to or not).
• Increasing your shelf life.
• Seizing the night.

Communication Tip
If great lovemaking leaves you speechless, feel free to:
1. Use Morse code.
2. Use flash cards.
3. Leave a note.
4. Point.

Is Sex Becoming Routine?
The warning signs.
1. Lately, during lovemaking, you find yourself wondering whether you left the oven on.
2. Instead of a caress, your latest expression of sexual endearment is a sultry . . . shrug.
3. You always make love at the same time (the first day after Lent).

4. Your new energy-conservation program occurs mostly during sex.
5. And your lover hasn't noticed.
6. When making love, you no longer bother getting undressed.
7. And neither of you notices.

For Health-Conscious Lovers
The benefits of a doctor-recommended sex life.

Outer Beauty	Inner Beauty
Whiter teeth	Pinker gums
Diminishes bloat	Diminished anxiety
Flattens the tummy	Improves digestion
Promotes weight loss	Induces that "lighter" feeling
Restores flexibility	Fights aging
Clears the skin	Cleanses the soul

The Respectful Lover
During lovemaking, pause and observe a moment of silence:
1. In honor of a former fiancé who also made you feel this way (or nearly this way).
2. To honor the memory of the Unknown Lover (the one you met at a party, had a night of unbelievable sex with, said she'd call when she got back from her business trip but never did, and you forgot to get her last name).
3. To consider an appropriate answer when your lover asks,
• "Was it good for you?"
• "Will we be seeing each other again?"

Fond Memories
How to keep a lover near who's far away:
"We keep a sex-activated tape recorder under the bed. When he's away on a business trip, I play back the good parts."
           – Beth, accountant
"I keep a lock of her hair with me at all times. It covers my bald spot."
           – Gary, detective
"I keep a beaker of her bath water on my desk. My co-workers think I should get a photo instead."
           – John, legal assistant

"I go in the garage and lay my head on his bicycle seat."
— Sonya, cosmetician

After-Sex Activities

If Sex Was Good	If Sex Was Great
Ask for an engagement ring	Ask for a raise
Light his cigarette	Don't whine about second-hand smoke
Rate your partner's performance	Demand an encore
Whisper sweet nothings in your lover's ear	While your lover is still awake*
Cuddle and give your lover more hugs and kisses	Cuddle and give your lover more closet space

*For best results

Sex and the Basic Food Groups: Part IV

Mexican: Courage to be sexually adventurous (doing it with the television off and the lights on). Also regulates the rate of intercourse for couples who do it to a Latin beat.

Dish	Application
Tostada	Fosters decadence in prudes.
Burrito	Dispels jitters cause by personal design defects (cellulite, stretch marks, astigmatism); prevents the "bends" caused by ending sex too abruptly.
Enchilada	Provides protection against impotence cause by rap music.

What I Did For Sex

"Learned to play golf."
— Cynthia, mistress
"Learned to play tennis."
— Max, gigolo
"Learned to play."
— Morris, psychiatrist

The Respectful Lover

During sex, pause and observe a moment of silence when:

• You find it simply impossible to moan anymore.
• You achieve what you thought was unachievable (an eight orgasm without Maalox).
• You're unable to talk with your mouth full (you're busy giving love bites).
• You think you're starting to levitate.
• Your think you might hear your boyfriend.
• You can't recall your lover's name.

Especially Distracting Moment In Sex

"After our housewarming party, while on the patio enjoying some of the most incredibly wild sex ever, my husband called out from the bedroom, 'Are you ever coming to bed?'"
        – Margaret, roofer

The Full-Service Lover: Poll #32

In addition to great lovemaking, what else is important?
"He must also do windows, and not leave streaks."
        – Nicole, chef
"Communications. She must be knowledgeable about our new tax laws."
        – Roland, security guard
"I like a man who can make me laugh in bed (unless I'm fast asleep, then it's very annoying)."
        – Gretchen, craftsperson
"He must be able to get things for me wholesale."
        – Rita, retired

What I Changed For Love

"Political parties (from Republican to Democratic). The men are more fun. And so's the food.
        – Jessica, legislative assistant
"My underwear. From blah briefs to flamboyant boxers."
        – Ahmed, philosopher

MONTHLY QUALITY OF LIFE® CHECKUP

•Number of sexual encounters: 1___   3___   58___
None____   (NOTE: if "None" see below**)
•Duration of each sexual encounter: 1 hour___   18 minutes___
3.6 minutes___
Until the realtor showing the house caught us___
•Number of sexual encounters that were satisfactory: All___
Some___   Only those that occurred (sob) when I was alone___
•Orgasms per encounter: 1___   2___
Couldn't count, ran out of fingers___
•Did the earth move?   Yes___   No___
•Did trumpets sound?   Yes___   No___
•Did bedsprings squeak? Yes___   No___
•After each sexual encounter did you note an improvement in:
Complexion___?
Blood pressure___?
Flexibility___?
Ability to digest fried foods___?
Golf game___?
•Number of times you thought about sex on compsny time:
1___   3___   7___   Often, my boss kept making passes at me

**NOTE: Celibacy stinks: Yes___   No___

Signed_____

Witnessed_____

JUNE

•Erotic goals for June:

1. Improve bondage technique
2. Buy more dental floss (waxed)

For singles made anxious by a summer alone, the deadline looms—June is the last official month to find true love, one that will last either until you both tire of each other or until Labor Day, whichever comes first. Most of the good partners are taken by July, so time is precious. Wise shoppers spend the first two weeks of June looking for Mr. or Ms. Right. If unsuccessful, they spend the second two weeks looking for Mr. or Ms. Right Now. But how to find that special someone? Personals? Beware of false advertising (i.e. "Me: Wealthy bachelor. You: Attractive doormat. Object: Lust"). Fix-up by parents? Social suicide. Not to despair, however, love happens when you least expect it. The following are six true-life success stories:

Couple*	How They Met
Kiki and Cheech	Mosh pit at Republican fundraiser.
Al and Monica	As he departed the White House luncheon, a smitten Al inserted his business card in her chicken salad. She called that afternoon.
Kelly and Dom	Their hands touched when they both reached for the last copy of "Bambi" at Block Buster Video. They decided to watch it on her VCR.
Sol and Becky	Shared a cab to Brooklyn. Magic happened.
Deepak and Lulu	Beach. She rear-ended his dune buggy.
Demi and Leonardo	Both fleeing paparazzi.

*Names used are real. Our correspndents have nothing to hide.

Official aphrodisiac of the Month:
Gazpacho salad and Valium

What Every Bride Should Know
The five most frequent causes of wedding night fatigue:
1. Dancing with the guests
2. Changing into your travel clothes
3. Carrying each other over the threshold
4. Reviving the groom
5. Returning gifts

Tips for the June Bride
Obstacles to wonderful wedding-night lovemaking.

Not Serious	Serious
Best man came along.	You're thankful.
Gifts a disappointment—four coffeemakers.	Gifts a major disappointment—four coffeemakers (two of them your in-laws).
Groom slightly injured—fell off top of wedding cake.	Groom on floor—tried to carry you over threshold.
Groom inexperienced (but shows promise).	Groom inexperienced (but refuses to admit it).
Groom not yet warmed up.	You are.

The Enlightened Lover
When buying an air conditioner to stay cool during sex, consult the following purchasing guide.

Size of You and Lover	BTUs Needed
Average (combined weight: 300 lbs.)	7,000
Above average (combined weight: 540 lbs.)	14,000
Below average (combined weight: 76 lbs.)	50

Variables	Extra BTU's Needed
One lover sort of hairy	3,000
One lover very active during climax	1,500
But highly energy-efficient	600
Bed faces north	800

Gem of the Month
A string of cultured pearls to the lover who never:
• Steals your share of the blanket.
• Complains when you have a "headache" (as long as it's real) and cheerfully takes a cold shower instead.

- Forgets that your favorite aphrodisiac is halvah.
- Mixes business with pleasure (unless it's the only way to cope with office politics).
- If sex was wonderful, forgets to express deep appreciation either by:
- Applauding
- Staying for breakfast.

Sex For Nature Lovers

The ideal outdoor partner:
- Can do it in a narrow place (like on a hiking trail).
- Can locate your erogenous zones (even under a waterfall).
- Needs only one hand for lovemaking (if the other must be used to swat bugs).
- Won't leave you for something better (like a handsome hunter).
- Is an expert at spotting poison ivy (unless it's already under you).
- Can start a fire by rubbing two things together.

The Reluctant Bride

Proper ways to tactfully decline sex on your wedding night.
1. *If you're goal-oriented:* "We have to inventory the gifts."
2. *If you're conservative:* "Let's wait until we know each other better."
3. *If you enjoy being the center of attention:* "Relax, we're still on the receiving line."
4. *If you're punitive:* "There was a distinct lack of enthusiasm when you said, 'I do.'"
5. *If you're pre-occupied:* "Start without me, I'll catch up."
6. *If you're honest:* "I'm still saving myself."

More Honeymoon Facts

- Most popular sexual aids:
1. In the Poconos: A heart-shaped tub
2. In West Palm Beach: Metamucil
- Two most frequent causes of wedding night jitters:
1. Bargain revolving bed (must be rotated by bellhop)
2. Hotel error (chocolate square on pillow a laxative)
- Mistake most often made by inexperienced lover:
Failing to remove Walkman

Some Honeymoon Tips

Most frequent cause of wedding-night jitters:
- For groom—bride placing an egg timer on the nightstand
- For bride—groom placing a photo of his mother on the nightstand

Sexual errors most often made by inexperienced lovers:
- Not sleeping in the same bed
- Asking the bellhop for assistance
- Expecting the heart-shaped bed to pump

Great Moments In Sex

The discovery by a not-too-terribly-bright, over-anxious, kind-of-lonely male that phone sex was the ultimate form of birth control.

A Lover's Biggest Fear

Before sex: *"I'll forget my mantra."*
　　　　　– Zagreb, reflexologist
During sex: *"I'll run out of steam."*
　　　　　– Enrique, captain, tug boat
"I'll run out of popcorn."
　　　　　– Imelda, city planner
After sex: *"He'll pitch a story."*
　　　　　– Lois, producer
"My cab won't start."
　　　　　– Jason, driver
"His meter won't stop."
　　　　　– Emily, Jason's passenger

Those First-Night Jitters

How do you cope?*

"I release tension by furiously chewing bubble gum while she has her way with me."
　　　　　– Dino, sign painter

"Reese's Pieces, herbal tea and Viagra."
　　　　　– Laurie, greengrocer

"Do the same thing I do on a roller coaster—cover my eyes until it's over."
　　　　　– Les, graphologist

"Do it only in the daytime. Who ever heard of first-afternoon jitters?"

— Gilda, sandhog

*According to a random survey of shoppers conducted at the Paramus, New Jersey, mall.

Cautious Bride-To-Be Countdown
First things to do after getting engaged.
1. Break the news to:
Your parents.
Your other lover.
2. Tell your friends.
3. Run a Dun & Bradstreet on:
Him
His parents.
4. Stop checking the personal ads.
5. Read the pre-nup carefully.
6. Have the ring appraised.

The Dieter's Guide to Weight Loss During Sex

Activity	Calories Burned
Doing it for the first time:	
This week	55
This year	84
Ever	258

How Long Can a Lover Go Without Sex? Part II
The second three weeks:

Week 4. First damp dream. Awaken in sweat and discover you've made love to your pillow.

Week 5. Sociopathic behavior: blow horn the instant light changes; in stores, whine if not serviced immediately. Force cat to change its own litter. You need sex badly.

Week 6. Weaken and call old lover who you found boring—but built. Five-minute conversation reminds you why it ended. Make first call to an erotic "900" number. For $25, get six minutes of salesperson trying to sell you land in the Poconos. Astrology beckons.

What I Got for Sex
"A discount on my dental work."
— Rudolph, lineman
"A quarter-share in a really neat summer house."
— Jacqueline, executive assistant
"Nothing, absolutely nothing (sob)."
— Jason, appliance salesman

What Every Bride Should Know
Possible obstacles to an ideal wedding night:

Not serious	Serious
Groom has a headache.	It's a migraine.
Both had a bit too much to drink.	It was coffee.
Parents calling to see if you've arrived safely.	They're calling from the next room.
You're reclined on the nuptial bed in your sexiest outfit, afire with anticipation.	Groom still recovering from carrying you across the threshold.
He ran off (with bridesmaid).	He ran off (with best man).

Your Second Honeymoon
What to do that you didn't do on your fist.
1. Let the chauffeur carry your spouse over the threshold, you'll need your strength.
2. Spend more time making love.
• You probably have less stamina but a better technique.
• This is not the time to improve your golf game.
• Your spouse may be heavier—there'll be more to love.
3. Bring reading glasses (you may want to order room service).
4. Spend lots of time on foreplay (it's a digestive aid).
5. Tip the bellhop better (he's older).
6. Call the kids.

Beauty Breakthrough
Researchers confirm that four or more non-superficial orgasms a week:
• Significantly reduce split ends.
• Discourage signs of aging such as:

Hearing loss.
Telltale gray.
Purchasing "relaxed fit" jeans.
• Banish crow's feet.
• Increase one's interest in sex.

The Leg Cramp

A transient sex-related affliction that may be temporarily incapacitating.

Cause	Cure
Constricting garment	Loosen offending garter
Attempting position that defies gravity (the double cartwheel)	Attempt more conservative position such as double missionary (both partners on bottom)
Insufficient warm-up before sex	Fitness machine, or use partner as free weight
Insatiable partner	Exorcist

Personal Bests

"Seven climaxes on the first night of my honeymoon. My wife couldn't believe it and made me start all over."

— Norman, postal employee

"Despite a handicap,* I engaged in all 19 positions cited in the *Munich Book of Lust.*"

— Eddie, board-certified bartender

*Six under par.

The Bedside Eater: Part II

Blueberry parfait (aphrodisiac for the dessert lover):

Erotic Claim

Refreshes sexual appetite, improves circulation, makes lovers who've been in bed for an entire weekend appear less haggard; decreases incidence of side-stitch caused by overexertion while changing position.

Scientific Evidence

Observes report formation of new and much better capillaries, rg̃uction of triglycerides and lower heart rate even during moments of extreme sexual crisis (you're about to break curfew).

What I Do During Sex

"Wonder why we don't do this more often, it feels so good."
> – Meg, carrier pilot

"Moan in measured tones."
> – Lawrence, accountant

"Who can remember? The room is so dark."
> – Jill, self-employed

National Abstinence Week

Six ways to celebrate.
1. Ignore it.
2. Learn a skill that uses similar muscles (like making a pizza or riding a motorcycle).
3. Confine public displays of affection with your partner to wearing matching sweatshirts.
4. Work off nervous "deprival" energy by doing your Christmas shopping early.
5. Put away your lover's picture.
6. Volunteer to help recovering sex addicts.

In Your Lover's Bedroom

It's a bad sign if on the night table:

He has:	**She has:**
A photo of his mother	A photo of her cat
Mercenary magazine	*Bride's* magazine
A time clock	An egg time
Tic Tacs	Valium
His briefcase	Her Filofax
A pyramid	A Ouija board
The Rise and Fall of the Third Reich	*Miss Manner's Guide to Etiquette*
A camera	A tape recorder

June Emergency Diet
To fit into your bathing suit by tomorrow:

Suggested Activity	Calories burned
Call in sick	11
Convince lover to call in sick:	
If lover has strong sense of responsibility	43
But is oversexed	$1/2$
Ten hours of sex (per partner)	4,874
Without rest stops	9,000
The eleventh hour:	
Trying again	361
If lover not yet ready	2,594
Giving lover a pep talk	75

Honeymoon Ritual for the Bride: Part I
Advice on how to handle the sheltered groom. If on your wedding night he loses his virginity,* it's customary the next morning to put money under his pillow.
*First time only.

How Great Was It?
Frequently used after-sex phrase indicating a less than delighted partner:
"Did I miss anything?"

How Did You Meet? Part II
"At work. After reading his resumé I knew he wasn't right for the job, but perfect for me. The interview was wonderful."
> – Marjorie, personnel director

"At a restaurant. He stuck his business card into my tuna salad and walked away. I dig smooth men."
> – Kathryn, ordained glove model

"Speed trap."
> – Gloria, state trooper

Music to Your Lover's Ears
Things to say in the evening to a lover who experienced a) a dreadful day at the office plus b) a lunch of pan-fried calamari that defied copious doses of Maalox and c) dreadful rush hour traffic:

- "How about a cold glass of Chablis?"
- "I've got a warm bath waiting."
- "I cancelled our guest."
- "You just lie there, I'll do everything."
- "You've been accepted at Harvard."

Love Poll #6

Of 200 honeymoon couples interviewed at Niagara Fall, 61% believed in a no-fault wet spot.

Sexual Etiquette

During lovemaking, it is permissible to talk on the phone only if it's:*

- Your mom
- Your spouse
- Your lover's spouse
- 911
- Your broker

*Caller may be put on hold during orgasm.

Astounding Moment In Sex

"Realizing that sex could be a valid way to relate with the opposite sex!"

– Heather, remarkable talent

From Our Lover's Glossary

Empty Nest Syndrome. The moment when the last child leaves the house and the remaining two people (usually known as husband and wife), after they wave a tearful goodbye, realize they can have all the sex they want, whenever they want, in any part of the house without worrying about privacy. Unfortunately many such couples, in those first few weeks of freedom, experience what is known in medical terminology as "overdoing it" and attempt to compensate for 18 years of deprival. Alas, they usually go insane.

The Conservative Lover

Sexually explicit sex—some guidelines.

Activity	Sinful	Virtuous
Office gossip	X	
Magical back rubs		X
Using baby oil	X	
Anything kinky with:		
A partner (business)	X	
A partner (lover)		X
Bathing together		X
Both using same bar of soap	X	

Tips For Novice Lovers

Sex in the shower or under a waterfall, making love in a hot tub, and skinny dipping are great ways to get your feet wet with a new lover.

Sex Without Tears

What to do if your lover can't get enough of you.

Affliction	Remedy
I'm too gorgeous: my lover can't stop gazing at me	Gain weight. Cease exercising and eat more pound cake
I'm too creative: my lover can't wait to see what's next	Cool it. Confine lovemaking to the same time each night, in the same place, on the same sheet
I'm so irresistible my lover jumps me the moment I get home	Work late

Lover's Quote Of The Day

"On our honeymoon we simply couldn't stop doing it. When we finally left the room, we discovered that postage rates had gone up—twice."

– Nathan and Nancy, marathoners

Advisory For Honeymooners
What to expect after:

3 Hours of Sex	5 Hours of Sex
Bedsores	Bunions
Dehydration	Fermentation
Heat exhaustion	Heat stroke
Hunger	Malnutrition
Significant weight loss	Dwarfism
Afterglow	Meltdown
A rematch	A rebirth

The Enlightened Lover
The difference between:
An act of God
Makes the earth quake
An act of Goddess
Makes the bed quake

Some Enchanted Evening
Some statements indicating he or she may be falling under your spell.
- "Don't look at me like that."
- "Cut it out, people are staring."
- "Meet me under the table in 20 seconds."
- "I'll get dinner."
- "I'll get the waiter."
- "Do you like children?"

Sexual Etiquette
If you must talk during sex:

Do Be	Do Not
Interesting	Mumble
Romantic	Wake the children
Brief	Speak with your mouth full

Lovemaking Tip For June Brides
The average honeymoon couple can survive on nothing but sex, chocolate ice cream and a multi-vitamin capsule for up to 11 days. The above-average couple can dispense with the vitamins.

Three Thoughts for Today
1. Even moderate sex can help you fit into your bathing suit.
2. Good sex can help you look good in it.
3. Great sex should make you get out of it.

The Dieter's Guide to Weight Loss During Sex
The slimming effect of lovemaking.

Activity	Calories Burned
If climax was:	
"Intense"	95
"Really special"	33
"Awesome"	195
"Quite acceptable"	11
"So nice"	58
"Off the charts"	166
"Worth the wait"	
10 minutes	67
3 hours	481
"Worth every penny"	230

The Diplomatic Lover
The question: Do you think I've put on weight?"
When asked: After undressing, just before sex.
By whom: Your partner.
Your choice of answers:
Good: "No."
Better: "Only, thank goodness, in the right places."
Tactful: "It's difficult to tell by moonlight."
Romantic: "About one pound, which we're about to work off."

Honeymoon Helpers
Three nonchemical sexual aids.
1. A terrific caterer.
2. An ocean view.
3. Advice from a wise bridesmaid.
Two reasons for wedding-night jitters.
1. For bride: When lifted over the threshold, groom winced.
2. For groom: The cost of the ring.
Sexual error most often made.
• Telling friends where you are (unless a third opinion is desired).

From Our Lover's Glossary
Really safe sex. Refusing, after dazzling lovemaking, to sign the prenuptial agreement that is placed before you by your smitten partner because you can't read the fine print.

Morning Etiquette
As a considerate lover, you should:
• Brew the coffee.
• Kiss your lover awake.
• Serve freshly squeezed orange juice.
• Prepare the bran.
• Never make the bed with your lover still in it.

Fond Memories
Never allow a great lover to depart your bedroom without leaving:
• A photo
• A phone number
• A sample

Thought for Lovers Who Overdo It
Having too much sex is like:
• Having too little cholesterol.
• Having too much money.
• Being too thin.
• Playing Chopin too well.
• Owning too many Van Goghs.
• Having too high an IQ.
• Getting into the college of your choice.
• Looking too good in a bathing suit.
• Looking even better out of it.

Prediction for Today
You will meet your new lover at a garage sale. His wife will give you a terrific price.

Tip for Cautious Brides
Acceptable reasons for declining sex on your wedding night if:
You're absent-minded: *"I forgot your condoms."*
You flew United: *"The airline lost my diaphragm."*

Unusual Benefits Of Sex

"It helped me get chosen as a contestant on a TV game show."
— Myrna, roofer

"The IRS auditor changed her mind and allowed me to take my new pool table as a medical deduction."
— Donald, marketing

"Extra-favorable treatment from an insurance adjuster."
— Meg, secretary

"A free contraceptive. She said she never left home without it."
— Barry, toll collector

Try Something Different Tonight: New Lovers Only

Find each other's birthmark or erogenous zones.

Okay to Use	Against the Rules
Nightlight	Floodlight
Intuition	Bribe
Fingertips	Sonar
Magnifying glass	Divining rod

Put Your Lover On Probation

If he or she:

• Turns down your request to make love five or more times in one month.

• Constantly falls asleep just as you're getting interested.

• Keeps forgetting what turns you on.

• Experiences more than two power failures a week.

• Starts moonlighting.

• Fails to keep you warm on cold nights.

• Needs a flowerpot to make you feel the earth move.

Svelte Lovers Confess

"It was sex that enabled us to lose weight in all the right places: Paris (-2 lbs.); Maui (-3 lbs); the Poconos (-7 lbs.); Bermuda (-4 lbs.); Brooklyn (-2_ lbs.); our new leather workout room (-6 lbs.)."
— Franco and Margo, teammates

Review Questions (answers below)

1. First Aid: A lover who overheats during sex should be ___?

2. Easy-care: In referring to a lover's virtues, what does the term low maintenance mean?

3. Concentration: List the three during-sex distractions most likely to occur in the suburbs.

1. (a) Wiped with a cool damp cloth (b) Given water (c) Commended

2. (a) Can start without you (b) Never needs oiling

3. (a) Bell (the door) (b) Bell (ice cream truck) (c) Zealous tax assessor tapping on skylight.

Not To Worry

After lovemaking, while lying there with your partner, basking in the afterglow, it's comforting to know that:

• Your relaxed, "floaty" feeling is nothing to feel guilty about.

• If you're patient and wait long enough, you'll get your breath back.

• Those alarming sighs of pleasure may be coming from you.

• It's okay if your partner can still move to ask for more.

• It's Saturday and you don't have to go to work.

Sexual Points On Your Marriage License: Part I

(The more serious the violation, the more points.)

Violation	Points
Wanting sex when your partner doesn't want it	3
Not wanting sex when your partner wants it	7
Can't decide	50
Asking your neighbor if she could accommodate you	22
Both want sex at the same time but the kids are off from school today	11

The Bedside Eater

Body Part	Most Likely to Taste Like:
Inside wrist	Shrimp pâté
Backs of fingers	Link breakfast sausages
Fingertips	Tapas
Nape of neck	Goat cheese with red and yellow tomatoes on a bed of arugula
Thighs (hers)	Beef brochettes
Thighs (his)	Steamed sea bass or, if he's petite, curried chicken wings

The Contented Lover

"It is usually after a third climax that my world visibly brightens. My lover insists it's the new halogen night lamp, but I say it's the afterglow."
— Lynda K., consultant

Temporarily Celibate?

As Good as Sex	Nearly as Good as Sex
Your team wins the Series	Your bathing suit finally fits
No cavities	No debts
No line at the Dairy Queen	No line at the cash machine
Finding a great hairdresser	Finding a great plumber
The car is really fixed	No water in the basement
"It's a girl!"	"Triplets!"

Tip for the Shy Bride Having Second Thoughts

An acceptable excuse for not having sex on your wedding night: "My diaphragm's locked in the hotel safe."

Tip for the Newlywed

"How did I get to know my husband better? On our honeymoon, I walked a mile in his shoes. It wasn't easy, they were still tied to the car bumper."
— Dottie, rocket scientist

Scenic Views

Reasons why, before lovemaking, one couple enjoys standing in front of their full-length mirror without any clothes on.

- "It gets us in the mood."
- "I can relish his shoulders."
- "I can savor her pretty knees."
- "I can take her measurements, 38-22-38, and play the lottery."
- "We play show and tell."

The Bedside Explorer: Part I

An erotic adventure for the intrepid lover.

Expedition 1. (Albert's Ascent)

Recommended equipment: the lips

Begin kissing lover's ankle. Travel north, very slowly, past the calf to the knee. Stop. Linger. Examine the patella: is it cute? Tasty? Nibblable? Good. Now proceed farther north to the thigh. Lightly kiss, then go on to base camp.

Our Second Honeymoon

Testimonial from a senior couple, who said they never had so much fun:

- In a Winnebago
- On a cruise
- In Florida
- Not playing shuffleboard
- On a heart-shaped bed
- Without our grandchildren
              – The Winstons, retired

Advice for Newlyweds

Don't overdo it. You know you've been making love too long if:

- The wet spot starts to dry.
- You begin to quote scripture.
- Your mind begins to wander (and you start wondering which gifts to return).
- Your parents go on their second honeymoon. . .and join you.

Not-So-Great Moment In Last Flings

"In the middle of lovemaking, when she extended her hand to admire her new engagement ring, she got really offended when I asked, 'Did he give you a real diamond?'"

      – Ricardo, lifeguard

Just as It Was Getting Good: Part II

More frequently heard answers to "Why'd you stop?"

If your partner:	You'll hear:
Is conservative.	"I'm saving myself."
Is awed.	"I didn't know what I was missing."
Is exhausted.	"I didn't know what you were missing."
Is getting antsy.	"Enough, already."
Is religious.	"Our divorce just came through."

Lovemaking—The Technical Aspects: Part II

Change positions when:
- One of you has fallen off the bed.
- You can't see the time.
- You can't see your partner.

Q. During an especially fiery orgasm, all 10 of your press-on nails loosen and stick in his back. Should you apologize?
A. *No, if*: He didn't notice.
Yes, if: It woke him.

The Paranoid Lover

Frequent thought among insecure people moments before they undress for the first time in front of a new lover:
Should have spent more time at the gym.

The Inquisitive Lover

Q. After sex, who gets to use the bathroom first?
A. The lover who sleeps the fastest.

Did You Know?

The primary source of nourishment for honeymoon couple reluctant to leave their room:

Honeymoon Site	Nourishment Source
Niagara Falls	The bottle of Champagne they brought along in their luggage
The Poconos	The mints on their pillows
Bermuda	Room service
Any Days Inn	Domino's or Taco Bell
Syosset, Long Island	Mom

Loving Couples

Six reasons our test couples gave for having sex (other than "We're trying to start a family").

1. Practice makes perfect.
2. We can't help it.
3. We need the exercise but we can't afford health club dues.
4. Why waste a king-size bed?
5. To remind ourselves that all the good ones really are married.
6. If we didn't have sex, I'd feel guilty about co-signing his loan.

Time-Management Advisory: Part II

How soon after sex should you	Wait at least
Suggest a rematch	1 hour
Tell him you're getting:	
Very fond of him1 minute	
Married	1 week
Confess this will be your:	
First time	5 minutes
Last time	5 weeks
Apologize for:	
Taking so long	10 seconds
Not taking long enough	10 minutes

Tonight's Health Tip

How to achieve total fitness in 15 minutes.

For Him

Gently and lingeringly kiss her knees, then her thighs on all four sides (preferably after she's removed her jeans). Thighs are an ex-

cellent source of calcium, as well as the perfect low-cholesterol midnight snack.
For Her
Gently and lingeringly nibble his shoulders (avoid those distracting tufts of hair). Not only an excellent source of roughage, but considered by the Dutch Dental Association to be an effective way to fight plaque.

What We Did for Sex
"Sent both kids away to summer camp."
           – Marge and Frank

Reassurance for the Jittery
When getting undressed with a new partner and you're nervous about those few extra pounds, don't be.
• You carry them well.
• They're difficult to see by candlelight.
• Most people look thinner when they're lying down.
• You'll need them if the mattress is extra firm.
• They'll give you more bounce.
• They'll probably come off during sex.

The Patient Lover
How Long Should You Wait

To operate heavy machinery:	After Good sex	After Great Sex
Your juicer	5 minutes	10 minutes
Your truck	1 hour	5 hours
To look in the mirror	5 minutes	1 minute
To look for:		
An earring	10 minutes	20 minutes
A contact lens	15 minutes	1 hour

Are You Insatiable?
Research indicates that couples who have sex 20 or more times weekly:
• Can't get enough of each other.
• Probably take vitamin E.
• Lose their ability to metabolize fruitcake.

- Are seldom aware of what's going on in the world.
- Usually don't have children.
- Probably like on a cul-de-sac.
- Have no shame.

Telltale Signs of a Happy Sex Life
1. A cheerful disposition.
2. Sleeping peacefully.
3. Eating sensibly.
4. Loving thy neighbor.
5. Liking thy in-laws.

What I Did for Love
"Made her my favorite dish."
> – Lance Charmeuse, chef

The Dieter's Guide to Weight Loss During Sex
Your wedding night.

Making Love	Calories Burned
If it's the first time for both of you	125
But you're both adventurous	166
And fearless	524

Words to the Wise Lover
When journeying from your partner's lips to your partner's knees, always stop at the scenic overlook.

Sex Poll #10
What's the best thing about sleeping with your lover?
"Staying up all night."
> – Melba, track and field star

"Her wake-up call: one long, then two short. . .moans."
> – Allen, financial advisor

"I can't tell you, this is a family calendar."
> – Trudy, astrologer and cocktail waitress

Guide For Brides

Our exclusive post wedding night checklist (fill out in the privacy of your morning shower):

Was it everything you thought it would be?
__ Yes __ No __ Not sure

Was he everything you thought he would be?
__ A bit less __ A bit more

Was he considerate?
__ Asked, "Was it good for you?"__ Waited for an answer

Do you still want him to be the father of your children?
__ Yes __ No __ He already is

The Enlightened Lover

Frequent during-sex utterances:

- *"Things might go better if you removed your headphones."*
- *"This is so depraved. Don't you dare stop."*
- *"This is better than sex!"*
- *"Uncle!"*
- *"Uncle?"*

Treat Him Like Royalty

Give him his weight in:

- Metamucil (if he's a health fanatic)
- Spare engine parts (if he's a car nut)
- Gold (if he's a great lover)
- Sex (if you're a great lover)

Lovemaking Tips: Part I

To a Lover Who:	Suggested Gratuity
Helped you experience another orgasmic episode when you were certain you never would.	$5.75
Calmed your first-night jitters.	$2.00
Is service-oriented (keeps your feet warm before, during and after sex).	$1.25
Reads romantic poetry aloud by the light of your afterglow.	$1.75
Wants to try again.	$2.50
And again.	$7.00

Quotes of the Night

Actual after-sex utterances of impressed sex partners.*
"Keep me in mind for the next time."
"I'm listed."
"Whew!"
"Can't wait to tell my friends."
"Bartender, another round!"
"Are we still on for Bermuda?"
*Source: Files of the Justice Department.

The Enlightened Lover

Should you sleep with him, or just nap a little?
Neither if, before you go to bed, he refuses to shower with you because he's afraid he'll get his ponytail wet.

From Our Lover's Glossary

Beginner's Luck. *1.* When, on his wedding night, and inexperienced groom, just by clutching a rabbit's foot, brings his bride to ecstasy no fewer than six times. *2.* When, on the first date, (a) dinner, (b) sex and (c) your partner, all go off without a hitch.

Great Moment in Lovemaking

"When we discovered that the quiet, reserved couple that everyone in the community suspected of having loads of wanton, torrid sex . . . was us!"
– Bess and Gary, antique dealers

Pillow Talk

The cuddle. A post-lovemaking procedure in which both partners, to facilitate the onset of sleep, press against each other and murmur sweet nothings until they fall asleep. This maneuver should not be attempted if the site of your lovemaking has been a restaurant banquette.

Our Technical Adviser Suggests . . .

1. A gentle, up-and-down flopping motion of either hand is the standard signal used by exhausted lovers to indicate that sex was awesome.

2. A minor case of first-night jitters can almost always be remedied through prayer (applies to all religions).

3. On satin sheets, deck shoes provided the best traction.

4. Using a squeegee to wipe sweat from a lover's brow is unromantic.

The Well-Equipped Lover

Three must-have items if your sun-burned partner peels during sex:

1. A sense of humor.
2. Safety goggles.
3. A Dustbuster.

Sexual Points On Your Marriage License: Part I

The more serious the violation, the more points

Violation	Points
During a sexual time-out:	
Failure to yield TV clicker	4
Eyeing laptop computer longingly	9
Achieving liftoff during orgasm	0
But in the wrong direction	10
Rolling over and going to sleep immediately after sex	4
Habitual offender	12

Fore-Play Tips For Golfing Lovers

Things to do to perk up the game.

• *In the golf cart:* Sit on his lap.

• *While waiting to tee off:* Nibble your partner's neck.

• *While walking to the next hole:* Always hold hands.

• *After a putt:* Compliment his birdie.

• *If stuck in a sand trap:* Make love (pretend you're at the beach).

• *After a hole in one:* Carry him over the threshold (of the clubhouse).

Shocking Your Lover

When should you whisper lewd suggestions in his or her ear?

Event	Yes	No
Funeral of a relative?		X
Funeral of a wealthy aunt?	X	
While touring the White House?	X	
During Bible studies class?	X	
When meeting his or her parents?		X
Wedding:		
Yours		X
His		X

How Often Do You Make Love? Part IV

Frequency Rate

6-9 times weekly (second honeymooners and in-shape civilians only)

What It Means

Love life quite healthy. Partners still your heart's desire, but outside activities such as bowling league and sleep compete. You're both beginning to find the "energy-saving" position most rewarding (both partners on bottom).

Are You Covered?

Check your health insurance. If last night's sex was too glorious, the silly grin that will cover your face for the next several days will have to be surgically removed—especially if you live in a conservative community.

The Road to Great Sex

Six unusual couples reveal their secret.

1. "Jello, bit of whipped cream on the side."
2. "Use the right workout video (our favorites—*Sweatin' to Sex* * and *Spanking Masters of Guam*)."
3. "Always take 'Yes' for an answer."
4. "We have a great dental plan; it gives us peace of mind."
5. Change positions at least three times an hour (enables us to get well done on all four sides)."
6. "A splash of Joy in our morning coffee."

*Not available in any store.

Tipping Advice For Newlyweds

After he brings in the luggage and carries her over the threshold, the bellman should be given an extra generous gratuity if he remembers to go back for the groom.

Great Moments of Relief in Sex

"When I realized those scary, animal-like noises were just me moaning."

        — Thomas, reverend

"When I realized those hot flashes were only his butler taking pictures."

        — Harriet, parlor maid

"He promised not to hold it against me."

        — Cornelia, pharmacist

Words of Relief

Overheard from a woman who, after twenty-two years of marriage, got a divorce, met a new partner and is ecstatically happy, especially with her sex life:

"They don't make lovers like they used to, thank God."

A Guide To Vehicular Sex

SAAB

Advantages

Excellent handling: safe to enjoy foreplay an intercourse while negotiating a hairpin S-curve.

Disadvantages

Hair-trigger horn may sound when lovers engage in classic "front seat" position: his feet on floor, her feet on steering wheel (also known as the "Women's Movement").

When The Unthinkable Happens

Event	What to Do
Your lovemaking gets so hot that you set off the sprinklers.	Share an umbrella.
Intense lovemaking leaves you speechless.	Let your fingers do the talking.

The Art of Romance
Five valid excuses for not having sex on your wedding night.
1. "We forgot how."
2. "I'm saving myself."
3. "My wife expects me home."
4. "My parents are in the next room."
5. "I'm in labor."

A Lover's Hobby
A few reasons why, in addition to stamps, sex should be a favorite pastime:
• You can enjoy it with only a high-school education.
• No worrying about court fees.
• It promotes intimacy.
• What to wear is never a concern.
• It's been known to feel better than golf.
• You can't overdo it.

Are You Being Too Celibate?
Researchers suggest you may be suffering from clinical sexual deprival if you have five or more of the following symptoms:
• Difficulty concentrating.
• Insomnia (especially during after-dinner speeches).
• A change in appetite (from, for example, foods rich in fun, to cauliflower).
• Thoughts either of death or calling a 900 number.
• 70 or more pounds overweight and your only explanation is that you're eating too much.
• In your wallet you still keep a photo of your last lover (and it's life-size).

Secret Weapons Of Successful Lovers
(A random sampling.)
• An intimate hideaway in Vermont
• A charge account with a florist
• Bedroom eyes
• Treating every time like the first. . .no, wait, the second time
• Original poetry (It's unethical to recycle a poem written for a previous lover unless the creative juices have dried up.)

- Always remembers:
- Valentine's Day
- Anniversaries and birthdays
- To leave the seat down

The Enlightened Lover
Some common distractions and their possible disturbing effect on lovemaking.

Easy to Ignore	Not So Easy
Salivating partner	Dripping faucet
Upstairs neighbor having a party	With your lover
Call of migrating geese	Call of nature
Telephone	Audible message
Technical errors	Equipment failure

The Lust-Intensive Honeymoon
"We spent 14 days in sunny Bermuda, yet with great effort, and room service, we managed to achieve that healthy indoor look. Our friends were so jealous."
— Fred and Gloria

The Language of Flowers: Part V

To the lover who:	Send:
Helps you balance your check-book	Magnolias
Always smell so good	Jasmines
And tastes even better	Lilacs
Drinks wine from your slipper	Queens Anne's lace
And tomato juice from your sandal	A bib

Tip from a Sadder but Wiser Honeymooner
"Be wary of budget bridal suites. During sex, whenever we got really excited:
1. Plaster from the ceiling would fall and hit my husband's back.
2. The wallpaper would peel.
3. And we could see into the next room."
— Eve, bank teller

Your First Night Together

Eight things a new partner may not be able to do:
1. Get totally relaxed.
2. Oral sex (even if you look the other way).
3. Floors.
4. Go all the way.
5. Easily experience a climax.
6. Find the light switch for the bathroom.
7. Stay over.
8. Leave.

Obstacles to Perfect Sex

1. Stress
2. Trying to be perfect
3. Fear of intimacy
4. A stubborn zipper
5. Three margaritas
6. No partner

Love Signs

Horoscope For A Carnal Cancer
- *Ruling passion:* making love with someone just for their mind
- *Ruling body lotion:* peanut oil
- *Chief sexual asset:* come-hither eyes
- *Governing erogenous zone:* nape of your swan-like neck
- *Aphrodisiac of choice:* triple-decker club sandwich (baked Virginia ham, turkey, Swiss cheese, hold the mayo)
- *Ruling sexual activity:* administering love bites to a deserving partner
- *Ideal time for sex:* you're always on call

Lovemaking: The Spinoffs

- All the personal attention
- The memories
- Greater self-confidence
- The definitive antidote of stress
- Healthier appetite
- Instant gratification
- Teamwork

- Lower cholesterol
- Reduced plaque
- Energy conservation (you can do it in the dark)

What We Did on Our Honeymoon

"Went on a cruise."
> – Debbie and Donny

"Went white-water rafting."
> – Kate and Karl

"Went to the Grand Canyon."
> – Betty and Boyd

"Went on and on."
> – Laura and Lauritz

Guide For Clockwatching Lovers

Average time between moans:	
Honeymooners	3 seconds
If married 25 years	3 months
Usual time that elapses between working couples:	
Getting into bed and falling asleep	3.5 minutes
Getting into bed, having sex and falling asleep	3.9 minutes
Time one partner can spend on the phone during sex until the other partner gets peeved:	
Business call	4.5 minutes
Personal call	5 minutes

National Statistics

In the heat of passion, the
Aroused American Male Needs
- 2 seconds to remove his shoes
- 3 seconds to remove the rest of his clothing.
- 1_ seconds to get into bed.

Aroused American Female Needs
- 7 seconds to say, "I'll be right back," then goes into the bathroom.
- 5 minutes to remove her makeup, then 3 more minutes to put some back on.
- 6 minutes to arrange her hair, 4 minutes to rearrange it.

Sad Fact of Love

A congressional report shows that among two-career couples married twenty years or more:
1. Calling in sick at 8 A.M; then
2. Staying in bed and making love until 11 A.M.; then
3. Dressing each other; and
4. Going out for a deliciously sinful brunch

accounted for only 3_ workdays lost last year in the United States.

What Do the Professionals Do?

Problem

Making love with my partner gets so exciting that as I approach orgasm, I can never decide where to put my chewing gum.

Solutions

1. *Neat:* Swallow it.
2. *Less neat:* Place on bedpost. Afterward, gum can be rechewed to quell postsexual nervousness.
3. *Weird:* Put gum behind lover's ear. It will intensify that feeling of togetherness and commitment.

The Enlightened Lover

First things usually done after lovemaking.

If it was great:	If it was just so-so:
Wonder where the time went.	Consult your watch.
Recover from whisker burn.	Recover from a slow burn.
Schedule a rematch.	Schedule a rehearsal.
Whisper "You've worn me out."	Whisper "It's your turn to do the dishes."

Love Signs

Horoscope for Consummate Cancer.
* *Ruling passion:* transforming bedroom into a petting zoo
* *Ruling sexual turnoff:* lovers with a paper route
* *Chief sexual asset:* a steamy past
* *Governing erogenous zone:* bucket seats
* *Aphrodisiac:* popcorn (popped)
* *Ruling sexual activity:* changing position without stopping
* *Ideal time for sex:* moments before the guests arrive

A Lover's Nutritional Guide

To maintain your strength during sex:

After

1. One hour of torrid sex (unable to recall year you graduated high school)
2. Two hours of bliss (total rapture—your eyebrows are somehow now on backward)
3. Three hours of ecstasy (utter moral degradation—unable to see what's wrong with wearing a blue suit with brown shoes)

You will need

1. Herring in cream sauce or a large bowl of rigatoni
2. Buffalo chicken wings (for best results rub barbecue sauce on your pule points)
3. A poultice of warm risotto or bathe forehead with fennel soup

Love Signs: Cancer

(June 22-July 22)

Opposite love sign: A callipygous Capricorn. (Accept no substitutes.)

Outstanding sexual quality: You've been around, but always show mercy toward a new partner.

Most attractive physical feature: A forehead that never gets a headache from too much champagne.

Ruling sexual turnoff: Partners who try to arouse you with artificial stimulants (like conversation).

Ruling sexual turn-on: Partners who know their place (beside you).

Ideal place for sex: Whenever it's taboo, like Cairo and your sex therapist's office.

Alternative Love Signs: Cancer

(June 22-July 22)

Most attractive feature: Buns officially classified as the fourteenth wonder of the modern world.

Turn-on: A partner with "come hither" bedroom eyes, all of Willie Nelson's CDs and a condo on the beach.

Turn-offs: Hard-to-please lovers who complain your beauty's only skin deep.

Ideal romantic adventure: Making love while skydiving, then having simultaneous orgasms that make the parachutes open (you hope).

Favorite sexual fantasy: Putting it in "Park" and making love on the hood of an idling Jaguar while waiting for the light to change.

The Language of Flowers: Part II
To the lover:
Against whom you snuggled until you fell asleep

Who drove you:	Send:
• Up a wall	A huge bouquet of morning glories
• Up a wall, then, gently, and exquisitely, helped you down	Ivy
	White roses, one dozen

Great Moments During Climax
"Seeing my life flash before my eyes."
> – Velma, meter maid

"Reaching that point of no return."
> – Paul, travel agent

"Fireworks (in season)."
> – Agnes, beekeeper

A Lover's Bedroom: Part II
Also nice to have.

Item	Function
Mallomars	Keeps up strength, revives exhausted lovers.
Tanning lotion	To avoid that indoor look.
Calculator	To keep track of earned bonus miles.
Drapes	Something to grab on to should sex get out of control.
Spatula	The utensil of choice for separating lovers after sex.

Shocking Moment In Lovemaking
"At first I was ecstatic: after hours of wondrous lovemaking, this divine, beautiful creature said she wanted me to be the father of her children. . .all she had to do was obtain custody of them from her husband."
> – Yves, test pilot

Passion Alert For Newlyweds

Preoccupied by a sexy spouse? The drawbacks of too much chemistry:

1. Thinking of sex on company time.
2. Neglecting friends.
3. When doing laundry, feeling too weak to separate whites from colors.
4. Forgetting to return your parents' phone calls.
5. Guilt (caused by giving in to Temptation, twice a day).
6. Poor job attitude (grinning when a customer complains about the melons).
7. Bed sores.

June Bride Alert

Words often uttered by an overexcited groom:
"This is all happening too fast, could we speed things up?"

Midsummer's Night Resolutions

1. *Easy to break:* no more sex with someone just for their mind.
2. *Not as easy to break:* no more sex with someone just for their body.

Midsummer Night's Resolution

Make more time for sex, even if it means:
• Setting the alarm an hour earlier.
• Ordering the kids to sleep later.
• Holding up the car pool.
• Shorter lunches.
• Leaving work early.
• Occasionally skipping poker night.
• Less golf.
• Early retirement.

From Our Honeymooner's Glossary

Comeback. A heroic effort made by a bridegroom, usually on his wedding night, when, although exhausted by (a) the day's events and (b) counting the gifts and (c) having already satisfied his bride (twice), he attempts, with utter disregard for personal safety, to satisfy her again before breakfast, without so much as a bran muffin.

After-Sex Tip for Overheated Lovers
If lovemaking was truly hot (both of you are actually glowing*), cool off by:
Sipping iced tea
Turning up the air conditioner
Retiring to the "No Smoking" section of the bed
*Applies especially to first-night honeymooners either at Niagara Falls or in the Poconos.

On Your Lover's Mind
When, in the heat of sexual passion, your lover calls out your name, be happy. Even if you aren't there, it shows your lover's still thinking of you.

The Mysterious Lover: Poll #47
Where do you keep a secret diary you don't want your spouse to find?
"Anywhere, he can't read."
   – Hillary, concierge
"Under the hood of my Buick, taped to the battery."
   – Steve, realtor
"In my head—I never allow him to look in my eyes."
   – Caroline, dentist
"In my bra, silly."
   – Norma, hostess

Reminder
Science now tells us that doing it under the bed is no guarantee that you won't get pregnant.

The Beneficial Energies Of Sex: Part II

Activity	Benefits
Arousal	Encourages deep breathing
Intercourse:	
Slow	Increases total muscle mass
Fast	Increases heart muscle mass
Quite fast	Achieves target heart rate
Orgasm:	
Small	Makes eyes shine; strengthens puny lashes
Big	Nasal decongestant

Breaking the Ice

The first thing I do with a new lover.

"Ask him his sign."
> — Georgette, secretary

"Show him my wedding album."
> — Madge, attorney

"Introduce her to my mother."
> — Chuck, federal agent

"Sit down and schmooze a little."
> — Hobart, accountant

"Send a bottle of wine over to his side of the bed."
Renata, crane operator

Tip For Honeymooners

Words most likely to cause an exhausted groom to either (a) experience first-night jitters, or (b) think annulment, when uttered by his panting bride after the first three hours of nonstop sex:

"Thank goodness the night is still young."*

*"Thank goodness the knight is still young" is a less frightening alternative.

Why Did You Take an Older Lover? Poll #44

"She yells at me, spanks me, makes me clean up my room and cuts my meat. I love being mothered."
> — Carlos, 51, playboy

"He can't pick up the phone to break our date. He's too weak."
— Mimi, 40, IRS agent
"The young ones all want me to put them through law school."
— Raoul, 67, magnate
"I've always wanted my own, personal historical marker."
— Ursula, 71, nurse
"The young ones aren't doing it anymore."
— Virna, 50, sculptor

Emergency Weight-Loss Tip

To fit into your new bathing suit by the July 4th weekend:

You must	Calories consumed
1. Shut off your phone	3
2. Change the sheets	70
3. Get into bed with your partner	22
4. Spend one hour slowly arousing each other	258
5. Watch yourselves in amazement in your ceiling mirror	133
6. Settle only for simultaneous orgasm	801
7. Check the scale	50

The Dieter's Guide to Weight Loss During Sex

Activity	Calories Burned
Making love outdoors while leaning against a:	
Tree	74
Sapling	3
Rosebush	458
Bull:	
Sleeping	106
Awake	500

Some Sexual Atrocities

1. Using the same sheet for two different lovers.*
2. Getting aroused with your current lover by thinking about a past lover.
3. Calling out the wrong lover's name.
4. Sleeping with someone just for a recipe.
5. Starting what your partner can't finish.
6. Abstinence (unless it makes the heart grow fonder).
*Unless they know each other.

Honeymoon Ritual for the Bride: Part II
Advice for brides with back problems:
Toss the bouquet with both hands.
Let him carry the luggage.
Let him carry you over the threshold.
When in bed, let him do all the work.
When out of bed, let him return the gifts.

Loving Couples
How we celebrated our first six months of great sex.
"The usual stuff: First a picnic, then we went bowling. Afterwards, we showered by candlelight, then we sipped Dom Perignon in front of a video cassette of a crackling fire (it was August), read poetry to each other and, finally, we got into bed and dozed off. We were, alas, too exhausted for sex. Maybe next time."
— Trini and Fenton
"Brought our mattress in for its 1,000-mile checkup."
— Stacy and Tracy

National Passion Week
To celebrate:
• Give the butler the week off.
• Miss no opportunities to cuddle.
• Have breakfast in bed with your lover at least twice (but not on the same morning if you're dieting).
• Make love at an unusual time, such as (a) high noon, (b) before cocktails, (c) during high tea.
• Give your lover the key to your heart.
• Better yet, give your lover the key to your apartment.

With a New Lover?
You know you've struck sexual gold when:
• Your climaxes cause your makeup to flake.
• You say, "I've never felt this way before". . .and mean it.
• During lovemaking the windows fog.
• He or she says, "What else can I do for you?" and you're stumped.
• You stop thinking about your ex.

Summer Beauty Tip

When making love in your convertible, protect skin from premature aging by keeping the top up.

Midyear Recap

Your previous six months in sex.
Best lover __ Phone __ Fax __
Did you need an appointment?
Yes __ No __ Sometimes __
Best sexual experience _____
Best month _____Why _____
Have I improved?   Yes __ No __ Not sure __
Fantasy for this year _____
Is it coming true?   Yes __ No __ I hope not __

Warning for an Over-Optimistic Bride

Something to keep in mind on your wedding night, especially if your groom is a stockbroker:
Past performance is no guarantee of future results.

In Case You're Not Sure

Researchers tell us that any climax that:
• clears the mind of negative thoughts
• exorcises demons
• clears the body of negative thoughts (the Pepto-Bismol effect)
• induces onlookers to toss confetti
• drives you to a state of unspeakable ecstasy similar to the one you experience when your mortgage if paid off
• separates you from your dentures
• is as, or nearly as, satisfying as a freshly baked onion bagel is a good one.

Not Just A Sex Object

Additional uses for an everyday lover:
1. Making your ex jealous.
2. Walking your dog on dreary mornings.
3. Guarding your house when you're away.
4. Refinishing that table you found at a yard sale.
5. Warming up the car on cold mornings.

6. Reading you a bedtime story when you can't get to sleep.
7. (If he has hairy legs) a scratching post for your cat.
8. Splitting the wedding expenses.

Love on the Run
How busy couples cope with too little time.
"We skip foreplay and get right to the good stuff."
        — Daphne, umpire
"We do it wherever we can get some privacy—we're grinning because we were just in the lavatory of our local Taco Bell."
        — Dean, slacks buyer
"I go to her office—she fits me in between meetings and her manicurist."
        — Eli, messenger

Q. Are your doing it as often as you should?
A. The national average for couples who have been together three or more years is 3.8 times weekly, which compares rather favorably with the figures for Panama (2.6), Finland (2.3) and North Korea (.8). Newlyweds have the highest frequency rate (14.7) times weekly, slightly more if it's a first marriage); next, newly divorced lawyers (10.9 times weekly) and, finally, residents of trailer parks not hooked up to cable TV (9.4 times per week).

Pillow Talk
Lover's Leap. 1. A cliff, ledge or other high place from which depressed lovers jump. (Lovers who are afraid of heights may use a chair.) 2. Any passion emergency in which an athletic person, in one single motion, makes a house call by springing from his or her bed to that of a lover who's in dire need of sex.

Tip For Vacationing Lovers
Sex: Don't leave home without it.

From a Lover's Scrapbook: Part I
How others preserve those special memories.
"Pressed the petals from the first flower my lover gave me into a book of love sonnets."
        — Audrey, illustrator

"Wore a throw rug from the chest hair my lover kept shedding on that first hot summer night."

— Karen, beautician

"Incorporated all the messages she left on my answering machine into my first novel."

— Sam, being sued

Anxiety and Lovemaking

Research shows that

Each time:	From your life, subtract:
Your lover can't explain where she's been for the past 3 days	4 minutes
But she suddenly has a terrific tan	30 minutes
You discover a suspicious credit-card receipt	7 minutes
You find strange lipstick marks on your lover's:	
Shirt collar	10 minutes
Neck	40 minutes

Did You Know?

Having sex at bedtime* is the perfect all-natural substitute for:
• A fatty midnight snack (like hot milk or pork chops).
• A possibly addictive sleeping pill.
• Reading a trashy novel that, unlike sex, doesn't improve your mind.
• Wearing a night repair gel.
• Going to bed alone.
• A nightcap.
*It will also improve the quality of your dreams.

Above and Beyond the Call of Duty: Part I

Five erogenous zones for the adventurous lover:
1. Hospital
2. No parking
3. No loading
4. No standing
5. "Oh!" zone

Sexual Demerits: Part II

Host infractions.

Violation	Demerits Earned
Lumpy mattress	12
Narrow bed	17
With squeaky springs	8
No mirror on ceiling	10
Wrong wine (the rule: red with swarthy lovers, white with all the rest)	22
Disgusting aphrodisiac (macaroni-and-cheese casserole)	30
Unearned headache	18

Summer Beauty Tip

Avoiding the sun and making love indoors:
Helps the skin retain moisture longer.
Protects the skin against damaging ultra-violet rays.
Prevents sweat from being released into the ozone layer.
Saves the price of a new bathing suit.

Health Tip for Lovers

If your lover's on top, and wearing pearls, it's a good idea to safeguard sensitive eyes by wearing protective eyewear.

Spelling Bee for Lovers

G-R-E-A-T S-E-X spells relief from:

• Migraines.
• Insomnia (and enduring those late-night infomercials).
• Constantly calling friends to see if they want to have dinner.
• Listening to them say no.
• The haunting fear that your face-lift was in vain.
• Scary dreams.
• Another night of
• TV dinners
• *Night Line.*

Our National Pastime

Acting on your sexual urges is normal and healthy unless it in-volves:

The stranger in front of you at the cash machine.
The lifeguard.
The au pair.
An appearance on a talk show.
Our national security.

The Dieter's Guide to Weight Loss During Sex

Activity	Calories Burned
Finally discovering lover's:	
"G" spot	46
"Gee!" spot	255

"Not Tonight, Dear"

Don't feel quite up to it? Ease feelings of rejection by offering your lover some equally erotic alternatives:
• A hot toddy
• A cold shower
• Warm milk
• An intense game of Scrabble
• A bedtime story
• A rain check
• Fig Newtons
• A surrogate

Great News for Plant-Loving Lovers

The right sexual partner can turn into a vegetable.

From Our Lover's Glossary

Traveling Companion. A partner who, when you fall out of bed during extra-vigorous sex, clings to and stays with you, even if you slide into the kitchen. This eliminates the possibility that sexual activity might be interrupted.

Lover No-Nos

1. Talking in your sleep about past loves (unless it's a nightmare).
2. Turning on TV and withholding sex until they announce the baseball score.
3. Replying "Whose?" when your partner holds you close and whispers, "Do you like children?"

4. Interrupting sex to replenish the bird feeder.
5. Replying "Have to win a bet" when asked by an amazed partner, "How do you last so long?"
6. Runny eggs.

Family Values and Sex
After three hours of fantastic lovemaking ("He made me feel the way I've never felt before," was the way one woman* put it), 52% of agnostic lovers and 27% of atheistic lovers were willing to concede that a Higher Power might exist.
*Her previous partners were Conservatives.

MONTHLY QUALITY OF LIFE® CHECKUP

We did it 5 times____   15 times____   22 times____
Too embarrassed to say____

• Favorite position:
Customary: Man on top, woman on bottom____
Working couple: Man on bottom, woman trying to see the time____
Aerobic: Both on top____
• Favorite locations:
Bed____
Jacuzzi____
Patio____
Kitchen____ (bonus point if sex makes refrigerator magnets clatter to floor)
Mud room____
• Which of the following best describes how you felt after sex:
Pleasantly tired____
Kind of floaty____
Like a beached whale____
All wet and sweaty____
Wondering where my contact lens went____
Delightfully sinful____
Delightfully sticky____

Signed_____

Witnessed_____

JULY

•Erotic goal for July
1. Make more time for erotic pleasures
2. Learn to speed read sex manual

The favorite month of patriotic lovers since, with the right partner, it is possible to create fireworks in the bedroom without violating local ordinances. ("I was cleaning my husband and he went off," claimed one startled woman when authorities came to investigate.) A word of caution, however: there may be couples who suddenly find themselves indifferent to sex, due to a condition known as "Independence Day Jitters," an affliction caused by eating improperly-cooked food at July Fourth picnics. A man in Oswego, NY, after eating undercooked meat at a neighbor's barbecue, suffered from what the Center for Disease Control referred to as "Hamburger patty-related erectile difficulties," rendering him incapable of having sex unless he clutched a seeded bun. And a bride in Detroit, after partaking of egg salad left out in the sun, was unable to engage in connubial bliss without a laxative.*

Medical note: In rare instances, the onset of food poisoning caused by eating, say, undercooked hot dogs, can be reversed during a #9 climax (Both partners experience and "out of body" orgasm and suddenly find themselves in the automotive-supply department of a Walmart).

Official aphrodisiacs of the Month:
Deviled ham and pound cake

*Use only as directed.

What I Did For Sex

"Made wild, passionate love in a hot-air balloon. We almost got carried away."

    – Scott Winters, bank examiner

Midyear Review

Tear out and send to lover

How Am I Doing?	Excellent	Good	Fair
Friendliness of service	___	___	___
Speed of service	___	___	___
Quality of service	___	___	___
Quantity of service	___	___	___
Appearance	___	___	___
Value for money	___	___	___

You see me because I'm:

___ Fun to be with ___ A sex object ___ Both

Traveler's Advisory

Nationality	Outstanding
Italian	Warm-blooded
Spanish	Hot-blooded
French	Take their time
British	Take a bit too much time
Japanese	Attention to detail
German	On-time performance
Swedish	Extra-long nights
Swiss	The peaks
Austrian	The valleys

Gem of the Month

Rubies to that jewel of a lover who:
• You can always count on for great suggestions, especially
1. "Buy low, sell high."
2. "A little more to the left."
3. "Let's change positions."
• Is sweet (gently removes your headphones before whispering sweet nothings in your ear).
• Never forgets to celebrate

1. Your birthday.
2. Each time you lose your virginity.

Accuracy Tip
When your partner's lovemaking technique drives you out of your mind and up a wall, use an approved hi-tech sex toy, like a radar gun, to determine if he's speeding.

Midyear Satisfaction Questionnaire
Detach and present to partner
1. How happy are you with our sex life?
___ecstatic ___reasonably content ___wish I didn't have to beg so much ___what sex life?
2. What's the nicest thing about making love with me?
___you're always up for anything ___those barking sounds during climax ___ our new king-size bed ___you're so much more skillful than my ex ___service with a smile
3. Is there anything you'd change?
___positions ___our mating time ___the sheets
4. To what do you attribute our blissful sex life?
___your cooking ___luck ___chemistry ___I'm hardly ever home

What Causes First-Time Jitters: Part I

Him	Her
"Will her cat attack my back?"	"Will his dog maul my purse?"
"Do my shorts have that tattered look?"	"Does my bra have that lived-in look?"
"Why didn't I start my diet sooner?"	"Why didn't he start his diet sooner?"

Pillow Talk
Automated Teller. A lover, usually in the banking industry who, during sex, mechanically repeats the same thing over and over again. Phrases often used if sex is:
Good: *"Your deposit's safe."*
Very good: *"Increase credit line."*
Great: *"I love banking by male."*

Great Moments In Outdoor Sex

"Making love under the stars."
> – Henry and Arlene, space shuttle astronauts

"Making love under a tree."
> – Holly and Wilbur, mom and pop lumberjacks

"Making love under a Bonsai tree."
> – Leda and Chuck, pygmies

Summer Lovemaking

"After getting back from the beach, if we both feel sexual, my boyfriend and I go into the bedroom, stand in front of the full-length mirror and hold a swimsuit contest. The one who removes theirs first wins."
> – Candy, starlet

What I Did For Love

"Took him to a tailor. I couldn't let that gorgeous build go to waste."
> – Jessica, wealthy divorcée

"Six years. She swore we'd never get caught."
> – Chuck, embezzler

"Coached her son's Little League team. She rewarded me whenever they won."
> – Bernie, stockbroker

"Nothing. I'm still waiting for the right one to come along."
> – Cynthia, therapist

Five Reasons to Laugh During Sex

1. She's tickling you.
2. You'd better because she told a joke and she's your boss.
3. He can't get his bicycle pants off.
4. He's eating rum-raisin ice cream ... from your navel.
5. Everybody thinks you're still just friends.

Pillow Talk

The purr. A lovemaking-related sound, often mistaken for an idling refrigerator motor, emitted by contented lovers to indicate the presence of animal magnetism.

What Do the Professionals Do?
The Problem
Whenever I'm on top, my head hits the hanging plant above the bed.
The Solution
1. Wear a ski cap.
2. Redecorate.
3. Lower the head.

From Our Book of Sexual Records
Highest IQ ever measured on a lover: With no medical training whatsoever, and using only an abacus, Ernie M. of Grand Rapids, Michigan, determined that the odds of getting his partner pregnant while making love in the back-to-back position would be 1 in 649,734,099.

After-Sex Etiquette
A shrug is never an appropriate response when your lover asks, "Was it good for you?"
*Three exceptions: 1. You're still speechless from a Level 6 climax (911 calls you). 2. You're trying to be mysterious. 3. You speak body language.

Midyear Satisfaction Survey
Detach and send to spouse, lover or both
1. How satisfied are you with our love life? If it got any better:
___we'd never get out of bed ___I'd believe in a Higher Power ___I'd never even touch the TV clicker
2. What do you most enjoy when we make love?
___the way the springs creak ___the way my eyes light up when you say, "Roll over, it's your turn." ___the view ___the position
3. What is our biggest sexual problem?
___finding enough time for lovemaking ___too few hours in the night ___that stupid march music
4. To what do you attribute our happy sex life?
___we work at it ___luck ___the kids finally have their own apartment

The Dangers of Excess

Researchers suggest that after too many climaxes (23) within an eight-hour period, 77% of all lovers:
- Are unable to recall their Social Security number.
- Bear a striking resemblance to their passport photo.
- Could care less about resuming trade relations with Cuba.
- Experience dizziness if they stand too quickly.
- Can't wait to do it again.

Need Motivation?

Seven wholesale and non-lustful reasons for having sex:
1. To generate warmth
2. Marital obligation
3. Cellulite control
4. Humanitarianism
5. Biological clock ticking
6. Patriotism
7. Weight control (considered a definitive Sunday morning brunch substitute)

Tips for Seagoing Lovers

Sex on a barge can make you sluggish.
Sex on a raft can make you feel intimate.
Sex on a yacht can make you list.
Sex in a canoe can make you tipsy.

How to Make Your Lover See Fireworks

If you:	Lover will see:
Slowly undress lover while nibbling vital erogenous zones	Roman candles
Gently cuddle against lover and whisper sweet nothings into either ear	Rockets
Perform any lovemaking act that's labor intensive	Sparklers
Cause lover to experience a grade-4 climax (one that sets off your home-security device)	Pinwheels

Eight Reasons to Be Ecstatic During Sex

1. You're with your favorite lover.
2. So is your lover.
3. The practice is making you perfect.
4. Your sunburn doesn't hurt.
5. You're burning off your lunch (•7.50 worth of Carvel).
6. The night is still young.
7. You could be at work.
8. The fireworks.

A Perfect Day for Fireworks

If you:	Lover (theoretically) will see:
Gently bite your lover's ear.	Sparklers.
Tell your lover to lie back while you do wondrous things with your hands.	A cherry bomb.
Spend 15 minutes rubbing your lover's feet with exotic oils (like Valvoline).	Rockets.
Respond generously when your lover asks, "Ready for more?"	Pinwheels
Take a shower together.	A flasher.

Terms of Endearment

Use:	When you:
"Darling"	Want your lover to do something extraordinary for you during sex, as in, "Please don't fall asleep yet, Darling."
"Baby"	Feel extra-loving toward your partner as in, "That was so nice, Baby."
"Sweetheart"	Can't recall your partner's name.
"Babykins"	Regress.

Advice for Happily Married Couples
A weekend away from children can cause bedsores.

The Satisfying Lover
Is one who, no matter how:
• Energetic the lovemaking, can still go dancing afterwards.
• Cramped the bed, can still turn in a stellar performance.
• Demanding the partner:
a. Does not cry out for warm milk
b. Does cry out.

Communication Tip
Things often said by really hot lovers.
During Sex:
"What fireworks!"
After Sex
"Your fire works!"

The Bedside Eater: Part I
Professional lovers reveal their favorite during-sex foods.
"Spaghetti with Red Clam Sauce. It gives me the strength to go on...and on...and on."
       – Jessica, tour guide and temptress
"Oysters Rockefeller. It gives me the strength to keep up with a woman who can go on...and on...and on."
       – Barry, ironworker

Air Traveler's Advisory
Six reasons to have sex aloft.
1. On any flight over two hours, it's a lovely way to pass the time.
2. It'll take your mind off the inferior:
• Inflight movie.
• Food.
3. You automatically earn bonus miles.
4. With the right partner, it's like getting a free seat upgrade.
5. If you make love in the lavatory, it's the preferred way to fly standup.
6. You won't miss your connection.

Celibacy Alert

Our eight official excuses for declining sex.
1. Wife wearing rollers (afraid they'll pick up local FM station).
2. Too much to drink.
3. Not enough to drink.
4. Saving yourself for a) marriage or b) when you reach the motel.
5. Punishing partner for making you a golf widow.
6. Moaning will break your vow of silence.
7. Astrologer forbade it.
8. You'll hate yourself in the morning.

Your Stress Quotient

Event	Degree of Stress
(Scale to 500)	
You're at your new lover's place and:	
The bathroom door doesn't lock	11
It locks but from the outside	146
No toilet paper	49
Some toilet paper (4 sheets left)	48
You're afraid to ask for more	100
The toilet won't flush	49
It does, and begins to overflow	278
Leading you to believe that you won't create a good impression	500

The Language of Botany: Part II

To a lover who:	Send:
Instead of a Solarflex, uses you to achieve total fitness	Forget-me-nots
Has sex with you just for your body	Daisies
Has sex with you for your mind	A shrub
Has sex with you for your mind *and* your body	A new lawn

Achieving Climax

If you're	Level of difficulty
Aroused	1
Distracted by:	
A special request	3
Gremlins	7
Heartburn	10
Slightly bored with partner	5
Stalled in your present job	9
On a conference call	15

Tip for Commuting Lovers

No matter how much fun it is to drive to work, morning sex can make it even better because:

• It gives you something to think about in bumper-to-bumper traffic.

• It gives you something to talk about if you car pool.

• It gives you something to sing about if your radio doesn't work.

During-Sex Communication: Part I

Speaking may break the spell. Shrugging your shoulders is ambivalent. Instead we recommend our exclusive Tap System. (Affix this page to your headboard.)

Number of taps on lover's head	Translation
1	"That's getting me very hot."
3	"That's the spot!"
4	"'O Sole Mio'" (Italian sex only)
5	"'Be My Love'" (all other sex)
7	"Are we still on for Aruba?"
$9^1/_2$	Mixed message.

Not to Worry

Fertility experts suggest that having sex only for the purpose of reproduction doesn't make the act less pleasurable unless:

• You try more than 22 times a week.

• You're not being paid union scale.

• The test tube's too small.

Sex Without Tears

To prevent confusion, never try to whisper sweet nothings into both ears at once.

> ## Tip Regarding Ultra-Marathon Lovemaking
> It is in the sixth hour of sex that you may begin to hear a strange chirping sound. Not to work...it may only be you either begging for mercy or trying to fly.

An Expert Lover's Eight Secret Weapons

1. Flowers
2. The right cologne
3. Perfect hushpuppies
4. Moonlight
5. Charm
6. Technique
7. Patience
8. Baser instincts

Sex Poll #19

Lovers divulge the source of their during-sex wet spot.

"Early morning dew. We love the great outdoors."
> – Cheryl and Frankie, campers

"A combination of hormones. Mine are flowing, my boyfriend's are raging. We never get into bed without a set of oars."
> – Desiree, homecoming queen

"The Amazon. Next time we move our sleeping bag inland."
> – Magda and Zorro, botanists, the rain forest

"An Amazon. That's why I married her."
> – Rodney, flautist

The Lover's Herb Garden: Part I

Remedies for the dysfunctional partner:

If Partner	Appropriate Herb
Becomes violently ill when you ask how he feels about S&M.	Queen of the Meadow or Marshmallow.
Embarrassed to show you what feels good (even with the lights off).	Rose Hips or Ginseng.
Doesn't get excited when you put on high heels and a revealing chemise.	Blessed Thistle or Poke Weed.
Is not in the mood.	Necklace.

Thought for Tonight

When beginning a new relationship, observe a moment of silence to honor the memory of a previous lover who taught you enough, in and out of bed, to make your present lover fall in love with you.

Advice for Cautious Lovers

Four warning signs of sexual enfeeblement:
1. Decreased aversion to airline food
2. Equipment failure
3. Early retirement
4. Computer worship

A Lover's Guarantee

Absolute satisfaction or your

Cards___	Flowers___	Candy___
Wine___	Ring___	Jewelry___
Books___	Kitchen utensils___	
Love letters___	Stuffed animals___	Photos___
Plants___	Recipes___	Phone number___

cheerfully returned. (Big-ticket items to be negotiated.)

The Enlightened Lover

With the right woman, nearly any man can be good in bed. With the wrong woman, he may be great.*

     – The Suburban Sex Manual

*Or improve significantly.

Good News for Vain Lovers

Skin blemishes? Our consulting dermatologist suggests a pleasant way to camouflage them completely: During sex, cover them either with (a) makeup or (b) your partner or (c) a sleeping mask.

Keys to a Golden Sex Life After 65

1. Keep your retirement plans a secret from your children.
2. Change the oil regularly on your Winnebago.

Suburban Sex: Part I

Romance tip for commuting wives.

When, in the evening, he greets you at the door wearing only

1. Black high heels
2. A demi-bra
3. A thong bikini
4. A glass of champagne
5. A smile

a) don't panic but b) do check the house number.

The Busy Lover

Pressed for time? The following are sex-compatible activities.

1. Flossing (use lover's hair for greater intimacy).
2. Talking on the phone (cordless provides the most flexibility).
3. Listening to a motivational tape.
4. Working out (a Best Bet if your lover cooperates).
5. Networking (exchange recipes and/or business cards).
6. Ordering in (person whose mouth is *not* busy does ordering).

What We Did for Sex

"We love Italian food, so we tried the pasta position (al dente). Afterward, we both felt like wet noodles."

     – Gino and Gina, honeymooners

Adventures In Love

Great romantic getaways (all lover-tested):

Money No Object	On a Budget
Venice	Any local canal
Cannes	A local motel with hourly rates
The Pyramids	The Poconos
The Pampas, Argentina	Casper, Wyoming
Fiji Islands	Niagara Falls
Bermuda	Your hot tub
Monte Carlo	Atlantic City
A riverbank, the Nile, Egypt	A savings bank, Enid, Oklahoma

A Lover's Dilemma

Q. Between business trips, tennis lessons, health club visits, golf, night school, Little League coaching, volunteer work, the car pool and my needlepoint, our sex life consists of "rain checks" left on each other's pillow. As of this writing, we haven't made love since May 1992. Any suggestions?

A. It's not the frequency but, rather, the quality of sex that counts. Couples who have only so-so sex nine times weekly (only two hours per encounter) may be less satisfied than the couple who enjoys quality sex monthly or once a year, on their anniversary. Stop berating yourselves.

The Enlightened Lover

Secret formula of the great lover-mathematicians:

$$\frac{\text{NMx (size of bed)}}{\text{"Ohhhhhhhhhhh"}} = \text{●●●●●●●●●●●●●●●●●●●}*$$

*The number of minutes you have sex multiplied by the size of the bed in square inches divided by the total number of orgasms experienced by you and your lover will give you a winning lottery number.

Suburban Sex: Part II

Romance tip for commuting husbands.

When, in the evening, she greets you at the door wearing only

1. Black high heels
2. A Demi-bra

3. A thong bikini
4. A glass of champagne
5. A smile
do not ask, "Is the lady of the house in?"

Caution
Three major warning signs of too much sex:
1. Guilt
2. Fitness
3. Smiling at strangers

The Ideal Traveling Companion
Is a lover who:
• Doesn't need lots of rest stops.
• Can read a map.
• Enjoys getting lost.
• Has an all-terrain body (can make love at campsites).
• Ignores early checkout times.
• Doesn't need a map to identify points of interest.
• Doesn't need a compass to determine position.

Tip for a Lonely Night
Our technical adviser says that one pint of ice cream makes the perfect lover substitute. It's smooth, creamy and melts when warmed. (For those with a cholesterol problem, frozen yogurt will work, but not as well, unless you're partial to slender lovers.)

One Reason for First Night Jitters
"The more I drank, the uglier he got. I mean, hey, I thought it was supposed to be the other way around."
        — Taffy, economist

Sin Taxes for 1995: Part I
The official Congressional guide.
Sin Tax
Smoking
Before sex: As a foreplay substitute $8.40
During sex: To mask the smell of garlic $7.54

352

To enhance the sexual experience	$4.54
To remind you of an old flame	$1.00
After sex: To relax	$2.40
Peer pressure	$2.50
As a substitute for afterglow	$8.50

Sexual Points on Your Marriage License: Part II
(The more serious the violation, the more points.)

Violation	Points
Coming to bed with wet hair	27
Hogging the quilt:	
In the summer	9
In the winter	45
Failure to:	
Communicate	21
Use Binaca	31
Use Odor Eaters	49

Try Something Different Tonight
Be inventive. At the height of ecstasy, whisper in your lover's ear:
"Darling, I'm getting out of breath, may I borrow some of yours?"

The Candid Lover: Part II
Should you tell a new partner everything?

If you've had:	Tell	Let partner guess
A face-lift		X
Eyelids done	X	
A hair transplant:		
Just one	X	
Many		X
Suction lipectomy		X
Chemical peel	X	
A tummy tuck		X
A sex-change operation		X

Senior Sex
Often heard in the better retirement communities after especially wonderful lovemaking:
"I want you to be the grandmother of my children."

Mid-Year Satisfaction Survey

Detach and send to spouse or lover

1. Over all, how satisfied are you with my performance?
___ Very satisfied   ___ Satisfied   ___ Dissatisfied
___ Starting to answer personal ads

2. Which of my talents do you consider most outstanding?
___ Those stress-relieving back rubs
___ The way I wake you up in the morning (neck nibbles)
___ My minestrone

3. How do you think we can improve our sex life?
___ Have more of it ___ Have a lot more of it___ At least try it once in a while ___ Stop watching game shows

From Our Lover's Glossary

Unwelcome sexual advance. One that occurs at an inappropriate moment such as while the recipient is:
• Performing open heart surgery
• Undergoing open heart surgery
• Running to catch a bus
• Leaving for her honeymoon
• Sky diving
• Interviewing for a job
• Talking to a divorce lawyer

Safe Sex

• Flirting
• Tasting each other's soup
• Cutting each other's steak
• Playing footsies under the table
• Dancing for hours to Tony Bennett
• Rubbing her back with sun-tan lotion
• Watching the seals mate at the zoo
• Asking him to come over and help you move a sofa
• Strolling along a moonlit beach discussing Schopenhauer
• Just saying "Maybe"

The Bedside Eater
Aphrodisiac of the Day
Fettucine with lobster, garlic and parsley sauce (if there's a weight problem, parsley may be omitted)
Erotic Effect
Perks up and has an ever so slightly warming effect upon the southern erogenous zones
Aphrodisiac of the Night
A doggie bag
Erotic Effect
Lights a fire under frosty lovers, enables quicker activation of the fondle reflex, and permits wild lovemaking even with the gardener watching

The Bedside Eater
Aphrodisiac of the Morning
Two eggs, any style, with hash browns, toast and coffee (no substitutions).
Erotic effect
Raises the erogenous zones to see level, thus rendering them findable during lovemaking at dawn
Aphrodisiac of the Evening
Garlic chicken with lemon, rosemary and pepper.
Erotic Effect
Takes lover's breath away if you can't

A Lover's Alternatives
Our unregistered dietitian tells us that two hours of sex with a highly skilled lover will have the same weight-loss effect as:
- 3 hours of running
- 4 hours of walking
- 1 afternoon on a StairMaster
- 1 week on a high-protein, low-fat diet
- 50 laps in an olympic-size pool
- 23 holes of golf
- 3 hours of sex with a lover of average skills

Trade Secret

Too much of a good thing? Your lover's about to go into ecstasy overdose if he or she:

• Begins to wave a little white flag of truce, feebly.
• Has an erogenous zone that's actually pulsating.
• Is demanding overtime
• Is promising to put you through grad school.
• Has lost contact with reality (reaches out and tries to touch you while you're in the kitchen getting a snack.)

Not Sure About Last Night?

In the morning

Love yourself if
It felt so right.
You don't know what came over you.
You just couldn't say "no."
There was so much chemistry.
You can't resist a woman out of uniform.

Hate yourself if
It felt sooooo right.
You know very well what came over you.
Just couldn't say "no more."
There was so much champagne.
You can't resist a man in uniform.

Relationship Rules of Thumb

If you have:	Make him or her a:
Fantastic sex with someone with whom you have nothing in common	Lover (or personal trainer).
Ordinary sex with someone with whom you have everything in common	Friendly lover.
Extraordinary sex with someone with whom you have everything in common	Spouse.

The Bedside Explorer: Part II

An erotic adventure for the daring lover.
Expedition 2. (Linda's Descent)
Recommended equipment: fingertips, baby oil, pedometer
Place lover on stomach (not yours). Start behind the neck. Begin strolling with your fingers in a southeasterly direction. Tarry at the

waist. Anything of interest? Proceed farther. Traipse lightly over the buttocks. Note how callipygian. Return to base camp.

Good News for Dieting Lovers
In theory, great sex should leave you too exhausted to:
1. Walk all the way to the kitchen for a midnight snack.
2. Tear open a flavor-sealed bag of potato chips with your bare hands.

The Six Healthiest Things About Good Sex
1. It exercises the heart.
2. It relieves stress.
3. It clears up the skin.
4. It improves stamina and endurance.
5. It keeps the weight down.
6. It's one of the few ways to cook without using oil.

From a Lover's Scrapbook: Part II
More of how others preserve those special memories.
"Keep a bottle of her perfume under my pillow. When I'm feeling really nostalgic, I take a sip."
    – David, financial planner
"When we begin to make love, I start the recorder that's under the bed. Then I play the tape when there's nothing good on TV."
    – Karla, welder
"Framed the guest towel he used."
    – Peggy, flight attendant

Visiting Your Lover? Part I
Six things never to leave home without.
1. Credit card: if sex is good, celebrate by taking her out to dinner.
2. Filofax: something to thumb through if sex is not so good.
3. Booties: should one of you get cold feet.
4. Paperback: to read if your partner habitually dozes off directly after (or before) lovemaking.
5. Ziploc bag: to keep your cookies fresh.
6. A chaperone: to help you fight temptation.

The Tactical Partner

Five things never to say to a (male) partner who is having erectile difficulties.

1. "Better luck next time."
2. "Gosh, maybe I broke it."
3. "That's okay, I'll start without you."
4. "I'm every inch (oops, sorry) a lady."
5. "Hello, Mr. Doubtfire."

One thing you may say: "Let's try it anyway."

The Traveling Lover

Camper maintenance tips for the sexually active:

• Change the oil every 3,000 miles.
• Change the air in the tires every 1,000 miles.
• Change the sheets every 500 miles.

Ten Things to Be Happy About During Sex

• The challenge.
• The guests aren't here yet.
• You could be at work.
• The nightlife.
• The kids are at camp.
• Being asked, "How do you last so long?"
• Not really knowing.
• It's so affordable.
• The first two hours.
• Those last five minutes.

The Inquiring Lover

Question asked after:

Good Sex

Where did the time go?

Great Sex

Where did my earrings go?*

*After an out-of-body orgasm (superb sex only), the question "Where did *you* go? is not unusual.

Common Lovemaking Difficulties

The Problem:	The Solution:
He makes love like a tank in battle.	Stop reminding him of Desert Storm
Our love life is getting monotonous.	During climax, change his facial expression.
My partner doesn't know what I like and I'm too shy to ask.	Use flash cards or show him your press clippings.
He doesn't satisfy me during intercourse.	As long as he satisfies you during sex.

Health-Care Advisory

When sex in the morning leaves you too relaxed to...
• Open your eyes
• Get out of bed and greet the day
• Open the closet and select an outfit
• Face the thought of commuting
• Do an honest day's work
...it's permissible to call in sick.

Just So You Know

Three questions to ask a super-energetic lover who a) can't get enough of you and b) is wearing you out.
1. "Has it been that long?"
2. "Are you always like this when your team wins?"
3. "Is it me or the coffee?"

The Dieter's Guide to Weight Loss During Sex

Activity	Calories Burned
Finally telling your lover about your past:	
Edited	27
Unedited	145
If your past is rated:	
G	35
PG	61
R	143
X	466

Lovemaking Tips: Part II

To a Lover Who:	Suggested Gratuity
Never teases when you make lots of noise.	$2.00
Nor teases when you're inarticulate.	$3.00
Is low-maintenance (brings own champagne and massage oil).	$2.25
Is supportive (lip-syncs your moans).	$1.25
Never says, "Start without me."	$10.00

Midyear Review

The considerate lover is one who never:
• Yawns during sex without covering his or her mouth.
• Makes love like a moose in heat.
• Falls asleep until sex is over (or nearly over).
• Is too tired to make love.
• Needs winding.
• Leaves you unsatisfied.
• Rushes into sex.
• Rushes out of it, either.

The Responsive Lover

Six non-threatening answers when a jealous partner asks, "Why are you so good?"
1. "I studied U.S. Government printing office publication #567 entitled, *Lord, It's Been So Long.*"
2. "You inspire me to greatness." (Works only if said with a straight face.)
3. "I went to the right boarding school."
4. "It...it...just comes to me."
5. "I watch soaps a lot."
6. "Because I'm so bad."

The Bedside Adviser

Make a late-night phone call to an ex-lover only if:
1. He or she can't trace the call.
2. The rates are cheaper.
3. You broke up amicably.
4. You're lonely.
5. You're having trouble getting to sleep.
6. You're certain your current lover's fast asleep.

The Inquiring Lover

What is your favorite form of birth control?

"Avoiding temptation. I date only women I meet through personal ads."

> – John, beadle

"Celibacy. I date eunuchs."

> – Claudia, recovering sex addict

"Phone sex."

> – Nina, stockbroker

"I don't tell them my last name."

> – Terry, parking lot attendant

Sex Al Fresco: Part I

A favorite outdoor pastime, combining human nature with mother nature. Some comments below from those who indulge.

Advantages	Disadvantages
"Lots of fresh air."	"Clouds of gnats."
"Making love on moss is ever so erotic."	"Ants, they tickle."
"Being at one with the birds and the bees."	"Gawking crows."
"Twinkling stars intensify orgasm."	"Weather may turn on you."
"No early checkout time."	"Game warden demanding permit."

The Enlightened Lover

The first time you make love on your lunch hour, be prepared.

If:	Bring your own:
You have very little time.	Lunch.
It's a cheap motel.	Television.
If it's a seedy motel.	Towel.
It's spur-of-the-moment.	Lover.
You're not sure of the outcome.	Car.

The Language of Flowers: Part VI

To the lover who:	Send:
Figures out what you like during sex	Cosmos
Took the initiative during sex	Impatiens
Made you smile in your sleep	Sunflowers
Can't stay angry	Hollyhocks
Can't stay	Weeds

From Our Lover's Glossary

Exhaust fumes. An after-sex haze, often mistaken for smog (especially in Los Angeles), that hovers in the air space above exhausted lovers who have engaged in three or more hours of nonstop sex. Researchers think that such haze, although nonpolluting, may be caused by heavy breathing.

The Joy of Loving

Statement uttered by a well-known philosopher-lover after experiencing great lovemaking for the first time in eight months:
I had sex, therefore I am...and smiling."

Sex-Life Improvers

1. The kids are away at a) summer camp or b) college or c) the Peace Corps.
2. A fireplace.
3. Nat King Cole tapes.
4. A mini-cam.*
5. Great stamina.
6. Ignoring the doorbell.
*Also considered a teaching aid if used to make a sex-help video.

Q. How soon after sex is it safe to fall asleep?

A. The more you've satisfied your lover, the quicker you may doze off. If you don't want to offend, see below:

Post-Orgasmic State of Lover	You May Fall Asleep in:
Smile on face	10 minutes
Song on lips	5 minutes
Trance	1 minute
Babbling Yiddish proverbs	30 seconds

Advice for Busy Lovers

Pressed for time? Save precious minutes by:

- Removing clothes *before* you see each other.
- Showering together.
- Omitting foreplay.
- Emitting shorter moans.

Reminder for the Open Road

When making love in your ear, if you and your lover truly want the sky to be the limit, don't forget to open the sunroof. (It will also help you tan more evenly.)

Not-Too-Bright Moment in Sex

"I thought permitting an obese but cuddly partner to lie on top of me during lovemaking was what they meant by carbohydrate loading."

– Regina, marathoner

Exciting Destinations

A mini-guide to exotic romance.

For the	Visit
View	Nepal
Beer	Australia
Beaches	Tahiti
Shopping	Hong Kong
Intimacy (and castles)	Luxembourg
Wine	France
Women*	Italy
Song	Wales

*For the men: a tie between Spain and Texas.

Stolen Sexual Moments

Our favorite locations.

Easy	Takes Courage
The beach at Waikiki	The beach on a surfboard
Last row of a movie theater	Last row of a roller coaster
Your bedroom, kids in college	Your bedroom, kids in the family room
Your boss's office, door locked	Your boss's office, your boss knocking on the door
In the shower	Under Niagara Falls

What I Did For Love

"Changed my religion."
(What I did for sex? Changed my will.)
> — Ernesto Flynn, tennis instructor

Reminder

When you make love indoors, the ceiling's the limit.
When you make love outdoors, the sky's the limit.

Sexual Rule of Thumb

A watched lover never boils.*
*Exception: exhibitionists.

What Do You Do After Sex?

"Tell the neighbors in our hallway to go back inside, we were just rehearsing a play."
> — Svetlova, hairdresser

"I don't know, I'm usually asleep."
> — Greg, plumber

"Take photos of the damage for the insurance company. We're very lusty lovers."
> — Hans and Greta, acrobats

Question Often Asked After Sex

"What do you do for an encore?"
"Give him my autograph (unless he's a producer, then I give him my heart and soul, and head sheet)."
> — Cassandra, starlet

"Make my special buttermilk-raspberry waffles (unless we make love in the evening, then it's my spring lamb with fresh-mint vinaigretteCnothing's too good for my landlady)."
— Rick, copywriter
"Sing 'Stardust' (but only if I've gotten my second wind and my partner's an astronaut)."
— Donald, interior decorator
"Try again if the applause was sufficient."
— Imelda, beauty contestant

Point to Ponder
After two hours of fervent lovemaking, most lovers, if they're still turned on to each other, exhibit a shockingly depraved indifference to:
- The issue of school prayer.
- Recycling.
- Whether they have adequate life insurance.
- Politics.
- Reducing the deficit.
- A balanced a) budget and b) diet.
- Our immigration policy.
- The condition of the room.

How Often Do You Make Love? Part V
Frequency Rate
9-12 times weekly (honeymooners and world class athletes only)
What It Means
Very healthy love life; still turned on by each other (arousal time, 7.9 seconds), cutting-edge orgasms (an acceptable substitute for afternoon tea). Both partners probably engaged in nondemanding profession such as retirement or civil service.

Sexual Etiquette
No matter how eager to please, the thoughtful lover waits until after sex before asking partner* to fill out a customer satisfaction survey.
*Exception: Can be filled out during sex if partner knows shorthand.

An Insufficiently Satisfying Sex Life?

In case you can't tell the indicators:
- Whining
- Joining coalitions
- Dry skin
- an over-abundant interest in sports
- Injudicious consumption of ice cream
- A feeling of being singled out by fate
- Watching too much television
- Frequent colds (sex contains vitamin C)
- A single bed

Trouble Shooting

What to do if your partner isn't working properly, and before calling customer service:

1. Read the instructions.
2. Shake him.
3. If no response, check the equipment. Is anything broken? Bent? Frayed?
4. Is he experiencing a power outage from too much sex? (Indicator: speckled bands across the face). If so, install either a pacemaker or medicate with chicken à la king.
5. Or perhaps you just forgot to plug him in.

From Our Lover's Glossary

Sex Patch. An object worn on the arm which enables one to indulge in ultra-safe sex without a partner. Throughout the day the patch lets the wearer experience a series of time-released orgasms that not only prevent feelings of sexual deprival, but enable an executive to get through a tedious business meeting with a grin on his or her face.*
*And some good ideas to contribute.

Great Moments in Afterplay

"Trying to lift him off me without waking him. He's such a light sleeper."
    – Gail, clinical psychologist
"Carefully wiping my fingerprints off my partner. He's married."
    – Cyndi, chiropractor

"Trying to guess where my loafers landed when I kicked them off."
– Bernie, bookseller
"Untying him."
– Jane, gunsmith

Maintenance Tip
To keep your partner running smoothly, change the water in your waterbed every 500 miles.

Breaking the Ice: Part I
Some during-sex conversation starters.

Situation	What to Say
In bed.	"Your side or mine?"
Steamy sex makes the room fog up.	"Guess who?"
Onset of a major orgasm.	"Would you mind timing me?"
You're growing speechless.	"Can I see your notes?"
After sex, when you turn the lights on.	"Haven't we met before?"

Midyear Review
Best lover _____ Why? _____
Speed of Service ___ Fair ___ Good ___ Excellent
Have to make an appointment? ___ Yes ___ No ___ Sometimes
Best things about your lover (use back of sheet if you need more room) _____
How have you improved? _____
Fantasy for the next six months _____
Would you tell it to your lover? ___ Yes ___ Better not
Plan to write your memoirs? ___ Yes ___ No

Sexual Points on Your Marriage License: Part II
The more serious the violation, the more points.

Moving Violations	Points
During sex, making an improper turn while changing positions:	
U-turn	4
K-turn	8

367

Speeding during intercourse:

1-5 mph above legal limit	2
6-10 mph above legal limit	3

Failure to yield to a partner demanding:

A coffee break	2
A recommendation	8

Advanced Etiquette for Lovers

Experts do not consider...
• "I've had a better offer."
• "Can I get back to you?"
• "May I bring a date?"
• "Who else is coming?"
• "Why me?"
...ideal responses when a sensitive lover asks for a date.*
*We prefer: "How about a rain check?"

Sex: Some Regional Differences

In	79% of all couples believe that oral sex is
California	The work of the partner.
Utah	The work of the Devil.
Vermont	Work.
Mississippi	Talking about it.
North Carolina	A Shoney's breakfast buffet.

A Guide to Vehicular Sex

Jeep
Advantages
Four-wheel drive provides offroad capabilities and greater privacy. Possible to make love in the middle of a stream.
Disadvantages
Unless lover on top wears a copper derby, tight suspension may cause head injuries when going over rough roads.

Love Poll #9

Responses to the question "How do you feel after a great night of lovemaking?":
- "My usually great tennis serve...well...frankly...stinks."
- "Unable to use a cash machine without assistance."
- "Like purring."
- "Floaty."
- "Like a Cheddar cheese omelet with corned beef hash and French fries."

Lover's Etiquette
When a really special climax sends you to heaven, always leave an address and phone number where you can be reached.

What I Got Because of Great Sex

Great lovers confess.

"Four husbands, a house in Beverly Hills, several lovers, five children, two Lincolns and absolutely no financial worries."
> – Tawny, housewife

"Finally a sponsor."
> – André, immigrant awaiting his green card

"First prize in the swimsuit competition."
> – Elvira, brewmaster

Pre-Arrival Checklist

What to do before your lover arrives.
1. Ice the champagne.
2. Place book of poetry on night table.
3. Light the candles.
4. Draw the shades.
5. Water your plants.
6. Run a bubble bath.
7. Prepare the music. (For extra romance, hire musicians.)
8. Turn on your answering machine (but turn off the volume, you don't want your lover hearing embarrassing messages).
9. Improve the ambianceCrearrange your refrigerator magnets.
10. Suck in.

Intimacy Tip

It's easier to see the soul of a partner who:
1. Is open, honest and communicative.
2. Is secure within himself or herself.
3. Wears a mesh body stocking.
4. Is radioactive.

Reawaken Your Sex Life: Part III

Locations for experienced lovers.

For the Pleasure	For the Challenge
Hammock (canvas)	Hammock (rope)
Ping-pong table	Ping-pong table (net up)
The attic	Your old crib
Top of tooled-leather desk	Top of roll-top desk
Any wet bar	Any salad bar
Clothes closet	Broom closet
Porch glider	Hang glider
Moss	Mulch

The Desert Island Lover

If you could pick just one perfect partner to be stranded with, select one who:
• Looks great in a bathing suit.
• Is not easily distracted when the tide comes in.
• Is always on call.
• Is endlessly inventive.
• Can swim...and surf.
• No longer worries about waking the neighbors.
• Can build a fire by rubbing two bodies together.
• Can make you hear the ocean just by holding him or her up to your ear.

Warm Weather Drinks for Lovers: Part I

Type of drink	Application
Mai tai	Ice-breaker for inhibited lovers
Frozen daiquiri	Makes blind dates dressed in cruisewear more bearable
Piña colada	Courage to make late-night phone calls to former lovers
Bloody Mary	Alternate source of potassium and celery
Martini	Alternate way to make the earth move

One Secret of Marital Bliss

Some love-related statistics. Researchers tell us that couples who make love six to eight times a week report a:

- 45% decrease in arguments over money.
- 58% decrease in arguments over politics.
- 63% decrease in arguments over how to raise their children.
- 70% decrease in arguments over in-laws.
- Major decrease in arguments over investment strategies.
- 91% decrease in arguments over sex.
- 100% increase in being late for social engagements.

The Keys to Great Sex

1. Avoid partners:
- Who begin sex with a flip chart.
- Whose idea of foreplay is feeding their tropical fish.
- Who need glasses to read a sex manual.
- Who need a sex manual.
- Who end sex with a recap.
2. Always screen your calls.

Trust Is ...

- Leaving your diary where he'd be tempted to read it (unless you keep two sets of books).
- Believing that he worked late even though the moment he gets home he 1) offers you flowers then 2) takes a shower.
- Believing that the red blotch on her neck really was made by a low-flying woodpecker.

• Being secure in the knowledge that when she's on a business trip, the reason she doesn't answer her hotel room phone at 1:45 a.m. is because she's in a deep sleep.

• Not locking the bathroom door.

• Hiding the package containing her birthday gift where she can find it.

Love Signs

Horoscope For a Lusty Leo

• *Ruling passion:* doing it till you ferment
• *Ruling body lotion:* whipped cream (or yogurt for Leos into health)
• *Chief sexual asset:* bedroom eyes
• *Governing erogenous zone:* your press-on nails
• *Aphrodisiac of choice:* fresh air
• *Ruling sexual activity:* purring
• *Ideal time for sex:* league night

Is Your Lover Insatiable?

Yes if:

1. On more than one occasion you've been awakened by lovemaking even though:

a. You're a sound sleeper, and

b. So is your lover.

2. To your lover, the phrase "handyman's special" doesn't refer to a house.

3. When getting in bed:

You say	*Your lover says*
"Good night."	"All night."

Love Signs

Horoscope for a Loving Leo:

• *Ruling passion:* spoiling your lover for others
• *Ruling sexual turnoff:* grovelers
• *Chief sexual asset:* a working fireplace
• *Governing erogenous zone:* Paris when it sizzles
• *Aphrodisiacs:* smell of pine needles and new money
• *Ruling sexual activity:* helping the needy
• *Ideal time for sex:* the company picnic

Are You a Jaded Lover?

The warning signs

1. After only 70 minutes of sex, you're wondering what's on television.

2. During sex, you discreetly snack on the crumbs in bed.

3. You keep your eyes closed so you can better concentrate on your career.

4. You prefer the bottom position so you can watch the ceiling fan go round and round.

5. You have sex only so you have something to talk about in the commuter van.

6. Lately, you notice you and your partner always have sex in the same two places:
    1. In the bedroom.
    2. Below the neck.

Love Signs: Leo the Lion

Opposite love sign: An amorous Aquarius. When tired, however, you may substitute a virtuous Virgo.

Outstanding sexual quality: A thick mane of hair that, no matter how wanton the sex, never comes off.

Most attractive physical feature: Four dimpled cheeks.

Ruling sexual turnoff: Partners who rush into sex before your nails dry.

Ruling sexual turn-on: A thorough physical by a dynamite-looking internist.

Ideal place for sex: A Ford Explorer (as long as the driver keeps at least one hand on you).

Love Signs: Leo the Tigress

Most attractive features: Toes and high arches that would satisfy the most demanding foot fetishist.

Turn-on: A partner who looks good in tight leather pants and great when he or she peels them off.

Turn-off: A lover who instantly stops smiling when you ask how he or she feels about kids.

Ideal romantic adventure: Touring the south of France on a bicycle built for two (you and a new lover in each new town).

Favorite sexual fantasy: Making love in an undiscovered gold mine with a partner who just happens to have a pick and shovel.

The Enlightened Lover

A normal, healthy woman can experience as many as 14 quality orgasms in one hour, more if her lover's in the room. A fit male is also capable of achieving multiple orgasms, but not in such quantity; after his fifth in 20 minutes, he will assume he's on NATO maneuvers.

Pillow Talk

Good deed. An act of kindness in which you have sex with your spouse even though:

- You have a) sunburn or b) heartburn.
- Spouse has gained 60 pounds (and not from your cooking).
- You're tired (just had a session with your lover).
- You're exhausted (just went food shopping).
- It would mean perspiring.
- You already have a child.
- It's not your special time.
- It would spoil you (fifth time that day).
- It's not in the pre-nup agreement.

The Well-Compensated Lover; Part I

A tipping guide for the extra-talented partner.

To the lover who	Suggested gratuity
Can give a professional massage	$1.00
Without causing an oil spill	$1.50
Washes your windows without leaving streaks	.50
Is knowledgeable about aphrodisiacs (can open and shred a coconut during sex)	.75
Knows enough to wait until after sex to make the bed	.50
Knows how to remove candle wax from your night table	1.00
Is really great in bed (always helps you, after sex, plan your shopping list)	2.00

374

Tip for the Lonely Lover

When you sit in your bedroom, contemplating your queen-or-king-size bed
You have the right attitude
If you think: "Gee, there's always room for one more."
You have the wrong attitude
If you think: "Gosh I really don't need such a huge bed."

New Age Sex

Strangest after-sex utterance ever uttered:
"You just wore out your welcome, please come again."
– Storm, chakra interpreter

Sexual Etiquette

During sex, if you're too shy to tell your lover what turns you on, it's okay to:
• Make him guess.
• Make him work harder.
• Point.
• Quote your therapist.

What Do the Professionals Do?

Problem: During lovemaking, your partner's pet keeps climbing on the bed and offering suggestions.

If partner's pet is a:	Solution
Needy little Pekingese	Repel with a fan.
Psychotic parrot that "talks" and ruins your concentration	Force-feed bird with crackers.
Playful Akita who gets between the two of you	Teach dog, on command, to fetch the mailbox.
Jealous cat who sharpens its claws on your back	Be open-minded. Let it watch (it will love you all the more).

Sex at the Beach

Why some people avoid it:
"Impossible to find a really comfortable sand dune."
– Irma S.

"The lifeguard rushes over whenever we go down for the third time."
                    – Sue S.
"Instead of tanning, my partner fades."
                    – Jessica H.

Thought for Tonight
The one good thing about your spouse having an affair is that you finally get to raise the kids your way.

Lovers at First Sight: Part I
What first attracted you to your lover?
"Her body, her mind, her face, and a mean right cross. I love assertive women."
                    – Dabney, florist
"Her 320-line personal in New York Magazine. I figured she must be rich."
                    – Craig, busboy and psychic friend
"He had a fully stocked gourmet kitchen, and I was living in a rooming house. It was paradise. I never knew that other than a hammer, there was an actual utensil for pressing garlic."
                    – Alyse, actress

Tip for Quarrelsome Lovers
A good fight can make the sex even better unless the fight's about:
• Money.
• That new dent in the Mercedes.
• The person you were caught in bed with and why wasn't I included.
• Directions.
• Whether to get a divorce.
• Sex (whether to have it).
• Religion (whether there is a goddess).

How Do I Love Thee?: Part I

Let me count the weighs.

Weight Lost	Where	How
3 lbs.	*Queen Elizabeth 2,* Caribbean cruise	We did it on seven tropical beaches.
4 lbs.	Lanai, secluded island paradise	Nothing else to do, it poured.
5 lbs.	Arizona, Canyon Ranch	Instead of hiking, we stayed in our room.
7 lbs.	New Orleans, during Mardi Gras	Doing it on, and underneath, several floats.

The Language of Flowers: Part III

To the lover who helped you achieve:	Send:
The beautiful clear skin you've always dreamed of (and such person is not a dermatologist)	Lilies of the valley
Ecstasy	A dozen roses

Midyear Break

Day of rest: instead of making love, consider these just-as-sensuous alternatives.

• Freshen up your bedroom: get either a) new sheets or b) a new lover.
• Redo your resumé (an erotic Best Bet).
• Plan a romantic getaway weekend. (Tip: Avoid inns where solicitous owner keeps knocking on your door to ask, "How are things?")
• Be healthily dissolute: spend the day sleeping late, watching television, eating chocolate and baking bread.
• Count the moments until tomorrow.

Survival Advice for Lovers

Thinking about a great—or even a very good—sexual experience can help you survive:
• Your 50th birthday
• A boring business lunch
• A rainy day at the beach

- Any commute longer than 15 minutes
- Working for a living
- Dealing with a bureaucrat
- The wait until the next great sexual experience

For the Lover on a Budget
Sex is a thoughtful yet inexpensive way to repay a friend who:
- When you were away, fed your cat.
- Helped you redecorate your apartment.
- Taught you how to roller blade.
- Typed your resumé.
- Prepared your income tax.
- Let you win at pinochle.
- Helped you resist temptation.
- Talked you out of your virginity.

Sexy Signals: Poll #45
How do you let someone you've just met know you're interested?
- "Ask if she's ever considered being a model. If that doesn't work, I ask if she's ever considered driving a cab."
- "I drop my wallet. If she picks it up, hands it to me and smiles, I ask her out. If she picks it up and runs, I chase her."
- "I tell him how virile he'd look in red, then splash burgundy all over his jacket."
- "Ask her to sit on my lap so I can guess her weight (I'm turned down only by the light ones)."

Secrets of the Great Lovers
Perfect lovemaking begins by:
1. *Eliminating distractions:* Unplug your fax.
2. *Ensuring privacy:* If in-laws are visiting, hand a "Do Not Disturb" sign on the bedroom doorknob.
3. *Warming up:* Spend quality time (at least 20 minutes) on kissing and fondling each other in all the wrong places.
4. *Opening yourselves to new experiences:* Devote at least 5 minutes to slowly undressing each other (one minute acceptable if you're wearing bathing suits.)
5. *Avoiding temptation:* Unplug the television set.

Water Sports

The eight stages of pre-arousal:
1. Running the bathwater
2. Adding bubble powder
3. Adding your lover
4. Uncorking the champagne
5. Soaping each other up
6. Mental stimulation (flirting)
7. Physical stimulation (embracing the rubber duck)
8. Erotic stimulation (embracing each other)

Spicing Up Your Sex Life: Part III

A gastrome's guide.

Condiment	Application
Oregano	Prolongs shelf life of the lover lacking in stamina.
Paprika	Makes lover tangier, more flavorsome—especially if sprinkled on chest.
Salt substitute	Turns bland lover into love slave (unproven claim).
Tabasco	Re-invigorates the lover who's had a busy day; quickens recovery time.

Intrusive Moment in Sex

"On our second honeymoon, in the middle of making steamy, passionate, ever-so-fervid, moan-inducing love on satin sheets covering a canopied bed in a luxurious room with its own fireplace (lit) in a romantic country inn nestled deep in the AdirondacksCthe slightly oversolicitous innkeeper knocked on our door (for the third time that evening) to ask, 'How is everything?'"

– Cindy and Edgar

379

The Enlightened Lover
How to tell a reluctant partner that you want sex
- For *shelter*: "Let's get under the covers."
- For *comfort*: "My skin feels so dry."
- For *entertainment*: "Darling, I'm bored."
- For *job benefits*: "It'll clear my head so I can better help you with your resumé."
- For *the freedom*: "It'll give me an excuse to get undressed."

Tip for Naive Lovers
When traveling, remember: suspicious motel managers almost never consider a package of condoms to be luggage.

Above and Beyond the Call of Duty: Part II
To remove stains from a dozing lover:

Stain	Use
Gravy: If hairy	Woolite
If not	Damp cloth
Grease: Spareribs	Soap, hot water
Other	Fantastik
Clam sauce: White	Saliva
Red	Club soda
Perspiration	Sponge

The Beneficial Energies of Sex: Part III

Activity	Benefit
Kissing lover's lips	Boosts lover's ego
Kissing lover's neck	Makes lover bubble mysteriously
Praising lover's performance:	
During sex	Increases lover's self-confidence
After sex	Gives lover courage to ask for rematch
Orgasm	Relieves stress
Multiple orgasms	Increases mathematical ability

Sex Poll #32

A sampling of responses from those asked, "What do you think is nearly as good as sex?"
- "Listening to Sousa marches."
   – Lamont, Justice of the Peace
- "My children."
   – Molly, realtor
- Going to tag sales."
   – Vernon, plasterer
- "A credit balance on my Visa card."
   – Merwin, security guard and poet
- "Sleeping late...in my bed."
   – Paula, bartender

Sex—Our Real National Pastime: Part II

Biggest worry during arousal:
For Mature Women
Labor pains
For Immature Men
Growing pains

Handy Love Guide #4

Determining sexually related stress (Scale: 1 to 100.)

Some Random Events	Degree of Stress
Lover inert (moves only to reach for a Tums)	60
Not sure you're satisfying lover because he or she is also:	
Studying the instructions accompanying:	
WordPerfect	55
Meditating	32
Setting the VCR to record a favorite soap	70
Frequency rate inferior to that of the:	
Rest of America	41
Couple next door	80

How Do You Lure Your Partner Into the Bedroom?

"I take off my clothes, hide in the closet and murmur, 'Help!'"
   – Masie, model

"Better yet, ask me how I lure my partner out of the bedroom. She's a nympho."
> — Gregory, union organizer

"Put on a sexy peignoir, stretch myself out on the bed and turn on the Knicks game.
> — Monica, school bus driver

"Hand him a boarding pass."
> — Patricia, stewardess

Summer Beauty Tip

Avoid wrinkles and age spots by:

1. Finding your lover
2. Going inside the house
3. Turning on the air-conditioner
4. Getting undressed
5. Staying in bed and doing it until the summer is over

From Our Treasury of Sexual Knowledge

1. The vigor of an underpowered lover can be greatly increased by drinking Ovaltine.
2. Researcher have found sex to be habit-forming.
3. Constant pampering and tender loving care will greatly add to the resale value of a new lover.

The Dieter's Guide to Weight Loss During Sex

Outdoor Lovemaking	Calories Burned
In a canoe	56
On white water	203
On an Adirondack chair	33
With extra-wide armrests	141
While backpacking:	
With backpacks off	87
With backpacks on	300
In your bedroom but with windows wide open:	
In summer	24
In winter	389

Sex: Seven Reasons Not to Deny Yourself
1. You've earned it.
2. It's fun.
3. Two hours of really robust lovemaking will enable you to enjoy that extra pat of butter.
4. Those new sheets on the bed are just too tempting.
5. It's the perfect combination of action and romance (and comedy if you've been married 10 or more years).
6. It's an ideal way to get on your partner's good side.
7. It soon may be subject to government recall.

Love at First Sight
What caused it?
"Her honesty. She was the first one who ever went out with me for my money."
> — Nelson, millionaire

"His line. He smelled like a brewery and said, "This bod's for you.""
> — Daphne, cowgirl

To Enhance Your Love Life:
Things Worth Doing Well
- A back and foot massage.
- Meat loaf.
- When applying cologne, knowing the difference between just enough and...an asthma attack.
- The tango.
- Kissing your partner awake.
- Fitting into a bikini.
- Making up for lost time.
- Making up for last time.

Summer Maintenance Tip
To prevent overheating, baste your partner twice daily.

If partner is:	Use:
Japanese	Sake
Chinese	Soy sauce
American	Any fruit beverage or beer
French	Bordeaux
English	Tea
Italian	Spumoni
Spanish	Olive oil
Californian	Mineral water

Early-Bird Special
Morning sex: the advantages.
- You and the sun get to rise together
- Still sleepy enough to enjoy it
- Makes the morning memorable
- Makes the commute tolerable
- Facilitates digestion of breakfast
- Contributes to a more positive outlook
- May elevate job performance
- And contribute to superior customer service

The one disadvantage: fainting at your workstation

Midyear Report
tear out and send to your lover

How Do I Rate in Bed?	Excellent	Good	Fair
Ability to relieve stress and tension	___	___	___
Spontaneity	___	___	___
Commitment to service	___	___	___
Creativity	___	___	___
Communication (verbal)	___	___	___
Communication (just sighing)	___	___	___
Flexibility (mental)	___	___	___
Flexibility (physical: bending over backward to please you)	___	___	___

The Bright Side

The nice thing about making love:

• In a restaurant: Always something to look forward toCif sex isn't great, you can enjoy the dessert cart.
• Outdoors, in the mountains: The sky's the limit.
• Outdoors, the desert: No worrying what the neighbors will think.
• On an airliner: You're already walking on air, kind of.
• On your terrace: You can wave to passing astronauts.
• In your bedroom: Familiarity breeds content.

Question of the Night

Q. Can an orgasm ever be too intense?
A. Only one that:

• Ruins your nylons.
• Causes the wallpaper to peel.
• Makes the Neighborhood Watch peer into the window and ask, "How's everything?"
• Rearranges the furniture.
• Makes your CD player skip.
• Makes you swallow your chewing gum.

The First Time: Lovers' Poll #47

What can't-fail arousal technique do you use on a new lover?
"I dim the lights, put on a Mel Torme CD, pour two glasses of imported champagne, open the hide-a-bed, slip out of something comfortable, tell her about my troubled childhood and hope for the best."

— Kurt, copywriter

"I alternate; a love bite, then an info-bite, then a love bite, then an info-bite. You get the idea."

— Prudence, historian

"The Wonderbra."

— Myra, barmaid

Summer Lover-Care Tip:
To prevent fading, remove partner from direct sunlight after three or more hours of sex.

"The Sex Was So Great That I..."
Some testimonials from:

Her

"Told him my deepest, darkest fantasy."

"Gave him my phone number."

"Gave him a salary increase."

"Let him stay the night."

"Posted his bail."

"Introduced him to my husband."

Him

"Didn't even flinch (except the part about the Vegematic.)"

"Put it on the Rolodex."

"Gave her a refund."

"Didn't snore."

"Didn't skip out."

"Treated the three of us to dinner."

The Guest Lover
The perfect visiting lover never:
• Makes toll calls from the host's phone.*
• Snoops in partner's closets or drawers.
• Hurts partner's feelings by arriving with a friend.
• Cancels at the last minute (or too late for partner to get someone with similar skills).
• Gets up in the middle of sex to check to see if the car's okay.
*Except to call for reinforcements.

Disappointing Moments in Lovemaking
"When he took his clothes off, my new, computer-literate boyfriend turned out (alas) to be Microsoft."
              – Jade, CEO, huge corporation

The Truly Ideal Partner
In addition to being a wonderful lover, also:
• After morning sex, knows the perfect restorative (French toast, maple syrup and a gift certificate for a facial).
• Loads the dishwasher without being nagged.
• Understands the fine print in your insurance policy.
• Knows what never to eat on an airplane (the Swiss steak).
• Knows how to make money in a declining stock market.
• After evening sex, knows the perfect restorative (a stack of Oreos and a good night's sleep).

When Lovemaking Gets Too Intense

What to do:

• Dig your nails into your partner's back (or chest, depending on the position).

• Start your own glee club (moan in harmony).

• Check your heart rate. (If it's over 200 beats per minute, congratulations! Call the *Guinness Book of Records*.)

• If you're driving, stop the car. It's the best way to avoid potholes.

• Blush.

One thing not to do: feel guilty.

MONTHLY QUALITY OF LIFE® CHECKUP

•Frequency of lovemaking: twice weekly___ twice, weakly___
•Quality of lovemaking:
Outstanding___
Quite lovely___
So-so___
Had to grit my teeth___
•If I could try something new it would be:
Doing it with the lights on___
Bondage___
Spanking___
Phone sex___
Cybersex___
A nymphomaniac___
•If I could tell my partner one thing to improve our sex life it would be:
Go slower___
Stop expecting me to do everything___
Get rid of your chewing gum before blowing in my ear___
Cease wearing those day-of-the-week boxer shorts___
Buy better handcuffs___
Give me more closet space___

Signed_____

Witnessed_____

AUGUST

•Erotic goal for August:
1. Try new position
2. Increase flexibility

Confirmed sun worshippers spend every moment of August basking in the sun, trying to store up enough of a tan to last through the winter. Hence, we recommend taking your partner (or a juicy lifeguard), finding a deserted beach and making wild, passionate love on a queen-size sand dune. (For inspiration see either *From Here to Eternity*—the beach scene with Burt and Debby or *Beach Blanket Bingo*—director's cut with Frankie and Annette.) And no need to worry. Dermatologists agree that even the most fervid sexual encounter runs off a mere 5% of one's tan, even less for those wearing sunscreen.

Afraid of being seen: Don snorkling gear and head for the ocean. Lovers of extrme sex have nothing but praise for an underwater climax, which can be particularly pleasurable if you're watched by a curious squid.

•Alert for couples with kids at camp: Soon they will be back. So make the best of your time alone.

Official aphrodisiac of the Month:
Strawberry shortcake

The Responsible Partner

He	She
Warms her up	Warms up
Tries	Encourages
Keeps up	Keeps count
Comes up with new and exciting things to do	Refrains from laughing when he does
Answers the doorbell	Informs the Welcome Wagon that it's not a good time

Emergency Sex: Part II

Is called for:
- To reassure lover that all is well.
- When a clear mind is needed to study for finals.
- To compensate for a rough afternoon at the mall.
- Something to do between cocktails and dinner.
- Or dinner and bed.
- To burn off a taco (120 calories).

Health Tip for Lovers

"Because it contains so little fiber, morning sex, while highly recommended,* is no substitute for a breakfast that includes at least three pieces of fruit."

         – Binky Fleck, registered dietician

*Because it is low in calories and high in riboflavin.

Gem of the Month

A sardonyx cameo pin to the lover who always leaves:
- A smile on your face.
- You satisfied.
- Something to the imagination (for next time).
- An emergency number where he or she can be reached (in case you're on your honeymoon).
- Directions (in case you need to make a house call).
- Instructions (so you know what to do once you get there).
- A ring on your finger...but never in the bathtub.

How Do You Know If You're Achieving Your Fitness Goals?

(Asked of several people who make love eight times weekly.)

• "My love handles disappeared (but now my husband has nothing to hold on to)."
• "I must be, my bicycle pants are getting looser."
• "My paunch disappeared."
• "I'm getting stronger. After sex, when he falls asleep, I can lift him off me without too much trouble."
• "In the supermarket, I push my grocery cart with more confidence."
• "I use a heart rate monitor, her name is Mary Lou."

Compensating a Perfect Partner

To a Sensual Lover

Who Introduced You To	Suggested Gratuity
Chocolate-covered strawberries	$1.50
Beluga caviar	$1.75
Wheatina	10¢
Extra-chewy brownies	50¢
Billie Holiday	$2.50
Hillary Clinton	$2.00
Peanut brittle	50¢
Waxed floss	$1.75

Considerate Lovers

She: Never leaves the seat down when leaving the bathroom.
He: Never puts the seat up while she's still on it.

The Undistinguished Lover

During-sex statement most likely to suggest that you may not be totally satisfying your partner:
"We can still be friends."

Words to the Wise Lover

Never confess that you're having an affair if your spouse has:
• A heart condition
• A weapon

- A bad temper
- All the money
- Martial skills
- A great lawyer

Some National Averages: Part I

4: The height in feet of the average out-of-body climax.

12: The number of "ms" in the "Ummmmmmmmmmmm" muttered by a contented sex partner moments before dozing off.

2.89: The number of square inches in the average erogenous zone.

6: The number of sexual encores the average 22-year-old male is capable of before going into cardiac arrest.

8: The number of sexual encores the average 22-year-old female is capable of experiencing before uttering, "Gee, this is nice!"

306: The maximum gross weight at which the average lover, during even the hottest sex, is no longer able to get carried away.

Six Great Moments in Sex

1. Your partner didn't lie about her vital statistics.
2. Your partner finds your bikini line charming.
3. Discovering that your during-lovemaking groans are actually good for the ozone layer.
4. Your ex is taking the kids for the weekend.
5. So is your lover's ex.
6. The right answer when you utter, "Mirror, mirror, on the ceiling, who's the fairest one of all?"

Is Your lover Just Lying There?

Is he listless? Does she lack enthusiasm? Some possible reasons:
- Depressed (his team lost).
- Can't recall why she's there (also known as memory loss).
- Rigid personality (you forgot to make an appointment).
- Distracted by
- World events.
- Peeling wallpaper.
- Fear of failure.
- Prefers a midnight snack, instead.
- You're not in the mood.

Official Table of Comparisons
Calories do count, but which ones?

Regular Activity		Comparable Sexual Activity	
Backstroke (swimming)	164	Backstroke (foreplay)	205
Climbing a hill:		Climbing a lover:	
Little	26	Little	38
Big	190	Big	270
Sleeping alone	6	Sleeping together	133
Sitting on sofa	24	Sitting on partner's lap	38
Sewing a dress	46	Sowing wild oats	443
Singing	14	Moaning	41
Walking fast	85	Breathing fast	116
Badminton	110	Bad sex	8

Sorry About Last Night
If lovemaking was less than terrific, check the appropriate reason and send to your lover.

___ Bad sunburn
___ Distracted by traffic noise
___ Indian food (never again)
___ Prowler
___ I don't accept walk-in applicants
___ Let's try again on _____

Know Your Sexual Law
Failure to satisfy. A lover is guilty of such offense and the offended party may sue when, during sex, such lover:
1. Also (a) watches television out of the corner of his or her eye to determine if the home team is winning or (b) tries to recall the theme song from *Bonanza*; or
2. Keeps answering the phone unless such a person is expecting a call from his or her (a) spouse or (b) agent; or
3. Asks, "Is it good for you?" and, before you can answer without perjuring yourself, dozes off.

The Enlightened Lover
The three most frequent causes of a during-sex wet spot.
1. Perspiration.
2. A steamy past.
3. Roof needs fixing.

Good News for Melancholy Lovers

Hate pills? Skinny dipping à deux in a hot tub is one of the few over-the-counter antidepressants that:
• Has been approved by the FDA.
• Doesn't come in a bottle.
• Won't irritate your stomach.

Sad Moment in Sex

"After lovemaking, I used to reach for a Camel. Now, instead, I put my nicotine patch back on and suck on a lollipop. It's really (sob) not the same."
— Marcy, computer sales

Common Sex-Related Afflictions

All minor and transient: one attack confers immunity forever.

Affliction	Probable Cause
Eye strain	Weak night-light
Whiplash	Abrupt stops while earning bonus miles
Shock	Out-of-bed orgasm
Breathing difficulties	Lover keeps taking your breath away
Dark circles under eyes	Too much passion-mascara-running
Guilt	Too much pleasure

Reminder for Outdoor Lovers

Smokey the Bear says 31% of all forest fires are started by careless campers. The other 69% are started by heat from careless campers making love on dry leaves.

Sexual Ethics

You should never have sex with someone only because he or she has:
• A great body
• A superior mind
• Celebrity status
• A well-stocked refrigerator
• Bedroom eyes

- An ocean view
- Air conditioning
- A corner office
- Exceptional genes

After-Sex Etiquette
If sex was labor-intensive, it is the partner who labored hardest who's entitled to:
- First aid (or at least a little nap).
- A sponge bath.
- An extra helping of strawberry shortcake.
- Vitamins.
- Skip tonight's dinner party.
- Be excused from taking out the garbage, making the bed and trying again too soon.
- Retirement benefits.

The Enlightened Lover
What to give to a first-time lover who has:

Everything	Very little
A sumptuous breakfast	A glazed doughnut
A perfumed thank-you note	A perfumed list (of why you're tied up for the next four months)
Your best good-bye kiss	Your best wishes
Another date	Excuses
Your phone number	Your friend's phone number
An invitation to move in	An invitation to move on

Approved Avoidance Techniques
It is permissible to ask for a rain check when:
- You're 8½ months pregnant.
- Your back is acting up.
- Your partner's acting out.
- You're afraid your lover's sunburn might be contagious.
- It's the last game of the World Series.
- Your new partner's references don't check out.
- Your old partner's back in town.

Conserve Your Energy

No sex today. Instead, some sexual alternatives:
- Fake it.
- Distribute campaign literature.
- Visit a moonlight seashore?but only make mudpies.
- Do laundry together (intimate but safe).
- Work a different muscle group.

Pillow Talk

Right-of-weigh. The right of two lovers to dispense with a bathroom scale and, instead, try to guess each other's weight by using their hands.

All-terrain partner. One who is flexible enough to have sex in any location, be it on-road (in a car) or off-road (on a sofa), and doesn't need sneakers to achieve maximum traction.

The Well-Compensated Lover: Part II

A tipping guide for that extra-special lover.

To the lover who	Suggested gratuity
Is kind to your:	
Children	$2.00
Cat	3.25
Can light a fire:	
In your fireplace	1.75
In you	5.00
Helped you quit smoking:	
Cigarettes	4.00
After a ferociously hot climax	6.00

From Our Lover's Glossary

Out-of-body climax. 1. *In sex.* Similar to one that is in-body except the climaxer gains more altitude. While in the throes of rapture, the lover experiencing such event may go beyond the limits of the bed and, in a fit of ecstasy, rise and orbit the bedroom until such lover's partner indicates, either by signaling or an offer of milk and cookies, that it's safe to come down. 2. *In sports.* Hang gliding.

Some Remedies for a Blah Sex Life
• Try a new and exciting location:
1. At your next cocktail party, on the coats in the bedroom (you
can always work the room later).
2. A BBYOS* motel room.
• Indulge at a new and exciting time: Instead of 11:34 p.m., do it
either in the morning (good) or now (better yet).
• Change your attitude:
1. Don't visit a restaurant only to eat. A dimly lit corner is the
perfect place to a) renew your vows and b) cop feels.
2. Fight often?it'll make the chemistry more compelling.
*Better bring your own sheet.

Sex Without Tears
Rolling over and going to sleep directly after sex is not the best
way to show your tender side.

When the Unthinkable Happens
Event
During ever-so-steamy sex, you call out a name other than that of
your lover.
What To Do
1) Deny it.
2) Placate lover by promising to work on unusual muscle group.
3) Make it into a joke.
4) Hope lover laughs.

The Dieter's Guide to Weight Loss During Sex

Activity	Calories Burned
Traveling from lover's mouth to lover's knees:	
Using lips only	24
Also using hands	55
Taking most direct route	73
Making lots of U-turns	154

The Prescient Lover: Part I

Why I suspected our romance might not last:
"He had a pay phone next to his bed."
      – Shirley, ski instructor
"Those preprinted thank-you notes she'd hand me after I was especially wonderful in bed. (The raised lettering, though, was kind of nice.)"
      – Henry, drill press operator
"That name tag she always wore when she got into bed saying, 'Hi, I'm your partner.'"
      – Geraldo, tour guide

During-Sex Communication: Part II

More ways to talk to your lover without breaking the spell:

Number of taps on lover's head	Translation
9	"How about breaking for dinner?"
10	"No way, I'm getting close."
13	"Is the baby crying?"
14	"No, that's me."
15	"That was a moan of pleasure."
16	"Twelve o'clock and all is well."

What I Do When I Meet a New Lover

"Stop seeing other women (but stay friendly with them just in case)."
      – Roberto, blackjack dealer
"Gain about 400 pounds. All we do is eat, watch television and do it."
      – Judy, office manager

"Give thanks, they're so hard to find."
— Dennis, paralegal
"Start buying shelter magazines but read them in secret. I don't want to scare him off."
— Valerie, editor

Remedial Lust: Part I

How long will you live?

Each time you:	To your life, add:
Have intercourse	1 hour
Have an orgasm	2 hours
Cause an orgasm	5 hours
Fake an orgasm	21 minutes
Anticipate having terrific sex	2 hours
But are disappointed	1 second

Nothing in Common?

Don't despair. You may still be lovers if:
• You speak the same language.
• You share the same zip code.
• The chemistry's there.
• It's mainly for the exercise.
• You're doing it for the challenge.
• You're doing it for the practice.

The Five Biggest Post-Sex Lies

1. *"Wow!"*
2. *"Oh, wow!"*
3. *"That never happened before."*
4. *"I'll call you."*
5. *"I could never have done it without you."*

From Our Book of Sexual Leasts

Least promising reaction by a lover to a new partner after canceling a business lunch, renting a motel room and having sex at noon.
"For this I missed a meal?"

Sexual Etiquette 101

After an especially hot session with your lover, it's considered appropriate to bring up the subject of:
• Marriage.
• Better living conditions (like new curtains for the bedroom).
• No more Hamburger Helper.
• A raise.
• Your parents coming to stay for the weekend.
• More help with the household chores.
• More of the same.

Words to the Wise Lover

• Let your partner decide if you're too tired for sex.
• Trust in God, but ask to see your partner's vasectomy scar.
• Once in a while, think about doing the unthinkable?it can improve a bland sex life.
• Getting into bed with cold feet is an unpleasant way to break the ice.
• Always wait until after sex to ask, "How was I?"

Famous Last Words

Things often said after sex:
• "Were you paying attention?"
• "Where *did* the time go?"
• "Where's my earring?"
• "When do we eat?"
• "Switch off the light on your way out."

Sexual Etiquette

No matter how pressed for time, the considerate lover never begins to dress until sex is over.

For Lovers Who Are Watching Their Weight

Try our special 200-calorie Sunday brunch:
• *For gargling:* Listerine
• *For drinking:* orange juice (6 oz.)
• *For sipping:* coffee (no cream, no sugar)
• *For eating:* a bagel (no butter, dab of jelly)
• *For nibbling:* your lover (artificial sweetener only)

It's a Lover's Question
Q. For how long should the effect of a Level 8 climax last?
A. For men, the feeling may be dispelled rather quickly?in less than one minute. For women, however, especially if the kids are at camp, that post-orgasmic "Cloud 9" effect may very well carry over into the next day, resulting in an at-peace-with-the-world attitude that, in extreme cases, may prompt her to treat her co-workers to coffee."

Air Traveler's Advisory
Six obstacles to sex aloft:
1. Suspicious looks when you ask for a blanket.
2. Partner would rather watch the inflight movie.
3. Midair turbulence may hinder your on-time performance.
4. Nosy child keeps asking what you're doing.
5. You're flying tourist class (in first class they draw the curtain).
6. Stress (the oxygen masks have dropped).

The First Time
Pre-sex statement by a demanding partner most likely to make a vulnerable male a) insecure and b) terminally impotent:
"You should know, I'm impossible to please."

What Causes First-Time Jitters: Part II

His	Hers
"Should have flossed."	"Should have waxed."
"How long can I hold in my stomach?"	"How long can I hold out my chest?"
"I can't think of her name."	"I can't think of his name."
"She'll be too great in bed."	"No I won't."

The Enlightened Lover
How to determine what turns your lover on.
Acceptable: Guess.
Good: Ask your lover.
Better: Ask your lover's seven most recent lovers.
Best: Sign language.
Terrific: Body language.

From Our Lover's Glossary

Wet tips. Objects at the end of a woman's just-washed hair that she sometimes brings to bed. In the course of writhing, squirming and other sex-related activities, these tips may lash her partner into a mild state of unconsciousness. Sensitive men find little consolation in the fact that such condition, according to experts, is caused by inefficient blow-drying, the result of her eagerness to get into bed and commence lovemaking.

Lovers at First Sight: Part II

What first attracted you to your lover?

"He knew how to waltz and where the good tag sales were."
        – Myrtle, divorcee

"Her warranty?60 nights or 60 meals. Who could resist?"
        – Brett, lawyer

"We met while surfing in Hawaii; fell in love instantly when we realized we were on the exact same wave length."
        – Wilma and Ambrose, happy couple

The Enlightened Lover

If your partner can't get enough of you:
• Make love more often.
• Invite him or her to take bigger bites.
• Gain weight.

When It's Difficult to Think About Sex

• While operating heavy machinery
• During root canal
• While holding an unopened letter from the IRS in your hand
• The weekend your in-laws visit
• While trying to fake a convincing climax
• In the third hour of a bad blind date
• While watching the Disney Channel

The Bedside Explorer: Part III

An erotic adventure for the bold lover.
Expedition 3 (Mordecai's Traverse)
Equipment recommended: all-terrain tongue

Place lover on back. Gently slide tongue east to west, then west to east, back and forth, forth and back. Observe all agreed-upon lines of latitude and feel free to rappel down any overhang. The first person to grow dizzy gets the honor of planting the flag.

The Dieter's Guide to Weight Loss During Sex

Activity	Calories Burned
Faking orgasm (includes all supplementary activities such as tears of joy, flailing, and issuing small-craft warning):	
If you went to acting school:	
In California	74
In Indianapolis	23
In New York	300

Warm Weather Drinks for Lovers: Part II

Type of drink	Application
Margarita	Makes lover giggle in all the right places during sex
Screwdriver	Vitamin C minimizes danger of catching cold when making love in a draft
Tom Collins	Permits amicable resolution of sexual conflicts (Who am I?)
Shirley Temple	Elevates morality
Rusty nail	Nightcap

The Romantic Outdoors

No matches? Survival tip for lovers stranded in the woods:
Good Way to Start a Fire
Rub two sticks together
Great Way to Keep It Going
Rub two bodies together

Our Lovers Master Class

Answers to the question: "How, after sex, do I get a reluctant partner to leave?"

"If it's the morning, prepare a less-than-perfect breakfast. Forget pancakes and eggs Benedict; serve egg salad on matzo with a cup of weak tea. He'll be gone in no time."

– Jane, feminist sex therapist

"If she's savvy, a gentle hint should suffice. Dress her, open the front door and hand her her car keys."

– Mario, author, Lawyers in Heat

"Explain you have to make a phone call and would he mind waiting on the lawn."

– Joanne, Director, Bronx Foreplay Center

The Enlightened Lover
Things often said after sex by
A Satisfied Partner:
"I'm crazy about you, baby."
An Egomaniacal Partner:
"And you were very good, too."

The Erotic Motorist
A guide to in-vehicle affection:

Activity	Appropriate Time
Kissing partner's neck	While waiting for light to turn green
Holding hands	During traffic jams (to ease stress)
Inter-seat fondle	When stuck behind slow-moving Winnebago (to keep calm)
Caressing knee	During skids (to intensify passion)
Earlobe nibble	When pulled over by state trooper (to alleviate anxiety)
Starting all over again	While making a U-turn

The Prudent Lover
Our technical adviser suggests keeping an oxygen bottle handy should awesome sex take your lover's breath away.*
*Another climax will bring it back.

Great Moments in Lovemaking
"The rehearsal."
> – Raymond, set designer

"The performance."
> – Serena, "New Face" of 1993

"The encore."
> – Matthew, props

Environmentally Responsible Sex Tip
Outdoor lovers, especially if they're (a) Earth-friendly and (b) messy, always put a blanket down before making love.*
*It protects the topsoil against (a) oil spills and (b) perspiration.

Truly Enlightened Lovers

During Sex—Leave Lights	On	Off
If you like to watch your partner:		
Blush		X
Glow	X	
Worry about bumping into furniture when you get a midnight snack	X	
Are embarrassed by your sexual fantasies		X
Hear a helicopter hovering above your skylight:		
And it's paparazzi		X
Your rescuers	X	

Wise Couples Know
After sex, if you've been together for 10 or more years, the best way to keep from drifting apart is to avoid lying in the wet spot.

Rest Period
Only a little sex today. Recommended:
• Strip Monopoly.
• No petting below the collarbone (to prevent degeneration of moral values).
• No candlelit bubble baths unless suitably attired (wet suits).
• Stick to low-impact arousal (listen to romantic instead of disco music).
• Call your mother.

Security Tip for Uninhibited Lovers
To prevent unauthorized purchases:
"During an especially perfervid climax, while in the throes of bliss, the practice of shouting one's credit card number should, if possible, be curtailed until one is thoroughly acquainted with one's lover."

     – Credit Card Security Association

Myth or Fact?

Conventional Wisdom Suggests	Myth	Fact
The best time to have sex is at night.	X	
Sex with a hairy partner can rub away one's tan.	X	X
Men reach their sexual peak at age 17; women, sometime in their late 70s.		X
Sometimes it's the other way around.	X	
You can tell if a person will be good in bed by the way they eat lobster.		X
After a true grade-6 climax (total clearing of the sinuses), a rainbow should appear.		X

The Inquiring Lover
Q. There's so much chemistry between my lover and me that during sex I lose all control and shriek, bite, moan, knock over the night table, clutch at the sheets and once actually flung a pillow out the window (luckily it just missed the mail carrier). Am I missing anything?
A. Yes. Inhibitions.

Great Moments in Afterplay
"Returning my phone calls."
     – Lois, 911 operator
"Feeling all relaxed, then rolling over and falling asleep."
     – Kim, starlet
"Hindsight."
     – Murray, Kim's lover

Caution

Researchers tell us that the worst time to
- Make a career decision
- Invest in penny stocks
- Accept an offer of marriage
- Try to thread a needle
- Catch up on your reading
- Sign whatever's put in front of you
- Remove a cinder from your partner's eye
- Land an aircraft

is 3 seconds before you climax.

The Dieter's Guide to Weight Loss During Sex

Activity	Calories Burned
Making love on horseback (by gait):	
Canter	60
Trot	92
Full gallop	155
Bareback	350
Sidesaddle	9
Neck-and-neck	145

Lovemaking Tips: Part III

To a Lover Who:	Suggested Gratuity
Helped you work off the Spaghetti Bolognese you had for lunch.	50¢
Often makes you late for work.	$1.75
Always understands when you've had a rough day (and lets you sleep during love-making).	$1.50
Ruined you for other, lesser lovers.	$25.00
Doesn't charge for travel time	$3.00

The Enlightened Lover

After a new conquest, no matter how proud you are of your sexual prowess, it's never a good idea to carve a notch on your mattress, especially if you sleep on a waterbed.

Sex at the Beach

Avoid sunburn by using our exclusive "Sun-screen" position:
You on the bottom, lifeguard on top.
Note: You'll get even more protection from the sun if a crowd gathers around.

Weight-Loss Fact

Scrubbing a floor on your hands and knees will expend a mere 7 to 8 calories per minute whereas scrubbing the back of a lover who is soaking in a bathtub can expend up to 15 calories per minute*?even more if (a) you're thorough and (b) you use your lips instead of a loofah.

*100 calories per minute if lover is soaking facedown.

The Enlightened Lover

Sexual dysfunction? You know you're cured when your sex therapist calls you for either (a) advice or (b) a date.

Sex Al Fresco: Part II

Before you indulge outdoors, consider the following.

Pro	Con
Singing birds	Buzzing mosquitoes
Flowers	Ragweed
Morning dew	Acid rain
Field mist	Field mice
Low-floating clouds	Low-flying aircraft
Summer: alfalfa	Fall: mud
Shade trees	Gypsy moths
Hanging ivy	Poison ivy

Lovemaking: The Possibilities

"The loss of a prominent beer gut, even one caused by oceans of Guinness stout, during three hours of high-octane sex is not unheard of."

— Gaylord S., unregistered nutritionist

Suggested Service Charges

How much should you charge your lover for

A photo of you	$4.00
Wallet-size	$3.25

Watering plants and getting the mail while lover's:

On a business trip (Chicago)	$10.00
On a pleasure trip (honeymoon)	$500.00
Cooking his or her favorite dish	$8.00
If it involves peeling onions	$12.00
Calling in sick for lover	$2.00
Pretending to be lover's mother	$4.50
Replacing a lost key to your place	$3.00

Thought for the Day

"Sex is God's way of telling us to play less golf."

Phone Sex

Advantages	Disadvantages
Convenience of shopping by phone is the privacy of your own home.	Not the best way to find that special someone.
Very safe.	Unless you're calling from a public pay phone.
Caller decides when sex is over.	Caller may be "put on hold" at crucial moment.
Caller can fake it without insulting partner	Expensive if (a) you're slow to grow aroused or (b) the person on the other end stutters.

More Stolen Sexual Moments

• Accompany her into the dressing room at any candlelit Victoria's Secret store. Help her try things on.
• In your host's guest room at a dinner party?if you're going to be longer than 10 minutes, ask for a doggy bag.
• During a picnic under the stars—at the planetarium.
• In your own bedroom?when your dinner guests simply won't leave.
• While standing behind him on a cash machine line?be discreet.
• In the back of your car?for privacy, place a "Just Married" sign in the rear window.

Q. My husband, a dentist, refuses to make love to me for two days before a big root canal. He says it would sap his strength. Is this true?

A. There is absolutely no scientific evidence indicating that sex saps one's strength, although many dentists, two days after sex, prefer to do only inlays.

What I Did for Love

"Went on a diet and used my lover as a between-meal snack. I lost 47 pounds the first weekend."

– Tracy, registered nutritionist

"Ignored the alarm clock?and kept my lover a prisoner in his own bed."

– Penelope, morning person

"Married well."

– Boris, exchange student

Protocol Tip for Patriotic Lovers

Those who are making love while watching a televised sporting event:

Need not
Stand when they play our National Anthem
But should
At least place one hand over each other's heart

Sex Poll #45

What are the benefits of sex in the workplace? (Asked of several dedicated employees.)

"My assistant lowered his salary demands."

– Holly, attorney

"It was an excellent way to verify her resumé."

– Winston, account executive

"Job security...I made a videotape."

– Natasha, executive assistant

"Great benefits: Blue Cross, Blue Shield and blue Mercedes."

– Scott, fashion assistant

The Unstoppable Lover

A true romantic never allows...

- Grief (his team lost the pennant)
- Gloating (her team won it)
- A bad day at work
- Late-staying guests
- Indigestion
- Bad news from his or her (a) stockbroker or (b) bookie
- Homework
- A vow of abstinence
- Strange footsteps (mice)

...to interfere with lovemaking.

After-Sex Music

(To a new lover's ears)

- "I'd love to see you again."
- "I didn't know I was multi-orgasmic."
- "My PMS is gone (for now)."
- "My faith in personal ads is renewed."
- "Want to move in?"
- "I think I'm in love."
- "Here's a little something for your trouble."

How to Revive an Exhausted Lover

Good: tuna casserole or a chilled kiwi (apply as poultice to affected areas)

Better: smelling salts

Best: mouth-to-mouth resuscitation

Can't fail: strip search

Positively won't fail: whispering sweet but suggestive nothings into his or her ear (like "Dinner's ready")

Advice from the Experts

During sex, prevent confusion by using the same partner for foreplay, intercourse and arousal. Use more than one partner only if your lover is a specialist.

The Passionate Motorist

A guide to vehicular lovemaking.

Activity	Ideal Time
Blowing in lover's ear	When lover is searching for toll money
Closing eyes to better enjoy lover's caresses.	Only after vehicle has come to a complete stop
Touching lover's favorite erogenous zone	While lover is asking directions
Pinching lover's cheeks	Never while lover is trying to parallel park

The Conservative Lover

Advice for couples who do not approve of having sex, especially with each other, but still want children:

• Keep the lights off
• Try to think about something pleasant
• Just grit each other's teeth and bear it.

Sin Taxes for 1995: Part II

Sin Tax	
Drinking	
Before sex: To make your partner more attractive	15¢
During sex: To relieve performance anxiety	25¢
To justify performance anxiety	$5.00
After sex: To whet your appetite for	
Dinner	10¢
Breakfast	$7.65
To toast that it's over	$10.00

Thought for Tonight

Second-wind alert for the woman who's drop-dead gorgeous:
If, when you undress, you take your partner's breath away, remember, for best results, to put it back.*
*Especially if he's asthmatic.

What I Did for Love

"Finally got up the courage to take the initiative during sex?he almost fainted."

> – Olivia Krill, NASA

Practical Sex Tips

Things getting dull? Use Turtle Wax to perk up the shine on your lover's forehead.

Overdid it? Use lemon juice to remove mildew from a worn-out partner.

Accident? Remove gravy stains from a dozing lover by sponging with a cloth dipped in vinegar.

Perspiration? Soak entire lover in cool seltzer.

Great Moments in Afterplay

"Being thinner."

> – Laura, countess

"He tells me how good I was until I fall asleep. Then he tells me how great he was."

> – Norrie, judge

"Listening to the applause."

> – Harvey, guitar maintenance

"The view."

> – Egbert, forest ranger

The Bedside Eater: Part II

Olympic lovers reveal their favorite during-sex foods.

"Free-Range Risotto Primavera. It helps me maintain my reputation for good service and reliability."

> – Max, attorney

"Brown Rice and Bean Sprouts. My partner likes me wispy."

> – Jason, dancer

"Lots of Chocolate Mud Pie. For energy and stamina, plus plenty of bottled water in case of fireworks."

> – Penelope, nutritionist

The Day After the Night Before

A thank-you note to an outstanding lover should:

1. Not be mimeographed.
2. Be handwritten.

3. Not begin, "Dear Resident."

4. Contain sufficient postage (otherwise, unromantic Post Office will not deliver).

5. Mention at least one detail of what happened in bed to prove you were really there.*

*Examples: (a) "The rose on the pillow really perked my libido."
(b) "Breakfasting on chablis and flapjacks was unique."

Great Outdoors Alert

To avoid the attention of

- Deer
- Chipmunks
- Insects
- Raccoons
- Nature photographers
- Spy satellites
- Low-flying helicopters
- Environmentalists

partners with animal magnetism should avoid the woods when making love.

The Difference Between Good Sex and So-so Sex

Good	So-So
Fortifies one's belief in God	Fortifies one's belief in aspirin
Uncovers new erogenous zones	Can't seem to find the old ones
Spontaneous combustion	Just a few sparks
Can't keep your mind off how good you feel	Can't keep your mind off the cold chicken in the refrigerator
Afterward you sing in the shower	Afterward you just hum a little

What Do the Professionals Do?

The Problem

During sex, my partner's dog keeps jumping on the bed and interfering with our lovemaking. It's distracting and drives us crazy, especially when he tries to bury his bone. Is there anything we can do?

The Solution

Get a spot remover.

Fitness Tip for Women

Constantly pushing an aroused lover away from you until your nails dry can do more for your upper arms than 20 push-ups.*
*And he'll learn to be more patient.

Secrets of the Great Lovers

During sex. Never interrupt your partner to make corrections. It can:
• Stifle creativity.
• Make him lose his place.
After sex. To establish a warm, communicative mood, always ask questions like:
• "How was I?"
• "Can you see the time?"
• "What's for dinner?"

What Do the Professionals Do?

Q. As someone who is memory-challenged, I often call out the wrong partner's name during moments of extreme passion. How can I stop this very embarrassing act?
A. Before sex, write her name where you'll be able to see it:
1. On the ceiling.
2. On the mirror.
3. On her forehead.
4. On your shirt cuff.
5. On a check.

From Our Lover's Glossary

A true romantic. One who believes that the shortest distance between two points is your sternum

A Guide to Vehicular Sex

Ford Taurus
Advantages
Capacious trunk permits "kinky" sex, especially if lover doesn't have a spare tire.
Disadvantages
Limited warranty: doesn't cover rust and/or wet spots.

Hot-Weather Tip for Lovers

To keep cool during sex:
1. Drink plenty of water during arousal.
2. Do it in the shade (under the boardwalk or a beach umbrella is best).
3. Remove your tie.
4. Take off your shirt.
5. If you want to look crisp during intercourse, wear seersucker.
6. If you don't want to burn, put down the sun reflector.
7. The person on top should use a sun screen.

The Art of Romance

The Performance Lover
Lasts up to three hours
Needs a high-test partner
Breathes efficiently
Handles superbly
Many moving parts
Manual shift

The Regular Lover
Just one hour
Can run on regular
May gasp on hills
May skid on curves
Just one
Automatic

A Lover's Rituals

During sex, always observe a moment of silence:
• Moments before orgasm?so you can better concentrate.
• Moments after orgasm?so you can better savor the pleasure.
• If you're smitten by the sight of your partner in nothing but a wedding ring (honeymooners and retirees, especially).
• If you think you hear the garage door opening.

From Our Lover's Glossary

Sheet Music. The sounds emanating from a bed upon which two partners find themselves making love in perfect harmony.

Sexual Etiquette

Four appropriate questions after aerobic sex.
1. "Have a nice workout?"
2. "Share a towel?"
3. "Wow! Have you been eating your Wheaties?"
4. "What do we tell the people beneath us?"

Sex on the Beach

"Between a man and a woman, there is no such thing as the innocent application of sun-tan lotion, especially if the shoulder straps of her bathing suit must be lowered. Caressing the body with a lubricious substance must be respected for the erotic event that it is."

— Malibu Chamber of Commerce

Fact

Next to a show of hands, the four most reliable indicators of a wonderfully unmanageable love life are:
1. A perpetual grin
2. Never quite finding time to do laundry
3. Fewer workouts at the gym
4. A flat stomach

The Confident Lover

Makes love wonderfully even:
• With indigestion
• With a cluster headache
• During an argument
• With tennis elbow
• While wearing a seat belt (vehicular sex only)
• With in-laws coaching
• With the wrong music playing (marches)
• In the wrong position (both on the bottom)

Caring For Your Lover

To the Lover Who:	Give:
You make ache with pleasure.	An aspirin.
You drive crazy with pleasure.	A straitjacket.
Always pleads for more.	Nonstop service.
During sex, always sees too many stars.	A pair of Ray-Bans.
After sex, always wears a blissful smile.	Dental floss.
You drive up a wall.	CPR.
Can't get enough of you.	A lock of your hair.

420

The Secret Signal

How do you know when your partner wants sex?

"She picks me up, throws me down on the counter, and has her way with me (sometimes even before I've shut off the meat slicer)."

     – Alfred, deli owner

"He calls me a cupcake."

     – Cynthia, baker

"She clutches my head to her bosom and practices her nursing technique (we're expecting)."

     – Alvin, firefighter

"Something (I think it's my husband) goes bump in the night."

     – Harriet, realtor

True Love Is . . .

• Opening a joint checking account.
• Pointing out that his weight is creeping up before his paunch reaches critical mass.
• Sharing (equally):
1. The last piece of cheesecake.
2. The last piece of floss.
• Calling out, "You!" when she asks, "Mirror, mirror, on the wall, who has the highest cheekbones of all?"
• Trudging out for ice cream and pickles at 4 A.M. because you're a) pregnant and b) don't wish to disturb him.

The Enlightened Lover

To prolong pleasure, simply think about nonerotic topics.

To delay climax for:	Think about:
1 minute	Last Sunday's sermon
2 minutes	An ailing stock portfolio
3 minutes	Your neighbor's spouse
4 minutes	Improving your golf swing
5 minutes	Standing on line at the post office

Breaking the Ice: Part II

More during-sex conversation starters

Situation	What to Say
While admiring lover's body.	"Is this how you stay so thin?"
Your Airedale is making lover sneeze.	"I think he likes you."
Intense lovemaking?your heads keep bumping the headboard.	"I see we have the same taste in aspirin."
Lover instinctively knows how to arouse you.	"With whom did you study?"
After lovemaking.	"Do you come here often?"

From Our Book of Sexual Records

Fastest rate of intercourse (land speed): Husband-wife team Benny and Flo, of Salt Lake City, Utah, claims an unofficial 19.6 mph, or Mach .0008, achieved with the aid of little booster rockets and a tail wind.

In-Bed Fashion Tip for Lovers

During sex, it's acceptable to wear sunglasses* or ski goggles to protect sensitive eyes from the glare of a lover's afterglow.
*Designer frames only.

The Well-Informed Lover

Favorite ways to celebrate romance.

Activity	Possible Drawback
A candlelight dinner for two	Small portions
Making love in front of a fire on a bearskin rug	Animal rights activists may picket your living room
Slow dancing in the moonlight on the terrace of your hotel	Waiters keep cutting in
A romantic stroll in the rain	Pneumonia
Holding hands on the beach and watching an oceanside sunset	Confrontation with a person whose sandcastle you crushed

More Secrets of the Great Lovers

Make your partner feel Needed	By Asking for help with
Before sex	1. Making the *salade niçoise*
	2. Finding the right music
	3. A stubborn necklace clasp
During sex	1. Sharing in the position decision
	2. Ignoring your pager
	3. Mentioning him or her in your diary

What Do the Professionals Do?
Problem
A discrepancy in sexual drive: he wants it only five times a week, I need it at least twice a day (even more during my busy season).
Solution
Romantic:
Work out a compromise:
Practical:
Start without him.

Great Moments in Afterplay
"Realizing how good it was."
— Sean, gunsmith
"The guilt."
— Maureen, librarian
"Getting my second wind."
— Tina, student
"Wringing out my sweatband."
— Randolph, personal trainer-in-residence to L.A. royalty

Moodbreakers
Three questions never to ask.
1. *As you begin lovemaking*: "How long is this going to take?"

2. *During lovemaking*: "Have you heard anything about tomorrow's weather?"
3. *After lovemaking*: "Was it good for me?"

More Review Questions
1. Interruptions: From whom is it permissible to take a phone call during sex without offending your partner?
2. Senior citizens: Of the 743 possibilities, name the only two sexual positions endorsed by the President's Commission on the Aging.
1. Either (a) your tailor or (b) your broker (up market only).
2. Indoors: Woman on top, man trying to remember her.
    Outdoors: Woman on bottom, man over the hill.

The Lover's Herb Garden: Part II
More remedies for the dysfunctional partner:

If partner	Appropriate Herb
A type "A" personality (changes position every 30 seconds)	Slippery Elm (also cures diaper rash)
Gets turned on only when you do it in places where you might be caught (in your car during an oil change)	Bee Pollen or Irish Moss
Can't experience a rich, satisfying climax without first hearing a weather report	Aloe Vera or Wild Yam

Helpful Hint for Moist Lovers
Always keep a box of non-scented facial tissues on the night table to dab away tears from:
- Hay fever
- Laughter
- Ecstasy
- Remorse (that you didn't do this sooner)
- Onions (great snack)
- Happiness
- Gratitude (if it's been over a year, you'll need a sponge)
- Love bites

Love Signs

Horoscope For A Venal Virgo
- *Ruling passion:* thinking thin
- *Ruling body lotion:* non-dairy creamer
- *Chief sexual asset:* great legs and yummy knees
- *Governing erogenous zone:* your glorious thighs
- *Aphrodisiac of choice:* boiled pike, chopped really fine
- *Ruling sexual activity:* making high-pitched sounds
- *Ideal time for sex:* after 5 P.M., but before 7 P.M.

When Your Lover Has a Fragile Ego

Be kind.

If Your Partner Asks:	Don't Reply:
"Was it good for you?"	"What's for dinner?"
"Was I too loud?"	"Turn up the TV."
"Why are you doing that?"	"Research and development."
"Can I help you?"	"Just browsing."
"How was I?"	"You meant well."
"Did I take too long?"	"Hand me my watch."

Love Signs

Horoscope for a Vigorous Virgo.
- *Ruling passion:* experiencing lovers of different faiths
- *Ruling sexual turnoff:* a blue handbag with brown shoes
- *Chief sexual asset:* expert cuddler
- *Governing erogenous zone:* any sandy cove in North America
- *Aphrodisiac:* fried matzoh
- *Ruling sexual activity:* performing miracles
- *Ideal time for sex:* any idle moment

Overheard After Marvelous Sex

"Where am I?"
> – Matt, explorer

"I'll pay for the night stand, vase, Champagne flutes, headboard, lamp and your wrist watch."
> – Marla, deprived of sex for a long time

"Darling, you can breathe now."
> – Kate, snorkling instructor

"Snap out of it!"
> – Lorenzo, hypnotist

Love Signs: Amorous Virgo

Opposite love sign: A perfervid Pisces with a great body.

Outstanding sexual qualities: Experience, dedication, willingness to learn, and perfect teeth.

Most attractive physical feature: Bedroom eyes that work just as well at the office.

Ruling sexual turnoff: A date who, after dinner, instantly grabs the check and hands it to you.

Ruling sexual turn-on: Meeting "cute" prospects (at the deli, for instance, you find yourselves competing for the same whitefish).

Ideal place for sex: At the beach, while being rescued by (or from) a bronzed lifeguard.

Love Signs: Regular Virgo

Most attractive feature: Blind dates love you (you look so much better in person than you sound over the phone).

Turn-on: Spending three or four sizzling hours in bed with your lover, forgiving each other after a really intense phone fight.

Turn-off: Partners who ask, "You're not doing this out of pity, are you?"

Ideal romantic adventure: Shipwrecked with your lover on a remote South Sea island containing nothing but palm trees and a Wal-Mart.

Favorite sexual fantasy: Calling your ex during sex and letting your partner say hello.

The Language of Flowers: Part IV

To the lover who:	Send:
Finally got it right	One white orchid
Gave you an all-over body massage, knew just where to linger *and* tossed in a Jiffy Lube	Jonquils

Minimal Frequency Rates
A guide for the sexual minimalist.

If you:	You can get away with:
Love your partner's body	4 times a week
Love only your partner's mind	Twice a month
Are on a budget (too much pleasure makes you feel guilty)	Once every 2 weeks
Are career-oriented	Once a week
Are married to an animal:	
A tiger	Once a night
A pussycat	Once a week
A wrestler	Once an hour

Advice for Active Lovers
After making extraordinary love, wait approximately one hour before trying to:
- Swim (relaxing in a Jacuzzi okay)
- Hike
- Bowl (for money)
- Operate heavy machinery (your blender, for instance)
- Follow any recipe that requires a whisk
- Drive a stick shift
- Collect your senses
- Plan your estate
- Try again (unless it's with a different partner)

The Morning After a Not-So-Great Night
Lovers' rights activists insist it's unfair to punish a sex partner who performed less than adequately by making him empty your dishwasher, take out the garbage, and seek professional help.

Traveling Lovers
Our favorite romantic getaway:
"Venice. We make love in a gondola while the oarsman sings 'Volare.'"

> — Luella and Denise, owners,
> mom-and-mom travel agency

"Anywhere exotic, as long as they have MTV."

> — Sid and Nancy, flight attendants

"Niagara Falls. Then we can do it in our favorite position (me on top, hubby over a barrel)."
— Gretchen and Bryan, honeymooners
"Speeding cross-country on Rt. 80 with the cops in hot pursuit."
— Doug and Myra, fugitives

Lover's Formula
TDA + CHI x MOM ? HFYHBDS = BUCKS*
*Time Devoted to Arousal plus the Combined Height in Inches of each partner multiplied by the Money Owed on Mortgage divided by How Fast Your Hearts Beat During Sex will nearly always give you a winning lottery number.

A Fact
New research indicates that 87% of all women holding a managerial position feel they do not need permission from their lover to have an orgasm.

Energy Alert
Our technical adviser calculated that during a genuine climax, it takes an additional:
- 11 calories to call out your lover's name
- 64 calories to let out a rebel yell (regional)
- 149 calories to keep your eyes open
- 17 calories to moan
- 25 calories to stifle a yawn
- 104 calories to stifle a yawn not your own
- 135 calories to ignore a jealous Akita
- 400 calories to ignore a jealous lover

The Language of Flowers: Part VII

To the lover who:	Send:
After lovemaking, is always there with a warm washcloth to help you fight chills	Geraniums
Never forgets your name, even in the heat of passion	Snapdragons
Is constantly helping you remove the fat not susceptible to ordinary exercise	A window box

Are You with the Right Lover?

You are if he or she:

• Sees your inner beauty even if the lights are off.

• Thinks that love handles are a turn-on.

• Believes that making too much love is like having too much money.

• Assures you that the best way to improve circulation is on a revolving bed.

• Loves you for your body and your mind (although there's a tendency to concentrate on the former during sex).

• Sees nothing wrong with eating spareribs in bed.

• Believes there's only one cure for temptation.

Lover's Poll: #49

When sleeping with your lover, what is the:

Best Thing

"Snuggling against his big hairy chest. He's a hunk."

　　　 – Laura, CEO

"The way she makes me fall asleep. I wish I could bottle it."

　　　 – Herbie, artist

"The convenience. If I need to make love, he's right next to me."

　　　 – Ethel, cartoonist

Worst Thing

"She takes up most of the bed, it's terribly emasculating."

　　　 – Butch, pipefitter

"When he tosses and turns, his ponytail tickles my nose."

　　　 – Bill, policeman

"Her snoring. I can hear it even if she's sleeping in the upper bunk."

　　　 – Joe, mail carrier

Financial Tip for Noon-Time Lovers

After sex, it may be difficult to emit sighs of contentment, lay your head on your partner's shoulder, snuggle against each other, whisper how wonderful it was and make plans for the future if the motel charges by the hour.

Pillow Talk

Casual sex. Any spontaneous, unplanned sexual encounter between two lovers who may or may not know each other when it occurs:

- On a bank line
- In a museum
- At a Dunkin' Donuts
- In the parking lot of any mall
- While commuting
- Upon finally finding a working cash machine

Pillow Talk

During-glow. That stage of sex, preceding afterglow, when, if conditions are right, both lovers begin to emit gamma rays and make themselves understood chiefly through grunts and moaning. It is at this stage of lovemaking that couples are cautioned against making major business decisions.

Good News for Allergy Sufferers!

Great sex

Does not:	But may:
Make you sneeze.	Make your eyes water.
Make your eyes itch.	Make you weep.
Contain pollen.	Get your dander up.
Make your nose run.	Raise dust.
Cause asthma.	Induce shortness of breath.
Cause hives.	Cause rosier cheeks.
Cause heat rash.	Cause a meltdown.*

*A positive sign.

Ice Breakers

Eight pre-lovemaking questions sure to warm up your partner.
1. After a wonderful time in the restaurant: "So, how much did my share of dinner come to?"
2. As partner undresses: "How do you stay so thin?"
3. As you get a better look: "Are those what they call love handles?"
4. As you're getting into bed: "What side of the bed do you like?"
5. As your partner's getting into bed: "What's the password?"
6. Once you're both in bed: "Hold all calls?"
7. Moments before beginning sex: "Sure you're up for this?"
8. If you practice cautious sex: "So, where's the hidden camera?"

Our Favorite Fibs

Before sex:
1. "I don't usually do this so quickly, it must be that moon.
2. "I should be getting home, my plants will be wondering where I am."

During sex:
1. "I can stop at any time."
2. "How about 3:47 A.M.?"

After sex:
1. "I didn't think we were going to do this tonight."
2. "I'm glad we waited."
3. "I'm glad I saved myself."

How Do I Love Thee?: Part II

Let me count more weighs.

Weight Lost	Where	How
½ lb.	Bedroom	Quickie in front of the mirror.
2 lbs.	Our living room, on the floor	Christened the new oriental carpet.
3 lbs.	Terrace	Against the window box?the petunias thrived.

The Seaside Lover

Comparable to a booth in a three-star restaurant or the rear seat of a Bentley, the beach is a high-romance setting. Some considerations:

Turn-Ons	Turn-Offs
Sea air	Bathers with gruesome bodies
Lifeguards	Tourists
A chance to tan all over	Sun blisters
Sand dunes	Sand flies
Sound of the ocean	Sound of dune buggies
Partner in bathing suit	Partner in bathing suit

The Enlightened Lover
Too much sex can be a dangerous thing. It can cause:
• An increased desire for sweets (human and non-human).
• A glazed expression.
• Indifference to work.
• High motel bills.
• Romantic evenings.
• Dinner to be late.
• Excessive happiness.
• Gossip.
• A craving for more.

Assessing the Merits of a New Lover
Can he or she:
1. Keep you warm without a blanket?___ Yes ___ No
2. Find your erogenous zones in the dark?   ___Yes ___ No
3. Function during a crisis such as
     Mosquitos? ___ Yes ___No
     Skyrocketing interest rates? ___ Yes ___ No
4. Tolerate quirky behavior? (You love to watch TV during fore-play)   ___ Yes
     ___ No
5. Turn into a tiger? ___ Yes ___ No
     Turn into a lion?___ Yes ___ No

Nutritional Tip for Marathon Lovers
If, after three hours of high-powered sex your partner turns into an animal, don't panic: it may be feeding time.
We recommend
• *For strength:* corn popovers*
• *For endurance:* kasha
• *For cardiovascular health:* ratatouille
• *For mental health:* apple pie
• *For the libido (regular):* oysters
• *For the libido (inflated):* Gruyère soufflé
*Or cottage fries if you're watching your weight.

Visiting Your Lover? Part II
Five more things never to leave home without.

1. To-do list—in case your partner's sexually demanding.
2. Breath mints—if you stay over, to prevent morning mouth.
3. Swiss army knife—use the nail file to groom yourself if your partner's taking too long in the bathroom.
4. Tape measure—an infallibly accurate way to determine if you're measurably thinner after sex.
5. Lucky charm—it can't hurt.

Suggestion for the Cautious Lover

Never confess you're having an affair (especially in public) if you suspect your partner has a:
- Non-forgiving nature.
- Winning lottery ticket.
- Weakish heart.
- Bad temper.
- Tape recorder going.
- Tough lawyer.

Tip for Neurotics
For better, more carefree sex, keep a photo of your therapist next to the bed.

Are You Insatiable?

You are if:
1. The phrase "time out" is not in your vocabulary.
2. Your lover frequently asks for:
   a. Mercy; and/or
   b. Your autograph
3. You've had to give past lovers:
   a. Mouth-to-mouth resuscitation
   b. A sabbatical
   c. Pension benefits

Moments After Perfect Sex

The guidelines:
- *Your heart rate:* elevated.
- *The spirit:* invigorated.
- *All muscle groups:* toned.
- *Your appetite:* enormous.

- *Your mind:* focused.
- *Your eyes:* crossed.
- *Your partner:* asleep.
- *The bed:* a shambles.
- *Regrets:* none.

Passionate Couples Confess

"After our second simultaneous climax, we were so relieved when we realized that our blurred vision was actually the windows fogged up."

> – Elvira and Butch, newlyweds

"After our third simultaneous climax, we were so relieved when we realized that our blurred vision was caused by tears of joy."

> – Ramona and Trigger, second honeymooners

Love at First Sight

What first attracted you to your lover?

"His biceps, triceps and forceps. I always wanted to marry a hunky surgeon."

> – Carmela, nurse

"My ringside table at Chippendale's."

> – Gidget, diesel mechanic

Regular Sex: Some Benefits

	Good	Very Good	Superior
Aerobic conditioning		X	
Alternate to bowling			X
Upper body muscle toning		X	
Lower body muscle toning	X		
Coping with another tax hike			X
Improved conversational skills	X		
Creative expression:			
At the office	X		
In bed			X

Reawaken Your Sex Life: Part IV

Some alternate locations.

Location	Advantages	Disadvantages
Futon	Goes anywhere. Easily rolls up after lovemaking.	Moves if not anchored down. During a steamy coupling, you may hit the wall.
Adirondack chair	Sturdily built. Seat angle invites many interesting positions.	Splinters.
Dining Table	Portion control.	None.

Lovers' Quarrel?

One solution:

"We constantly fought about money until we began to have sex."
         – Don and Mary

Wine and Your Sexual Fantasies: Part I

Type of Wine	Application
Burgundy	Releases libido, stimulates long-repressed but highly creative erotic fantasies?especially the embarrassing ones.
Bordeaux	Gives you new insights into how to implement these fantasies, particularly those involving leather and/or naugahyde.

Guide for the Out-of-Practice Lover

After long-term sexual deprival?what to expect from your first climax if, since your last one:

It's been	Reaction
One month	Earth will most definitely tilt
Two months	You'll go into orbit
Three months	And earn bonus miles
Four months	Sudden belief in a higher power (a God)
Five months	Sudden belief in a high power (your lover)

The Inquiring Lover

Q. What should I do when my partner declines an invitation to join me in a nice warm jacuzzi?

A. Take a cold shower.

Q. Is prolonged sexual deprival harmful?

A. Yes.

Q. What are the chief symptoms of prolonged sexual deprival?

A. 1. Clean living.

　　2. Celibacy.

Lovers' Poll #71

To what do you attribute your glowing, healthy skin?

"I'm a giving person. I gave up smoking, I give at the office and I give in to my wife at least four times a week?she can't keep her hands off me."

　　　　　– Don, cargo handler

"A thirty-minute Night Line workout with my husband four times a week. He's a human night-repair gel."

　　　　　– Gina, Don's wife

The Dieter's Guide to Weight Loss During Sex

Mental health experts tell us that sex-related guilt burns even more calories than guilt caused by never calling your mother.

Activity	Calories Burned
Thoughts of sleeping with your therapist	31
Thoughts of just rubbing against your therapist	7

Sleeping with your therapist:

As part of your treatment (the transference)	216
As part of your therapist's treatment (the counter transference)	390
For a reduced fee	21

The Inquisitive Lover

Question	Answer
"How many does that make?"	"My computer's down."
"Am I the best?"	"I was a novice till I met you."
"Was it good for you?"	"You made me lose the place in the book I was reading."
"Do I make you happy?"	"I laughed in all the right places."
"How about a rematch?"	"Call for an appointment."

Ten Things To Be Happy About After Sex: Part II

1. You had film in the camera.
2. You hiccups finally stopped.
3. You didn't run overtime.
4. There's still some ice cream left.
5. Tonight, you'll sleep.
6. Your cholesterol's down.
7. It feels so good yet doesn't hurt the environment.
8. The baby didn't wake up.
9. For once, your psychic was right.
10. You saved the best for last.

Senior Lovers Take Heed

The only problem with short-term memory loss:
"In the middle of sex with my new girlfriend, I suddenly remembered that I already had a perfectly good wife."
— Murray, shuffleboard coach (ret.)

Why I Hate Sex

"After four hours of doing it and doing it, we get so icky, especially on a warm summer night."
— Floyd, accountant

"It leads to other things, like four daughters, three sons and incredible tuition bills."

> – Norman, spice merchant

"Because it keeps me looking younger than I really am, I have to pay full fare on public transportation. The drivers never believe I'm 71."

> – Shirley, senior partner

"I never get any."

> – Cecilia, attorney

Orgasm: Five Benefits

1. If you're an insomniac, it will help you sleep the night through.
2. If you're concerned with your heart, a Level 10 climax* proves you've nothing to worry about.
3. If you're all stuffed up, a big one will drain your sinuses.
4. It's a nice way to break the ice.
5. It'll make your partner feel productive.

*Cracks the ugly vase your aunt gave you as a wedding gift.

Summer Beauty Tip

Studies show that at the moment of orgasm, a truly warm-blooded woman can lose up to 30% of her tan. (It is regained, however, during that stage of lovemaking known as "afterglow," in which she's at her most luminous.)

Gifts for the Perfect Lover

Romantic	Practical
A silk robe	A reference
Flowers	Lunch
A Gershwin CD	A bank CD
An ascot	A tie
A book of poetry	A pop-up sex manual
Lots of space	Closet space
A weekend in Paris	A free-seat upgrade

How Too Much Lust Affects Us

Our technical adviser reports that by the fifth hour of nonstop sex:
• 87% of all lovers, when asked, are unable to name our Secretary of Commerce.
• 99% of all lovers cannot do square roots without a calculator.
• 100% of all lovers don't care about the rebels?anywhere.
• 89% of all lovers note a definite decrease in their sex drive.

Was It Good for Us?

How proper couples felt after 15 minutes of reasonably satisfying sex?the result of our poll in Des Moines:
• "It sure whetted our appetite."
• "Perfectly willing to try again, in a week or two."
• "Quite nice. The way I imagine we'll feel when we finally sell our house?it's been on the market so long."
• "Really super. As though I'd just test driven a Lexus."
• "It's like...well...having a really special golf experience."
• "Never you mind, it's none of your business."
• "Like we found something super at a flea market."

For Ultra-Romantic Encounters

Night table necessities for advanced lovers:
1. Alarm clock (to awaken your sexual powers).
2. Makeup kit (for during-sex touch-ups).
3. Speakerphone (for hands-free discussions during lovemaking).
4. Feather (for tactile arousal).
5. Steaming bowl of New England clam chowder (the latest in sexual aromatherapy).
6. Ceramic cat (provides companionship without (a) exciting allergies or (b) jumping up on a startled lover's back).
7. Breathalyzer (to determine, during sex, how excited partner is). Digital readout indicates: 1. "Panting." 2. "Gasping." 3."Huffing." 4."Puffing." 5. "Need sushi."

The Enlightened Lover

Two during-sex questions that will either:
1. Bolster his ego: "Honey, why did you stop?" or
2. Deflate his ego: "Honey, why don't you stop?"

MONTHLY QUALITY OF LIFE® CHECKUP

•Despite the heat wave we did it: Once___   Twice___
53 times___(we thrive in humidity)
•Who perspired the most:
Me___
My partner___
The poor guy who cooled us by waving a palm frond___
•Our favorite part of sex was when we:
Slowly undressed each other___
Did it while wearing flip-flops___
Simultaneously blew in each other's ear (but wrenched our backs)___
Told each other our e-mail passwords___
Licked each other all over (the ultimate body moisturizer)___
Fell off the chaise lounge___
Realized we could make as much noise as we want because the kids were at camp___
•Favorite thing to do after sex:
Take more ginseng___
Fall asleep in each other's arms___
Straighten the pictures___
Vacuum___

Signed_____

Witnessed_____

SEPTEMBER

•Erotic goals for September:
1. Encourage partner to be more intimate during lovemaking.
2. Convince partner to reveal his last name.

At last! The kids are back in school so you can give each other your undivided attention. Use this month to re-excite your marriage by spending more time on hot, steamy sex (NOTE: May be difficult if spouse
(a) has back problems, or
(b) coaches Little League.)

Feeling sinful? Call in sick and cuddle in bed, getting up only to cook only a romantic breakfast (unregistered nutritionist's choice: Colt 45, french toast and Mallomars®) and check your e-mail. Out of practice? Who isn't? Not to worry however. Evidence shows that even among time-pressed working couples who make love just twice a year (St. Patrick's Day and Purim) it takes but a mere 33 seconds to remember what to do.** Out of shape? Try these three special perk-up-your-sex-life exercises recommended by Dr. Sid, our sports medicine expert:
1. Sit-ups. Tones tummy muscles, enables you to sit up quickly during sex to check an incoming fax.
2. Bench presses. For upper-body strength. Makes it easrier to carry partners into the bedroom, even if he's still wearing his knapsack.
3. Spinning. Provides cardiovascular workout necessary to get out of there fast of you hear the garage door opening and a voice call, "Honey, I'm home."
**Lab studies of divorcees who suddenly meet a hunky Club Med lifeguard confirm this.

Aphrodisiac of the Month:
Turkey croquettes

The Dieter's Guide to Weight Loss During Sex
Approaching orgasm.

Activity	Calories Burned
Quivering	19
Trembling	25
Actually vibrating:	
Low impact	31
High impact	40
False alarm	278

Sexual Demerits: Part III
All-purpose during-sex infractions.

Violation	Demerits Earned
Failure to flip lover when done on one side	8
Fibbing:*	
"You're the best I've ever been with"	26
"I never knew it could feel this way"	37
Failure to give full attention:	
During sex at night—reading mattress tag	˙33
During morning sex—reading back of cereal box	78

*Mitigating circumstance: lover has a weak ego.

Don't Forget
This is the month the kids go back to school and the perfect time to resume those noontime trysts with your (a) spouse or (b) lover or (c) both.

Gem of the Month
An uncut sapphire to the lover who relieved your first-night jitters by:
- Being patient and understanding.
- Holding you close and assuring you it's going to be okay.
- Singing Elizabethan love songs while strumming a lute.
- Luxuriously massaging your back with corn oil (low in cholesterol).
- Calming your fears by going only part of the way.
- Waiting until the next night to go the rest of the way.
- Waiting until the next week to go all the way.

Still On Good Terms? Part I
For committed recyclers, eight uses for an old lover:
1. A mailing address
2. Credenza, sofa or piano mover
3. A fourth at bridge
4. Recipe tester
5. Party guest
6. Blind date for a needy friend
7. An escort when times are tough
8. Strictly platonic . . . sex

Quality-of-Sex Tip
Those who use sex to keep fit should never think of a lover who's been:
• Divorced
• Widowed
• With at least three lovers before you
• With you for more than five years
as used exercise equipment.

The Well-Rounded Lover
In addition to a king- or at least queen-size bed (satin sheets a bonus), he or she has:
• An extra toothbrush
• Extra dental floss
• Hot water
• Air-conditioning
• A well-stocked refrigerator
• An assortment of take-out menus (for when the fridge is empty)
• No curfew
• Talent

For Speedier Sexual Service: Part II

Standard during-sex abbreviations.

Use:	When you mean:
"Y.A.A.B.I."	You are a bad influence.
"M.M.M.M.M."	My my my my.
"I.E."	I'm exhausted.
"M.A.W."	Make a wish.
"H.I.G.?"	How's it going?
"I.R.T.F.M.F.M."	I remember that from my first marriage.
"W.H.L.!"	We have liftoff!

The Prudent Lover

It is permissible to take the Fifth Amendment if, during sex, your partner asks:

• Why are we doing this?
• How do you feel about children?
• Is that your real height?
• Were you faking it?
• What are you thinking about?
• Who are you thinking about?
• Does it get any better than this?
• So . . . what really turns you on?
• How was I?

Are You Too Lustful: Part II

(Answering yes to even one question means your soul may be in danger.)

1. Have you ever had sex not for reproduction but for the sheer pleasure of it?
___ No ___ Yes, and what a revelation!

2. At the end of a rough day, have you ever turned down a beer and, instead, used sex to help you unwind?
___ No ___ Yes, and it was less filling.

3. Are you too spontaneous? Have you ever arrived home and made love with your spouse even though it wasn't your special time?
___ No ___ Yes, but I was instantly forgiven.

From Our Lover's Glossary

Silent Partner. One who, during sex, is afraid to make noise because he or she:
- Thinks it's uncouth.
- Might wake the kids.
- Is too inhibited.
- Is in the country illegally.

The Art of Romance

A dozen roses to a lover who, during sex, never complains:
- That you're not doing your share of the work.*
- If you occasionally make irrelevant remarks such as "You moan just like my high-school sweetheart."
- When you demand "a moment of silence" so you can a) fantasize or b) change positions.
- If you lose your place and have to start over again.
- If you achieve ecstasy first (as long as she achieves ecstasy last).

*"I'm saving my strength for your orgasm," is a satisfactory excuse.

Performance Anxiety

His Biggest Fear
She'll be too good in bed.
She'll want to be on top and I won't be able to see the playoffs.
I won't be able to tell if she's had an orgasm.

Her Biggest Fear
I'll be too good in bed.
He'll want to be on top and I won't be able to see the time.
Neither will I.

The Dieter's Guide to Weight Loss During Sex

Activity	Calories Burned
Multiple orgasms (within a 2-hour period):	
For a woman (per orgasm)	61
If complexion suddenly clears, add	27
If she breaks a nail	100
For a man	
The first	45
The third	126
The sixth (and he lives)*	400

*But may result in transient brain damage (a sudden incapacity to figure out his fair share of a restaurant check).

Love Poll #45

According to our sampling of 1,000 couples, when it comes to sex lovers argue most about:

• When they last had it	19%
• Why they had it	14%
• With whom they last had it	25%
• Whether to have it again	45%
• How much to have	32%
• What to watch while having it	19%
• When to stop	55%
• Whether there's a draft in the room	24%
• Money	41%

How to Tell

After the first time you make love, should you get together again?
Yes, if your partner says:
"I'd better check my pulse."
"Did you see the fireworks?"
"I feel so close to you."
"Oh God, I forgot how good it feels."
"I feel great."
No, if your partner says:
"I'd better check my messages."
"Did you see my car keys?"
"This bed is too narrow."
"Oh, God, I forgot to shut the iron off."
"I feel a draft."

During-Sex Demerits

Activity	Demerits
Giggling in the wrong places	5
Moaning in the wrong places	20
Cuddling your cat, instead of your partner	12
Thinking about the office	9
Chewing gum	3
Consulting your watch	20
Turning a good day into a bad night	50
Compulsive behavior (scrubbing the tiles while bathing with your lover)	25

"Not Tonight, Dear"

The six approved responses.

If you're	Reply
1. Patient	"How about tomorrow morning?"
2. Annoyed	"But I shaved."
3. Disappointed	"I thought I made a reservation."
4. Desperate	"But it's been so long."
5. An optimist	"That's okay, the night's still young."
6. Relieved	"Whenever."

Older Women With Younger Men

Advantages

He'll learn from her experience—older women are better in *and* out of bed.

An older woman is more understanding—she won't giggle if he experiences performance anxiety.

If they have nothing in common, they can talk about his mother.

Disadvantages

He'll be embarrassed if he tires before she does.

She may ruin him for younger women.

If they have nothing in common, she can be his mother.

Great Moments in Lovemaking

September 4, 1990, 11:35 P.M.: The discovery by two not completely experienced lovers that the back-to-back position ensures a novel and completely fail-safe method of birth control.

The Bedside Eater: Part III

Barbecued spare ribs (aphrodisiac for the beef lover):

Erotic Claim

Improves manual dexterity; enables a lover who has just given a three-hour massage to recapture feeling in fingertips and wrist without seeking professional help.

Scientific Evidence

Quite a bit. CAT scan of bed used by participating lovers revealed no trace of disappointment.

After-Sex Etiquette

After lovemaking, any partner who believes that the sex was just too much should feel free to take some home in a doggy bag.

Timesaving Tips For Busy Lovers

"An egg timer besides the bed keeps the sex short, and to the point."
    – Charlotte, model
"I remove most of my clothes while she's parking the car. It's just a short walk from the garage to the bedroom."
    – Bobby, actor
"I schedule sex precisely, usually from 11:05 to 11:22 P.M. If my partner's not there, I start without him."
    – Pamela, TV producer
"Wearing a phone headset leaves my hands free to fondle my partner and conduct business."
    – Mark, sales manager

Last-Minute Touches

Things to do before a new lover arrives.
1. Make sure you have plenty of ice cubes (for drinks and sprains caused by overdoing it.
2. Remove items from your medicine chest that you don't want her to see (like a pregnancy tester, especially if you're a male).
3. Light candles (overhead lighting can be cruel).
4. Hide your good jewelry (until you know him or her better).
5. Promise yourself you won't feel guilty if
• The sex turns out to be too good.
• He brings you a really expensive gift. ("You shouldn't have," is the correct response.)

Older Men With Younger Women

Advantages

Younger women are usually cheaper to date.
Older men usually spend more time on foreplay.
A younger woman is more flexible, can bend to accommodate his bad back.
If they have nothing in common, they can talk about sex.

Disadvantages
Older men can't digest French fries.
Hearing loss may hinder their ability to follow instructions.
She may bend too far.
If they have nothing in common, they can *only* talk about sex.

The Art of Romance
For making love in your car, we suggest either the:
Convenience position:
Woman on bottom
Man using cruise control
or
Out-of-gas position:
Woman on top
Man pushing

Sexual Rule of Thumb
After making love, "I think so" is not the best way to express your enthusiasm if your partner asks, "Was it good for you?"

The Inquiring Lover
What did you do on your summer vacation?
"By never leaving our hotel room, we achieved that healthy indoor pallor so sought after by those whose skin is sensitive to sunlight."
— Moishe and Olga, enjoying their third honeymoon
"Brought home two great souvenirs—-a tribal mask and a life-guard named Herb."
— Patty, florist

Time For Romance
At last! Children go back to school this month. Use your free time to:
• Enjoy the peace and quiet.
• Watch your favorite soap opera without interruptions.
• Get in touch with your inner self.
• Make up for lost lovemaking time (and meet your spouse during the day to do what you couldn't do while your kids were home on summer vacation).

Things to Be Thankful For After Sex: Part I
- The housekeeper didn't knock.
- You fell asleep first.
- He really is the man your mother warned you about.
- You didn't fall off the pedestal he put you on.
- The earth moved.

When To Change Positions
Researchers tell us that couples who remain in the same position for two or more hours have to be surgically separated (not covered by Medicare). Use these guidelines to decide when to switch:
1. Onset of mildew (on lover, not mattress)
2. Sighting of any mirage, such as an oasis or long-lost in-law
3. No feeling in the right leg (*and* it's turning magenta)
4. Design rubbing off decorator sheets

What I Did During Sex
"Showered her body with kisses."
> — Fernando, playwright

"Peppered his main frame with love bytes."
> — Alicia, computer jockey

The Dieter's Guide to Weight Loss During Sex
The positions.

Activity	Calories Burned
Usual:	
Male partner on top, female partner on bottom	47
Reversed	135
Unusual:	
Both on top	388
(For accuracy, add 24 calories if not certain how you got there.)	
Highly unusual:	
Both out of control	500

From Our Lover's Glossary
Tenure. A status granted to a teaching lover who, after a probationary period (five hours to five weeks, depending on the lover's expertise), receives certain privileges including:

1. Keys to your place.
2. A personal drawer and closet space.
3. Greater intimacy (a shelf in the bathroom).
4. Sleepover dates.
5. Midnight snacks when lovemaking continues into the wee small hours.
6. The right to see you without makeup.
7. A full partnership in the TV remote control.

Relationship Alert: Poll #60

How do you (diplomatically) get rid of unwanted lovers?

"I report them to the immigration authorities."
> – Alison, hostess

"Transfer them to the Middle East."
> – Raymond, supervisor, CIA

"No problem. The way out of a man's heart is also through his stomach. I can't cook."
> – Rita, osteopath

"Propose."
> – Christopher, baggage handler

To Serve You Better

Card to be filled out by your partner after lovemaking

	Excellent	Good	Average
Greeting	___	___	___
Quality of hug	___	___	___
How did I look?	___	___	___
Bedroom ambiance	___	___	___
Quality of lovemaking	___	___	___
Portion size	___	___	___

Is it likely you'll call within a week? ___ yes ___ no

Making the Last Move

He	She
Says how great it was.	Agrees.
Turns on the television.	Adjusts the color.
Calls and makes dinner reservations.	Decides where.
Hangs up or folds all clothing removed in haste.	Makes the bed.
Runs the water for their bath.	Gets the rubber duck.
Picks up any loose change dropped on the floor.	Tosses another log on the fire.

After-Sex Etiquette

It is the lover who did the most work who gets to:
• Lie there longest.
• Use the fluffiest towel.
• Linger in the bathroom longer.
• Watch while the other lover makes the bed.
• Hear the sounds of breakfast being made.
• See the Polaroids first.
• Take the most vitamins.

Memorable Moments in Lovemaking

Sad
"I chose a lover who was, alas, politically correct."
Happy
"I chose a lover who was, can I say it's politically erect."

The Prescient Lover: Part II

Why I was absolutely certain our romance wouldn't last:
"He kept borrowing my perfume."
– Marilyn, pediatrician
"Her answer was, well, painfully candid when I asked her, 'Am I the best you've ever been with?'"
– Alain, golf pro
"Just moments before sex, she'd always look deep into my eyes and say, 'Wake me when it's over.'"
– Morton, nice guy

Embarrassing (But Nice) Moments in Sex

• *"Forgetting my vow of celibacy."*
• "Neighbors pounding on the wall, wanting to know if everything's all right (it sure was)."
• "Shower clogs flew off during a Level 9 climax."*
• "Broke the ceiling fixture during an out-of-body orgasm."
• "After unbelievably wondrous sex, I tried to insert both legs into the same trouser leg."
• *"Partner moved the wrong way while switching positions. We ended up in Atlanta."*
*Spit curls straighten.

The Art of Romance

When did you realize your partner was an animal in bed?
"After ten minutes of kissing her back, she began to purr."
    – Luciano, baker
"She growled and bared her teeth when I asked if she'd share the pretzels."
    – Melvin, welder
"He turned chicken when I asked how he felt about bondage."
    – Arlene, housewife
"I left a rose on his pillow. He ate it."
    – Martha, real-estate appraiser

Remedial Lust: Part II

How long will you live?

Each time you:	To your life, add:
Receive a gentle love bite	8 minutes
Have sex with someone for their:	
Mind	5 minutes
Body	57 minutes
Both	3 days
Do it for the first time	20 minutes
Do it for the last time	1 minute

How Long Should Sex Take?

With a good lover, it will take quite a while.
With a great lover, it should take forever.

Lover Benefits Package

You are entitled to a bonus* whenever you must work extra hard during sex to:

• Arouse your lover.
• Keep your love interested.
• Fulfill your lover's fantasies.
• Achieve your fitness goals.
• Pass a kidney stone.
• Achieve lift-off.
• Keep your chin up.

*Breakfast, lunch or dinner in bed.

Sexual Energy: How It Is Channeled

Activity:	Effect:
Mild flirting	Boosts ego of flirtee
Intense eye contact	May cause flirters to break down
During-sex communication	Increases verbal skills
After-sex communication	Increases mumbling skills
Nibbling partner's earlobe	Giggling
Climax (ordinary)	May cause partner to hit the ceiling
Climax (extraordinary)	Will cause partner to see UFOs

Sexual Etiquette 101

Q. I love my husband but sometimes, after three hours of lovemaking, I want to stop (I'm a housewife and need my beauty rest) but don't want to hurt his feelings. Can you help?
— Audrey, Lansing, Michigan

A. You have several choices:
Tactful: "This is fun, but I have to get up early."
Gracious: "How about a nightcap?"
Guilt-inducing: "Guess what I found in your drawer."
Caring: "Sweetie, you'll wear yourself out."
Ego-inflating: "You're too much man for me."
Flattering: "You're too much husband for me."

From Our Lover's Glossary

Casual sex. *1.* Lovemaking without an appointment. *2.* Sex with someone you want to sleep with but may not want to know.

When the Unthinkable Happens

Event	What to Do
Partner complains that you make too much noise during lovemaking.	It's not your fault that you're oversexed. Give partner the silent treatment.
Your friends think that because you're dating a Republican, you hardly ever do it.	Kiss and tell.

Problem Lovers: Part I

Fatal Flaw	Symptom
Mood-wrecker	After tenderly kissing your neck and holding you close, whispers, "Let's go bowling."
Ambitions	Thinks sex with you is a terrific career move, just because you're a head hunter.
Neglectful	Doesn't open the car door and help you in with the groceries . . . unless you're carrying pretzels and a six-pack.

Sex Poll #78

How do you pass the time if sex isn't as exciting as usual?
"If I'm on the bottom, I watch my partner's bald spot move back and forth, back and forth. It's quite amusing."
— Joan, visiting nurse
"Worry about what others might be thinking."
— Jimmy, outpatient
"Try to remember what I was wearing the last time I had sex."
— Tracy, pageant contestant

What Do the Professionals Do?

The Problem
In the middle of feverish lovemaking, your new partner exhibits a frightening lack of sexual sophistication (asks, "Where do babies come from?").
The Solution
Be honest. Explain that the stork or, during the holiday season, Santa brings them, then continue.

458

Pillow Talk

Probationary lover. One who does not yet have:
- Seniority
- A personal drawer
- Space in your closet
- Space on your toothbrush holder
- Keys to your apartment
- Your cash-machine code
- Your undivided attention
- Tenure

After-Sex Testimonials

Participants tell how they felt.
"Like a believer."
> – B.J., 44, heiress

"Like a well-driven Porsche."
> – Seymour, 37, accountant

"The way a piano must feel upon which a consummate artist has just played several Chopin Études."
> – Kiki, 19, Wendy's employee

"Sort of floaty and magical. My eyes are sort of crossed, and I think how wonderful my parents were to have had me."
> – Cecile, 34, outpatient

"Embarrassed if I yelped too much."
> – Evelyn, 38, sex therapist

"Like a ravaged daffodil."
> –Norbert, 24, haberdasher

Sex Without Tears

Bedsores and minor irritations are best avoided by lubricating your lover at least three times per hour of sex at those points most subject to friction.

Recommended Lubricant	Apply to:
Jergens lotion	Palms
Baby oil	Elbows, knees
Margarine	Tip of nose, heels
Peanut oil	Tip of tongue
Champagne	Vocal cords
Engine oil	Hips

How Long Should You Wait to Have Sex?

After:	Wait:
Eating a tossed salad	10 minutes
Fried food	1 hour
Skiing cross country	2 hours
Downhill	45 minutes
Meeting a new lover through	
a friend	1 week
In a bar	1 month
Undressing in a warm bedroom	5 minutes
Cold bedroom	1 second

When to Think About Sex

A few suggestions to make those dull moments more bearable.
- *At a football game*—during half-time.
- *At a baseball game*—between innings.
- *Commuting to work*—while waiting for the trooper to finish writing a speeding ticket.
- *At work*—during any meeting lasting three or more minutes.
- *At the mall*—when there's nothing on sale.
- *While playing golf*—between putts.
- *After sex*—while waiting for the bathroom.
- *During sex*—while waiting for your partner.

The Enlightened Lover

After-sex question most often asked by:

A great lover
"Is everything all right?"

A so-so lover
"Is anything all right?"

Inside a Lover's Fortune Cookie

You will be successful in love, the moment you stop:
1. Wearing that "I Love Bingo" sweatshirt.
2. Answering personal ads from "multi-faceted individuals who love to laugh."

460

In the Wee Small Hours

Lonely? It's okay to call an ex-lover if:
• You miss his hands or her body.
• You need your robe back.
• You can't quite recall why you broke up.
• You just want to hear his or her voice.
• Even if it's only an answering machine.
• You broke up amicably and you know he'd love to hear from you.
• You didn't break up amicably but you know she doesn't have caller ID.

More Benefits of Sex

Sexual Activity	Benefit
Flirting (mild)	Renews elasticity of skin around eyes
Flirting (intense)	Reverses visible signs of aging
Arousal	Reduces pore size
Foreplay (regular)	More positive self-image, with or without a mirrored ceiling
Foreplay (imaginative)	Deepens dimples
Intercourse	Improves breathing technique

Communication Tip

While lover is on top: reach up and touch someone.

Good Grooming Tip for Tonight

Before seeing your lover, your alternate lover's fingerprints can be easily removed by wiping your skin thoroughly with olive oil (second pressing okay).

Thought for the Happy Lover

After wonderful sex, if you smile and the whole world smiles back at you, there's an excellent chance you forgot to pull the shades.

Endangered Species
Q. Our kids are leaving for college, how do we avoid the "Empty Nest" syndrome?
A. By becoming love birds.

The Inquiring Lover
Q. My husband of seventeen years claims I make him feel like a sex object. True, we do it six times a week and, when we eat dinner, I ask him to hurry so we can finish and go to the bedroom. But he's such a hunk. What's a wife to do?
— Matilda C., homemaker
A. Show you value him for more than just sex. During lovemaking for example, as him:
1. About his day at the office.
2. What movies he's seen lately.
3. When he's going to start earning more money.

The Good Sexual Samaritan
1. Is patient (does not keep glancing at the egg timer if the other person's taking too long to climax).
2. Knows CPR should the earth actually move during climax.
3. Keeps track of orgasms so neither partner is in danger of having too many.
4. Willingly assists a fatigued partner when switching positions.
5. Gives rain checks in the event of a football game on TV.
6. Cheerfully lies on the wet spot.

Pillow Talk
Tailgating. Spooning.
Hydroplaning. A during-sex event in which, owing to slippery conditions caused by satin sheets or frozen yogurt, one or both partners lose traction and slide into the next room.
Warranty. The assurance that a new lover will function with only minimal upkeep for at least six months or 180 climaxes, whichever comes first.

The Considerate Partner

It's time to stop if your lover is:
• Yawning
• Consulting his or her watch
• Worried about getting the laundry out of the dryer
• Bickering with the gardener
• Waving a flag of truce
• Checking the Yellow Pages under "Pest Control"
• Consulting a timetable

Sex for the Busy Couple

Suggested after-dinner schedule:

10:00 P.M. Give the secret "I'm ready for sex signal" (smile knowingly or shut off your P.C.).

10:11. Foreplay. Consists of tossing to see who gets the good side of the bed (the side that is already warm, or doesn't sag).

10:14. Panting. (Health tip: Between pants, take long sips of bottled water.)

10:19. Communication. (Choose either from: "Oh, oh, oh" or "When are you going to get a real job?").

10:24. He says: "All done."

10:25. She says: "Good boy."

10:30. The big question: "What do you want to watch?"

The Candid Lover: Part I

Questions often asked by a new partner.

Question	Good Reply	Bad Reply
When did you lose your virginity?	Moments ago.	Several partners ago.
Are you allergic to anything?	Dogs.	Nudity.
What's your favorite sport?	Climbing over you to get a snack.	Golf.
Do you mind performing oral sex?	Depends.	Depends on where.

The Enlightened Lover

A true romantic never permits
- A backache
- Lack of partner enthusiasm (he's watching *Jeopardy*)
- Visitors
- A losing lottery ticket
- Last week's triple bypass
- A bad-hair day
- The wrong night
- The wrong apartment

to interfere with lovemaking

Tip for the Dual Lover

Before going home to your other lover:

Remove	Method
Cat hair	Adhesive
Hickey	Feather boa or blusher
Aroma of:	
Shaving lotion	Rub face with Listerine
Perfume	Soak clothing in bourbon
Bite marks	Self-tanning lotion
Fingerprints	Ajax

Tips for Senior Lovers

1. You're only as young as you feel.
2. You're only as old as your lover feels.
3. Avoid Florida in August.

Not in Touch with Your Feelings?: Part I

An official guide to sex-related guilt.

You've slept with someone: Should you feel guilty?

	Yes	No
Because you had to (it was your wedding night).		X
Because you really needed sex.		X
Because they really needed sex.		X
Only to release excess energy.		X
To see if you should sleep with them again.		X
Because of their body.		X

What I Did to Avoid Sex

"Went out only with the men my mother fixed me up with."
— Adrienne, social worker
"Fantasized about my present job. That really worked."
— Marty, car salesman
"Suppressed all feelings of lust. Boy, did that hurt."
— Trish, police officer
"Nothing, absolutely nothing, and I'm deliriously happy."
— Fifi, astrophysicist

Lovers' Poll: #65

Why I'm abstaining from sex:
"Too broke to call a 900 number."
— Peter, plasterer
"Wife left me—and she took my heart, my soul and the bed."
— Herman, shoe salesman
"My mind's on other things."
— Jessica, studying for her law finals
"We've decided to adopt instead."
— Alice and Adam, retired
"Stuck with really homely tentmates."
— Marvin, Marine on bivouac

Distractions

Activity	Difficulty Factor
Making love to the sound of:	
Wind chimes	2
Chamber music	1
Traffic whizzing by your motel room	8
Sermon: live	10
televised	9.5
The couple next door	15
Your partner's jingling bracelets	5
Adoring fans	1

After-Sex Etiquette

To regain your rightful share of the bed, use:
• *The push*—both hands open, palms against lover's back, foot against wall for leverage.

- *The jab*—elbow into lover's ribs, repeat if necessary.
- *The double poke*—both knees against lover's back.
- *The tilt (a drastic measure)*—incline mattress at 45° angle, observe lover roll into next room.

The Inquisitive Lover

Q. Whenever we have especially passionate sex, our bed speaks alarmingly. Not only is this distracting, but the people next door have sought an injunction. When we took the bed back to the dealer, he said it was normal. What should we do?

A. Either:

1. Use a jacuzzi.
2. Check for mice.

The Inquisitive Lover

Q. My wife, a real-estate agent, refuses to make love for at least one week before selling a house. She says she'll need all her strength for the closing. Does that sound right?

A. Not really. Studies show that sex has no effect on strength (although at the moment of orgasm, research suggests that we may lose up to 27% of our IQ, temporarily).

Sex in America: Part I*

Do you think you are getting enough sex?

Yes	46%	No	21%
Not sure	15%	What is enough?	18%

What do you argue about more?

Sex	12%	Money	88%

What do you have more of?

Sex	79%	Money	21%

*Based on our telephone poll of 1,000 registered lovers

From Our Emergency Sex Manual

Her mother's sick? He has to work late? When your lover cancels at the last minute, use the time productively to:

1. Hold your teddy bear close and cry on its shoulder.
2. Finally do that three weeks worth of laundry.
3. See if that easy-to-follow recipe for lemon chicken salad is really easy to follow.

4. Finally call your parents (first take 22 sips of a reasonably flinty Chardonnay if you're an only child).
5. Sort your shopping coupons.
6. Draft a personal ad (just in case).
7. Find out the real reason why your lover canceled.

Sad Moments in Afterplay

"Watching him carve our initials on the tree we did it under. I'm a member of the Sierra Club."
> – Margo, union organizer

"Watching her (sob) carve another notch on her belt."
> – Mario, personal trainer-in-waiting to a megastar

The Bedside Eater

Aphrodisiac of the Night	Erotic Effect
Mallomars	Provoke torrid thoughts, yet still allow you to operate heavy machinery

Aphrodisiac of the Night	Erotic Effect
Candygram	Turns a timorous mouse into a sensuous vixen and a bashful male into a hot-blooded Galahad

Life: Part III

With Sex	Without Sex
Making love can always turn a bad day into a good night	Have to resort to bowling and potato chips
Little notes to lover	Little notes to landlord
Afterflow from lovemaking	Afterglow from chili
In your bedroom: the "greatest show on earth"	Must visit the circus
Lovers' quarrels	Community activism
Fantasies	Dreams

From Our Lover's Glossary

Love slave. *1*. One who exhibits a depraved indifference to celibacy. *2*. One under the domination of an erotic power, such as a fiercely attractive and expert lover, over which that person has little or no control. The signs:

• Having sex as often as possible.
• Ignoring other just-as-fun activities, such as golf, frisbee and fishing.
• Smiling at nothing.
• A significantly improved cardiovascular system.
• Telling friends.

Frequent Lovemaking*: The Benefits

• It's addictive.
• It's heart smart.
• What to wear is never a problem.
• It readies one for military service.
• That constant feeling of walking on air (even in heels).
• Breathtaking views without looking out the window (applies to in-shape partners only).
• Immediate gratification.
*Based on the U.S. average of twice weekly for married couples; 16 times weekly for engaged couples.

The Enlightened Lover

You know you have a great love life when:

• Your complexion glows.
• You neglect your health club workouts (instead, you opt for better ones, in your bedroom).
• You buy a new set of sheets (designer, of course).
• You even consider the purchase of a new mattress.
• You're rapidly achieving a healthy indoor look.
• You no longer need warm milk to fall asleep.

Undressing Each Other: Part I

Problems for the male partner on a scale of 1 to 20.

Removing	Difficulty Level
Her jeans:	
Relaxed fit	4
Skin tight	8
Legs not waxed	17
Her bra:	
Back closure	5
Front closure	4
But he thinks it's a back closure	10
Her shoulder bag	2
If it contains her Filofax	15

The Bedside Explorer: Part IV

An erotic adventure for the dauntless lover.

Expedition 4 (Lola's Lift-Off)

Equipment recommended: nerve

Begin wherever your lover asks you to. Continue until one of you reaches the top.

The Bedside Eater

Aphrodisiac of the Morning

Erotic Application

Éclair (acceptable alternative: brownie).

The one form of oral sex permissible on one's coffee break.

Aphrodisiac of the Night

Erotic Application

Carrots (raw, boiled or puréed).

Improve night vision—allows lovers to find each other's erogenous zones without using halogen.

Really Great Moments in Sex

"I finally met the man my mother warned me about."
> – Rhonda, fashion consultant

"I'm the man!"
> – Yves, photographer ·

Ideal Working Conditions

A caring lover always provides:

• A king-size bed (two twin beds tied together is not acceptable).
• Fitted sheets (so they don't bunch up during frantic sex).
• Health care (plenty of chocolate brownies on the night table).
• Floss (so you can floss after each brownie).
• Severance pay (in the form of cab fare; gas money or supper money if you decide not to stay the night).
• A toothbrush if you decide to stay the night.

Fashion Tips

How do you show your lover your tender side?

"I treat him just like his mother treats him, except for the nagging."

> – Estelle, blackjack dealer

"I'm supportive. She's been out of work, so I pay her dues to NOW."

> – Al, arbitrager

"I turn over."

> – Vicky, homemaker

Sexual Etiquette

When you meet that special someone at a party, you may, if you can't wait, ravish each other in your host's bathroom so long as you:

• Excuse yourselves ("We'll return in a moment," is sufficient).
• Allow the couple already in the bathroom to finish.
• Take no more than 10 minutes.
• Use only the guest towels
• Clean up afterward.
• Flush.
• Look reasonably sheepish when you emerge.

Traveler's Advisory #2

Most recommended position for in-flight lovers:
Woman on bottom
Man earning bonus miles

The Dieter's Guide to Weight Loss During Sex

Activity	Calories Burned
Making love in front of a mirror:	
For pleasure	127
For knowledge (to spot what you're doing wrong)	251
If mirror is:	
Floor length, add	63
On ceiling, add	79
Hand-held	175

Sexual Demerits: Part III

Some typical during-sex electronic infractions.

Offense	Number of Demerits
Watching television while making love	6
And actually following the story line	25
Failure to relinquish channel selector during foreplay	8
Excessive clicking during moments of exquisite passion	5
Constantly flipping during intercourse	10

Are You Oversexed?

The five warning signs:

1. You sometimes call in well so you can enjoy all-day sex with your lover.
2. After 3 hours of sex, your lover begs you to go to work.
3. After 4 hours of sex, your lover begs you for (a) a breather or (b) lunch.
4. You frequently make your lover see stars such as (a) Sirius or (b) Madonna.
5. You still haven't married.

Sexual Fact

Researchers tell us there is no such thing as a bad climax. Even if it makes you forget
- To phone home
- To be depressed
- You're a lady
- He's a gentleman

- Why you're having sex
- To offer your partner refreshments
- Who's boss

Taking Precautions

Items to shed before sex	Why
Item	Partner on the bottom may swallow them.
Pearls	In the missionary position, friction causes gold to overheat and melt.
Navel ring	Assures partner you plan to stay awhile.
Shoes	
Inhibitions	The only way to experience truly wild sex.

Approved Excuses: Part II

For Him	For Her
Too tired	Not our special time
Lower-back pain	Nails still wet
In mourning (car's in shop)	Roast in oven
Game on	Don't need sex (already sleepy)
Too cold	Too hot
League night	Favorite movie on
We'll wake the kids	We'll wake the neighbors

When the Unthinkable Happens

The Problem

While undressing your lover, you peek and discover a "wrong" designer label. You find yourself distraught and barely able to continue making love.

Why It Happened

You picked the wrong lover. Next time, don't be so democratic. (Or at least turn out the lights before you begin to make love.)

Trade Secret

If the phone rings while you're making love, no matter how curious you are, it's better to wait until after you've both climaxed to check your answering machine.

Did You Know?

62% of all sex-related stress fractures occur when, during exceptionally vigorous moments, a tall partner's unprotected head slams repeatedly against the headboard. Defense: wear a bicycle helmet.

Quality Time: Part I

Questions often asked by busy couples after sex: "Where did the time go?" Some answers.

Activity	Minutes Consumed
Making sure the kids are asleep	2
Reading them a bedtime story if they're not:	
Little Red Riding Hood	11
Hansel and Gretel	14
Tiptoeing back to the bedroom	3
Waking up dozing spouse:	
With gentle kisses	2½
With your elbow	¼

Magic Numbers: Part III

10 pounds per square inch: The average cheek-to-cheek pressure when you slow dance with an attractive partner.

8: The number of minutes a full-service lover devotes to a foot massage.

2: The volume, in ounces, of oil consumed during a foot massage.

13: How many seconds the average lover goes without breathing during a Level 7 climax (you experience weightlessness).

14: The number of minutes one spends on the phone telling a best friend about an absolutely terrific new lover.

40: The number of minutes one spends on the phone telling a best friend about a perfectly awful new lover.

Reminder

It's early, but not *too*, early, to begin worrying if you don't yet have a date for New Year's Eve.

Great Moments in Marathon Lovemaking

"Realizing we'd stayed in bed so long that we'd have to pay $47.65 in overdue library book fines."

> — Elvis and Dolly, trapeze artists

"My partner asking what all the shouting is about."

> — Emily, t'ai chi instructor

"Thinking sweat."

> — Herman, philosopher

From Our Book of Sexual Records

Loudest moan of sex-related pleasure: The most audible moan of pleasure on record was that of Heidi G., of Zermatt, Switzerland. She was heard three miles away by her husband, Hansel, who was driving home in a car with a broken muffler.

Something to Keep in Mind

According to the Lover's Code of Responsibility, your partner receives combat pay if, during sex:

- Your cat jumps on the bed.
- The dog starts barking when you begin to moan.
- Your spouse comes home early from a business trip.
- Dried flowers cause an allergic reaction.
- The bed moves more than 11 inches in any direction.
- You're also holding a tag sale.
- Marauding Jehovah's Witnesses try to leave literature."
- You change positions every 42 seconds.
- Your housekeeper interrupts to ask, "How many for dinner?"

Our To-Do List

Thing to make after lovemaking that is:

- Good: An intimate candlelight dinner for two.
- Great: Vacation plans.
- Superior: Future plans.
- So-so: Re-stringing pearls.

Lover's Poll #78

Some typical replies to that inevitable during-sex question:
"Where'd you learn that?"
"Watching afternoon soaps. *General Hospital,* especially."
> – Kirk, househusband

"My high-school sweetheart. He's now my gynecologist."
> – Edna, social worker

"A client. It was the only way I could close the sale."
> – Lester, vacuum-cleaner salesman (door-to-door)

"Charm school."
> – Bunny, debutante

Food and Sex: Part I

The voracious eater.

Dining Habits

Eats with face only inches from plate. Tip of nose makes small craters in mashed potatoes. Licks plate clean, then belches appreciatively.

Type of Partner

Unbelievable. Leaves no erogenous zone wanting. Possesses a kissing technique known to provide adult-strength hay fever relief. Has made many partners late for work, but they never complain.

In-Bed Advice: Part I

Should you make love *under* your quilt?

Pros

1. Under-quilt snugginess provides greater feeling of intimacy and closeness.

2. Under-quilt lovemaking preserves body heat.

3. Erogenous zones less accessible but certain to be warm when finally found.

Cons

1. Freedom of movement will be curtailed, specially if quilt is stuffed with goosedown.

2. Lack of oxygen almost sure to cause dizziness.

3. A really small lover may get lost in the quilt and never again be found.

Sexual Burnout: The Symptoms

• Exhaustion after only the first minute of sex (even if you're not overworked).
• Lackadaisical attitude toward your partner's orgasm (and irritability if it's too loud).
• Abdicating responsibility for your own orgasm.
• Sudden intolerance to partner's usual during-sex demands such as:
"More!"
"Much more."
"A little less."
"Could we try it with our clothes off?"

Overcoming Mental Blocks to Sexual Pleasure

If Your Inner Critic Says:	You should:
I don't feel good about myself in this position.	Ask your partner to get off your leg, it's numb.
I'm not being assertive enough.	Change your therapist.
During sex, I often feel my lover doesn't know who I am.	Point to the business card taped to your forehead.
I'm much too shy during sex.	Cease holding open rehearsals.

Romantic Criteria

You know you're a great lover if your partner keeps coming back for more, although you:
• Never remember birthdays.
• Have a paunch.
• Keep only catsup and several packs of preowned crackers in the refrigerator—and you never go out to dinner.
• Life like a poet (no sheet on the bed, towels you can see through).
• Reside in a two-fare zone.
• Always leave the seat up.
• Adore garlic
• Are not yet legally separated.

During-Sex Fantasies

Should you feel guilty if, to heighten arousal:

You Think About	Yes	No
A new Mercedes convertible		X
Stuffed with starlets	X	
Your partner		X
And how you wish he was with you	X	
An ex-lover	X	
If he called that afternoon	X	
What it would be like to be with two lovers		X
Your partner and his twin	X	
Your partner and your twin		X

Six Embarrassing Sexual Moments

"Heartburn from love bites."

"Got lost among lover's houseplants while blazing new sexual trails."

"It was hay fever season and I couldn't stop sneezing."

"Edible underwear turned out to be indigestible."

"I set off the sprinkler."

"Created a wet spot the size of Lake Tahoe."

In-Bed Advice: Part II

Or should you make love *on* your quilt?

Pros

1. Easier to see the ceiling mirror—and the stars.

2. Helpful neighbors who peer in your window will be able to see what you're doing wrong.

3. Unlimited freedom of movement allows esoteric positions for the fidgety partner.

Cons

1. Loss of heat makes lovers less energy-efficient.

2. Less body protection makes lovers vulnerable to external forces such as playful cat and meteor showers.

3. Constant whining of partner pathologically susceptible to drafts.

The Enlightened Lover

Four ways to tell your partner that he or she is not great in bed:

1. Quietly
2. Diplomatically

3. Not in a public place
4. Fax

Disappointing Moments in Lovemaking

"Too much passion. We kept sliding off our new satin sheets. Next time, we wear deck shoes."

— Irene, customer service representative

"Holding hands and trying to watch a gorgeous sunset through a stained-glass window."

— George and Gilda, church proprietors

"On a romantic cruise for two under a beautiful starry night sky, our canoe tipped over and all the candles went out."

— Megan and Oolak, explorers

Getting Away from It All

Fall weekend tip—privacy or charm?

Motel	Inn
Nobody cares what you do once they run your card through the machine.	Must wipe feet, beware of breakable "period pieces."
TV in room—you can turn it on immediately after sex.	Shelf of mildewed books. Must talk to partner after sex.
Privacy. Discreet desk clerk leaves you free to roam the grounds and stroll in peace.	Trapped. Over-friendly owner can't wait to show you the decor and the herb garden.

Communication

Common during-sex fibs.
1. "You're wearing me out."
2. "I don't usually do this so soon, it must be the moon."
3. "You make me feel like such:
    a) a man."
    b) a woman."
    c) an animal."
4. "I never fake it."
5. "You can stop at any time."

The Dieter's Guide to Weight Loss During Sex

You don't always have to be in bed to experience a rich orgasm.

Activity	Calories Burned
Discovering an undiscovered restaurant	83
A short bank line	90
A refund from the IRS	120
A promotion	31
With raise	231
Sudden departure of in-law who had planned to stay two weeks	500
No cavities	204

Lover Alert

At last! The days are getting shorter, the nights are growing longer—more time to devote to lovemaking. Compare:

The Ritual	Summer	Fall
Opening the champagne	3 minutes	7 minutes
Preparing the bath	8 minutes	12 minutes
Removing clothes	1 minute	5 minutes
Lighting candles	2 minutes	5 minutes
Decanting massage oil	1 minute	3 minutes
Placing name cards on pillows	2 minutes	4 minutes
Sex	45 minutes	2 hours

The Art of Romance

The sexual half-time—alternate bedside amusements.

If you're	Use
Lonely	A telephone
A bird watcher	Binoculars
Tense	A jump rope
Exhausted	A sleeping mask
A gastronome	Carrot sticks (with low-cal dip)
Wondering where the time went	A checklist
Handy	A power tool

Recession Lovemaking

Some tips:

• Instead of paying dues, use your bedroom as a health club.

• A leftover lover, when reheated and served the next day, makes a

perfect noontime snack.
- Install energy-efficient windows if, during sex, your lover proves an unreliable heat source.
- Take advantage of early bird specials—make love before 5:00 P.M.
- Before changing them, use both sides of the sheets.

Our Frequent Lover Program: Part I

Each Time Your Partner	Bonus Points*
Tells you how:	
Wonderful you are	8
To drive	$^1/_4$
Plays:	
Hard to get	3
Easy to get	7
Sinatra	10
Communicates by:	
Whispering in your ear	4
Moaning	8
Nagging	$^1/_2$

*Partner needs 50 points for a free ride.

Reminder for Forgetful Lovers
Thinking about sex at least three times a day can:
- Lower your blood pressure.
- Enable you to sleep better.
- Give more meaning to your life.
- Take your mind off the latest Middle East crisis.
- Keep you sane.
- Improve your sex life.

Love Signs
Horoscope for a Lascivious Libra
- *Ruling passion:* bewitching lifeguards
- *Ruling body lotion:* chocolate syrup except for special evenings (then it's Ovaltine).
- *Chief sexual asset:* poise
- *Governing erogenous zone:* a big one
- *Aphrodisiac of choice:* red sangria (white makes you critical)

- *Ruling sexual activity:* moaning fortissimo and embarrassing your partner
- *Ideal time for sex:* dear season

Reminder for the Sensitive
During sex-questions never to ask a lover who is honest:
1. Where'd you learn that?
2. Are we doing it as often as we should?
3. Am I the best you've ever been with?
4. Why are you laughing?
5. Do you think I've gained weight?
6. Can you tell I had garlic?
7. Am I your first?
8. Am I your first on these sheets?
9. Was that real or faked?
10. Where do we go from here?

Love Signs
Horoscope for a Luscious Libra.
- *Ruling passion:* sex and cute puppies
- *Ruling sexual turnoff:* working for a living
- *Chief sexual asset:* many in-bed job skills
- *Governing erogenous zone:* any soft surface
- *Aphrodisiac:* the contents of an Italian bakery
- *Ruling sexual activity:* turning bad days into good nights
- *Ideal time for sex:* a sizzling weekend tryst

Reminder
Today is the first day of autumn. Time to switch to:
1. A down comforter.
2. Flannel pajamas.
3. Your wool bathrobe.
4. A winter-weight lover (one who is at least 10 to 15 pounds over-weight will keep you warm even when the thermometer dips below freezing).
5. Cold-weather sex—you do it:
- Under the covers.
- As often as possible to maintain body heat.
- As rapidly as possible to produce body heat.

Love Signs: Regular Libra

Opposite love sign: An ardent Aries but, if none available, don't be too quick to spurn an ardent pint of vanilla fudge.

Outstanding sexual quality: With minimal coaxing will yield to temptation but still respect yourself in the morning.

Most attractive physical feature: A complexion that passes muster in even the cruelest light (and sparkles after sex).

Ruling sexual turnoff: Politically correct partners who, in bed, respond to only one movement—affirmative action.

Ruling sexual turn-on: Petite partners—they eat less.

Ideal place for sex: The lavatory of a corporate jet.

Love Signs: Irregular Libra

Most attractive feature: All-American good looks that work just as well in Venice, Tangiers, Manila and the Bronx.

Turn-on: Sleepless nights because of a new lover.

Turnoff: Sleepless nights because of a new baby.

Ideal romantic adventure: Journeying underground and, with your lover, turning an ice cave into a steam bath.

Favorite sexual fantasy: Winning a custody battle (he gets the friends, you get the dog).

It's okay to talk about sex on the first date—it'll keep the relationship platonic."
— Chlorinda Ford, Ph.D.

Post-Sexual Bliss

How soon after sex does one generally fall asleep?

If the quality of sex was:	You will be asleep in:
Good (smile of contentment on face)	7 to 9 minutes
Terrific (cannot say "You're the best" clearly)	5 minutes
Beyond belief (during climax, your bird panicked)	3 minutes
Out of this world (during climax, your slipper socks flew off)	11 seconds

Great Climaxes We Have Known

"We woke the kids."
                    – Rudyard and Faith
"The earth moved."
                    – Veronica and Lyle
"The earth got out of our way!"
                    – Gilda and Norbert

Just So You Know

During-sex utterances likely to diminish passion:
- "So, big boy, how was your day?"
- "You're nearly the best I've ever been with."
- "Ummm, that's my watch, not a birthmark."
- "Make yourself at home, I'll be right back."
- "Calm down, you're mussing my hair."
- "Better go check on the baby."
- "Do you smell gas?"
- "Is that a wet spot . . . or duck sauce?"

Perking Up Your Sex Life

How do our panel of lovers cure the blahs?
"We do everything they only leave to the imagination in those Gothic romance novels (you should see our bodice bill)."
                    – Adolph, drill press operator
"If her boyfriend's not in the mood, I take pity and invite my room-mate to join Oscar and me, we're loose."
                    – Clarissa, auditor
"I lie there with my arms at my sides, perfectly motionless. It forces him to be creative."
                    – Jodie, manager

When Do You Think About Sex?

(Exit poll at a midwest Kmart.)
- "Sunday morning. Our new minister is a) so sexy and b) so un-married and I feel c) so guilty."
- "Whenever my husband and I visit a petting zoo."
- "On the phone when I'm talking to an American Express cus-tomer-service rep. Their voices are so sexy."
- "Standing in front of a salad bar."

• "Whenever my new assistant stretches out on the conference table, arches his back and bats his eyelashes. He calls it a 'desk job.'"
• When I'm not getting any."

What I Did for Love
"Let my fingers do the walking—all over my lover."
> – Lorna F., overseas operator

Know Your Sexual Law
The Abandoned Partner: A partner is deemed "abandoned" and may sue for damages when the other partner:
1. Curls up and goes to sleep:
    a. Moments after sex; or
    b. Moments before sex (aggravated abandonment).
2. Jumps up during partner's climax to:
    a. Start the coffee; or
    b. Order a ski parka from Eddie Bauer.
3. During foreplay, also tries to adjust TV antenna.
4. Leaves him or her at a scenic overlook.

The Lover Bonus Package
To the lover who called you at the last minute and rescued you from:

An evening of
• One sad little TV dinner
• Watching television (because of boredom and loneliness)
• Doing a laundry, then sleeping alone

Give
• Buttercups
• A bottle of premier cru Bordeaux
• Your full cooperation

The Benefits of Sex: A Testimonial
"At night, when I'm in bed and have aches and pains and sleeplessness, I turn to aspirin-free Bufferin. If that doesn't work, I roll over and turn to aspirin-free Martin. He's my lover."
> – Jacqueline, librarian

Quote of the Month

"Our lovemaking makes my husband speechless. Now if it would only make him snore less."

> – Wife who hasn't had a good night's sleep since 1989

Pressed for Time?

How busy couples make more time for lovemaking.

"We read only book reviews, never books."

> – Fred and Millie

"We never wear underwear. It takes but three seconds to undress each other."

> – Lynda and Arturo

"We quit our jobs."

> – Sanford and Sonya

"We have a rule: Never spend more than one hour on foreplay."

> – Don and Nancy

Love Poll #7

The unofficial results of the annual Mayor's Conference Survey:

• 68% of the men felt that it was wrong, during sex, to permit a cat on the bed unless it assists.

• 8% of the women resented their partner's dog keeping time with its tail.

• 30% of the men were sure their partner had not faked orgasm if her eyes were crossed (although scientific evidence shows otherwise).

• 61% of the women felt that, during sex, their partner came in handy.

The Enlightened Lover

Suggested breakdown concerning division of labor.

If one partner:	The other should:
Waters the plants.	Walk the dog.
Sets the alarm.	Lock the doors.
Prepares the bed.	Open the wine.
Hangs the mistletoe (seasonal).	Get under it.
Stokes the fire.	Warm the bed.
Says prayers.	Grant them.

Our Slumber Expert Tells Us

The most complete and healthful sleep is one that's experienced after sex. Unlike regular sleep, which rests only a small part (1/4) of the brain and very few muscles, true post-orgasmic slumber* is often deeper, richer and refreshes and rejuvenates the entire mind, most of the spirit and nearly 87% of the body.

*Occasionally mistaken for a coma.

From Our Lover's Glossary

Chemistry. An initial, possibly binding attraction between two people which, if they aren't careful, can lead to woeful excesses such as:

• An inability to keep their hands off each other.
• Doing it more than 8_ times a week.
• Neglecting friends.
• Puffy eyes from too little sleep.
• Smiling at strangers.
• Walking on Cloud 9 without a safety belt.
• Marriage

Did You Know?

Our research couples tell us that one hour of intensive sexual activity burns the same amount of calories as:

• Shaving your legs 500 times.
• Searching, after sex, for a lost contact lens.
• Running in place on a treadmill for 46 minutes.
• Shaking your partner awake after a passionate nooner so she won't return to work late.
• Feeling around for the light switch in the bathroom of a new lover's apartment at midnight.
• Making ordinary love for 1_ hours.
• Trying to pry the lid off a pint of Häagen-Dazs while it's still frozen.

From Our Lover's Glossary

Aromatherapy. When a sexually-transmitted fragrance a) enhances lovemaking and/or b) seduces a partner not afflicted with a stuffy nose. Essential "sniff points" are divided into two categories:

1. Bodily, including:
• Hair, behind the ear lobe and behind the knees.
• Nape of the neck and other unmentionable places.*
2. Culinary, particularly:
• An oven in which an apple pie is baking.
• A pan in which Canadian bacon is frying.
• A pot in which white bean soup is simmering.
*Mmmmmm, something smells good," indicates the treatment is working nicely.

Pillow talk
Sport sex. The use of sexual activity to replace exercises such as running, tennis, squash or cooking, which, due to injuries, one is no longer able to enjoy. Common sports-related injuries that are eased by sexual workouts include:
• Aging
• Athlete's foot
• Tennis elbow
• Jogger's knee
• Charleyhorses
• Failure to score

Thought for Today
Send one dozen roses to the lover who:
• Makes your eyes shimmer.
• Makes your windows fog up (and your glasses).
• Takes out the garbage (before sex).
• Found your other birthmark.
• Never rushes.
• Keeps you warm.
• Serves you breakfast in bed (without getting up).
• Responds to visual stimuli such as:
a. You
b. Flash cards
• Doesn't need a road map to go all the way.

What I Did for Great Sex
"Came out of retirement."
                    – Edwina, nurse

"Found a girl just like the girl that married dear old dad."
> – Ethan, brain surgeon

"Waived the prenuptial agreement."
> – Kyle, dentist

Tip for the Guilt-Ridden Lover
If, after a night of wondrous, passionate, uncontrolled, even lustful sex, you can't face yourself:
1. Lie face down on the bed. This will prevent you from looking up at the ceiling mirror.
2. Be comforted in the knowledge that you must have been doing something right.
3. Eat a nourishing breakfast—you're going to need it.
4. Don't ever do it again—until the next time.
5. Face your lover—and smile.

Why I Love Sex

"It helps me decide if I'm with the woman I want to be the governess of my children."
> – Jeff, astronaut

"It helps me determine if I'm finally with the man my astrologer warned me about."
> – Karen, healer

"It gives me an excuse to lie down in the middle of the afternoon."
> – Theresa, pilot, USN

"I love doing seventeen things at once."
> – Wayne, chef

"It gives me great pleasure to do the Lord's work."
> – Priscilla, Lady

"My Intentions Are Honorable"

Can mean that a person:
• Isn't just a gold digger.
• Will not take sexual advantage when you have six or more beers and invite him to join you in a game of strip poker.
• Wants you for more than just your body, your mind, sex, breakfast and a ride on the back of your new motorcycle.
• Desires a serious relationship instead of just a one-night stand (not to worry if she leaves in the morning without telling you her

last name, address or phone number—it could mean only that she's shy).

• Won't try to see your driver's license to determine your real age.

A Guide to Vehicular Sex
Any Compact
Advantages
Smaller size encourages greater intimacy and (Bonus!) vehicle easier to push if you run out of gas.
Disadvantages
Minimal legroom: difficult to drive with jeans around ankles.

Love Poll #11
The results of a survey in which 1,000 people were asked, "How did you meet your lover?"

• Through a relative	14%
• In a museum	3%
• Mail order	9%
• At a party	16%
• Word of mouth	3%
• Recruiting poster	2%
• Through a friend	41%
• Through an enemy	10%

Be a Kinder, Gentler Lover
1. If your partner wants to see you again, don't show off by consulting your engagement book.
2. If your partner calls out your name during sex, don't pretend you didn't hear (or worse, ask "What do you want?").
3. Wait until after sex to run an errand (unless it's for more potato chips—an approved and, for some couples, a vital aphrodisiac).
4. Never ask, "How was I?" in the middle of sex. It may confuse your partner.

A Happy Couple Shares Their Secret
"After really tiring lovemaking, we just kind of lie there, then gather our strength, put it in a pile and use it either to make love again or put the kids through college."
 – Julia and Jim, parents.

The Curious Lover

Q. Is it ever proper to read a lover's diary?
A. Yes, but only to find out:
- If he's literate.
- If he really bowls on Thursday night until 2 A.M.
- About his or her past.
- If those moans are real.
- Why it's on the best-seller list.

Men Who Love Women: The Positions

"Her on the bottom, me kneeling at her feet. Don't try this at home."
> — Virgil, stunt man

"Me on the bottom, her on a pedestal."
> — Raul, dancer

"Me on the bottom, her on a lazy Susan (she's petite)."
> — George, caterer

The Enlightened Lover

The approved stages of intercourse:
- Ignition
- Cautious optimism
- Acceleration
- Demonic possession
- Lift-off
- Sizzle
- Fizzle

Lovemaking: The Essentials

- Clock with illuminated face—to see if you've spent sufficient time on foreplay.
- Ice bucket—for chilling champagne and mild sprains.
- Bathroom scale—to see how much your bathroom weighs.
- Mattress pad—for absolutely-have-to-have-Chinese-food-during-sex addicts (keeps unsightly duck sauce stains from soaking in).
- Balloons—for a festive touch.
- Tennis racket—to perfect topspin when one hand is free.
- Rolodex—to call in a substitute lover.

For the Absent-Minded Lover
An official sequence for sex:
1. Swearing-in ceremony
2. Foreplay
3. Rest
4. Resume foreplay
5. Check the pot roast
6. Intercourse
7. Rest, take a vitamin, let the dog out.
8. Begin orgasm
9. Turn off television
10. Finish orgasm
11. Let dog in

Mental Wellness Tip for Commuters
When you get home tonight, remember that even one hour of warm, romantic lovemaking can compensate for the stress caused by:
• Stop and go traffic.
• The bizarre people in your van pool.
• The strange sound coming from under the hood of your car.
• During-work sexual fantasies constantly interrupted by phone calls from your husband.
• The curry you had at lunch.
• A speeding ticket.

Handy Love Guide #8
Are you in love, or in lust, with your partner?
In Lust
Sex: All the time.
You only have a single bed but who cares.
Can't wait to get your hands on your partner.
Any excuse to have sex.
In Love
Sex: Whenever you can make time.
Need a queen size at least—you also use bed for sleeping.
Never want to take them off, especially on frosty nights.
Don't need an excuse.

Secret Signals for Lovers

For those partners who lose their powers of speech during sex—
our alternate communication system.

Number of Taps on the Headboard*	What They Mean
1	"I'm Ready."
2	"What's taking you so long?"
3	"Do it slower."
4	"See who's at the door."
5	"It was just the dog."
6	"How about sharing the covers?"

*Or partner's head if you haven't a headboard.

What Do the Professionals Do?

The Problem	The Solution
We always make love at the same time (autumn).	Try a different season.
We always make love on the same surface.	Turn the mattress over.
We always make love in the same position.	Get a porch swing.
Sometimes my lover is lethargic.	Get jumper cables.

The Diplomatic Lover

Nonthreatening answers to six during-sex questions.

Question	Suggested Answer
"Why did you stop?"	"You wore me out."
"When did you learn that?"	"Just now."
"How does that feel?"	"Allowing for inflation, like a million dollars."
"You didn't climax?"	"I like to leave something to the imagination."
"Why are your eyes closed?"	"Easier to see the spots in front of them."
"How do you last so long?"	"Black coffee."

Quote of the Day

"One of the nice things about having remote control TV is that it helps avoid having to talk to your partner after, and sometimes during, sex."

– Imelda, investment adviser

Tips for the Sexually Deprived

Finally with a new lover? Here are a few sexual points to remember, especially if it's been a long time.

Before sex begins:

• Invite your new lover to call you by your first name.

During sex:

• Unless you're compulsive, it's not necessary to make love in the exact order. Sometimes, a climax may occur before orgasm.

After sex:

• To tell if sex was good—a change of outlook (for the better).

• To tell if sex was great—a change of hair color (no more mousy brown).

• To tell if sex was long—a change of seasons.

Daytime Lovemaking

The advantages:

• Much easier to see what you're doing.

• It's so wicked.

• It works up an appetite for supper.

• You still have the evening should you need more time.

• You can work on your tan (bedrooms with skylights only).

• You can work on your technique (bedrooms with ceiling mirrors only).

• Afterward, the stores are still open—you can shop.

One disadvantage: Stage fright.

Our Favorite Times

(To fantasize about sex.)

• While waiting for the next available customer-service rep.

• When stalled in bumper-to-bumper traffic.

• When you've finally reached the top of your profession (and you're wondering what else is there?).

• While listening to Chopin.

• On the first week of your diet (consider all the great partners you'll meet when you lose 10 pounds).

• At the restaurant (while checking out that cute guy who sent a bottle of mineral water to your table.)

• While having it (optional).

MONTHLY QUALITY OF LIFE® CHECKUP

•Number of sexual encounters: 4___   7___   15___
Does thinking about an old lover during an after-dinner speech count?___
•In addition to pleasure I found this month's sex an excellent source of:
Exercise___
Vitamins A, B, D, and E___
Stress relief___
Cellulite removal___
Guilt___
•I feel the following factors are important when choosing a lover:
Cares about me___
Has a working fireplace___
Has an airconditioned bedroom___
Makes housecalls___
Is close to public transportation (I don't have a car)
Makes sure I am satisfied___
Always has a stamp when I need one___

Signed_____

Witnessed_____

OCTOBER

•Erotic goal for October:
1. Have more creative sexual fantasies
2. Stop drinking cough syrup just to get buzzed

The ancient Mongols believed that couples who had lots of sex in October (at least twice weekly, more if you have a home office) would experience good luck *and* no cavities for the rest of the year.* Take this opportunity to buy a new mattress, designer sheets and spend the next 31 days breaking them in. (Privacy tip: On Halloween night, to discourage trick-or-treaters, hang a "Do Not Disturb" sign on the door and hire a pit bull.) The temptation, however, to overdo it may be great, particularly if your partner is extra-delicious, so be on guard for six telltale signs of too much sex:
1. You start wearing plaids with stripes.
2. Curious co-workers asking about those red bite marks on your neck.
3. Fluid retention.
4. A mysterious craving for Cocoa Pebbles.
5. No longer needing warm milk to fall asleep.
6. Attention Deficit Disorder.
•See "National Geographic," vol. 4, 284: Sex in Central Asia," Chapter VII: "Lust in a Yurt."

Official aphrodisiac of the Month:
Eggplant Parmigiana

Afterplay

Three ways to recover from orgasm:
• Take the rest of your clothes off (a best bet).
• Set the snooze alarm.
• Return to your novel.

The Dieter's Guide to Weight Loss During Sex

Activity	Calories Burned
Achieving orgasm for:	
A skeptic	41
An optimist	6
A pessimist	145

Guide For the Well-Rounded Lover

The signs that you are growing more dependent on sex:
• Having it even when you don't need it.
• Impaired thinking (indifference to local property taxes).
• Leaving work early to rendezvous with a lover.
• Morning-after regrets (that you didn't do it more).
• Moral degradation (lustful thoughts on company time).
• Secretive behavior (keeping a lover in a desk drawer).
• Bizarre behavior (missing social events where they serve food.)

Embarrassing Sexual Moments

"Called out the wrong lover's name. Fortunately, I saved the situation by convincing him it was his name."
           – Courtney, publicist
"While making love in the kitchen, my monocle fell into the Manhattan clam chowder."
           – Eric, sous-chef
"Trying to walk just moments after a Level 7 climax."*
           – Stacy, homemaker
*Any climax that blows at least two fuses.

The Candid Lover: Part II

More questions often asked by a new partner.

Question	Good Reply	Bad Reply
What part of you most needs improving?	My tummy and my biceps.	My self-respect.
How do you look without makeup?	Like I do now.	Like my passport photo.
What about me arouses you most?	Your shoulders.	Your business contacts.

Love: The Ups and Downs

Agony	Ecstasy
He didn't call when he said he would.	You get home and there's his message on your machine.
She doesn't return your phone call.	She surprises you and makes a house call instead.
Another cold shower, she's too tired to do it tonight.	A warm bath, she's caressing your neck with a loofah.
A lover's quarrel.	Making up in bed.

Maintaining Passion

It's easy to keep your love life from growing stale.
- Change the time ordinarily reserved for sex.
- Change the sheet ordinarily reserved for sex.
- Do volunteer work (wax your lover's legs).
- Set goals.
- Try organic sex (no additives, no preservatives, just you).
- Find a partner with a long shelf life.
- Try making love in a different room (lover in the kitchen, you in the bedroom).

Training a New Lover

Not as difficult as one might think, especially if both share a common goal and:

Trainer	Trainee
Is an expert	Is a quick study
Is patient	Is willing to grow
Uses flip charts	Pays attention
Is demanding	Loves a challenge
Is a good teacher	Does the homework
Is willing to stay after hours	Gets supper money

Question Often Asked by Disappointed Lovers

"Why me?"

Amazing Sexual Fact

For some strange reason, telling an insecure lover who happens to phone while you're enjoying fantastic, fabulous sex that "It's not the same without you" almost never makes that person feel better.

Five Things to Be Happy About During Sex

1. The wondrous aroma (you have a turkey in the oven).
2. Your partner noticed that you:
    - Bought new pillows.
    - Shed eight pounds.
3. You noticed that your partner:
    - Bought new, sexier underwear.
    - Isn't wearing it.
4. That what you suspected might be as long-lost erogenous zone, is.
5. You were home when your partner called.

What I Do for Love

"Wear the socks she knits for me—at least once."
> – Duane, longshoreman

"Cut his meat."
> – Simone, fishing guide

"Absolutely nothing. My boyfriend gives it to me for free."
> – Stella, merchant

503

Tomorrow Morning: A Best Bet

Moments before your lover leaves for work, pull him or her back into the bedroom (be persistent, use a lasso), get undressed and make love just once more. (It is not necessary, afterward, to eat breakfast again.)

Sweet Nothings: Part I

Two phrases certain to intensify passion.
• In the middle of sex:
"Please cover your mouth when you yawn."
• Toward the end of sex:
"I'm getting homesick."
• After sex:
"Did you make dinner reservations?"

Thought for Tonight

It's the perfect night for lovemaking if:
• You forgot to do it last night.
• You want to work off Sunday brunch
• There's nothing good on television
• You're having difficulty facing Monday morning.

Gem of the Month

One perfect opal to the lover who, during sex:
• Never complains no matter how long it takes you to finish (as long as there's a magazine handy).
• Never makes a fuss if you respond to voice mail.
• Never fails to uncover a long, lost erogenous zone.
• If it occurs in a sport other than the bedroom (the lavatory of an airliner, for instance), is careful not to wrinkle your slacks.
• Permits no artificial stimulants, not even conversation.

Sex Stoppers

Some mood-destroying statements.
"My boss expects me back from lunch."
"Pick up the pace, my biological clock's ticking."
"We really should get back to our guests."
"Tell me when you're done."
"Is whisker burn good for poison ivy?"

504

"Could you just turn up the radio?"
"Strike the set!"
"Should I leave my card . . . or my wife?"

Lover's Fortune Cookie
In love you will succeed beyond your wildest dreams, if you:
1. Lose 10 pounds.
2. Lose the polyester outfits.
3. Change hairdressers.
4. Stop believing that one size fits all.
5. Stop reading self-help books.
6. Walk your dog where the beautiful people meet.
7. Wear a miniskirt.
8. Win the lottery.

Sexual Etiquette
For first-time lovers who meet by fax:
1. Don't take each other for granted.
2. Shake hands (a firm grip indicates sincerity and nearly uncontrollable sexual energy).
3. If you find each other attractive, pause a moment to blink away tears of joy (and relief).
4. During arousal: network.
5. During intercourse: discuss Fannie Maes.
6. Afterward, to increase feelings of intimacy, exchange business cards (raised lettering suggests a lover of substance).

Mental Health Tip For Lovers
"Four hours of unceasingly glorious sex easily erases the psychic damage caused by the negative opinion of a judgmental hairdresser."

– *Journal of Erotic Angst*, Vol. 21, No. 4

National Ecstasy Week*
For this week, heighten your lovemaking pleasure by:
• Thinking lust.
• Increasing your frequency rate (from once to twice daily).
• Trying something wild (doing it at any approved hernia center).
• Eating rich chocolate while making love.

- Touching each other in forbidden places (like the local library or an undeserted beach).
- Being fearless in bed (and asking lover for suggestions).
- Introducing a new element into your love life (like a camcorder).
*Presidential proclamation pending.

The Inquiring Lover

Q. When composing a romantic letter to a new lover, is it ethical to plagiarize material from love letters I've written to former lovers? I mean, why should such good material go to waste?
A. There are no ethical consequences as long as:
1. You have a genuine case of writer's block.
2. You change the salutation ("Dearest, darling Clyde" is certain to fail if your new lover's name is Herman).
3. Such letter is written on stationary of equal or better quality.
4. You correct all grammatical errors.

From Our Lover's Glossary

"That was so nice." 1. Next to "Where am I?", the phrase most often uttered by a semicoherent, possibly speechless lover after 76 or more minutes of lovemaking during which time the earth moved . . . and moved . . . and moved. In some cases the speaker, due to a temporary loss of coordination, may slur the words, causing his or her partner to ask, "What did you say?"
2. The phrase most often uttered by an ecstatic partner after tasting his or her lover's first, but highly successful, attempt at making blueberry strudel.

Afterthoughts

At the end of exhausting but glorious lovemaking, aren't you glad that:
- This the weekend your ex has the kids?
- The phone didn't ring?
- There's still some fried chicken left?
- You got a workout without having to wear bicycle pants?
- Your partner discovered two new erogenous zones?
- You gave in to temptation?

Food and Sex: Part II

The noisy eater.

Dining Habits

When mouth is full makes strange whistling sounds, perhaps caused by breathing through meatballs. Shuns napkin and utensils; must be vacuumed between courses.

Type of Partner

Passionate but messy. Huge sexual appetite may startle partners used to Republicans, but they quickly adapt. Moments after a bed-shaking climax, asks: "Any pastrami left?"

Sex and the Conscientious Employee

A general guide to erotic thoughts permitted on company time.*

Permitted	Not permitted
Anticipating what you and your lover will do tonight	Recalling what you and your lover did this morning
Natural acts	Unnatural acts
Having your lover blow into your ear	Having your lover blow into both ears
Taking a nap with your lover	Taking a bath with your lover

*General information only. Consult your personnel department for specifics.

Tip For Insecure Lovers

During sex, for partners with first-night jitters, it is often just as difficult for a woman to let go of her purse as it is for a man to leave his golf bag in the other room.

Myth or Fact?: Part II

Conventional Wisdom Suggests	Myth	Fact
Thinking about sex while waiting for the next available customer service representative can make the time pass more pleasantly.		X
If you sniff a romantic lover's ear, you should smell cologne.	X	
Lovers who play spin the (deposit) bottle should, when they're finished, recycle.		X

First Things Done After Sex
If you went to bed with someone because:
Of their mind: Check your post-orgasm I.Q.—is it higher?
Of their body: Admire the results.
Of their money: Ask for workmen's compensation (or palimony).
You felt sorry: For them—see your therapist.
For yourself—see your clergyman.
Of their fame: Make sure the photos come out.

Overheard After Marvelous Sex
"You just passed your orals."
> – Kris, anthropology professor

"Let's hire a hall, a caterer and a photographer."
> – Ed, recovering bachelor

"You may get dressed now, Alan, the cavity's filled."
> – Dr. Ruth, dentist

The Language of Flowers: Part V
To the helpful but slightly dense lover who:
Arose in the middle of some very, almost prohibitively steamy lovemaking to check for prowlers
Send:
One wilted violet

The Telltale Signs of Great Sex
• You can't stop vibrating.
• You're wearing both shoes on the same foot.
• You can't recall the name of your hometown.
• You can't quite focus your eyes.
• You can't uncross them, either.

What We Did For Great Sex
Turned into bed potatoes."
> – Daphne and Roger, nice people

"Installed heavy-duty shocks in the Winnebago."
> – Ozzie and Grace, retired

"Each other."
> – Tammy and Clyde, on second honeymoon

The Misunderstood Lover
"After eight months of lessons, I asked my English teacher: Is there room for improvement? She said, 'Yes, step into my bedroom.'"
     – Josef, handsome Serbian immigrant

Our Frequent Lover Program: Part II
Each time your partner:

Improves your complexion:	
With sex	30
With Dove	4
Engages in spontaneous sex	11
With you	25
Makes you laugh in bed	7
For the wrong reason	1
Rises	22
And shines	50

Lovemaking Tips For Tonight

Change Positions:	To Avoid:
Once	Boredom
Twice	Bedsores
Three times	Leg cramps
Four times	A stale mate

What I Did For Love
"Sat through a football game."
    – Ellen R., flight attendant
"Sat through a ballet."
    – Irv K., stevedore

Reminder
The nice thing about going to bed angry is that it's so much fun to make up.

Amazing Facts About Robust Sexual Activity
During a lusty lover's orgasm:
1. The bed may shift its position by at least six inches.

2. The fact that the sheets are fitted is no guarantee they'll remain firmly attached to the mattress.

3. A night table next to the bed is not the best place to keep a genuine Ming vase.

4. The partner not having the orgasm may be:
   (a) curious
   (b) awed
   (c) envious
   (d) proud.

From Our Lover's Glossary

Rush Hour. A time of day, usually noon, when two people meet, usually at a motel with hourly or half-hourly rates, for the purpose of having sex. Because so much must be compressed into so short a time, those involved tend to omit the standard lovemaking preliminaries such as removing socks, whirlpool bath and planning a future together. Additionally, because there's less time to eat, smaller sandwiches are generally consumed by the participants, thus the reason for the weight loss commonly associated with what is known as a "nooner." (Note: In some areas of the country, this form of sexual conduct is called a "Working Lunch.")

Things to Be Happy About Before Sex

1. You're going to have it.
2. Your hairdresser was able to squeeze you in.
3. Your mother decided not to spend the weekend.
4. It's an excuse to buy:
   • Caviar (food for thought); or
   • Sara Lee (food for the soul).
5. Your nails are nearly dry.
6. The side effects.
7. The after effects.

What to Do Until Your Lover Comes

(Pre-arrival checklist.)

___ Vacuum and straighten up the bedroom.
___ Prepare the hors d'oeuvres.
___ Take off your apron.
___ Place the appropriate book of poetry on your nightstand.

___ Arrange the flowers.

___ Study yourself in a full-length mirror. Decide that your lover's lucky to be with you.

___ Review the movie schedules—in case sex ends early.

___ Sedate the cat.

___ Check to see if you turned the curling iron off.

Are You Addicted to Sex?

The five alarm signals.

1. Whenever you think about sex, the windows fog.
2. You'd actually rather make love than go to work.
3. You find your verbal skills significantly lower during orgasm.
4. And you don't care.
5. You frequently use sex as a substitute for:
   - Arguing
   - Communicating
   - Not having sex

What I Do for Sex

Information collected from graduate students at several top Ivy League schools.

"Type her thesis."
> – Elijah, doctoral candidate

"Putting her through med school."
> – Ross, husband

"Carry his books."
> – Kibbie, instructor

"Get research grants."
> – Martha, administrator

Lovemaking Ritual #9

Make love on a pile of golden leaves. Do this only at night if you don't have understanding neighbors. *Caution:* To avoid injury (a) be certain that leaves are no longer attached to the tree and (b) beware of the rake.

Sex Poll #87

What were your most annoying during-sex interruptions? (Asked of our panel of professional lovers.)

"Ummm . . . the butler kept asking for his wages."
"Our middle son demanding his allowance."
"A singing telegram. God, what a voice."
"The motel clerk calling to tell us our time was up."
"A peeping Tom I didn't recognize."
"The dog . . . no wait . . . my partner licking my hand."
"Telling the officer to put away his flashlight, we're married."

Looks Count
Some appearance-related benefits of a happy sex life.
"Thicker, shinier hair."
> — Barbara, hostess

"Longer, stronger nails."
> — Alma, mountain climber

"Whiter teeth, much brighter smile."
> — Montgomery, flight attendant

"Longer lashes."
> — Kimberly, beauty editor

"Longer lashes!"
> — Bart, masochist

The Inquiring Lover
Q. When invited for the first time by a man (whom I really like) for dinner at his apartment what should I a) know and b) bring?
A. If he actually cooks (i.e., makes a dish that requires heat), it means he really likes you, too. Some tips:
1. The moment you arrive, don't ask if you can make "just one phone call." (Unless it's to tell your roommate you arrived safely.)
2. In case he's making a red sauce, don't wear white.
3. Bring wine instead of flowers. He may not have a vase.
4. In the event things escalate:
   • Bring a toothbrush.
   • Wear great underwear.

The Male Virgin (Over 30)
Increasing in number are men who, owing to career demands, have never done it. Some advice for lucky women:

Do

Be gentle. No sudden or mysterious moves that might cause shin-splints.

Be reassuring. Emphasize how nice it will be once he stops trembling.

Encourage questions. You can always answer them later.

Do Not

Get fancy too soon. He'll be threatened.

Be too adventurous the first time. Save the banister for when he's a veteran.

Criticize unless it's constructive.

What to Do Until Your Lover Arrives

1. Check the sheets. Do they need changing or will vacuuming do?
2. Check the nightstand. There should be:
   - Pad and pencil to jot down during-sex thoughts
   - Stationery to communicate with lover when sex leaves you babbling
3. Check under the bed. Remove all souvenirs from past lovers such as crumpled tissues, old socks and empty Perrier bottles.
4. Place champagne in ice bucket.
5. Check beside the bed. Don't forget a flashlight for late-night trips to bathroom and kitchen.
6. Check the bed itself. Did you remember place cards?

The Language of Flowers: Part VIII

To the lover who:	Send:
Makes housecalls	A plant
Serves breakfast in bed	Carnations
Without getting up	Irises
Keeps your complexion clear	Marigolds
Makes you smile, especially during the good parts	Anything that blooms

Senior Citizens in Love

"I knew she was right for me. When we went to bed, she put her dentures in a half-full martini glass."

> – Ogden, retired railroad worker

"I knew he was right for me. It was in the third hour of sex that I found myself humming 'The Wabash Cannonball.'"
    – Bernadette, Ogden's paramour

Myth or Fact?

Conventional sexual wisdom suggests:	Myth	Fact
Only 1 out of 50 men is capable of thinking about sex when:		
Monday Night Football is on		X
A resilient woman can have up to 6 climaxes and still get up to fix an omelet		X
A weary man can have up to 6 climaxes and still eat that omelet	X	
Good sex can be habit-forming		X
Great sex can be addictive		X
Abstinence makes the heart grow fonder	X	

More Than Just a Sex Object

Eight uses for a perfect lover.
1. Travel companion.
2. Bartender at your cocktail parties.
3. Confidante.
4. Dishwasher unloader.
5. Cuddling, and warmth on frosty winter nights.
6. Furniture rearranger (ignore his whining when you can't make your mind).
7. Tax deduction.
8. Hired hand.

You Are With the Right Lover

If every time you have sex:
• Your toes curl downward.*
• Your teeth whiten.
• You achieve your target heart rate.
• You activate the a) smoke alarm or b) sprinkler.
• You forget you have guests waiting.
*Curling upward means the bed is too short.

The Socially Conscious Lover

Instead of tossing them out, consider donating your old lovers (if still usable) to friends or a worthy charity. (It may be tax-deductible—consult the IRS.)

Words to the Wise Lover

After counting their climaxes, grateful lovers count their blessings.

Believe It or Else

Whether by candlelight, or even if the room's completely dark, a truly skilled lover should be able to find all your erogenous zones without:
1. A contour map
2. A searchlight
3. Squinting

Note: Guiding your lover's hand is strictly prohibited. You may, however, offer verbal assistance such as "You're getting warmer" or "That's my 'gee' spot."

The Tactful Lover

Never:
1. When asked, "Am I as good as the other partners you've been with?", says "I'll let you know."
2. In the fourth hour of sex declares, "I've never had to work so hard before."
3. Gently puffs on his cigar when asked, "Are you losing interest in me?"
4. Responds to "Why aren't we having more fun in bed?" by reaching for the clicker.

Sexual Etiquette

Thing not to say the first time you see:
Her Without Makeup
"Never mind the Polaroid."
Him Without His Clothes
"I hate false advertising."

The Art of Romance
Showering cheek to cheek can be just as sexy as dancing cheek to cheek, unless:
- You can't agree on the water temperature.
- There's a 14-inch height difference.
- Neither of you has a sense of rhythm.

Sexual Etiquette
To make your lover feel wanted.
While making love, don't keep:
- Changing the channels, even if you have remote control
- Asking what's for dinner

Before making love, always:
- Pretend to be awake when he or she comes to bed
- Pretend to be grateful if he or she stays in bed.

After sex:
- Remain seated until lover comes to a complete stop.

The Seven Wonders of the Sexual World

Natural	Unnatural
Five times in one night	Recovering
Aphrodisiac (challah)	Aphrodisiac (scrod)
Guilt (Over too much sex)	Guilt (over too much celibacy)
Sex in an RV	While it's moving
Sexual marathons	Blisters
A miracle worker	Miracles
Cheating	Getting caught

Are You a Taciturn Lover?
Things often said in the middle of really hot sex—a sampling of our test couples.

"Did you remember to lock the door?"
> – Mabel, housewife

"Is it me, or my couch?"
> – Rodney, psychiatrist

"The phone is ringing, but this feels so good."
> – Cyril, writer

"I'll get it."
> – Shirley, Cyril's wife and realtor

Eavesdropping

Things often said after sex that was
Driving you up a wall: "You handle superbly."
Too good to be true: "Now I know I'm straight."
The first time in 5 months: "Thanks, I needed that."
Terrific but tiring: "Can we just lie here till November?"
Mind-blowing: "Sign here."
Unexpectedly wonderful: "Sign here."

Undressing Each Other: Part II

Problems for the female partner on a scale of 1 to 20.

Removing	Difficulty Level
His jeans:	
Over his cowboy boots	5
Over his head	19
Briefs	3
If he doesn't cooperate	12
Rolex	3
If you've only just met	9
Nipple ring	20

The Bedside Explorer: Part V

An erotic adventure for the courageous lover.

Expedition 5 (Klopman's Nuzzle)

Equipment recommended: The nose and, if available, non-skid socks

Begin at lover's neck, just under the earlobe. Sniff the delicate essence. Watch the sniffee grow aroused. Now proceed to the shoulders. Yummy? Fine, now travel south to the equator. Indulge in several more mighty yet delicate sniffs. Onward to the Torrid Zone. Stop. Now languish and observe a moment of silence.

Wine and Your Lover: The Basics

To the lover with:	Serve:
A big, bold libido	An assertive Gamay
A weak foreplay technique	An off-year Chinati
Potential	Any day-to-day red
A short shelf-life	A fortified Burgundy
Great hands	A velvet-bodied Bordeaux
The soul of a poet	Champagne
A beachfront house	Vintage champagne
Lots of enthusiasm	A perky Zinfandel

Lover's Etiquette

What to Say	When
"Excuse me." ("Oops!" also acceptable.)	While making love in a shower or the lavatory of an airliner, you step on your lover's foot.
"Sorry."	Aphrodisiac-induced burp (gassy lo mein)
"May I help you?"	If your lover is taking too long to find an erogenous zone.
"At last."	When your lover finds it.

Sex in America: Part II*

What is your opinion of orgasm?
- It's a great way to relieve stress — 96%
- I wish I had more — 87%
- I wish I had fewer — 2%
- I wish I knew — 19%
- One a day keeps the doctor away — 66%
- Two a day keeps the psychiatrist away — 94%
- It's our favorite way to end sex — 85%

*Based on another telephone poll of 1,000 registered lovers.

The Lover's Massage

A few of our favorite motion lotions.

Substance	Advantages
Baby oil	Perfect for Jiffy lubes. Eases upper and lower body tension, also not bad for relieving middle body tension.
Salad oil	Highly nutritious. Will add zest to the fig leaf worn by modest partners.
House dressing	All-natural, Earth friendly. Perfect for intimate picnics and couples who make love while hiking the Appalachian Trail. Leaves no unpleasant aftertaste.

Marital Aids

Our eight favorites:
1. A diamond tennis bracelet.
2. Crisp new designer sheets.
3. Drinks in the hot tub.
4. A second honeymoon (with an ocean view).
5. A spouse that can't get enough of you.
6. A fireplace.
7. A taboo on the words "backache" and "headache."
8. Privacy.

The Enlightened Lover

Approved reasons to enjoy vigorous sex:
• A good excuse to perspire
• Firms the inner thighs
• Rubs away dry skin cells
• Strengthens the circulatory system (especially if you chase your partner around the bed)
• It's safer than skiing
• Cheaper than bingo
• And Nature's own pacifier

Tip for the Masochist
When to hate yourself.
In the Morning if:
You wake up next to someone whose name you don't know.
At Noon if:
You wake up again and they're still there.

Not-So-Great Moment in Lovemaking
"When my new lover asked, after what I considered to be three hours of unspeakably stunning lovemaking, 'Do you happen to have any clothes that might fit me?'"
       – Dixie, postal inspector

Was It Great?
Favorite after-sex remarks indicating a delighted lover:
• "That was so nice."
• "Words fail me. That, my dear, is why I was moaning."
• "Must you go so soon?"
• "Love these palpitations."
• "Why don't you call me at my office?"
• "Zzzzz."
• "Who's your teacher?"
• "Your turn."

Tip For High-Level Executives
Always delegate low-priority jobs. Let your lover:
• Mix the martinis.
• Light the fireplace.
• Scrub the post-bubble bath ring from the bathtub.
• Carry you into the bedroom.
• Turn down the bed.
• Undress you.
• Do the moaning.
• After sex
• Light your cigarette.
• Warm up the car.

New Hope for the Hardworking Lover

Too tired to enjoy sex? But partner's feeling "amorous?" Give things a chance—consult our "All's Not Lost" chart below.

You will begin to melt	If, while soaking in a warm bath,
In 7 minutes	Your partner rubs your back while touching you in your favorite places.
In 4 minutes	Your partner hands you a glass of chilled white wine, beams and explains the kids are on a sleepover.

Q. Should I sleep with an old lover?
A. Only if you want to:
• Be reminded how good it was.
• Bring him or her up to date and demonstrate that noticeable improvement in your sexual technique.
• Compare your old lover with your new lover.
• Reminisce.
• Rethink your options.

The Enlightened Lover

You know you're not totally into lovemaking if you are:
• Constantly glancing at your watch.
• Thinking about
a. an old lover
b. gypsy moths
• Tweezing your eyebrows.
• Picturing your partner dressed.
• Busy reporting a lost or stole credit card.

> **Alert**
> Only 71 more shopping days and, worse, only 72 more mating nights until Christmas.

The Inquiring Lover

Q. After lovemaking, instead of just lying there inert, we balance a platter of chocolate chip cookies on whomever has the flattest stomach and feed them to each other. How do I know when he's ready to make love again?

A. Easy. Your lover will reach for you instead of the cookie.

Is He "New Lover" Material?

If, as you're both getting undressed, you say, "It's been so long since I've been with a man . . ."

• Continue if he replies, "It's been so long since I've been with a woman."

• Reconsider if he replies, "Me too."

Things to Be Thankful for After Sex: Part II

• She didn't notice when you ran to the bathroom to sneak a cigarette.

• He puts the seat back down.

• It was everything his ex-wife said it would be.

• She left nothing to the imagination.

Pillow Talk

Chocolate dependence. A state of positive intoxication achieved when one receives chocolate from one's lover in various likenesses (a Valentine heart, the Easter bunny, Santa Claus) and consumes such chocolate for the purpose of:

• Enhancing lovemaking

• Reminding one of one's lover

• Ruining one's appetite

• Bulking up for winter

• Compensating for overconsumption of leafy vegetables (known to cause decreased sex drive)

Seven Good Reasons to Have Sex Tonight

1. It's a good excuse for making popcorn.
2. It's a great excuse to build a fire.
3. It will keep your stomach flat.
4. Doctor's orders.
5. Partner's finally out of town.

6. The change will do you good.

7. It's too early to have it now.

Sexual Etiquette

No matter how aroused and ready to make love, both partners should take the time to:

1. Help each other undress.

2. Take care, in the frenzy of passion, not to twist an ankle when removing each other's cowboy boots.

3. Fold each other's clothes neatly.

4. If the aphrodisiac of choice is barbecued chicken wings, fill the fingerbowls.

5. Dismiss the servants.

6. Set the timer.

Holiday Alert

Time is getting short. Our gift suggestions.

To a lover who	Give
Always has to hunt around for your erogenous zone	A fishing license
Has cold feet because of:	
The weather	Bed socks
Sex	A sedative
You're not certain you want to stay with	A check (postdated)
Thinks you're too hot to handle	An oven mitt

Basking in the Afterglow: Lovers' Poll #80

Responses from outdoor lovers when asked, "What do you do after sex?"

We lie there, gaze skyward and watch the leaves change."

        – Emma and Murray, backpackers

"Resume picking apples. There's something about an orchard."

        – Tiffany and Kim, potters

"Race each other to the outhouse, what else?"

        – Fred and Nancy, farmers

"Gaze downward, hold hands and watch the leaves change."

        – Eve and Jerome, skydivers.

The Dieter's Guide to Weight Loss During Sex

Activity	Calories Burned
Sex with someone just for their:	
Mind	11
Body	220
Both	241*
Endurance	305
Perfect guacamole salad	56**

* Note 10-calorie synergy bonus.
** Margin of error: 3%.

Three Maxims
1. The larger the lovers, the smaller the bed.
2. The louder the moans,
   a. The thinner the walls and
   b. The more acute your neighbors' hearing.
3. In any tug-of-war for the blanket, the lover who is coldest will lose.

Sexual Disorders #6 and #7

Affliction	Cause
• Bruises	1. Making love on top of a cluttered desk
	2. Making love underneath a coconut tree
• Heat rash	1. Bargain pillowcases
	2. Attempting too vigorously to rekindle the flame
• Shock	Computer-generated "thinking of you" card

The Sexually Correct Thing

In the middle of the night, if you take a break from lovemaking and visit the kitchen for a snack, it is considered in appropriate to spend precious moments admiring or rearranging, by subject, your partner's collection of refrigerator magnets. It would suggest that you're less than totally involved.

Quality Time: Part II

Activity	Minutes Consumed
Whispering something sexy in partner's ear	$^1/_2$
Making quality love:	
That includes foreplay	22
But omits intercourse	2
Falling asleep:	
While thinking how wonderful it was	1
While thinking of all the things you must do tomorrow	20

From Our Lover's Glossary

Mid-sex crisis. An inability to perform because:
• An unstable ex is calling you collect.
• You didn't pass up the tomato-and-onion salad.
• You're allergic to the flowers on the pillow cases.
• Your new partner's idea of a "sex toy" is a vegetable peeler.
• Your spouse's marriage is in trouble.
• You can't remember if you shut the oven off.
• You're obsessed with your performance.

The Bedside Eater

Three tips for better lovemaking:
1. Vacuum the bed after eating pretzels.
2. Hose off your partner after eating spareribs.
3. Stay out of the way if partner's chewing bubble gum.

Bedchamber Music

For the modest woman seeking suitable music to drown out her moans during lovemaking.

Degree of Audibility	Appropriate Music
Not very (a dreamy "mmmmm")	Mozart: any late piano sonata
Discernible, but not alarmingly	Haydn: any quartet
Definitely audible	Vivaldi: any flute concerto
Piercing	Vivaldi: *Four Seasons*
Frighteningly so	Beethoven: *Fifth Symphony*
Deafening	Tchaikovsky: *1812 Overture*

Not-So-Great Moment in Sex
"After two months of the best, most passionate sex either of us had ever experienced, we discovered that our aphrodisiac was a placebo."
— Matt and Martha, research volunteers

Horticultural Thought For Today
Send an orchid to the lover who is:
• Energetic (without burning fossil fuel, keeps you cozy on chilly nights).
• Smitten (even though you've been married 10 years, still regards you as a sex object).
• Instructive (over and over again has taught you how to have a happy hour without the aid of alcohol).
• Considerate (re-adjusts your headphones if they fall off during climax).

The Over-Aroused Partner
Lack willpower? Partner too sexy? Eight things the typical lover thinks about to avoid a premature climax:
1. How much insurance is enough?
2. The Beach Boys
3. Alternate ways to achieve my target heart rate (like bouncing a check).
4. What's that noise coming from the cellar?
5. Heat exhaustion.
6. Is my silk blouse getting all wrinkled (it's a Ralph Lauren)?
7. NAFTA
8. The dinner guests waiting downstairs.

Magic Numbers: Part IV
15: The number of ounces of champagne required to mellow out a victim of first-night jitters.
3: The height in inches that your partner's eyebrows will raise the first time you take off your clothes and you're wearing a nipple ring (4 inches if she's led a sheltered life).
10: Distance in inches the average bed moves during simultaneous orgasm (only 2 inches if bed's on shag carpet).
22: The number of times a month you must have sex to keep your

complexion clear and glowing.

7: Number of inches a spouse jumps when you get into bed with cold knees

Sex on a Budget

A reference guide for couples just starting out as well as for retirees on a fixed income.

If you can't afford:	At least get:
Designer sheets	Sheets
Luxuriously fluffy towels	A sponge
A bidet	Indoor plumbing
Champagne and caviar	Wine cooler and Oreos
Candles	A night-light
An ocean view	A fish tank
A string quartet	A whistle
A bed	An air mattress

Three Ultimate During-Sex Distractions

1. Networking.
2. Researcher standing too close.
3. Jingling pocket change.

The Ultimate Sex Drive

Lovers planning a fall foliage tour should make sure their vehicle contains these essentials:

• *Suction-cup notepad*—to note the best places to make love (also useful if you need to laeve a sexual IOU).

• Visor organizer—*a handy place to keep (a) tissues to wipe away tears of joy or (b) sponge for tears of ecstasy.*

• *Wooden-bead seat cushion*—voted the "Object Most Fun to Make Love Upon" by the International Association of Off-Road Lovers.

• *Ice chest*—for basting the lover who overheats when going up hills.

Great Moments in Afterplay

"I carefully refold the airbag and push it back into the steering wheel."

— Lamont, long-haul trucker

"We toss a coin to see who makes the coffee."
— Agatha and Kirk, morning lovers
"We decide whether we should do it again by calling a psychic friend."
— Rachel and Bubba, astronauts

From Our Lover's Glossary

Yodels. *1.* A chocolate-covered during-sex aphrodisiac that, if used judiciously, provides each partner with sufficient energy to make love for up to two hours without having to order a meal from a Kentucky Fried Chicken franchise. *2.* The sounds emitted by a male partner in the final throes of orgasm who is wearing a lederhosen.

Hints You May Be With the Wrong Partner: Part I

• He makes you sleep in the guest room whenever you eat garlic.
• She insists your allergy to her perfume is "all in your head."
• He believes that "never let 'em see you sweat" applies especially to sex.
• She still insists that liver is good for you.
• He's gained 14 pounds, but still wears the same pants.
• You've been dating for two years and he still doesn't know what size jewelry you wear.

The Sexual Halftime

A brief (no longer than two hours) respite from lovemaking is recommended. It refreshes, energizes and better enables you to recall where you parked the car. What to do:
1. Splash cold water on face (to revive and smooth away those telltale pillow marks).
2. Check phone messages.
3. Consume high-energy snack (two out of three unregistered dietitians recommend brie and Vegemato).
4. Take another vitamin (better safe than weak).
5. Reset the applause meter and continue.

The Morning After a Perfect Night: Part I
"Eyes-only" love notes to make your lover blush.

What to Write	Probable Shade of Lover's Face
"You were great."	Standard, everyday red
"You were scrumptious."	Bright red
"You were an animal—specifically, a tiger."	Scarlet
"Thanks for keeping me warm without using a blanket."	Auburn
"I'm glad you make house calls."	Ruby

For Lovers Watching Their Weight
The committed, happy dieter finds it more satisfying to nosh on a lover (0 calories) than to nibble on a piece of sugarless candy (8 calories), eat a plum (a whopping 53 calories) or consume a 1-ounce piece of halvah (11,000 calories).

The Straight-A Lover: Part I
High marks to a partner who:
• Leaves nothing to the imagination (except the spots before your eyes during orgasm).
• Fibs charmingly when asked, "Do you think I've gained weight?"
• Replies, "You, of course," when asked, "How do you last so long?"
• Caused your therapist to declare you clinically happy.
• Has the right answer when asked "Where do we go from here?" and leads you either back into the bedroom or out for Italian food.
• Helped you renounce abstinence.

After Sublime Sex
Approved responses to "Where have you been all my life?"

If You're:	Answer:
A neighbor	"Next door."
Terrific in bed	"Gaining experience."
An immigrant	"In Europe."
An illegal immigrant	"In hiding."
An ex-convict	"Changing my image."
Liberated	"In therapy."
Newly liberated	"Married."

The Stressed-Out Lover
(Scale: 1 to 50)

During sex, each time you	Number of Stress Points
Are interrupted by:	
The housekeeper	14
A security guard'	27
An active toddler	38
Find an earring that isn't:	
Yours	31
His	44
Undress your partner with your eyes	3
And your contacts pop	42

A Guide to Vehicular Sex
Lincoln Town Car
Advantages
Two people can easily make love in spacious front or back seat or on roof, especially if there's a ski rack.
Disadvantages
Size makes vehicle difficult to conceal; tell-tale "bouncing" motions may be spotted by spouse or suspicious neighbor.

Six Embarrassing Sexual Moments
"My husband walked in."*
"My lover walked out."
"Thought she meant baseball when she invited me to engage in our national pastime."
"My wish came true."
"Knocked over the caddie while changing positions."
"Twins."
*"Served him right for showing up without a reservation."

Great Moments in Sex
"My divorce finally came through."
       – Maynard, golf pro
"Found out all the good ones aren't married."
       – Tipper, dancer

What I Did for Love

"Gave up smoking, without using a nicotine patch."
  – Claudia, dentist
"Gave up drinking, without using a nicotine patch (it didn't work)."
  – Leopold, nurse
"Five years. She swore they'd never give jail time for a white collar crime. (She also swore she'd wait.)"
  – Ernie, #7459200

To Make Romance More Affordable

Instead of:
• Candles, use moonlight—it's more seductive.
• Using an astrologer to decide when to make love, buy the "Farmer's Almanac," it's cheaper.
• Buying a dozen roses for your lover, pick them in a park or from your neighbor's garden."
• Mailing a love letter and wasting postage, write it in the grime on her windshield.
• Lavishly tipping a maitre d' get a good table by threatening him with bodily harm.
• An expensive weekend at a beach resort, stay in Cincinnati and hold a seashell to your ear.

Secrets of the Great Lovers

Experts reply to our question, "How do you keep sex fresh?"
• "I'm not afraid to make mistakes."
• "Lots of business trips . . . we hardly see each other."
• "We always do something wacky and different. Last night we took off our clothes."
• "Vary the location. Last week we made love once on the bed, twice under the bed and . . . let's see . . . again in front of her chaperone."
• "We never rehearse."
• "We never know what's going to happen next, I have tremendous mood swings."

When Your Lover Stays Over
He wants:
A little flashlight so he can find his way to the bathroom at 2:44
A.M. without stepping in the kitty litter
The photo of your alternate lover (the one where the eyes follow
you) turned to the wall
A bedtime story beginning: "You were terrific."
She wants:
Clean sheets, not simply flipped over or vacuumed
A clean and well-stocked bathroom, beginning with a full spool of
bathroom tissue
A bedtime story beginning: "I'll call you tomorrow."

The Dream House Effect
Good news for concerned lovers:
During torrid sexual moments, the sparks produced by one hard
body rubbing against the other do not contribute to global warming.

The Art of Romance
No lover? Some alternate ways to experience a nearly just-as-good
climax:
1. Finding a "prize" at a tag sale.
2. Winning the lottery.
3. Losing 10 real pounds (water loss doesn't count).
4. A credit balance on your MasterCard.
5. Taking delivery of your new car.
6. A job offer.
7. Getting into the college of your choice.
8. Watching weekend guests depart.

Stolen Sexual Moments
Difficult to find time for sex? Here are some time-saving tips from
passionate but busy couples.
1. Never play more than nine holes of golf.
2. Don't linger in restaurants: always ask for the check when the
waiter brings dessert.
3. Make love with the lights on . . . you'll find each other faster.
4. Always try to do two things at once: begin lovemaking, for in-

stance, while getting your flu shot.

5. Use both hands—you'll cover more ground in a shorter time.

6. Concentrate on the task at hand (during sex, keep your mind from wandering by wearing a sweat band).

7. Delegate responsibility: send the kids to the PTA meeting.

Sexual Etiquette

Six things never to say to a male who's experiencing erection difficulties.

1. "I'd better call for reinforcements."
2. "Frostbite?"
3. "Better luck next time."
4. "What's for dessert?"
5. "Let's hold a candlelight vigil."
6. "Upsy-daisy."

Which is Better?

Some tips on the size controversy.

A Petite Lover

Will look to you for security

Is cost effective (Eats less and can be smuggled free into movies)

Leaves plenty of room in bed

Short legs (must be dragged if you're in a hurry)

Easier to cover lots of ground with your lips

A Large Lover

Can make you feel secure

Consumes adult portions and must pay full ticket price

Takes up most of the bed

No problem, can easily keep up with you

Takes a longer time to kiss all over

Sex Without Tears

How to survive the insatiable lover.

1. Cheer up.
2. Take frequent rest breaks (fake sleep if you have to).
3. Drink lots of fluids (carrot juice is best, prevents dehydration and night blindness).
4. Avoid wearing musk (has been found to cause nymphomania in baton twirlers).

5. Wear slipper socks (relieves symptoms of too much chemistry).

Guide For the Guilt-Ridden
Hate yourself only if you:

Did it:	Didn't do it:
For a promotion	For lust
For mercy	For love
Out of curiosity	For pleasure
For the exercise only	To pamper yourself
For the practice	To relieve stress
To be different	Because you deserve it
For the heck of it	For the fun of it

The Enlightened Lover
Least difficult decision faced by highly sexed lovers:
Should we undress?
Very difficult decisions:
1. When to stop.
2. Whether to stop.
Most difficult decision:
When to dress.

Did You Know?
The four most energy-consuming after-sex activities

Will be:	If:
Untangling your clothes	You jumped on each other the moment you walked in the door
Finding that earring	If your partner swallowed it
Trying to stand upright	You both experienced a Level 4 simultaneous climax (equivalent to white water rafting the Colorado without a guide)
Shaking hands	You're congratulating each other

Fall Lovemaking Safety Tip
During foliage season, those who heighten their sexual pleasure by making love outdoors on a pile of leaves should watch out for:
• The neighbors
• The rake

Sexual Worsts

- *Worst way to banish lovemaking blahs:* Turn up the TV volume.
- *Worst seduction line:* "Don't you know me from somewhere?"
- *Worst reason to make love:* To keep partner from nagging.
- *Worst basis on which to select a life partner:* On the rebound (your canary died).
- *Worst way to make sure partner's faithful:* Helicopter surveillance.

Love Signs

Horoscope for a Sultry Scorpio
- *Ruling passion:* partners able to drive a stick shift
- *Ruling body lotion:* jello, al dente
- *Chief sexual asset:* your hauntingly beautiful grunts
- *Governing erogenous zone:* either your wrists or Tahiti
- *Aphrodisiac of choice:* elephant garlic
- *Ruling sexual activity:* mouth-to-mouth resuscitation
- *Ideal time for sex:* while contemplating a career change

What I Did Right After Great Sex

"Called L.L. Bean and ordered flannel sheets."
        – Alexandra, guru
"Accidentally stepped in kitty litter."
        – Tom, teamster
"Gave up celibacy."
        – Rex, vicar

Love Signs

Horoscope for a Sizzling Scorpio.
- *Ruling passion:* leaving the lights on, shades up
- *Ruling sexual turnoff:* doesn't exist
- *Chief sexual asset:* highly resistant to bedsores
- *Governing erogenous zone:* rear of a non-rental limo
- *Aphrodisiac:* any bulking agent, particularly celery
- *Ruling sexual activity:* making the world a better place
- *Ideal time for sex:* between phone calls

Shameful Moments in Sex

Confessions of those who over-indulged in marathon sex:

"We stayed in bed for so long we discovered our bell bottoms had gone out of style."

> – Nick and Veronica, soul mates

"Told our neighbor's kid to just slip the Girl Scout cookies under the door and go away."

> – Elwood and Dolly, passion freaks

Love Signs: Scorpio

Opposite love sign: A torrid Taurus with the stamina of a bull.

Outstanding sexual quality: Low maintenance.

Most attractive physical feature: Your body. You also have a gorgeous mind according to the guy who did your CAT scan.

Ruling sexual turnoff: Partners who go ballistic when you eat potato chips in bed.

Ruling sexual turn-on: Partners who can't get enough, so they just take more . . . and more . . . until you're too weak to protest.

Ideal place for sex: Your dentist's office—who can resist when he says, "Open wide."

The Well-Informed Lover

Things likely to cause arousal problems.

- A partner intent on explaining term insurance
- Insufficient foreplay (2.4 seconds)
- Prematurely initiating sex (3 days after his by-pass)
- Partner asking you to raise your feet so she can vacuum
- Prozac
- Taking too much
- Taking too little

After-Sex Etiquette

The debriefing: questions most often asked after sex.

"Who's name were you uttering?"

"How was I?"

"Am I the best you've ever been with?"

"Are you finished?"

"When do we eat?"

"Who walks the dog?"
"Do you still respect me?"
"How about a rematch?"

Great Moments in Afterplay
Things lovers most enjoy after sex:
• The silence
• Feeling drained yet full.
• Ordering in.
• Reheating the spaghetti.
• Helping each other up.
• Watching lover try to walk
• Trying again.
• Succeeding.

Football Season Lament
"It's always, somehow, more difficult to ease my husband off the couch and out of his pajamas when his team loses."*
     – Marjorie, football widow
*"But when his team wins, he puts on his special football helmet and chases me around the bedroom.")

Thoughtful Lovers
What they think about when the sex is:
Pretty good:
"Nothing, who can think?"
     – Brenda, nurse
Kinky:
"Gee, these boots are tight."
     – Roberto, tile installer
Great:
"Neat contact sport."
     – Daphne, flower child and actress

Still on Good Terms?
Reasons to remain with an older lover.
1. Knowledge. Can advise and assist when it comes to (a) the secrets of life and (b) those really difficult term papers.
2. Money. In all likelihood has a substantial Keogh.

3. Low cost. Significant travel discounts through AARP.
4. Wisdom. Knows what's truly meaningful like (a) money isn't everything and (b) all the important maître d's.
5. Experience. Has spent years perfecting his or her expert lovemaking technique.
6. Peace of mind. Has Medicare (can engage in vigorous lovemaking).

Love Signs: Scorpio

Most attractive feature: A vibrant sexual energy most lovers feel right down to their toes (and you make one heck of a flank steak).
Turn-ons: Watching partner undress very slowly, partner watching you undress very slowly, then comparing designer labels.
Turn-off: A partner with the wrong designer labels.
Ideal romantic adventure: Engaging in a wide range of sexual practices, especially those that include a breakfast buffet.
Favorite sexual fantasy: A scandal (your name is found in a "little black book" owned by a prominent madam).

The Enlightened Lover: Stamina

How soon after sex is it safe to:

Activity	Minutes
Fidget	5
Swim	30
Try again:	
Partners in shape	20
Partners not in shape	324
Operate heavy machinery:	
Toaster	4
Backhoe	78

When the Unthinkable Happens

The Problem	The Cause
Impotence	Goulash
Ants	Picnic
Too many climaxes	Miracle

The Enlightened Lover

If your partner isn't quite up to lovemaking tonight, try these persuasive reasons.

- The neighbors are doing it.
- I need you to warm me up.
- You don't know what you're missing. (*Note:* if you've been married 25 or more years, better not use.)
- You owe it to me. (This presumes (a) partner has already given you several rainchecks or (b) you did the dishes.)
- I won't tell you where I hid your bowling ball. (Our correspondents tell us this is most effective.)
- I need the practice.

Tips For the Impatient Lover

When you arrive at your partner's house, no matter how much you anticipate this night of love:

1. Never undress until you're completely inside (lest neighbors watering their lawn be shocked).

2. Always take a few moments to ask your partner how his or her day went. This will have a highly erotic effect as it proves you're not interested only in sex.

3. If your partner has a guest register, sign it before jumping into bed. It will show commitment.

Problem Lovers: Part II

Fatal Flaw	Symptom
Controlling	If pressed for time, orders you to skip foreplay and utter shorter moans.
Cheap	Always brings the same dozen roses.
Unromantic	For your last birthday, gave you pearls and a new vacuum cleaner.
Insensitive	When you say, "A little to the right, dear," he thinks you're talking about politics.

Their Innermost Feelings

How our participants felt after certifiably sublime lovemaking.

"Like nothing mattered except scrunching up against my lover and falling asleep."

— Wilma, tennis pro

"Really icky. Next time I'll try not to get so excited."

— Katherine, debutante

"Wondering aloud, 'Why don't we do this more often?'"

— Don and Margo, retired

"Glad we lied to the desk clerk."

— Duke and Emily, elopers

What Do the Professionals Do?

Problem

After only three hours of sex, we find that our elbows get so chafed that we actually have to stop. We've tried everything, even Cornhusker's Lotion. Alas, nothing seems to work.

Solution

There is obviously too much chemistry between you, so either:

1. Avoid sheets of man-made fiber (silk is best).
2. Switch to a deeper-pile carpet.
3. Put more straw on the ground.

Why Does Passion Fizzle?

Some leading causes of the blahs.

• Always doing it in the same place. Be bold—why not try the car or your front lawn at noon? (Bonus points if you live in a conservative community.)

• Middle-age spread. Chemistry turns into biology.

• Heredity (a recessive gene, usually carried by the male).

• Burnout (doing it too often when you first meet). If you make love seven or more times weekly, it will taper off to once a month by your 50th wedding anniversary.

• Routine (always making love at the exact same time). Why not change your office hours?

The Inquisitive Lover

Q. During the past 22 years of our marriage, we have made love every single night for a total of 8,035 times (we always celebrate

Leap Year by doing it twice). Are we abnormal?

A. Yes. Both of you, instead of reading *Jane Eyre,* are using sex as an unnatural sleep aid which, if continued, can be habit-forming. Stop it immediately.

Recession Lovemaking

How resourceful lovers earned extra money:

"Candlelight tours of our bedroom. For authenticity, we took turns lying in the bed."

— Marie and Guido ("Group rates available")

"Sold lemonade from our night stand. It was really difficult doing two things at once (making change while satisfying each other)."

— George and Barbara

Lovers' Poll: #70

After sex, if your new partner says, "You're my first in such a long time: and you ask why. Eight likely reasons.

1. "I was stuck in traffic."
2. "I'm picky, and all the good ones are either (a) married, (b) engaged, (c) my exes."
3. "My last lover referred to our bed as Never Never Land."
4. "Wasn't sure of my gender."
5. My career took up all my time."
6. "You're the first one able to pull my cowboy boots off."
7. "It's hard to meet Mr. Right when you take public transportation."
8. "Until watching Oprah, I thought sex was dirty."

You Know There's Chemistry

When:

• You often make love for purposes other than reproduction.

• Your friends want to know where you've been keeping yourself . . . and you're not quite sure.

• You both sleep straight through the night . . . like two spoons.

• You've actually attempted breakfast in bed . . . also in the spoon position.

• You throw out your beloved boxer shorts and buy the kind she likes . . . bikini briefs.

• You can't keep your hands off each other . . . even while consulting a marriage counselor.

The Enlightened Commuter: Love Poll #8

Results of a random sampling of people stuck in bumper-to-bumper traffic.

• 28 % of the men, if they were not in love with their partner, felt it was okay, during sex, to leave their socks on.

• 11% of the women, if not in love with their partner, felt it was better, during sex, if he left his socks on.

• 5% of the women felt they had better orgasms with men who had similar political convictions.

• 74% of the men were turned off by women who, during orgasm, engaged in stream-of-conscious yodeling.

Slaving over a Hot Lover

You are entitled to supper money when you have to work overtime to:
• Arouse a lover.
• Satisfy a lover.
• Earn bonus miles.
• Earn employee benefits.
• Interest lover in a new position.
• Convince lover it's your treat.
• Stay late to finish the job.

The Dieter's Guide to Weight Loss During Sex

Our official during-sex passion-intensity scale.

Activity	Calories Burned
If intense lovemaking causes:	
Hat to fall off	32
Makeup to flake	94
A sudden change of inseam	65
Watch to stop	21
Flowers to wilt	50
Windows to steam up	77
Sheets on bed to rumple	5
Both lovers to capsize the bed	87
Yet bravely continue	110

Reminder: Silence Can Be Golden

A few nice things about having sex with a silent partner:

- They don't snore.
- You can hear if the baby's crying.
- You can listen to the leaves outside rustle (very soothing).
- No noise complaints from the next-door neighbors.
- You can hear yourself think.
- There's nothing to disturb your concentration.
- It's much, much easier to perform unspeakable acts.

Conserving Our Natural Resources
Energy-efficient lovers:
- Never allow heat to escape from under the blanket.
- Use only natural energy to
- Flirt.
- Moan.
- Writhe.
- Laugh in the right places.
- Count the climaxes.
- Recycle (and use the same partner over and over again).

The Inquisitive Partner
After sex
Regular Lover Ask:
"Was it good for you?"
Lawyers Ask:
"Why was it good for you?"

Pillow Talk
Lover's block. An incapacity to perform one's sexual duties because of conscious or subconscious factors such as:
- Hidden resentment (partner rolls over and falls asleep either before sex or while leaving the restaurant).
- Panic reaction to during-sex inquiry ("How many children do you want?").
- Counterproductive aphrodisiac (herbal tea).
- Lack of privacy (your weekend to have the kids).
- Sexually transmitted aroma (too much cologne).
- Lover's G-spot in strange place (the kitchen).

The Official Guide For Clock-Watchers

During lovemaking, you may stop the clock only:

- To change the battery.
- To bring in a substitute.
- If either lover calls a time-out because of:

a. Leg cramp.

b. Snack time.

c. Scheduling conflict.

- To watch the sun rise.
- If the referee blows his whistle.

From Our Lover's Glossary

The teaching bed. A facility, usually queen-size or larger, upon which a highly skilled lover holds night classes for the partner who is less gifted or less experienced but eager to learn. Grading is usually done on a curve.

Some National Averages: Part II

3: The average calories in a strand of your lover's chest hair.*

5: The average distance in inches the earth moves during a Level 6 orgasm.

2$^1/_2$: The average distance in miles a pair of hands should travel during a perfect backrub.

153: The average volume, in drops, of tears of gratitude shed when a lover says, "You're the best I've ever been with."

11: The average number of phone calls a Hollywood agent takes during sex.

11: The average number of phone calls a Hollywood agent makes during sex.

*Caution: They're empty calories.

A Brief Guide to Flirting

While at a restaurant, reach under the table and squeeze your companion's knee.

Number of Squeezes	What It Signifies
1	"Don't look at me like that."
2	"I like you."
3	"Our soup's getting cold."
4	"You're making me blush."

| 5 | "Let's not order dessert." |
| 6 | "Oooh, that was not my knee." |

For Lovers with the Munchies

A gentle love bite of	Calories consumed
An Almond Joy	70
Partner's earlobe	1
Partner's calf	2
Partner is a roller bladder	1/2
Partner's tummy:	
Partner addicted to Nordic Track	2
Partner addicted to buffets	31
Candy corn in partner's navel	52

The Dieter's Guide to Weight Loss During Sex

Activity	Calories Burned
Rolling over and falling asleep:*	
After sex	26
During sex	80
While still in the restaurant	143
To avoid splitting the check	200

*No longer an exclusively male activity. More and more women, exhausted by demands of career and family, are allowing themselves a similar luxury.

The Art of Romance

The trained lover:	The untrained lover:
Knows about pacing; always leaves partner satisfied.	Peaks too early; always leaves partner wondering.
Is flexible.	Can't adjust.
Can last three hours.	Fades after one.
Likes adventure.	Needs an itinerary.
Gets carried away.	Gets carried out.

Sexual Demerits: Part IV

Some typical during-sex infractions.

Offense	Number of Demerits
Taking forever to come to bed	9
Coming to bed unprepared (still flossing)	6
Making negative comments ("Are you putting on weight?")	7
Not concentrating totally on The Act (simultaneously tossing bread to pigeons)	14
Finishing too soon	5
Taking forever	10

Tips For Out-of-Shape Lovers

Viewer discretion advised if:

• You're 20 to 25 pounds overweight.
• You're 15 to 20 pounds underweight.
• You've been neglecting those
  Sit ups
  Push ups
• You have cellulite (and you're a male)
• You're upper arms are going south
• Your thighs rub together (even when you ride a horse)

Quote of the Day

"I thought it was puppy love until I discovered he was an animal* in bed."

— Bambi, petting zoo owner

*A tiger, then a bear and, afterward as he toddled off to dreamland, a lamb.

Reminder for Couples

The bad news: The days are getting shorter, less time to enjoy yourselves in the sunroom.
The good news: The nights are getting longer, more time to enjoy yourselves in the bedroom.

Reminder

Three possible side effects of good sex:
Triplets

Thought For Tonight

Give an orchid to the lover who:

- Helps you spot-reduce.
- Monitors your vital signs.
- Gives you mouth-to-mouth resuscitation even when you don't need it.
- Often makes you late for the carpool.
- Never gets dressed until sex is over.
- Leaves you speechless (but can still read your lips).
- Took you to Acapulco for the weekend.
- Took you to Paradise for the night.

Terrible Moment in Lovemaking

"The day my wife came home with lipstick on her collar."
> – Norman, former homemaker

Disappointing Moments in Lovemaking

"Threw myself at him and missed, darn it."
> – Laura, former triathlon champion

"When she wasn't around, I read her diary. It was all about me!"
> – Jason, CIA agent

To Perk Up Tonight's Lovemaking

- Bring home fresh strawberries—bob for them in the Jacuzzi.
- Send the kids to a motel.
- Put on a mask.
- Enter your house via the bedroom window.
- Spend more time on foreplay—take the early train home.

"We're an Item"

Our favorite public displays of affection.

- *"He's trained. At cocktail parties I toss hors d'oeuvres in the air and he catches them in his mouth."*
- "When our neighbors barbecue, my boyfriend licks rib sauce from my fingers."
- "We do a smoldering tango down the cereal aisle of our supermarket."
- "At the Gap, she measures my inseam."

Trick or Treat?
The Tricks
1. Wear your mudpack while making love.
2. Give your lover a warm, wet kiss while wearing wax teeth.
3. Play "Ghost" and disappear immediately after sex.
The Treats
1. Take a bubble bath—bob for your lover.
2. Give your lover a back rub.
3. Stay awake during sex.

Ethics of Lovemaking
Feigning orgasm is acceptable only if:

Your lover's getting:	You're getting:
Excited	Squashed
Hungry	Fed up
Sweaty	Wet
Louder	Softer
Worn out	Sleepy
Creative	Seasick
On	Off

Advice For Lovers in Search of Privacy
Tonight, to ward off
- Flu
- Visitors
- Burglars
- The dog
- Your kids
- The Welcome Wagon
- Zealous trick-or-treaters

from your bedroom doorknob hang a
Good: Do Not Disturb sign
Better: Scarecrow

Our Exclusive Halloween Poll
How do you celebrate this night?
"We undress, get under the covers and take each other trick or treating. Oh, those Lady Fingers."
> – Peter, pastry chef

"We make love by the light of a smiling jack-o'-lantern. My husband's inhibited so just before the big moment we turn its face away."
　　　　　— Elizabeth, art historian
"Wax lips. They're the greatest."
　　　　　— Henry, state lawmaker

From Our Book of Sexual Secrets

Never rush sex:	Unless:
In the morning.	There's a schedule conflict (your co-car poolers have no patience).
In the afternoon.	You're on a budget (and have rented the bridal suite for only 15 minutes).
At night.	You've got tickets to a matinee. You must meet a deadline (your partner turns into a pumpkin at midnight and you're allergic to fruit.

Debriefing Our Lovers

(Check the phrase that applies most to your own lovemaking.)
"The sex was so hot that:
___ I lost my retainer."
___ The plants protested."
___ My tummy tuck (darn it) came undone."*
___ The people upstairs a) called and were b) envious."
___ The car windows fogged up."
___ It steamed open the mail."
___ The jack-o'-lantern smiled."
*Partner must pay for new one.

MONTHLY QUALITY OF LIFE® CHECKUP

•We had sex: Once___   Twice___   Four times___
Not at all (we both OD'd on Halloween candy___
•Quality of sex:
Good___
Very good___
Terrific___
Would have been better but his Halloween costume got in the way
(he was dressed as a lawyer)___
•Favorite sexual fantasy:
Being softly caressed by a pulchritudinous transvestite___
Making love in a downy meadow then afterward hoping we haven't
caught Lyme disease___
Sex aboard a 747 with a tender baggage handler___
A sunny, lazy afternoon in bed with my personal trainer___
Mud wrestling with four starlets___
Sex slave to a Marine battalion___
Being ravished in a dungeon by the Pillsbury Dough Boy___
Attending a mergers and acquisitions meeting braless___
A nooner with an affectionate Sherpa___
Trying on partner's false eyelashes___

Signed_____

Witnessed_____

NOVEMBER

•Erotic Goals for November:
1. Get partner to "open up" to me
2. Pay his bail if he's arrested for flashing

If they don't already have one, those who reside in colder climates (specifically but not exclusively women) should begin their search for a winter-weight lover. Not only do partners with a few extra pounds have more energy, but they'll keep you warm when the oil burner malfunctions. Women who are "always chilly" will be especially grateful for a large-size partner such as a hirsute tow-truck operator or, when the weather is truly frigid, a gallant lumberjack who will get into bed first and defrost the sheets.

Men, too, when the temperature drops, tend to discard their petite partner* and, instead, gravitate towards an "Earth Mother" type, one who radiates warmth, and, if necessary, can chop a cord of wood with a kitchen knife for kindling.

*Nutritional tip: Men who are committed to their petite lover need not despair. Even the thinnest woman can achieve "pleasing plumpness" simply by going on a diet of eclairs, potato salad and polenta for a week.

Official aphrodisiac of the Month:
20-pound roast turkey (or if your oven is small, a rock cornish hen)

Baby, It's Cold Outside!

Brrr. Time to switch to a winter-weight lover. One who can keep you warm on frosty nights.

For Minimal Warmth

Ideal weight: 159 to 185 pounds. Ideal deployment of body hair: shaggy on chest, modest on arms, wispy on shoulders. Heat output may be supplemented with hot-water bottle or Saint Bernard.

For Maximum Warmth

Ideal weight: 211 to 250 pounds. Ideal deployment of body hair: thick on chest, generous (but not apelike) on back. In an emergency, can also produce enough heat to warm a four-family dwelling.

The Lover's Nightstand

Basic	Advanced
Small radio to serenade lover	Mandolin
Lucky rabbit's foot (to ward off surprise visitors who saw your car in the driveway)	Amulet (has more power, and will make your car disappear entirely)
Book of Renaissance poetry (to help convey your most intimate feelings)	Thesaurus (to help you describe those indescribable feelings)
Thermometer(to detect changes in partner's temperature)	Compass (to detect changes in partner's position)

The Art of Romance

Four orgasms three climaxes within a one-hour period can create a feeling of well-being equivalent to either three months of intensive Zen or a bowl of warm lentil soup.

Gem of the Month

A topaz ring to an uninhibited but considerate lover who makes lots of noise during sex, but:

1. Provides you with earplugs.
2. Asks, "Am I disturbing you?"
3. If you have thin walls, writes a note of apology to each of your neighbors (explaining he was merely delivering a singing telegram).

4. Always takes a moment to comfort your frightened cat, especially if it's sitting there with its paws over its ears.
5. Promises to be less noisy the next time...but isn't.

Improve-Your-Love-Life Tip
Avoid distractions: At the beginning of football season, move the television out of, and your partner into, the bedroom
Note: Many cable companies offer a "lockout" feature that will prevent your set from picking up any major sporting event.

What Makes You Feel Sexy?: Lovers' Poll #44
"While he slowly undresses me, he gently and lingeringly sniffs me all over. It's called a scent strip."
    – Diana, blackjack dealer
"An after-dinner stroll along a moonlit beach after a night of...ooooh, I can't say it."
    – Tori, creative director
"If she rubs me long enough, my personal genie appears and grants her three wishes."
    – Matt, gynecologist

To Be a Well-Endowed Lower
Your nightstand should contain:
1. Pad and pencil-for those moments when you're speechless.
2. Liquid invigorant such as champagne, mineral water or seltzer.
3. Bowl of pop-in-lover's-mouth fruit (cherries, grapes, Raisinets or popcorn recommended).
4. Tiny flashlight-for late-night visits to bathroom.
5. Tweezers (the hair-in-mouth removal system of last resort).
6. Tissues (nonscented) for dabbing away tears of:
    • Joy
    • Laughter
    • Gratitude

The Dieter's Guide to Weight Loss During Sex

Activity	Calories Burned
Temporarily avoiding sex by feigning:	
Back pain	8
Sleep	22
Headache	
Ordinary	29
Migraine	45
Hangover	
From beer	19
From budget champagne	124
Cramps	71
If you're a man	300

What is More Important?

If lovemaking is going really well (two hours and you've not yet approached your peak), keep right on going, even if it means:
- Calling in sick at work
- Not showing up at a dinner party
- Canceling your tennis game
- Voting by proxy
- Canceling your hairdressing appointment
- Ignoring the doorbell when your guests arrive
- Paying the baby-sitter overtime.

Zen Thoughts For the Day
Any side of the bed is the right side when your lover is lying on the other side.

Looking for Someone New? Part I

Pickup Lines That	Might Work	Might Not
In a bar:		
"May I buy you a drink?"	X	
"May I buy you?"		X
In church:		
"Might I share your Bible?"	X	
"Repent!"		X
At a party:		
"Are you here with anybody?"	X	

557

"Don't you know me
from somewhere?"   X
"Stay away from the ham bologna."   X

More Sexual Worsts
• *Four worst ways to find out if your lover's been with another.*
1. Ask your lover.
2. Ask the neighbors.
3. Read his or her a) diary or b) mail.
4. Dust for fingerprints.
• *Worst kind of bedroom to make love in*:
Everything matches.
• *Two worst things to have to look for after wild sex*:
1. Your theater tickets.
2. Your partner.

Reminder
Three more warning signs of too little sex:
1. Obsession with a perfect gold swing
2. Insomnia
3. Running for office

Pillow Talk
The wake-up call. 1. Something said by one lover to another during sex, i.e., "Wake up, wake up!" 2. Something a lover leaves with you in the hope that, in the morning, you'll gently awaken such lover so that he or she won't be late for a) work or b) class or c) his or her wedding. Wake-up procedures favored by our technical adviser include:
• Holding a jellied slice of toast under sleeper's nose
• Kissing sleeper's neck
• Whispering sweet nothings into sleeper's ear ("Eggs are ready")

Guide for the Well-Rounded Lover

Lovemaking-odd symptoms:

Symptom	Cause
Feeling awkward during sex	Forgot to dismiss the housekeeper
Feeling awkward after sex	Too much noise during climax
Feeling overworked	Lover has too many erogenous zones
Reading during foreplay	Lover hasn't yet arrived
Low pulse rate	Lover doing it wrong
Rapid heart beat	Lover doing it right

Sex Speak: Part I

What Your Lover Says:	What Your Lover Means:
"I'm so close."	Now is the time to check my lottery ticket.
"Gosh, you do everything right."	Actually, I'm not that fussy.
"Love the way you do that."	It reminds me of my last lover.
"How many times does that make?"	Will we ever break for lunch?
"I...I can hardly catch my breath."	What was in those fajitas?
"Thanks for dinner."	Love those freebies.

Interruptions

It's okay to stop in the middle of sex only to:
• See if the baby's okay.
• Make a diary entry.
• Get a snack.
• Measure your pulse.
• Regain your composure.
• Change the tape in the minicam.
• Give the maid a chance to make up the room.
• Take a vacation day.
• Get your beauty sleep.

Great Climaxes I Have Known
Test lovers reveal the consequences of a gale-force orgasm.
"My pacemaker stopped (fortunately, my heart kicked in)."
— Edgar, retired
"I spilled my drink all over him. Luckily the waiter ran over with a dry shirt."
— Mary Ann, cosmetician
"It made my nicotine patch fly off, so I lit a cigarette. That first puff felt nearly as good as orgasm."
— Rex, paralegal
"Idiocy...and my skin cleared up."
— Victoria, jeweler

What I Did For Love
"Had sex with a Republican."
— Donna B., concerned citizen

The Dieter's Guide to Weight Loss During Sex
When your lover asks what really turns you on.

Activity	Calories Burned
Composing yourself	17
Putting on your thinking cap	22
Being completely honest	55
Calming shocked lover	200

Wine and Your Sexual Fantasies: Part II

Type of Wine	Application
Beaujolais Nouveau	Extra courage-enables you to share all fantasies with a meek lover (two glasses, minimum)
Chablis or Champagne	Provides the audacity to carry them out without guilt or having to consult your clergyman.

The Diplomatic Lover

Over-the-phone statements not likely to make a sensitive partner feel better:

Before Sex

"It won't be the same without you."

After Sex

"It wasn't the same without you."

Best Sex I Ever Had

"It was a contest to see who could have the most climaxes without growing mentally impaired. Thankfully, I lost."

      – Tiffani, philosophy instructor

"It was a controlled experiment. She got the orgasm, I got the placebo. It still felt great."

      – Irving, judge

"On a sofa bed-it opened into a casting couch."

      – Franco, model

"While Congress was in recess, we could finally take our time."

      – Amber, Senate aide

Thoughts for Tonight

Six things to think about while making love.

1. How nice your lover feels in your arms.
2. How happy you are.
3. How lucky you are to have met each other.
4. Wouldn't it be nice to have a king-size bed.
5. The cute little grunts your partner makes when you touch her "Right" spot.
6. Who you're going to vote for tomorrow.

Thought for the Day

Reesarchers have discovered that a full and happy sex life may significantly reduce the need to run for public office.

Great Moments in Afterplay

"We fold laundry."

      – Rhoda, interior decorator

"We make the bed."

      – Henri, concierge

"We reach out and touch each other."
            – Debbie, long-distance operator

From Our Lover's Glossary
Foreplay. The best way to preheat a non-microwavable lover to 102 F . While manual stimulation is still the preferred method, many of our panelists report excellent arousal results with wine and roses, freshly baked cookies or a ride in a stretch limo wearing nothing but the leather seats.

From Our Lover's Glossary
Mid-Sex Crisis. A during-lovemaking emergency in which one or both partners are temporarily unable to perform because of:
• Indigestion (the salsa syndrome).
• Guilt (have no right to so much pleasure).
• Exhaustion (forgot to carbohydrate load).
• Shock (partner finally told you what she really likes to do).
• Too much animal magnetism (the dog's on the bed).
• A counterproductive fantasy (picturing your dentist in his underwear).
• Strange noises (raccoons in the garbage, again).

Nice to Hear After Lovemaking
Good: "You're my first time in a long time."
Better: "You're my first."
Best: "You're my last."

Election Day
Things often said after sex:
Who'd you vote for?"

Setting the Mood

Ease into lovemaking gradually, by discussing:

Erotic Topics	Less Erotic
The sexual energy in caviar	The atomic energy in plutonium
How 30 minutes of vigorous sexual activity can lower cholesterol	How 30 minutes of vigorous aerobic activity might lower cholesterol
The ups and downs of intercourse	The ups and downs of interest rates
The juicy details	Sweet nothings
How sex without affection can be an empty experience	How affection without sex can be an empty experience

Guidelines for Lovers

Be sure to allow yourself enough rest between lovemaking sessions.

For every:	Rest:
4 hours of lovemaking	2 hours
6 hours of lovemaking	4 hours
9 hours of lovemaking	10 hours (a bit more if either lover begins to decompose)
24 hours of lovemaking (it's been done)	One day (more if either partner begins to ferment)

Great Moment in Sex

"In exchange for sex, she promised to replace my virginity with something better."
— Manfred, deacon-at-large

Believe It or Else

No matter how far apart the two of you are, sex can bring you together, especially if you both have it in the same room.

Eight More Things to be Happy About After Sex

1. No more liver spots.
2. You got your heart rate up.
3. You didn't reveal any military secrets.
4. There's still one chocolate-chip cookie left.

5. Your "dysfunction" was psychological.
6. You yielded to temptation.
7. Your instincts about him were right.
8. It still may not be over.

Sex in 1996 America
Findings from a telephone survey of 10,000 women voters.
- **Favorite position:**

The missionary (him on top, me trying to breathe)	11%
The missionary (me on top, him converting the heathen)	12%

- **Preferred during-sex activity:**

Receiving oral sex	77%
Giving oral sex	15%
Avoiding oral sex	8%

- **Preferred after-sex activity:**

Cuddling, then dozing off	69%
Socializing	2%
Shopping	10%
Avoiding the wet spot	19%

Sex Without Tears
Never:
1. Hate yourself in the morning. Wait till after lunch.
2. Continue lovemaking if your life begins to flash before your eyes. Instead, close them.
3. Assume that a great tennis partner will be a terrific lover.
4. Sleep with a person who wears
    - More than three gold chains
    - Training wheels

Making Love in Your Car-Some Statistics
1. If you wear a safety *and* shoulder straps:
    - Your chances of experiencing a yummy climax actually decrease 67%, but
    - Your chances of surviving a robust climax increase by 93%.
2. If you make love in the back seat:
    - Your chance of activating the driver's side airbag is only 4%, but
    - Your chance of activating the driver is 98%.

The Enlightened Lover
Researchers note that happily married couples who eat a balanced diet and make love five or more times a week develop an increased tolerance for sex.

From Our List of Sexual Worsts
Worst seduction line ever uttered by a male.
Who: Alvin (wouldn't give his last name)
When: January 14, 1991
Where: After-work watering hole, east side of Manhattan
To whom line addressed: Margot; beautiful, sophisticated, senior vice president of a multinational conglomerate
Line: "Would you like to come up and see my baseball cards?"
Was line successful? Yes.

Apologies
Sex not as good as usual? Want another chance? Simply detach and mail this form.

----------detach here----------

Sorry about last night. Next time I'll:
Let my toenails dry completely.
Go a little easier on the curry.
Turn on my answering machine.
Hang a "Do not bug us for your allowance" sign on the door.
Avoid wearing that overpowering scent.
Make certain my boyfriend's out of town.
Other

Familiarity Breeds . . .
Things a lover should never

Hear You Do	**See You Do**
Chew gum or speak with your mouth full of egg salad	Remove a piece of meat from between your teeth with tip of your fingernail
Gargle	Gargle
Blow your nose	Inspect the results
Get sick from drinking	Get sick from drinking
Whine about a zit	Squeeze it

The Enlightened Lover

The foolproof way to indicate that you're ready for sex is to take out your contact lenses so your lover can better see the glint in your eye.

Your New Lover

Things you:

Can Change	Can't Change
Weight	Height
Sexual experience	Sexual talent
The future	The past
The ending	The beginning

Reminder for Procrastinating Lovers

Now is the time to prepare your Christmas list.

If lover	We suggest
Is vain	A mirror
Is underweight	Chocolates
Likes to read after sex	A novel
Likes to read during sex	A bed lamp
Likes to stay the night	A toothbrush
Is always late	A wristwatch
Likes to see how long sex takes	A shockproof wristwatch
Has difficulty with commitment	A tattoo (your name)
Is perfect	An early Christmas bonus

Sex in America: Part III

The kinkiest sex we ever had? My husband and I did it in a voting booth. I told the guard that Bill was my political consultant. We pulled all the correct levers and our candidate won."

      – Trish, council woman

From Our Lover's Glossary

The Snuggle Reflex. An involuntary response to a human stimulus such as an extra-delicious, immensely cuddly partner against whose body you love to press, especially:

• On cold winter nights.

• When you have to get up in the morning to go to a job that you (a) don't really love or (b) despise.

• During the scary parts of the movie you rented.

Pre-Sexual Relaxation Techniques
Things to do after a long hard week.
Bring each other back to life by:
1. Soaking together in a bubble bath.
2. Fingertip massaging each other's feet.
3. Brushing each other's teeth.
Pamper each other with:
1. A rubdown with aromatic oils.
2. Chocolate-covered strawberries.
Achieve total rejuvenation by:
1. Sharing a glass of wine.
2. Spending the evening in bed.

Are You Having Too Much Sex?
The danger signals:
• Bedsores
• Craving for sweets (chocolate truffles, to be precise)
• Chafed elbows
• Decrease in social life
• Buying at retail
• Dark circles under eyes
• And don't care

The Morning After a Perfect Night
Know the dreaded symptoms of too much ecstasy.
• *At work:* Difficulty concentrating on the task at hand.
• *Current events:* Curious indifference to election outcome.
• *Attitude:* Humming love songs.
• *Comportment:* Spring in step, lilt in voice, eyes shining
• *Psychological:* Diminished hostility on bank lines.
• *Interpersonal:* Purchase of a) card containing likeness of cute animal plus warm sentiment, and b) 29¢ stamp.
• *Generosity:* Sharing a lottery ticket.

What I Did for Sex
"Practiced."
                    – Norma, designer

"Didn't give him a speeding ticket."
>   – Candice, highway patrol officer

"Took him to Palm Beach for the weekend."
>   – Hilary, bus driver

What I Did for Love

"Bought designer sheets that complement my new lover's hair."
>   – Olga, interior design consultant

"Finally left my first husband...at a scenic overlook."
>   – Kelly, researcher

"Finally left my parents."
>   – Barry, Kelly's new husband

Longevity and Lovemaking

Research shows that

Each time you:	To your life, add:
Do something strange and wonderful for your partner (like wait until after sex to retrieve your voice mail)	3 minutes
Experience a time-release orgasm (if you feel it the next day during sales conference-share it with the others)	5 minutes
Wake up with a smile on your face	7 minutes
At 2 a.m.	15 minutes

Tip for the Over-Enthusiastic Partner

When aroused, gushing with love is perfectly acceptable so long as you're willing, after sex, to:

1. Rinse off your partner.
2. Lie in the wet spot.
3. Mop up.

Sex Without Tears

Should he feel rejected if she says:

"Not tonight, dear, I'm too tired."	(yes)	no
"Not tonight, dear, it's not Veterans Day."	yes	(no)
"Not tonight, dear, I had my hair done."	(yes)	no
"Not tonight, dear, I'm in labor."	yes	(no)

Sexual Demerits: Part IV

Violation	Demerits Earned
Snoring:	
After sex	2
During sex	17
Over-the-calf black socks	11
Not removing them	26
More than 5 trips to the bathroom:	
Before sex	15
During sex	30
Leaving nothing to the imagination	6
Leaving too much to the imagination	21

From Our Book of Sexual Records

Most astonishing during-sex occurrence: Carlos D., of Norfolk, Virginia, and Machu Picchu, Peru, without ever having studied the language, began to moan rapturously in perfect Flemish when his lover, Jade, using only a pointer, took him on a three-hour sightseeing tour without ever leaving the bedroom.

The Diplomatic Lover

Fib: "I'm glad we waited."
White lie: "Sorry I took so long."
Misstatement: "Of course I'm going to leave my wife."
Falsehood: "Let's see, six partners, but they were nothing compared to you."
Untruth: "Of course I voted for you."
Lie: "It was a wrong number."

What Do the Professionals Do?

What to do when, during sex, the doorbell rings.
"If it's your blind date finally showing up, offer him refreshments and have him wait in the den until you're done."
  – Marilyn, executive director, the Moan Center
"Whisper in your partner's ear, 'They're playing our song,' and continue lovemaking."
  – Bentley, Counselor Emeritus,
   U.S. Body Rub Association

"Study the face of the person you're in bed with-make sure it's your spouse."
— Michele, therapist, The Spanking Center

Football Season Tip
How to reassure a partner obsessed with sports:
Don't worry, if we leave the door open, you'll still be able to see the TV from the bedroom."

Sex Without Tears
Should he feel rejected if she says:
"Not tonight, dear, I have a headache." (yes)   no
"Not tonight, dear, I have a cluster headache."   yes   (no)

Some Bedside Special Touches
Fresh flowers: Can make an old lover come alive.
Cordless phone: During lovemaking, allows greater freedom of movement if you're also talking to your broker.
Time: Obvious.
Calculator: See above.
Teddy bear: The lover-alternative of choice.
Candles: In cases of power failure.
Thermometer: To test for spring fever.

From Our Lover's Glossary
Guest lover. A substitute or additional lover who is called in if your current lover:
• Moonlights
• Is getting lonely
• Needs assistance
• Is working late
• Is waiting for his or her divorce to come through
• Needs a third opinion
• Has peaked
• Likes to kibitz
• Is not the jealous type

Olympian of the Year

A gold medal (gold-plated if you're strapped for cash) to the lover who:

• Knows the subtle difference between "a bit more" and "a little more."
• Likes a partner who's 5 pounds overweight.
• Always opens the car door for you.
• Puts you on a pedestal (unless the bed's available).
• When you come home after a hard day at work, always greets you at the door with a martini (and never fails to ask if you'd like one too).
• Always finishes in first place.

Pre-Lovemaking Relaxation Technique

We suggest slipping into something comfortable like:

• *To release tensions:* A hot tub.
• *To feel cozy:* Those warm, fleecy slipper socks.
• *For the tranquillity:* That soft, comfortable robe.
• *For the romance:* Your lover's lap.
• *For the climate:* Florida.

Today's "Eyes Only" Fax

(Check the phrase that applies and send to your lover at work.*)
Thinking of what we did last night is making me:

___Tingle all over
___Shed
___Shower extra carefully
___Consider going to confession
___Very, very hot
___Hear music (our song)
___Hear wedding bells
___Wish that I had another set of sheets
*Unless he or she works at the Pentagon

What I Did for Love

"Cleaned his hamster's cage."
　　　　— Laura M.
"Gave her cat a bath."
　　　　— Arthur K.

571

Good Places for Lovemaking

A new spot can make it seem like the "first time."

Location	Advantage
Elevator (caution: not a grain elevator)	Stares of envy from other riders; cozy space kindles feelings of intimacy
Picnic	Open space-no headboard or footboard to hinder movement
Swimming pool	Minimal gravity creates novel position possibilities
Front porch	Waving to passing motorists makes you feel warm inside

"Are You Coming to Bed?"

Your chances of having sex tonight, according to our consulting statistician.

If spouse gets into bed	Your chances of having sex are
When you do	91%
But clutching a teddy bear	63%
10 minutes after you	84%
With a snack	72%
35 minutes after you	26%
But asks, "Do you want to fool around?"	45%
One hour after you	4%
And wearing curlers	1%

Alternate Olympian of the Year

A silver medal to the lover who:
• Loves to cook your favorite dish (turkey hash).
• Knows how to take care of your infrastructure (with TLC).
• Assures you those fantastic lovemaking techniques were learned from a book.
• Is never intimated by that gleam in your eye.
• When he or she whispers in your ear, blows your mind.
• Helps you make it through the night.
• Always finishes in first place.

Fitness and the Baby Boomer
Suggested during-sex aphrodisiacs if you're:

Age 39 to 49	Age 50+
Popcorn	Leafy vegetables
Barbecued chicken wings	Vitamin B
Sirloin steak	Iron supplement
Any decent Beaujolais	Skim milk
Chili (extra powerful)	Nasal decongestant
Klondike Bar	Magnesium tablets
Eggnog	Prune juice

True Devotion
"I never play in a big game the night before I'm going to see my fiancée. It would make me too feeble to perform the way she expects me to."

— Major league fullback (who insisted on anonymity)

After-Sex Etiquette
You want to tell your lover how good it is, but the bedroom has:

Thick Walls	Thin Walls
Laugh	Giggle
Groan	Moan
Squeal	Chirp
Howl	Sigh
Grunt	Whimper
Wail	Squeak
Clap	Blink

First Aid for an Exhausted (but Happy) Lover
1. Do not move lover unless absolutely necessary (say, you rented the room for only an hour).
2. Check to see if lover is breathing. If so, ask if he or she would like to try again. If not, leave.
3. Apply cold compress if lover irrational from too many orgasms (free-associating or making "big band" sounds).
4. Carefully examine lover for physical signs such as change of height (from 6'1" to 4'3") or (worst case) mascara running.
5. Seek professional help only if partner has medical coverage.

Tip For Flu Season
Avoid over-the-counter remedies. Experts consider a time-release orgasm the only all-natural, FDA-approved, 12-hour decongestant that will get you through the day without sneezing (and it's tax deductible).

Sexual Etiquette
Unless you have to catch a plane, it's considered impolite to begin putting your makeup on before sex is completely over, even if you're fairly certain your partner won't (a) notice or (b) stop.

The Signs
You aren't having enough sex if your:
• Skin shows wrinkles, sun damage, muddiness and lines.
• Eyes look dull and bloodshot.
• Gait is listless, no spring in your step.
• Face resembles your photo I.D.
• Gums lose their sparkle.
• Lover complains that you haven't been sneaking out of the office enough.
• Weight starts creeping up.

Did You Know?
The four leading causes of guilt among happily monogamous couples are:
1. Excessive lust.
2. A frequency rate far above the national average.
3. Feeling insufficiently sorry for friends who haven't found the right one.
4. Lingering in bed on cold mornings even after the alarm goes off because your partner's body feels so deliciously warm.

The Bedside Eater
Aphrodisiac of the Day
Tortellini salad with (for best results) prosciutto and Italian dressing
Erotic Effect
Increases feelings of lust for one's spouse (and better enables busy

executives to schedule sex for that night without feeling guilty)
Aphrodisiac of the Night
Strawberry parfait and/or chocolate mousse
Erotic Effect
Helps the lover with a short shelf life rise to the occasion

The Enlightened Lover
How your partner truly feels about lovemaking.

Enjoys It	A Chore
Gives you long, languorous caresses.	Devotes four dabs per erogenous zone.
Smiles a lot.	Grimaces.
Asks if it's good for you.	Insists it's good for you.
Is totally involved in being with you.	Is also working a connect-the-dots place mat.
Feels great.	Feels a draft.
Is counting the moments.	On an abacus.

The Enlightened Lover
Statement least likely to calm a jealous lover:
"Those pictures were taken before I met you."

The Inquiring Lover
Responses to an often asked after-sex question: "What are you thinking about?"

Good	Not So Good
"Us."	"Must change my hairdresser."
"Gee, your whiskers make a great facial scrub."	"Could you please reach my night repair gel?"
"How really relaxed and tranquil I feel."	"Could you possibly get off my leg?"
"Sorry, can't speak yet."	"Need moussaka."
"Our steamy future."	"My steamy past."
"Does it get any better?"	"Overpopulation."

Fond Sexual Memories
How lovers preserve them.
"My partner gives me a nightly refresher course."
— Clint, moped mechanic
"Every time we make love, we carve a notch on the headboard-our friends think we have termites."
— Faye and Mark, newlyweds
"Wherever we did it-hotel, motel or inn-we took a matchbook, a towel and the bed. Now, in our golden years, we have a love museum."
— Sid and Cyd, retired tour guides

Great Moments in Afterplay
"Listening to him ask, 'What's for dinner?' as I'm nodding off to dreamland."
— Daisy, chemical engineer
"Gazing in the ceiling mirror to see if my lover's special 'anti-wrinkle' treatment really worked (it always does)."
— Felicia, southern belle
"Calling my mother and trying not to giggle when I explain why I'll be late for dinner."
— Elvis, welding teacher

Traveler's Advisory #3
For frequent fliers only.
Man on bottom
Woman either:
Flying standby, or
Trying to make a connecting flight (aisle seat only)

Helpful Hint to Make Your Love Life Easier
Before seeing a new lover, remove fingerprints of previous lover by wiping your body with a cloth lightly dampened in olive oil.

The Enlightened Lover
There can be little doubt that sex was good if you:
• Activated the smoke alarm.
• Ignored your beeper.
• Are having difficulty getting dressed.

- And walking a straight line.
- Totaled the bed.
- No longer have that "stuffed" feeling.
- Need jumper cables to get out of bed.

What Every Expert Lover Should Know
- Which wines go best with pizza (red with pepperoni; white with anchovy; rosé with Domino's).
- How to darn a seam ripped apart by passionate hands.
- How to play Chopin on the piano in the bedroom (for those quiet, romantic moments).
- That when it comes to lovemaking, it's better to give but not so bad to receive.
- That abstinence doesn't make the heart grow fonder.

Sexual Etiquette
Q. During sex at my lover's place, what do I do if the phone rings and she answers it?
A. If:
1. She says, "No thanks, I already have a no-fee credit card," relax.
2. She says, "Yes, I'm eating a balanced diet, Mom," ask to say hello.
3. She turns away and keep repeating in a low voice, "I can't talk now," causing your blood pressure to skyrocket to 167/166, feign nonchalance.
4. You hear frantic whispering and she asks you to wait in the other room, be gallant—finish having sex, then obey her wishes.

Survival Advice
Thinking about a wonderful sexual experience can help you endure:
- The bore seated next to you on an airliner.
- Being denied a) a mortgage or b) entrance to a hot disco.
- Looking at a co-worker's cat photos.
- An 8-mile traffic tie-up.
- The half-time show at a football game.
- The one you're having now.

Bed Manners
Always apologize if:
• You break your lover's bed (be especially contrite if the bed is borrowed).
• During an extravagant, climax-related gesture, you shatter a Ming vase (don't pretend not to notice).
• You address your lover by the wrong name (using an all-purpose endearment such as "darling," "honey" or "occupant" will alleviate this problem).
• You get your dates confused and show up a week early.

Know Your Sexual Law

Moving Violations	Points
Leaving the scene of an accident:	
Property damage (champagne glass	
made a ring on lover's night table)	3
Personal injury (hairdo ruined)	5
Failure to signal when changing positions	2
After lovemaking: drag-racing to bathroom	4
Perjury (pleading headache falsely)	7
Speeding through an erogenous zone	9
Tailgating	1

Facts of Love
Among couples who've been married 15 or more years, calling in sick and staying in bed all day to have sex accounts for (alas) only nine workdays lost each year in the United States.

Lighter Moments in Lovemaking
Before sex
"When I got so excited that I tried to pull my socks off over my head."
> – Clint, paralegal

During sex
"While in the middle of faking an orgasm, (needed to get it over with, I had a pie in the oven), I suddenly realized it was real!"
> – Abigail, Home Economics teacher

After sex
"When my fiancé offered to pay for the nail I broke while digging it into his back"
— Missy, aerobics instructor trainee.

The Eight Moments of Truth
The first time a new lover sees you:
1. Without makeup.
2. Nude in an especially cruel light (fluorescent).
3. Weep (particularly if your nose runs simultaneously).
4. Snore with your mouth open.
5. Get angry.
6. Floss.
7. Out of control (demonstrating your special "rebel yell" during moments of sexual ecstasy).
8. Eat lobster.

Our Survey of Sex in America: Part 600
How appealing to 1,500 lovers ages 21 to 61 is:

The Sexual Act	Very	Somewhat	Not at All
Intercourse	88%	11%	1%
Giving oral sex	77	13	10
With no expectation of receiving it	5	8	87
Sex with a stranger	3	12	85
Who turns out to be your spouse who's spent two weeks at a reducing spa	91	7	2

The Hot Breakfast
Did you know that shedding your robe and engaging in one impulsive and wild embrace with that person sitting across from you eating cereal and staring at the newspaper can:
• Burn up to 96 calories
• Lower cholesterol
• Increase pulse rate
• Aid digestion
• Make you late for work

All-Natural Sex

The EPA's guidelines.
• No clothes.
• No additives (curlers to bed, mudpack, night repair cream, an extra lover, etc.)
• No aphrodisiacs containing nitrites.
• Intimate apparel must be of all-natural fibers (includes slipper socks).
• Re kinky sex: naugahyde body suits prohibited.
• No animal testing (unless it's on your lover).
• All oil spills (salad or baby) must be properly contained.

From Our Lover's Glossary

Love knot. This configuration of two lovers who, owing to intense passion (or attempting an odd position), find themselves at the conclusion of sex hopelessly entangled and, in some instances, unable to separate without assistance.*

Common Love Knots	Cause
Figure eight	Too much creativity
Slipnot	Inexperience
Bowline	Simultaneous climax
Clove hitch	Moving from sofa to bed without stopping

*The fire department.

Tip for Lovers Who Work Together

Instead of a coffee break, why not take a sex break?
• It's less fattening than a pineapple Danish.
• Unlike caffeine, it won't make you nervous.
• Seven out of seven employees consider it the preferred method of on-the-job training.
• If you're careful, you can do it at your work station.
• It may be tax deductible (see IRS Form 3903, Moving Expenses).
• It's a legitimate form of Workmen's Compensation.

Memories

Reserve a special place in your heart for the first lover who
• Made it tingle.
• You did it with on an actual bed instead of:

- In a car.
- On a stairway.
- On a sofa.
- Against a sink.
- Brought out your sexuality.
- Made you ever so reluctant to put it back.
- Showed you how to feel better with less sleep.
- Helped you understand (finally) what all the fuss is about.

Our Survey of Sex in America: Part 746

How appealing to 1,500 lovers ages 21 to 61 is:

The Sexual Act	Very	Somewhat	Not at All
The Missionary position	78%	31%	9%
On a single bed	32	15	53
On a bar stool	2	3	95
Watching lover undress	73	22	5
At a wild party that's gotten out of hand	44	38	18
And he's wearing those day-of-the-week boxer shorts	5	12	83

Great Moments in Lovemaking

That wonderful and refreshing 10-minute pause between arousal and foreplay when, for extra energy, you go into the kitchen and finish the rest of the Italian cheesecake.

Wine and Your Lover: Advanced

To the lover who:	Serve:
Is aging well	A vintage Cabernet (cellared for at least 8 years)
Is soft yet full-bodied	A white, curvaceous Bordeaux
Is best at room temperature	Red Burgundy (premier cru)
Has a complex bouquet	A chilled Portuguese rosé
Displays a deep ruby color during afterglow	Trockenbeerenauslese, or any similarly rich dessert wine

Sex in Your Office

Seven tips to make it better.

1. Hold all calls.
2. Trading office gossip is an approved form of foreplay.
3. If partner is a subordinate, don't promise a raise until after sex.
4. If partner is a superior, ask for a raise (or a corner office) before sex.
5. Take notes.
6. Keep the door closed.
7. Clear it with legal.

The Diligent Employee

New guidelines covering lustful thinking on company time:

Permitted	Not Permitted
Daydreaming about what you and your lover did this morning	Making a call on company time to remind him
Ways to improve job performance	Ways to improve sexual performance
Wondering what it would be like to date your boss	Wondering what it would be like to sedate your boss
Satisfying your customers	Satisfying your lover
Starting your own family	Starting your own business

Relationship Alert: Poll #89

How did you know you were with the wrong lover?

"After two hours of lovemaking, I still felt as if I'd spent a quiet evening by myself."

> – Tod, court stenographer

"When I appeared before her in nothing but silk briefs, she asked, 'Why did you stop working out?'"

> – Paul, former Chippendale dancer

"After terrific sex, her first words when she woke up were always 'Are you still here?'"

> – Philo, usher

"I finally saw his paycheck."

> – Marlene, banker

Fitness Tip
Increase upper body strength by constantly pushing your aroused lover away:
- When you can't invite him in (the place is a mess).
- When you think you have something catching (cramps).
- Until you've finished an hour on your exercise bike.
- If you have to finish your sales report.
- If you're desperate to finish your novel-in-progress.
- When she won't take maybe for an answer.
- Until you at least get in the door.
- When her water's about to break.

Love Poll #9
Of 125 race car drivers, 14% thought safe sex means a bed with a roll bar.

Sweet Nothings: Part II
The eight most often uttered during sex:
1. "We're sliding off the bed."
2. "My feet are getting cold."
3. "Does it really get better than this?"
4. "Will it truly clear my complexion?"
5. "Could you possibly get off my leg?"
6. "Want to cut your property taxes?"
7. "I *know* this is helping my forehand."
8. "We have lift-off."

Great Moments in Lovemaking
"When I realized that my lover could be a wonderful source of sexual inspiration."
     – Julietta, photography
"When I realized that my lover could be an even better source of body heat."
     – same Julietta

At a Loss?
Eight ways to fill an awkward post-sex silence.
1. "Could you hand me my Pez dispenser?"
2. "Penny for your thought."

3. "Love your curtains."
4. "Sorry I took so long."
5. "Did I pass my driving test?"
6. "I'm speechless."
7. "Were you paying attention?"
8. "Shall we see to our guests?"

It Must Be Love
When were you certain that you and your lover were an item?
"She didn't get that 'Already he wants commitment' look on her face when I asked if we could make plans to go to Paris."
          – Charles, mail courier
"She introduced me to her parents, her A-list friends and, best of all, her doorman."
          – Sigmund, jeweler

From Our Lover's Glossary
"Check please." The only appropriate response when, in the middle of a candlelit dinner in a posh restaurant, your ravishing date suddenly realizes she's fiercely attracted to you, looks into your eyes, puts down her fork, begins to caress you under the table and utters, in a hoarse whisper, "Let's get a doggy bag."*
*"Let's blow this fire trap," is the alternate utterance.
Note: 98% of all men in this position fail to carefully add up the dinner check.

The Dieter's Guide to Weight Loss During Sex
Undressing a woman.

Activity	Calories Burned
Four difficult garments to remove by her aroused partner:	
Skin-tight jeans	68
Over cowboy boots	188
Turtleneck pullover	30
If she refuses to raise her arms	95
Power bra (latches in front)	86
If catch tamper-proof	150

When Is Lovemaking Over? Part II

Unofficially	Officially
Both lovers must keep coming up for air.	One lover hasn't breathed audibly since foreplay.
Only one thing left to try.	Nothing left to try.
Minor shift in mental focus (from lovemaking to mortgage payment).	Major shift in mental focus (from lovemaking to dinner).
Out of steam.	Out of whipped cream.
One partner sleeping.	One partner dozing.
Cheering section gone.	Partner gone.

The Enlightened Lover

Lovers who are at their proper body weight have an easier time achieving an out-of-body orgasms* than those who are 15 or more pounds overweight.

*Criteria: (1) Must rise at least 10 feet into the air (2) must not take partner along.

Shameful Moments in Sex

"After three hours we had a severe munchies attack and ate an entire smoked whitefish platter we'd prepared for guests. We're so ashamed."

        – Ursula and Horace, caterers

"We did it for so long the prime rate dropped, twice."

        – Rowena and Roberto, brokers

The Morning After the Night Before

You know it's been good when your new partner:

• Invited you to stay for breakfast.
• Cancels her lunch date.
• Doesn't banish you to the other room so she can check her messages.
• Doesn't care that you're the wrong sign.
• Asks if you have plans for Thanksgiving.
• And New Year's Eve.
• Frowns when you start to get dressed.

Scaring You Off: First-Date Advice
Be extra cautious if he or she:
- When you arrive, is playing a Bee Gees album.
- Asks, during cocktails, "How much do you make?"
- Confesses to being needy, lonely and a shopping fanatic.
- Reads, over dinner, an inspirational passage from *The Prophet*
- Talks only about past relationships.
- While slow-dancing, takes out a cellular phone and calls his broker or her psychic friend.
- Asks your sign.
- Doesn't laugh when you reply "Neon."

Tip for the Sensitive Male
When it comes to sex, nice guys finish last.

The Morning After
Was sex really as great as you thought it was? An informal checklist.
- Ravenous? ___
- But don't care that partner took the last cookie? ___
- Pictures on wall crooked? ___
- Partner able to walk upright unassisted? ___
- How about yourself? ___
- Can't recall title of the movie you rented? ___
- Can you find your car keys? ___

Tip for Marathon Lovers
Be responsible: If you plan to make love for five or more hours, avoid worry by hiring someone to take care of your pets, water the houseplants and take phone messages.

Fond Adieus
A pre-departure checklist.
He
___ Tells her how great it was.
___ Asks when he'll see her again.
___ Leaves a billet-doux in her purse.
___ Kisses her goodbye.
___ Says, "I can't wait till tonight."

She

___ Agrees.

___ Gives him a confirmed date.

___ Promises to fax him one.

___ Wipes the lipstick from his cheek.

___ Says, "Okay," and pulls him back inside.

Magic Moments

My best friend became my lover when:

• "One night we got really mellow and I tasted (a) the nape of her neck and (b) her roast loin of pork with sausage stuffing. I don't know what aroused me more."

• "The night I helped him with his master's thesis. It's difficult to remain just friends while reading Shakespeare's sonnets aloud in a hot tub."

• "She asked if she could borrow my Dirt Devil to vacuum the ashes of a dead relationship. I decided to comfort her."

• "My wife left me for his wife. (It worked out nicely all around.)"

The Enlightened Lover

Assumption	Myth	Fact
A great body always means great sex	X	
A fantastic climax can unclog mascara from eyelashes		X
Sex-related guilt is caused by:		
Experiencing too much pleasure	X	
Calling in sick to experience that pleasure		X
You know you're with an insatiable partner if you begin to:		
Mildew	X	
Ferment		X

Love Signs

Horoscope For A Steamy Sagittarius

• *Ruling passion:* lack of willpower

• *Ruling body lotion:* corn oil

• *Chief sexual asset:* ferociously high cheekbones

• *Governing erogenous zone:* all of them

• *Aphrodisiac of choice:* the chef's special

• *Ruling sexual activity*: sit-ups while wearing nothing but a tennis bracelet
• *Ideal time for sex*: twilight

Pillow Talk

Debriefing. The post-orgasmic interrogation of one's lover upon his or her return to Earth to assess, for scholarly purposes, the quality of the lovemaking. The seven most usual questions are:
1. Where am I?
2. Was it good for you?
3. Why not?
4. Could you possibly reach the Tic Tacs?
5. Who was that on the phone?
6. Will you help me look for my contact lenses?
7. When's dinner going to be ready?

Love Signs

Horoscope for a Smoldering Sagittarius.
• *Ruling passion*: Achieving total fitness, with a partner
• *Ruling sexual turnoff*: Meaningful conversation during sex
• *Chief sexual asset*: a dynamite retirement plan
• *Governing erogenous zone*: any theme park
• *Aphrodisiac*: either Wheatina with raisins or world peace
• *Ruling sexual activity*: a free introductory offer
• *Idea time for sex*: whenever your ex has the kids

Warning for New Lovers

Just met and you're crazy about each other? The dangers of too much sex:
1. Indifference to important social issues.
2. Indifference to job security (personal calls on company time).
3. A surge in your consumer spending (particularly on Champagne and flowers).
4. Singing on bank lines (and your face getting red when the teller chirps. "Somebody's happy.").
5. That telltale "inner glow" that could be mistaken for too many visits to a tanning salon.
6. Neglecting friends (they'll understand).

Love Signs: Steamy Sagittarius

Opposite love sign: Any juicy Gemini, especially one whose aphrodisiac specialty is a tuna melt.

Outstanding sexual quality: You know the difference between an unwelcome sexual advance and a quite welcome sexual advance.

Most attractive physical feature: Come-hither eyebrows.

Ruling sexual turnoff: Whistles from construction workers who can't carry a tune.

Ruling sexual turn-on: A partner who respects your honor, but knows when to make the first move (10:27 p.m.).

Ideal place for sex: Your zipper...oops...zip code.

Love Signs: Regular Sagittarius

Most attractive feature: Always ready to make love, even if it means getting back with your ex (just for the night).

Turn-on: Getting your partner away from the TV and back into the bedroom just by snapping your fingers.

Turn-offs: Bad-hair days and a partner who doesn't demand a rain check when you can't perform.

Ideal romantic adventure: Doing it in the first-class section of a speeding airplane, preferably the company jet.

Favorite sexual fantasy: Visiting Vienna and, for the healthy vibes, doing it on Freud's couch.

"During lovemaking, most lovers want tenderness, intimacy and honesty. A snack also comes in handy."
— Omar Stravinsky

When the Unthinkable Happens

The Problem	What to Do
Your realize, after 1 hour of fine lovemaking, that you're out of positions.	Start all over again.
You realize, after 2 hours of great lovemaking, your partner's turning into an animal.	It may be feeding time.
You realize, after 3 hours of incredible lovemaking, you're developing a crush on your partner.	Change positions.

The Language of Flowers: Part IX

To the lover who

Asks, as he's about to get into the shower with you, "Are you decent?"

Send:

Nothing. He is beyond help.

Inside a Lover's Fortune Cookie: Part III

"A pleasant surprise is in store for you, especially if you happen to be in bed with your dinner companion."

"You will be enormously successful in business, but tonight, it's time to make love."

"You display the wonderful traits of charm, courtesy, kindness and the ability to last for nearly two hours without a rest stop."

"Now is the time to try something different...but make sure you don't throw your back out."

Service for Inquiring Lovers

Call our toll-free Lover's Hotline (1-400 SATISFY) if you want to know:

• Which is better for your heart—sex in the morning or canasta.
• Eight magical things to do on your honeymoon night other than write thank-you notes (have your credit card ready).
• What to do when your partner overheats.
• What it means when your lover grins while asleep.
• How to fight temptation.

- How to tell if your partner faked it.
- Where the boys are (you'll need a touch-tone phone).

Breaking Up Is Easy to Do: Part I
When did you know it wasn't going to work out?
- "When she claimed she got yeast infections from eating too much rye bread."
- "He never spent weekends or holidays with me and always called me from a phone booth. It made me suspicious."
- "When, after the third time we made love, we drove to a day-care center and he said, 'If you still want to be the mother of my children, there they are.'"

Pillow Talk
The headache (faked). Like the "backache," a "headache" is considered a polite excuse for declining an invitation to have sex-especially if the person who does the inviting asks, "Can I bring a friend?" Under no circumstances may the person rejected ask for a doctor's note.

The Morning After a Perfect Night: Part II
"Eyes-only" postcards to make your lover blush.

What to Write	Probable Shade of Lover's Face
"Help, I'm still wobbly."	Magenta
"Can't wait to see you again."	Pink
"Even your snoring turned me on."	Roseate
"Last night we made history."	Plaid
"I'm sending this because I'm speechless."	Vermilion

The Dieter's Guide to Weight Loss During Sex

Activity	Calories Burned
Responding to a lover's request:	
To change positions	67
Without stopping	92
On bunk beds	312
One partner not very flexible	108
One partner in other room	200

Reminder

Today, give thanks for a lover who, with a bit of tender loving care, proper diet (no more than three helpings of stuffing), gentle instruction and lots of patience . . . may flower.

Sexual Turnoffs

A report from extra-sensitive lovers.
- "Perfumed faxes-I'm allergic."
- "Men who run into the bathroom during foreplay to check their hair."
- "Hearing the couple next to us. We live in a trailer park."
- "A platonic sex partner."
- "A partner who obeys me when I say, 'I can't take any more.'"
- "After-sex communication. I'm not good at receiving compliments."
- "Clumsy partners, they rub me the wrong way."

The Enlightened Lover

You know your sexual technique needs improving when, after sex, your partner says:
- "Were you upset about something?"
- "Let's rent a porno film."
- "It must have been the lighting."
- "We should do this again, I'll let you know with whom."
- "Perhaps we should just be friends."
- "Have you ever read *The Joy of Sex*?"
- "Hey, I'm still awake."

Arousal Problems

Six things likely to inhibit sexual desire:
1. Budget hot dogs
2. Wing tips
3. Strip searches in:
    - Mexico
    - Istanbul
4. Eggnog
5. Ugly wallpaper
6. Late-night collect calls from:
    - Your ex
    - 911

Survival Training for Lovers

The art of fantasy.

To survive:	Think about:
An excruciatingly boring business meeting	Making love in a secluded romantic area (like the top of the conference table)
A 3-hour layover in Atlanta	Being in bed with your lover
A 3-hour layover at O'Hare	Being anywhere with your lover
A commute on a packed train	Attending an orgy
Having to work overtime	Redoing your resume

Lover's Etiquette

Never stop in the middle of lovemaking unless:

- Your turkey needs basting (the one in the oven).
- Either partner experiences a leg cramp (side-stitch also acceptable).
- Someone else has to use the bathroom (cocktail party only).
- The boat tips over.
- A police officer shines a flashlight into your vehicle.
- One partner falls asleep.
- Neighbors start grazing outside your window.
- The timer goes off.

Sound Body Reminder

Sex:

- Works the major muscle groups.
- Is pretty good for the minor muscle groups, too.
- Is easy on your back.
- Is an affordable way to meet your fitness goals.
- Protects against ultraviolet rays (when your partner's on top of you).
- Best of all, can help you overcome smoking (it's nearly impossible to puff while panting).

Why Did You take a Younger Lover? Poll #25

"So we could talk about the same thing that I talk about with an older lover: myself."

– Ralph, 57, midlife crisis counselor

"He still lives at home and his mother bakes us great lemon pies."
 – Sheila, 49, chemist
"During lovemaking, my older lover kept losing his erection and then he'd fall asleep before I could find it."
 – Buffy, 26, flight attendant
"She has a curfew. If I bring her back early, I can go home and watch Letterman."
 – Sheldon, dentist

Early Sex Education
How inexperienced lovers learn about sex.
Rating scale:* Good **Better ***Best ?Questionable
• By observing:
 The birds and the bees. ?
 The neighbors.**
• By watching (afternoon soap operas).**
• By reading:
 Sex manuals. ?
 Tabloids.***
 Parents' old love letters.**

The Enlightened Lover
During arousal, 89% of all lovers lose their place in the book they're reading.

A Guide for Turkey Lovers

To the lover who's:	Give:
Noisy	A drumstick
Sensitive	The breast
Always changing positions	The wing
Too thin	Lots of stuffing
Terrific in bed	An extra helping
Pure	White meat
Conservative	Dark meat
A turkey	The wishbone

From Our Lover's Glossary

Surprise sex. Any sexual episode that occurs when one least expects it. For sex to be considered a true surprise (a) it must be sudden and (b) the surprise must not have had the slightest inkling of what was about to happen (i.e., caught with his or her pants down).

What Do Professional Lovers Say?

Just moments before kissing his lover's lips:
"Say, 'ahh.'"
> – Clark, gynecologist

Just moments before orgasm:
"Going, going, gone."
> – Monroe, auctioneer

Just moments after orgasms:
"I'm really wrecked."
> – Jack, train conductor

Did You Capture Your Partner's Heart?

It just may be love if he or she:
• Happily accepts collect calls from you.
• Knits you a sweater (that doesn't look like it was made by your mother).
• Calls at least twice daily, "just to hear your voice."
• Declines a free ticket to a sporting event, just to be with you.
• Gets gooseflesh when you hold hands.
• Calls you by a pet name (but, to avoid embarrassment, never in public).
• Gives you house keys.

Earlier Sex Education

How novice lovers learn about sex.
Rating Scale: *Good **Better ***Best ?Questionable
• Hands-on experience:
   Broadminded nanny.*
   Self-taught.**
• High school:
   Sex-education classes.*
   Dances.**

Dances (no chaperone).***
• Hands-off experience
  Listening to parents on the intercom.**

Warning!
New findings indicate there may be some hearing loss in lovers who, during sex, stay too close to a partner who yells.

What I Did Right After Great Sex
"Floated to earth without a parachute."
> – Penny, tango instructor

"Rolled over and slept—real late."
> – Olga, Scorpio

"Kept trying again till I realized my partner had gone."
> – Bruce, coach

"Righted the lamp."
> – Larry, editor

Great Moment in Sex
"Two hours on a king-size bed with my lover doing close-order drill."
> – Hector, USMC, retired

The Well-Endowed Lover
Four things a sophisticated lover should have:
1. A steamer to refresh clothing removed in haste and left in a pile on the floor all night.
2. A dictionary to look up those big words your partner uses during extra-torrid moments of arousal. (Like "Ooooof.")
3. A bottle of chilled Champagne, ideal for washing down annoying hair caught in the back of your throat (it's the friction of the bubbles, or something like that.)
4. A teeny wooden bridge-for staying dry while crossing the wet spot.

How Much Sex Is Enough?
According to a random survey:
"Either four times a week, or ten times a year, whichever meets the national quota."

"Until the statute of limitations runs out."
"Until she asks...no...wait...orders me to stop."
"When we being to ferment."
"I don't know, I never get enough."

Hints You May Be With the Wrong Partner: Part II
• He goes to work in a ski mask.
• She believes her stuffed animals have a soul.
• Her favorite cookbook is the local "Dining Out" guide.
• Nothing takes priority over watching *Star Trek*.
• Whenever you try to introduce a new position into your sex life-he already knows it.
• That "nails-across-the-blackboard" feeling when she talks baby talk to her toy terrier is getting worse.
• Although you've been sleeping with each other for eight months, he still refers to your lovemaking as "casual sex."

Food and Sex: Part III
The finicky eater.
Dining Habits
Chews each bite 10 times, even if it's soup. Eats corn on the cob kernel by kernel. Gently refolds napkin after each delicate wipe.
Type of Partner
Very slow, but very thorough. After two hours, many partners feel as if they've been curried. Before lovemaking puts a place card on each pillow, then spends hours arranging lover just so. Tries not to muss hair during orgasm; usually succeeds.

The Satisfied Lover
Eyes are the windows of the soul, especially after lovemaking.

If quality of climax was:	Lover's eyes will display:
Good	Just the whites
Better	Dilated pupils
Excellent	Double vision
The best	Your reflection
Off the charts	Appropriate phase of the moon*

*Or dollar signs.

For a Happy Sex Life

When in bed with your lover, never argue over:
- Money
- Politics
- Religion
- Who should check on
    The baby
    The strange noise downstairs
- Sex
- Whose car gets better gas mileage

The Straight-A Lover: Part II

Extra-high marks to a partner who, besides extraordinary sexual sensitivity, provides:

- Courtesy transportation. Not only takes you shopping but, when you're overcome by passion, carries you from the living room to the bedroom, often by the scenic route.
- While you're asleep, hugs, to give you warmth without weight.
- Bedside assistance. Brings you coffee, a seeded roll and juice (or a pretzel, ice cream and a pickle if you're pregnant) when you feel like brunching in bed.
- Emergency towing service. Helps you out of bed on frosty mornings when you're afraid to emerge from under the covers.

It's the Thought That Counts

First things thought after less-than-great sex by:

A Partner	Thought
Who's an optimist	"Maybe it'll be better next time."
Who's giving	"This person needs my help."
Who doesn't give up	"Wake up, we're going to try again."
With low self-esteem	"I don't excite her."
With high self-esteem	"He's had too many tacos."
Who's out of there	"It won't be the same without you."

Things to Be Grateful For
She doesn't love you only:
- For your Ford pickup.
- Because you smell so yummy after a shower.
- When you bring home a gift certificate to her favorite store.
- Because you're nice to her parents.
- For your ample stock portfolio.
- He doesn't love you only:
- For your money.
- Because you sniff him all over so thoroughly.
- When you say, "That's much too generous."
- Because your parents are so rich.
- For your ample hips.

The Dieter's Guide to Weight Loss After Sex
Hinting that sex is over (for now).

Activity	Calories Burned
Turning on the light	3
Getting dressed	19
Straightening up	37
Making the bed	48
With your lover still in it	175

Stolen Sexual Moments

Easy	Takes Nerve
In front of your fireplace	In front of your house
In a dark movie theater	Front seats at the Astrodome
The bathroom	The bathroom at a cocktail party
Your backyard, at midnight	Your backyard, during a barbecue
The bedroom	The bedroom of a model home*
When the kids are at school	When they're not

*Bonus points if you hear footsteps.

What Do the Professionals Do?

The problem

"Whew, I'm worn out. After 10 years of marriage, she still wants to make love at least six times a week plus twice on Saturday if she finishes food shopping early. I find three time weekly quite sufficient. What's a man to do?"

The solution

1. Hire a Guest Lover. In many areas, such service is available either through the Yellow Pages (dial 1-800-HELP-HER) or an unselfish neighbor.

2. Ask your in-laws to speak to her.

What Do Women Really Want?

The results of our poll of 1,000 women:

• 68% like it when a man undresses them before sex (but 41% hated it if he only uses his eyes).

• 89% hate it when a man dresses them after sex.

• 55% are willing to initiate sexual activity.

• 14% weren't sure of what to do if he responded. (Although 95% said he caught on very quickly.)

Missing You

Ways to preserve the memory of an absent lover.

"I keep a lock of his chest hair in my glove compartment."
            – Elizabeth, taxi driver

"After she leaves, I clasp a swatch of her still-damp washcloth next to my heart."
            – Tom, poet

"Savor the aroma emanating from her pillowcase."
            – Roger, wine merchant

"I wear his T-shirt till he returns from his business trip."
            – Ethel, carpenter

"I wear her nightgown till she returns from the kitchen."
            – Horace, parson

"Date his twin brother."
            – Sheila, nurse

Inexperienced Lovers' Poll #88

Percentage of novice lovers who thought safe sex meant:

Drawing the blinds	8%
Not telling him your first name	5%
Stopping when you were finished	14%
Keeping condoms in a safe	3%
Using a bundling board	2%
Making sure your partner was over 21	12%
Not overdoing it	2%
Doing it only with your spouse	54%

Q. Is it ethical to continue to engage in foreplay with someone while they're talking to your rival on the phone?
A. Yes, if:

• It doesn't cause you to stammer.
• There's nothing handy for your to read.
• It saves time.
• It's a speaker phone.
• The call isn't collect.

Who Must Have Sex?

Any U.S. citizen between the ages of 21 and 85 who is:

• On a honeymoon
• Qualified and able
• Involved with someone who feels that a night without sex is much like a day without sex (a hardship case)
• Not a member of any religious denomination that forbids sex
• A registered voter
• In his or her prime
• Still waiting to "peak"
• Not a conscientious objector

What Type of Lover are You?

Type A
Does it quickly, efficiently
Obsessed with on-time performance
Must try at least six positions
Fidgets
Thinks about partner's old lovers and worries, "Am I the best?"

Type B
Takes his or her time
Not a problem if orgasm takes longer than expected
Knows his or her limits
Writhes
Thinks positive

What Do Men Really Want?

The results of our poll of 1,000 men.
Percentage who preferred the following method of birth control:
• Condom-11%
• Diaphragm-25%
• Caution (back-to-back position)-3.1%
• Rhythm-0% (nobody knew what it was)
• Pill-86%
• Stress-9%

It Must Be Love

When were you certain that you and your lover were an item?
"He stopped asking to be reimbursed for the long-distance calls I made from his phone."
　　　　– Winifred, unemployed
"He invited me to call him by his first name."
　　　　– Catherine, divorce attorney
"She gave me my own closet space."
　　　　– Dan, Catherine's client

Making Up for Lost Time

Haven't seen each other for a while? Can't wait to get your hands on each other? Time-saving tips from our experts.
• Place a "No Appointment Necessary" sign at the foot of your bed.
• Begin foreplay on the elevator. Tell fellow passengers he's phobic about heights.
• Don't wait until you're in the bedroom. Leave a trail of underwear on the lawn.

• Instead of folding each other's clothes neatly, rip them off. It adds drama and you can always iron them in the morning.
• Kiss your lover hello on only two cheeks.

MONTHLY QUALITY OF LIFE® CHECKUP

•Favorite "special" position:

Defensive tackle (man cowering on bed, woman yelling, "Charge!")___

Nautical (Man on bottom, woman giving him 10 lashes)___(ease discomfort with chicken fat)

Both standing up___(If partner is too tall, it is permissible for male partner to stand on a hassock)

Republican (man on top, woman under him)___

Democrat (Woman on top, man under indictment)___

•Favorite marital aid:

Kama Sutra___

Heating pad___

The neighbors___

Baby oil___

Super vibrator (takes 15 AA batteries)___

Handcuffs___

Catalytic converter___

Potato masher (for that extra-stubborn cellulite)___

•Favorite after-sex activity:

Lie in each other's arms, gasping for breath___

Turn up volume on television___

Sleep___

Golf___

All of the above___

Signed_____

Witnessed_____

DECEMBER

•Erotic goals for the Month:
1. Make low budget film
2. Hope partner doesn't see camera hidden in headboard

Because holiday activity takes up so much time, wise couples have as much sex as possible during the first week of December, which leaves the rest of the month free for Christmas shopping and trimming the tree. If, for example, your sexual frequency rate conforms to The Official United States National Average (once every night, plus once in the morning if partner brushed his teeth*) simply have sex 60 times by December 7th and you're covered for the rest of the month! Of course the perfect lover deserves the perfect Christmas gift—some suggestions from Taffy, our gift counselor:

Gift	Application
Little mop	To remove those stubborn hairs that get caught in back of throat during sex.
Lantern	Provides touch of intimacy—enables lover to find way to bathroom in the middle of the night without stepping in kitty litter.
Beano	Allows magical stillness of post-coital bliss to endure without embarrassing seafoodgumbo related flatulence.
Tape measure	To see if Viagra is really working.

* Report by the Census Bureau to the Senate Sub-Committee on Pleasure (names of politicans were changed to protect privacy)

Official aphrodisiacs of the Month:
1. Eggnog
2. Fruitcake
3. Tupperware

Pillow Talk

Climax. This most sumptuous of orgasms is to be used only to celebrate special occasions (career change, passing driver's test, getting into the college of one's choice, etc.). It may occur by itself or be prompted by a series of small orgasms. At the moment of true climax, the person will "leave" his or her body and visit either several of the outlying planets, or Akron, Ohio.

Pillow Talk

Christmas bonus. A token of appreciation, usually of an erotic nature, given to one's lover for services rendered above and beyond the call of duty. Presentation of such bonus may or may not involve:
• A book of poetry
• Reading glasses
• A bed (queen-size minimum)
• Chocolate (for energy)
• Caviar (for protein)
• Arousal (for fun)
• Exhaustion (from sex)

Love Poll #56

The eight most popular during-sex utterances.*
1. "Please don't stop."
2. "Can you reach the phone?"
3. "Is it good for you?"
4. "Ohhhhhhhhhhhhhhhhhhhh."
5. "Am I making too much noise?"
6. "Let's split a lottery ticket."
7. "Where'd you learn that?"
8. "Can I use you as a reference?"
*Source: Electronic eavesdropping device surveilling a suspicious truck stop in Wichita, Kansas.

Gem of the Month

A turquoise pendant to the lover who:
• Is helpful—shows you the location of special erogenous zones with an anatomically correct hand puppet.
• Never complains—even when your heavy breathing wilts his favorite plant.

• Is considerate—always includes you during in-bed workouts.
• Is wise—knows exactly what to do should you succumb to sexual exhaustion (Baby Ruths and a cup of herbal tea).
• Respects your privacy—never asks where you've been when you return from an out-of-body climax.

From Our Lover's Glossary

"Thanks, I needed that." A phrase uttered after climax by a person who hasn't had sex for at least five months. Such person often wishes to express his or her joy and gratitude by getting up and (a) serving breakfast (or dinner, as the case may be) in bed or (b) dancing around the room, but only has enough energy to stretch luxuriously, grin and instantly fall asleep.

FYI—Arousal

Various reasons why people get aroused, according to a recent study by the Surgeon General.
• An attractive partner with a serious sexual technique.
• Fantasizing about an attractive partner with a serious sexual technique.
• Recalling the next day what happened last night with that partner with a serious sexual technique.
• Breaking 70 on a new golf course.
• A promotion with a salary increase.
• Legitimate tax shelters.
• Regularity.

Last-Minute Checklist for Better Sex

Before going to bed, make sure you:
___ Lower the shades.
___ Load the camera.
___ Take off your shoes (socks optional).
___ Hang garments that easily wrinkle.
___ Open the window (sex thrives on fresh air).
___ Take off your watch.
___ Remove curlers.
___ Turn down the furnace.
___ Turn up your furnace.

Don't Throw Them Away

Recycle an old, worn-out lover to help you:
• Find a new one.
• Move furniture.
• Network.
• Reminisce.

First Aid for the Uncommon Cold

"The moaning caused by one hour of high-impact sex can do more to clear the nasal passages than 98% of the over-the-counter cold remedies now available."
– Giselle M., M.D.

Sex Speak: Part II

What Your Lover Says:	What Your Lover Means:
"Thanks for having me."	Thanks for having me.
"That felt so good."	And so did the sex.
"Gee, I can hear the ocean."	Easy on the water bed.
"I'm glad we're at your place, it's so cozy."	Why should I use my electricity?
"You're so wonderful, I wish I could give you the moon."	It's just that I can't get my jeans down.

What I Got Just Moments After Great Sex

"My tax refund, it was the mailman's way of saying, 'Thanks.'"
– Laverne, dental hygienist
"Enlightenment, and my breath back."
– Vananda "Mel" Vishnu, free-lance swami
"An important phone call, dammit."
– Barbra, producer
"A role!"
– Arnold, actor
"Rave reviews."
– Penelope, courtesan

"Are You Coming to Bed, Dear?"

Chances of making love tonight:

If your spouse replies	Chances
"In a minute, my love."	37%
"Only if you want to fool around."	85%
"Zzzzzzzzzzzzzzz."	$1/2$%
"As soon as my mud pack dries."	9%
"Shall I open some champagne?"	67%
"Yes, just as soon as I take a nap."	4%

Are You Having Too Little Sex?

Some possible causes:
- Jury duty
- Inconsiderate lover (doesn't make house calls)
- Lazy lover (thinks sex is a spectator sport)
- Bargain bed (no legroom)
- Stress (Christmas shopping)
- More stress (Christmas shopping for the lover who has everything)
- Psychosis (Christmas shopping for the lover who has nothing)

When the Unthinkable Happens

The Problem

A time-release climax (experienced many hours after sex often not till the next night) occurs while you're attending a Chopin recital.

What to Do

1. Wait it out.
2. Stop feeling sorry for yourself.
3. Enjoy it.
4. Share it with the person on your left.

The Dieter's Guide to Weight Loss During Sex
The art of restraint while making love.

Activity	Calories Burned
Suppressing the urge to:	
Yawn	11
If your lover yawns first	60
Criticize	41
Check your watch	
If sex is good	55
Not so good	1

The Hesitant Lover
It's okay—some acceptable excuses for not having sex.

Excuse:	Use:
Headache	When you have one or can tell that one is on the way
Not in the mood	When you discover water in the basement of your new home
Already did it this month	When you're with an absent-minded partner
Let's rent a movie instead	If you prefer to be a spectator
It'll ruin my sunscreen	At the beach
I can feel contractions	In your ninth month

Advice for Cautious Lovers
"If it sounds too good to be true, it probably is," does not apply to the moan emitted by a lover in the final stages of a Level 15 climax.*

*Person having the climax actually experiences a change of inseam.

Breaking Up Is Easy to Do: Part II
When did you know it wasn't going to work out?
- "He was kind of needy. Whenever I'd go to the bathroom, he'd ask me to leave the door ajar so he could hold my hand."
- "He tried to buy my love with money, lavish gifts, trips to Europe and a BMW. I just wanted him to leave the toilet seat down."
- "When she asked my twenty-four-year-old son a) what he wanted to be when he grew up and b) for a date."

The Chemistry of Love

Clinicians tell us that just the thought of making love causes the body to release enough:

- Neuropeptides to discourage the purchase of stock options
- Pheromones to pollinate a tulip field
- White blood cells to neutralize an approaching Great Dane
- Water to significantly lessen a feeling of bloat
- Carbon dioxide to revive a dying bonsai tree
- Endorphins to stimulate new hair growth

The Art of Romance

Observe a moment of awed silence if the following should occur during sex.

- You have your fifth climax of the night.
- You and your lover finally connect.
- You finally master the art of changing position without:
    - a. Falling off the bed
    - b. Pulling a muscle
- You begin to grow hoarse.
- You think you hear the kids.
- The kids think they hear you.

The Art of Romance

What to give the lover who has everything:

1. More of the same.
2. A place to put it.

The Tired Lover

Partner wants to have sex. Again. We sympathize. Here are five tactful excuses for declining sex:

1. "I'm taking a vacation night."
2. "Other commitments (must save a rain forest)."
3. "Isn't our friendship enough?"
4. "On my coffee break."
5. "I've no time." (Use only during your busy season.)

Note: If all else fails, it is permissible to throw yourself on the mercy of your partner, so long as he or she isn't lying down.

Looking for Someone New? Part II

Pickup Lines That	Might Work	Might Not
At a Karaoke contest:		
"You mime like an angel."	X	
"May I pay for your acting lessons?"	X	
In a bookstore:		
"Are you into self-help?"	X	
"Self-abuse?"		X
At the beach:		
"I see you like an ocean view."	X	
"Would you like to practice the sun stroke?"		X

Male Dysfunction

The leading causes:
- Child support payments.
- Partner's dowry underfunded.
- Worried she'll be too good in bed.
- Partner asking "Do you like children?"
- Pressure to perform (partner also his boss).
- Fear of success.
- Feminist plot.

Only 20 Shopping Days till Christmas

A shopping list for lovers who have everything.

If Lover Is Romantic	If Lover Is Not So Romantic
Almond-flavored massage oil	Olive oil (3rd pressing)
Whipped cream	Vanishing cream
Ice-cream maker	Yogurt maker
Ostrich feather duster (for tickling)	Whisk broom

Review Questions

Questions

1. Health: Name at least two afflictions caused by too much sex.
2. Etiquette: After how many sexual encounters is one obliged to change the sheets?
3. Statistics: What is the average rate of intercourse for most American couples?

Answers
1. a. Stiff neck   b. Unemployment
2. In winter: 15 In summer: 3
3. 25 mph unless otherwise posted.

Sexual Demerits: Part V

Offense	Number of Demerits
Didn't call when he said he would	7
Frustratingly mysterious about past	5
Leaves a ring in the bathtub	6
Is self-centered (always tries to make small talk during your climaxes)	10
Undependable (sometimes has only one climax; other times, who knows?)	7
Too good in bed:	
Always makes you late for work	$1/4$
Gives you jet lag	$1/2$

Sex Poll #99

How do you know when you're overdoing it? (Asked of several cooperative lovers during their third hour of sex.)
"I begin to panic and worry that this night will never end."
        – Andrew, student with an 8 A.M. class
"I don't. This is my third partner since 11:20 P.M."
        – Abigail, test pilot
"I began to experience double vision and asked my partner, 'Was it good for you two?'"
        – Nicole, oboist

Six Things to Be Joyful About After Sex

1. All the hidden messages were under the blanket.
2. You can still make the 9 o'clock movie.
3. The religious experience (you can feel those endorphins flow).
4. You have a hickey (and you'll be able to play Show-and-Tell in the office tomorrow).
5. He doesn't snore.
6. You're not the person you used to be.

Found a New Lover?

Ways to purge yourself of the Ghost of Lovers Past.

1. Buy new underwear.
2. Vacuum under the bed to remove:
    a) Incriminating items (such as a pair of preowned nylons).
    b) Memories.
    c) An old lover.
3. Put away tell-tale photos (particularly the one of you and a past flame in the bathtub wearing just snorkle masks).
4. Hire a curse remover (in case you and your past lover parted on less than amicable terms).
5. Buy a new mattress (your old one can talk).

Advice to Men: The Unresponsive Woman

Most common causes:

Not Serious	Serious
Too much to drink	Too little to drink
Body's off-line (an affliction of computer operators)	Herbal tea bloat
Can't give herself permission	Can't give
You're doing it wrong (she can teach you)	You're still doing it wrong (and she's taught you)
Can't concentrate: distracted by dripping faucet	Can't concentrate: distracted by nails (still wet)

Things Often Said After High-Voltage Sex

During the year: "You've worn me out."
During this month: "You've just made my Christmas list."

Words to the Wise Lover

During sex, never use a yardstick to measure a lover's performance.

The Enlightened Lover

When making love with the lights on, it's easier to:
• Find those hard-to-get-at places.
• Read your lover's lips.
• Make notes.
• Tell when your lover's blushing.

- Say, "Hi!" to well-wishers.
- Tell when it's over.
- Be found by the neighborhood patrol.

Apologies for Last Night

If lovemaking was less than perfect, check where appropriate and send to lover.

----------detach here----------

___Turned off by your new "I'm ready for lovemaking" signal (wringing your hands and saying, "It's been three weeks").

___Mind was on other things (have a library book overdue).

___You kept yelling, "My stallion" (the name's Horace).

___Mixed signals (stop making me guess which way you want me to turn).

___In-law trouble (they were standing there).

___Still recovering from operation (sexual bypass).

Great Ways to Have Sex

For the:	We recommend:
Luxury	The rear seat of a moving limo.
Thrill	The front seat of a speeding limo.
Ambiance	Backstage at *Cats.*
Memories	Alumni day with your college sweetheart.
Excitement	Watching wrestling with the sound on.
Guidance	Watching MTV with the sound off.

After-Sex Etiquette

Three appropriate questions to ask someone if you went to bed with them just for their:

Body	Mind
"How did you know what I like?"	"Do you do volunteer work?"
"Is that you purring?"	"Do you speak any other languages?"
"Was it good for you?"	"Why was it good for you?"

The Dieter's Guide to Weight Loss During Sex
Trying again.

Activity	Calories Burned
Lovemaking after:	
Adequate recovery period (3 hours)	78
Inadequate recovery period (3 minutes)	450
Inadequate recovery period (but lover assists by feeding you chicken soup)	8

The Inquisitive Lover
Q. When I sleep with someone, must I close my eyes?
A. During regular sex, no. During a really wonderful climax, you'll probably have no choice.*
*At selected motels (those with hourly rates), it was found that 93% of all couples observed on closed-circuit TV shut their eyes during any climax that exceeded 4 on the Richter scale.

From Our Lover's Glossary
Sex While Under the Influence. Having glorious, completely and totally satisfying sex with someone while your senses and judgment are impaired by love. The result may be lovemaking of such intensity that:
• You forget your mantra.
• You leave fingerprints on each other.
• The neighbors begin to worry and call a constable.
• You hydroplane off the bed and find yourselves on the lawn.
• Your partner drops his sandwich.
• You decide to mention it on your resumé.

Lovers' Poll: #100
What do you do when:
He gets that look in his eye
"Instantly change into my sexiest chemise—I've got to get it while the getting's good."
"If we're out with friends I gently kick him under the table, he should know better."
"Hand him an I.O.U."
She gets that look in her eye
"Pretend I have a headache—you can't believe how many times a week she gets that look in her eye."

"Jump at my chance, she's usually on the phone."
"Hand her the Visine."

Rules of Financial Thumb

If your partner has:	Your life insurance should be:
A to-die figure.	Doubled.
A drop-dead smile.	Tripled.

The Enlightened Lover
Instead of getting up in the middle of lovemaking to let the dog out, simply hold him out the window and shake him.

After-Sex Quote of the Night
If lovemaking was:
- *Good:* "Please switch off the light on your way out."
- *Impressive:* "That's what I call room service."
- *Extraordinary:* "I'm listed."

The Next Best Thing
Six things to bed down with on a cold wintry night if your lover's not available.
1. A hot-water bottle
2. The latest bestseller
3. Chocolate-chip cookies
4. Flannel underwear
5. A cup of cocoa
6. A shoulder to cry on

Guide for Clock-Watching Lovers
During sex, you may call time out only to:
- Put more film in the camera.
- Wake a dozing lover.
- Sign for a parcel.
- Order from Domino's.
- Consult the manual.
- Leap up until the cramp in our leg disappears.
- Let the dog in.
- Lock in a low-mortgage rate.

$Fiscal Thought re Sex$

The best thing in life is free. It's the. . .
- Fresh flowers
- Satin sheets
- Deck shoes (to prevent slipping when on satin sheets)
- Champagne
- Caviar
- Kennel (so you and your partner can go off by yourselves)
- Cozy inn (the perfect getaway)

. . . that cost money.

From My Wife's Little Instruction Book

- Give people more than they expect. This applies particularly to me when selecting my Christmas present.
- Never be photographed holding an empty cocktail glass. They'll think you were too stupid to get a refill.

A Lover's List of Bests

- *Best reason to watch less television:* sex
- *Best way to banish bedroom blahs:* stop complaining about your job
- *Best basis on which to select a sex partner:*
    1. Love
    2. Trust fund
- *Best way to tell if your lover's been with another lover:* fingerprints
- *Best thing to think about in place of sex:* water in the basement

Happy Hour for Weight Watchers

In 60 Regular Minutes	In 60 Dietetic Minutes
Drink 2 white wines (+250 calories)	Get undressed (-80 calories)
Drink 2 beers (+300 calories)	Arouse lover (-150 calories)
Nibble on 20 pretzel sticks (+80 calories)	Nibble on one lover (-108 calories)
Talk to friends (-45 calories)	Moan (-70 calories)
Stir drink (-4 calories)	Stir lover (-111 calories)
Order another round (-11 calories)	Try again (-236 calories)

Tip for Eccentric Couples
Gravity-defying position for space cadets.
He: On bottom
She: Floating on air

The Enlightened Lover
If vigorous sexual activity leaves you comatose, you should:

Wait at least	Before
30 minutes	Taking your driver's test
2 hours	Running a marathon
1 day	Buying stock futures
3 hours	Purchasing new software
15 minutes	Resuming your golf game
5 minutes	Trying to walk
10 minutes	Trying to walk upright

Go for It?
Should you have sex with a friend? Score yourself.
1. Do you tingle when you're near this person? (+5)
2. Have you ever had fantasies about spending a weekend with this person at a cozy inn? (+8) On a kibbutz? (+9)
3. Do you suspect your feelings are reciprocated? (+11)
4. Have you ever gone to bed with this person? (+15)
5. What did you do in bed? Just sleep (-9) Just make love (+20)
6. After making love you went back to being just friends (-2) Just lovers (+12) Both (+20)
Scoring: 5 or less: just be friends. 10 or more: just be lovers.

When Do You Fantasize Most About Sex: Lovers' Poll #103
"While jogging. I get behind a guy with really cute buns and follow him for miles. It makes the hills bearable."
  – Penny, publicist
"At the mall. So many men, so few sales."
  – Trish, shoe salesperson
"Whenever those awful construction workers make lewd remarks about my perfect body and whistle at me."
  – Yolanda, secretary

"I know I'm not supposed to, but whenever my assistant crosses her legs I forget myself. Must get some sensitivity training."
— Brad, CEO
"While sitting on the pilot's lap."
— Greta, flight attendant

The Enlightened Lover

For better lovemaking tonight:

1. Remove shoes at least two hours before making love. This allows your feet to "breathe."

2. Undress at least one hour before making love. This allows the body to achieve room temperature and thus, bring out its full, delicious flavor.

3. Warm the bed* at least 15 minutes before making love. This allows you to get into bed with only a smile.

*Use either hot bricks or your lover.

Reminder

It's not too early to think about which lover you're going to spend New Year's Eve with. We suggest choosing a lover who can:

1. Lie in front of a crackling fire without melting.

2. Better yet, build a crackling fire.

3. Stay awake till midnight.

4. Make love before, during and after drinking champagne.

5. Look sexy in a party hat.

6. Give you that ultimate party favor.

The Holiday Spirit

What I'll do for Christmas.

"Give my lover a bear hug under the mistletoe."
— Sammy, secret service
"Give my lover a bare hug under our bed canopy."
— Pammy, fine arts major

A Few During-Sex Atrocities

1. Calling out the name of your personal trainer instead of your lover.

2. Failing to remove black over-the-calf business socks no matter how pressed for time you are.

3. Putting salt on a margarita glass.

4. Trying to get your partner in the mood with card tricks. (Unless it's the only thing that works.)

5. Forgetting to put film in the camcorder.

6. Cracking your gum.

7. Networking.

Words of Comfort

On-the-spot therapy to soothe a failed male lover's ego.

• "We'll try again, the moment I return from Europe."

• "Warmth, intimacy and great sex aren't everything, there's always dinner."

• "Perhaps I shouldn't have yelled at you."

• "We shouldn't have tried on a school night."

• "Could it be the cabin pressure?"

• "Maybe it's just asleep."

• "I think your last girlfriend was right."

• "Guess the honeymoon's over."

Seven Reasons to Take Your Lover to Dinner Tonight

1. Your divorce decree became final.

2. To celebrate this morning's lovemaking.

3. To reward her for helping you on with your clothes after this morning's lovemaking.

4. He's going to promote you.

5. It's easier than writing a "Dear John" letter.

6. She got her Christmas bonus—maybe she'll split the check.

7. He threatened to cook.

The Seven Natural Wonders of the Sexual World

1. Afterglow

2. A perfect back rub

3. Chocolate ice cream

4. Bubble baths

5. Room service

6. Cuddling

7. Elvis memorabilia

Sexual Myths #5 and 6
5. It is impossible to experience Paradise unless you go to heaven.
6. Eating sweets before sex will ruin your appetite.

Trade Secret
For bouncier, longer lasting sex, if you're with a:
Good lover
Turn your mattress once a month
Great lover
Turn your mattress once a week
Note: Don't try this while one of you is still in bed.

Amazing Sexual Fact
For some really strange reason, asking an insecure lover, after mediocre sex, to help you find a date for New Year's Eve almost never makes that person feel better.

The Fire Down Below
The Truth About Orgasm	Myth	Fact
You can always tell if:		
She's faking	X	
He's faking		X
A partner's silence is no indication of quality		X
Multiple orgasms can make:		
You slimmer		X
Your warts disappear	X	
You smile		X
They're generally experienced during sex	X	
And when you get your Christmas bonus		X

When You Just Need to Be Alone
Five ways to get a reluctant partner to leave.
1. Invite him to:
   • Meet your neighbors.
   • Help you paint the bathroom.
   • Your Dianetics meeting.
2. Reach in your refrigerator and ask if she's ever tasted jellied eels.
3. Turn on a home shopping channel—ask for her MasterCard.

4. Tell him the story of your life; spare no details.
5. Ask for a raise.

The Superior Lover
Is capable of achieving orgasm even:
• During a tax audit
• While listening to Wagner
• On a treadmill
• While fighting for the check
• With guests waiting

Pop Quiz for Lovers
Other than enthusiasm, what five elements must be present to achieve simultaneous orgasm?
1. Lust
2. Luck
3. A sense of timing
4. Teamwork
5. A partner

Sexual Rule of Thumb
Any orgasm that causes you to temporarily forget:
• The combination to your gym locker; or
• Your partner's birth sign; or
• Where you parked the car; or
• That you've got a roast in the oven; or
• Your manners
is a good one.

What I Do First When I Meet a New Lover
"Buy a whole new bed. I like to start fresh or, if I'm broke, I at least change the sheets."
        — Rebecca, mortgage consultant
"Hire a wizard to cast a spell over my mattress and remove the spirit of Lovers Past."
        — Ellery, bus washer
"Hold a bed-warming. I invite my new lover over for cocoa and gingersnaps. Afterwards, we enter the bedroom and we um. . . warm the bed."
        — Scott, maitre d'

How Did You Learn About Sex?

Candid replies from veteran lovers:
After years of on-the-job training, I finally married my boss."
> – Esther, executive assistant

"Patience. During lovemaking with my first two wives, I would just lie there and observe. Now I'm (a) a consummate lover and (b) happily married."
> – Frank, florist

"Had a last fling before I got married, then took a cram course on my honeymoon."
> – Bonnie, gunsmith

"Listened to my parents over the house intercom."
> – Ronald, veterinarian

Stupid Sex Tricks

- Changing positions without telling your partner.
- Not stopping when your hear the garage door opening.
- Trying to carry a 286-pound bride across the threshold.
- Jilting the boss's daughter.
- Returning with a newspaper in your mouth when your partner yells, "Fetch!"
- Mouth-to-mouth resuscitation with someone you've just met.
- Using a condom. . . again.
- Hoping that an inconvenient call of nature will just "go away."

Know The Sexual Self

Immediately after lovemaking, write down what was good, what worked best, what you didn't like and whether you achieved your target heart rate. Also ask yourself:
- Did I crave sweets? What kind? (White chocolate means sex was satisfying; dark chocolate also means sex was satisfying.)
- Did my mind go blank? (A definite plus.)
- Did we whisper sweet nothings to each other?
- Who whispered louder?
- How did my lover last so long?
- How did I last so long?

Amazing Facts About Sex

During lovemaking, far less energy will be expended if both partners are either:
• Just good friends; or
• Asleep

Benefits of Regular Sexual Activity

The 10 best responses from our reader survey.
1. "My psoriasis cleared up."
2. "Deeper, more restful sleep patterns."
3. "A feeling of serenity and calm, even at the mall."
4. "Much clearer, more youthful-looking skin."
5. "Lower blood pressure."
6. "Higher consciousness."
7. "Fewer migraines, especially in my head."
8. "A new Oldsmobile."
9. "Complimentary theater tickets."
10. "Tenure."

A Lover's Thought for the Day

It is entirely possible that Mother Nature gave us sex:
• As a low-cal alternative to between-meal snacks.
• As the perfect way to turn a bad day into a good night.
• Because it feels so good.
• So newlyweds wouldn't have to just ride horses on their honeymoon.
• Because it's all natural.
• As the remedy of choice for lust.
• So mortals might experience Paradise before going to heaven.
• Until She can come up with something better.

More Health Benefits of Sex

If each time you think about your lover

You Get	To Your Life Add
All misty eyed	5 hours
Aroused 5 days	5 days
Impatient for the weekend	3 days
An earache (from the wedding bells you hear)	2 hours
The urge to:	
Smile	1 hour
Mother him	1 day
All hot	3 hours
And bothered	6 hours

Secure Lovers

Are not afraid to:
• Leave the bed unmade after sex.
• Call in well and sleep late with each other.
• Arrive really late at a party because they were doing it on the exit ramp.
• Avoid starting a family because they're having too much fun with each other.
• Display their adult movie titles in a prominent place.
• Fight, then constantly re-fall in love with each other.
• Talk baby talk to each other in front of a) friends or b) their plants.
• Ask the waiter to repeat, in comprehensible English, the specials of the day.

Two Great Moments in Sex

1. "The day I discovered that I didn't need a Mercedes to fulfill my sex drive."
> – Dr. Fenwick Blinky

2. "Realizing that sleeping with someone didn't mean you had to close your eyes."
> – Julie, Spice Girl wannabe

The Wise Consumer

Researchers suggest that if you Christmas-shop for your lover directly *after* terrific sex, you will:
- Get strange looks from salesclerks.
- Make sounder purchasing decisions.
- Be less frantic.
- Be more generous.
- Tire more easily (only drawback).
- Note your hands trembling when turning catalog pages.
- Place phone orders in a huskier voice.

The Secret of Happiness

"A program of regular sexual activity can make even the most difficult lover easier to live with, especially if you see him or her only on weekends."

> – Dr. Amy Kasha, passion therapist,
> Rahway State Correctional Facility

Tip for Skeptical Lovers

Until you're better acquainted, it's permissible to use a lie detector to determine if a new partner really:
- Has a headache.
- Had a climax.
- Learned that trick from a manual.
- Really never felt that way before.
- Isn't an old one in disguise.
- Has a mirror on the ceiling only to check his bald spot.
- Is taking a phone call in the other room because he doesn't want to disturb you.
- Wants you for your money.

Are You Undersexed?

The six official criteria:
1. You don't understand what all the fuss is about.
2. You achieve sexual release through your credit cards.
3. During sex, you think about work.
4. During work, you think about work.
5. More than once the Neighborhood Watch has reported you for having insufficient sex.
6. Your partner takes no fewer than 47 cold showers a week.

Magic Numbers: Part V

25 watts: The maximum bulb to be used to illuminate sex if a) you're uncomfortable being naked in front of your partner and b) you have a picture window in the bedroom.

6: the number of cocktail franks the average partner burns off during 30 minutes of sex.

5: The number of minutes, after pressing the "Stop" button on an elevator, you can have sex with your co-passenger before the building staff grows suspicious.

The Enlightened Lover: His Recovery Time

Time required between orgasms for the average male.

Occupation	Minutes
Athlete:	
Football: Quarterback	31
Halfback	40
Baseball	52
Handball	3
Actor: Regular	64
Method	95
Lawyer: Divorce	21
Tax	105

Secrets of the Great Lovers

In bed, always be a good listener, even if:
• It's been a slow news day.
• Your lover isn't saying anything.

A Lover's Dilemma

Q. If you have two lovers, is it ethical to give both of them the same Christmas gifts?
A. Yes, but only if:
• Both lovers have similar taste.
• They don't live near each other (different zip codes).
• The gifts are exactly what they wanted.
• And (most important) the gifts were on sale.
No, if:
• They are not of the same sex.

Time Is Getting Short

Only ten more days until you give your lover that special Christmas bonus. For services wonderfully rendered throughout the year may we suggest:

• A book of poetry (try Keats) from which you can read when you're having trouble getting "in the mood."

• A box of tissues to absorb those tears of joy.

• A gourmet cookbook so, when you're hungry, your lover can prepare the perfect meal.

• A stepstool to make it easier for a weary lover to climb in or out of bed.

• A tote bag. When you fall asleep in front of the TV, it'll be easier for your lover to carry you to bed.

Public Service Announcement

Hooked on sex? Suspect addiction if:

• You need it just to function normally (without sex, for instance, you can't work the office copier).

• Missing sex makes you feel sad, empty and desperate for an apricot Danish (a classic symptom).

• Despite what the AMA says, you fervently believe a climax a day keeps the doctor away.

• Sex runs in your family (your parents had it).

• You continue to have it often despite the consequences (it's made you late for work and you think about it while snorkeling).

What Does Safe Sex Mean to You?

Our lovers explain.

"Praying, when I make an obscene call, that the person who answers doesn't have caller I. D.

— Louise, fortune teller

"Wearing a parachute when we achieve the heights of ecstasy."

— Esmeralda, financial planner

"Being certain, when we're rekindling the flame, that we're sitting in front, instead of in back, of a roaring fire."

— Jesse and Carlita, social workers

Acid Test That You're Over Your Ex

The phone rings. It's your ex begging to come back.

Presume nearly complete recovery if:

1. You're disappointed it's not someone selling:
    - Land; or
    - Magazine subscriptions; or
    - Penny stocks
2. You can't wait to get off the phone so you can resume:
    - Watering your plants; or
    - Sex with your new lover

'Tis the Season to Forgive

Forgive lover for:	Don't forgive lover for:
Leaving hair in the drain	Leaving hair in the drain that isn't his or hers
Ruining your hair during a passion attack	Answering the phone during that same attack
Requesting sex when it's not your special time	Begging
Taking forever to dress	Taking forever to undress
Letting the fire go out in the fireplace	Letting the fire go out in the other place

Really Great Climaxes We Have Known

"Blew out all the Hanukkah candles."
                    – Maggie and Mordecai
"Made the mistletoe bloom."
                    – Golda and Sean
"Actually had to put our stockbroker on hold."
                    – Alexis and Vinnie

Yuletide Tide

It is the lover who does the most work during sex who is automatically excused from strenuous holiday tasks like:
- Shopping for the person who has everything.
- Tying the Christmas tree on top of the car.
- Stringing Christmas lights.
- Wrapping gifts.
- Carrying and/or cutting the fruitcake.
- Door-to-door caroling.
- Playing Santa Claus.

- Dieting.
- Pushing the beds together when it's time for more sex.

It Came from Inner Space
Nine out of ten lovers who claim they were abducted by aliens discover, during therapy, that they merely experienced an out-of-body orgasm. Investigation of the typical incident reveals:
- The "strange being" turns out to be a partner covered with cold cream.
- The "strange craft" turns out to be a sleigh bed.
- The "bright objects" turn out to be a partner's gold teeth.

Sex With the Right Lover
Should give you orgasms that:
- Clear the cobwebs.
- Are:
    Earth friendly.
    Durable (last for more than 10 seconds).
- Do not leave you wanting.
- Come with a verbal guarantee.
- Make the pictures on the wall shake.
- Make you realize why you ended it with your last lover.

Night or Day
When is it better to have sex? The facts:

Daytime	Nighttime
Deliciously wicked	Quite acceptable
Lunch substitute	Midnight snack substitute
Can be habit-forming	Is a habit
Nice change of pace	Same old thing
Can also watch favorite soaps	Must watch reruns
Have to get into bed	Already in bed
Must get back to work	Must get back to sleep
If sex disappointing, can still go shopping	If sex disappointing, have to wait till morning

Reminder for the Generous
Tonight may be the perfect time to give a deserving lover his or her Christmas bonus.

The Enlightened Lover

If you need them, here are guilt-free reasons for making love.

• *If you're cold and out of firewood*—sex is the fastest way known to get warm quickly.

• *If you can't sleep*—sex is healthier, safer and less fattening than a sleeping potion.

• *If you feel aroused*—sex is an appropriate way to cope with this feeling.

• *If you've been pulled over by a state trooper*—sex is the approved adult-strength way to relieve stress.

Gift Ideas

For the bedroom that has everything.

• Hurricane lantern: The perfect back-up light source when rapture-induced panting blows the candles out.

• Juice extractor: When hooked up properly, can turn an ordinary sexual experience into one that's pretty good.

• Thunder gun: High pressure stream of water hoses off even the stickiest lover in seconds—the perfect timesaver if a realtor is showing your house.

• Booster cables: Apply clamps to lover's big toes, watch him start right up.

• Pen light: Allows you, during sex, to look up phone numbers without enduring the harsh glare of a lamp.

A Lover's Farewell

After-sex responses indicating your partner:

Will Be Seeing You Again	Won't Be Seeing You Again
"I'm making my special roasted pepper goulash tonight."	"Could you mail this letter when you leave?"
"Take my car."	"Take my card."
"Don't forget to call."	"Don't forget to write."
"What are you doing New Year's Eve?"	". . . of 2001?"
"Parting is such sweet sorrow."	Parting is so sweet, sorry."

635

Ultimate Stocking Stuffers

Men Name Their Favorites	Woman Name Their Favorites
"A new one-iron"	"A graphite driver"
"High-performance ski poles"	"A new laptop"
"A leather reading chair"	"Leather waterproof boots"
"A BMW bike"	"A Harley"
"A starlet"	"A rock star"
"My wife's great legs"	"A husband who will clean out the garage"

Tonight's Weight-Loss Bonus

Activity	Calories Consumed
Avoiding the wet spot	46

What I Did in the Throes of Pleasure

"Reshaped my nails on my lover's back."
> – Henrietta, lead guitar, Berlin Philharmonic

"Blushed."
> – Danny, peace activist

Couldn't be reached for comment.
> – John, lawmaker

Above and Beyond the Call of Duty

It is, indeed, the selfless partner who, after sex:
- *In the morning*—makes the coffee.
- *In the afternoon*—takes out the garbage.
- *In the late afternoon*—serves high tea.
- *In the evening*—walks the dog.
- *At night*—switches off the television.
- *At midnight*—wakes you up for more.

Tip for Concerned Lovers

Not to worry: Those hot flashes often experienced during frantic holiday season lovemaking may be either blinking Christmas lights or poorly made eggnog.

Today's Thought for Tonight

It's a perfect evening for making love if:
- Last evening wasn't.
- You need a reason to open that gift bottle of Dom Pérignon.
- The office Christmas party's turning out better than expected.
- You happen to be passing a motel with hourly rates.
- They finally installed your hot tub.
- Your bridge club canceled.
- You need the practice.

Yuletide Tip for Loving Couples

Seasonally correct responses to holiday lovemaking.*
1. As you're getting into bed: "O Holy Night."
2. When you're under the covers, your hands caressing your partner: "I Wonder as I Wander."
3. During lovemaking: "Hark! The Herald Angels Sing."
4. Afterward, when you're lying in each other's arms, about to doze off: "Silent Night."
*Each to be sung softly in your partner's ear.

The Bedside Eater

Aphrodisiac of the Day
A corner office
Erotic Effect
Makes one feel more desirable, permits lovemaking whenever the urge strikes. Increased pleasure caused by breathtaking view-induced orgasm.
Aphrodisiac of the Night
Ocean view
Erotic Effect
Nourishes libido, induces sexier vibes in both partners, trade winds may provoke extra-glorious climaxes.

Afterglow: The Eight Official Stages

1. That glazed look
2, Cessation of all movement except Earth's rotation
3. Perceptible reduction of plaque buildup
4. Hush falls over countryside (and neighbors finally cease banging on wall)

637

5. Arrival in promised land (oceanfront site)
6. Heaven
7. Sleep
8. Hunger pangs

Secrets of the Great Lovers
Romantic fantasies to heighten sexual bliss.

To enhance pleasure for	Consider the mystery of
10 minutes	The Nile at dawn
15 minutes	A New Mexican sunset
25 minutes	How a clutch works
35 minutes	Marrying well
40 minutes	The Sphinx
50 minutes	Perfect vichyssoise
1 minute	Why your lover is taking a phone call in the next room

Assorted Gifts for the Lover Who Has Everything
• More of it
• Gucci luggage to put it in

The After-Sex Feeding Frenzy
Making love excites the appetite. Gourmet lovers suggest

To a partner who:	Serve:
You drove crazy Nuts	
Is lying there, energy completely spent	Popovers
Is so overcome by the glories of sex that he's babbling incoherently	Hush puppies
Can't get enough of you	Passion fruit
Appreciates your lovely derriere	Sticky buns
Made you feel heavenly	Angel food cake
Made you feel wicked	Devil's food cake

Christmas Bonus Time
Some suggestions for a deserving lover.
1. Cash. (Vulgar and impersonal, yet if given a) with love and b) in any amount over $500.00 will seldom be rejected.
2. Negotiable securities (see above).

3. Jewelry. Lover's choice: 1) An engagement ring—size of the diamond is unimportant, it's the thought that counts. (Over two carats, however, is the recommended size.) 2) A watch with a face that glows in the dark. (No more constantly asking you, during lovemaking, "Can you see the time, dear?")

Food and Sex: Part IV
The insatiable eater.
Dining Habits
As earthy as a knish. Always demands seconds; hums appreciatively between courses. Late-night snacks, including lover, a specialty. Ice cream for breakfast? The very thing.
Type of Partner
The best. Nonstop, energetic and, if dinner isn't waiting, multiorgasmic. Effortlessly flips partners over when they're done on one side. Has made many lovers smile, possibly because of earlobes that taste like marzipan.

Reminder
Today is the last day to mail your lover a thank-you note if you want it to get there by Christmas.

Not in Touch with Your Feelings? Part II
A semi-official lover's guide to sex-related guilt.
During sex, to get excited, you've thought about things other than your lover, such as:

	Should you feel guilty?	
	Yes	No
A past lover.		X
Your other lover.	X	
Your lover's best friend.	X	
How you're finally getting in shape.		X
The meat loaf in the refrigerator.		X
Frank Perdue.	X	

What I Did After Really Great Sex
"Checked my watch and saw there was still time for more—it was even better than the first time, and I caught my plane!"
– Debby, Olympian

"Took a nice, long, relaxing bath. Then to show my gratitude, I left a ring in the bathtub—three carats, Tiffany setting. Now we're engaged."

> — Al, diplomat

"Finally got the courage to call my psychiatrist by her first name. She said it was okay, we'd reached a new level of intimacy."

> — Raoul, slowly improving

Are You Normal?

Test yourself. What do you experience during climax?

Normal	Abnormal
Fireworks	Candlelight vigil
Panting and gasping	Airbag opens
Nightingales singing	Ducks quacking
Like I'm going out of my mind	A nervous breakdown
Visions of sugarplums dancing in my head	But they're loaded with calories

Reminder for Today

What to do: Buy a postage stamp.

Why: This is the last day to mail your lover a thank-you-for a year-of incredible-pleasure card if you want it to get there by Christmas.

Pillow Talk

The time-release climax. Instead of one huge climax at the conclusion of sex, a series of pleasant little ones that occur unexpectedly throughout the day. Such climax is caused either by an unusually skilled lover or by luck.

Advantages	Disadvantages
Not as noisy.	You may mistakenly think it's heartburn.
May turn ho-hum morning commute into joy ride.	May shake your religious faith.
Will enhance coffee break.	May cause drowsiness during business meetings.

The First Day of Winter

Tips for outdoor sex.
• Keep warm: during sex, 68% of all body heat escapes through the pillow, so wear a hat. (The other 32% escapes through the fingertips, wear gloves.)
• Avoid frostbite; warm hands and feet by cuddling with a hairy partner.
• For can't-fail birth control, keep your snowshoes on.
• For extra efficiency during cross-country sex, wax your skis.
• For extra comfort during downhill sex, use a queen-size sled.

From Our Lover's Glossary

The probationary lover. A person who has not yet met (a) your children, (b) your friends or (c) your sexual standards; or to whom you have not yet given (a) first choice of nights, (b) space in your closet, (c) space on your toothbrush holder, (d) a key to your house or (e) the password.

Tonight's the Night

You will be unusually successful in love if you avoid partners who:
• Mistake your birthmark for an erogenous zone.
• Or, worse, mistake an erogenous zone for a birthmark.
• Rush through sex, even if you've extended your checkout time.
• Never ask romantic questions during sex (like "When are you going to ask your boss for a raise?").
• Always ask non-romantic questions during sex (like "Why aren't you earning more?").
• If the phone rings during sex, ask you to take a message.

Handy Holiday Love Guide

Determining sexually related stress (Scale: 1 to 100).

Event	Degree of Stress
You've waited until the last minute to buy your lover the perfect gift	95
You may have to go a bit over budget because he or she already has everything except:	
Ruby earrings	70
A silk scarf	19
A BMW	391
You can't get a clerk's attention	17
You've been trying since this morning	100

"Fa la la la la, la la la la"

Holiday lovemaking: Some extra-special reasons.

"To celebrate, after we've finished trimming the tree and before the kids get home from college."
— Myra and Phil, empty nesters

"As a reward for finishing our Christmas shopping. Poor compulsive Harry is totally impotent if he has even one gift left to buy."
— Gladys, florist

"It's my reward for drinking her egg nog; it's dreadful."
— Karl, public relations

"It's my gift for the man who has, well, nearly everything."
— Skeets, weather girl

Love Signs

Horoscope for a Concupiscent Capricorn
- *Ruling passion*: bubble baths for two
- *Ruling body lotion*: honey
- *Chief sexual asset*: attention to detail
- *Governing erogenous zone*: a beauteous, almond-shaped navel
- *Aphrodisiac of choice*: chilled apricot nectar except when with a Leo, then it's borscht
- *Ruling sexual activity*: flashbacks
- *Ideal time for sex*: when the kids are finally asleep

Things Often Said After Sex

"It's time to get up."

"Enough, already."

"Badly do I need some rum raisin ice cream."

"Will that be cash or charge?"

"Where's my other sock?"

"We'd better get back to the party."

"Your loan's just been approved."

Love Signs

Horoscope for a Cuddly Capricorn.

• *Ruling passion:* caring, sharing and leather
• *Ruling sexual turnoff:* cashiered politicians
• *Chief sexual asset:* a light touch
• *Governing erogenous zone:* Santa's workshop
• *Aphrodisiac:* a colossal Christmas bonus
• *Ruling sexual activity:* stirring deep desires
• *Ideal time for sex:* the instant your contacts come out

What I Did for Love

"Broke my vows of abstinence. . . and silence."

     – Arlo, librarian

"Learned to cook lobster bisque with crackers. It's her favorite after-sex snack."

     – Peter, pathologist

"Learned to sew. I had to—she kept tearing my clothes off."

     – Murray, stevedore

"You name it."

     – Olga, journalist

Love Sign: Capricorn

(December 22-January 19)

Opposite love sign: A curvaceous Cancer who nicely fills out the viewfinder of your camcorder.

Outstanding sexual quality: Secretly love it when accidentally touched (or brushed up against) while taking public transportation.

Most attractive physical feature: High cheekbones that get even higher during particularly excellent sex.

Ruling sexual turnoff: Dancing cheek to cheek in the dark and knocking over the breakfront.

Ruling sexual turn-on: A partner who, after all those holiday parties, can still fit down your chimney.

Ideal place for sex: You're adventurous—either the Bat Cave or Haiti.

Love Signs: Capricorn

(December 22-January 19)

Most attractive feature: A terrific metabolism. No matter how much fruitcake you eat, you still fit under the mistletoe.

Turn-on: Watching your lover undress through binoculars (he's painfully shy).

Turnoff: A partner who makes you lose weight in all the wrong places (cheap motels, Kmart dressing rooms—and your bust).

Ideal romantic adventure: Hiking through Europe with only your lover, your personal trainer and a psychic friend.

Favorite sexual fantasy: Making the researcher blush when he asks about your frequency rate.

Q. He likes it in the morning, I like it at night—what can we do?
A. There are three choices:

1. In the morning, let him do whatever he wants as long as he doesn't wake you.

2. At night, you do whatever you want to him as long as you don't wake him.

3. Compromise—meet at noon.

The Dieting Lover
Popular holiday drinks and how to compensate.

To burn off 6 ounces of:	You must:
Beer	Take forever to undress.
Irish coffee	Parade around for 1 hour in the slinky underwear your lover gave you.
Buttered rum	Tenderly nibble your lover's ear.
Eggnog	Tenderly nibble your own ear for 15 minutes (a Best Bet weight loss technique).
Champagne	Drive lover up a wall.
Mulled wine	Hit the jackpot.

The Environmentally Responsible Lover
To save electricity:
• Uses a dimmer switch
• Makes love by candlelight
To conserve heat:
• Uses weather stripping
• Makes love under the quilt
To preserve wildlife:
• Consumes only vegetarian aphrodisiacs
To save energy:
• Lets partner do all the work

Gift Certificate*
Christmas Gift Certificate No. 2005
detach here and send to lover
The bearer is entitled to the following.
• A 7-day in-home trial.
• A romantic candlelit dinner for two.
• A comprehensive program of holiday activities including:
___ A grab bag, with most of me in it.
___ A special "pucker-up" event under the mistletoe.
___ Slowly removing my personal gift wrapping.
___ Singing Christmas carols into each other's ears.
*Expires January 15th

Last-Minute Gift Idea

Sex*—it's an affordable gift for the lover who has:
• Nothing
• Everything
• Tension
• A great body
• Been extra-good to you
• The same gift for you

*Don't forget the trimmings: candlelight, moonlight, champagne and, under the mistletoe. . . you.

Last-Minute Stocking Stuffers

High-tech gifts for the perfect (or nearly perfect) lover.

Item	Application
Voice memo pad	Save valuable ideas that pop into partner's head during lovemak-ing.
Digital blood pressure monitor	Takes the guesswork out of try-ing to decide when climax is imminent.
Caller ID	Instantly answers the classic during-sex question: "Should I pick up the phone?"
Portable fan	Blows the cookie crumbs out of bed.

The Dieter's Guide to Weight Loss During Sex

Activity	Calories Burned
Regular intercourse (sort of cruising along)	49
Super intercourse (wild and crazy)	77
Getting emotional (appearance of sweat beads and winking at each other)	153
Off the charts (80% max. pulse rate)	200

The Enlightened Lover

The sounds of love.

If you hear:	It means:
Bells:	
Clanging	Things are going really well.
Jingling	Santa's getting closer.
A heavenly choir	Oops! Out-of-body climax.
Gregorian chants	You're doing it in the wrong place.
Strolling carolers	Close the drapes.
Chimes	Your guests are here.

You Are Not Alone

The 10 most common during-sex interruptions.

1. Letting the dog back in
2. Paperboy
3. Call of nature
4. Intrusive usher shining his flashlight
5. Dinner guests
6. Urgent fax
7. Overheating (room or lover)
8. Orgasm (impromptu)
9. Paparazzi
10. Carolers

What I'll Put Under the Christmas Tree

"A cellular phone. So my wife, during sex, can have greater freedom when she's taking calls. She works for Home Shopping Network."

— Seth, social worker

"Me. Gift-wrapped in a satin teddy, a gold tennis bracelet and my sexiest smile. I can't wait."

— Jennifer, FBI agent

"Me. But it's going to be tough. I'm 6'5" and 256 pounds and a tad claustrophobic."

— Sheldon, teamster

'Twas the Night Before Christmas

Stocking stuffers to enhance lovemaking:

Gift	Application
Silent butler	To brush away crumbs. Indispensable if you eat Ritz crackers in bed.
Welcome mat	Place it beside the bed. Makes even the most insecure lover feel wanted.
Ice bucket	To chill the massage oil if your lover needs sensitivity training.
Silver sugar bowl	For sweeter dreams.

More Last-Minute Stocking Stuffers

We suggest a:	For the partner who:
Talking wristwatch.	Has theater tickets.
Gift certificate.	Has nothing.
Fruitcake.	Has everything.
Digital thermometer.	Claims to suffer spring fever.
Personalized letter from Santa.	Still believes.
Candy cane.	Needs a pacifier.
Large-type Bible.	Is aging and chaste.

Bed Manners

The kinder, gentler lover never:

• Denigrates partner's sexual prowess (aloud).

• Falls asleep until *after* sex (unless other lover cooperates).

• Blames lover for a time-release orgasm (one that doesn't occur until sometime during breakfast).

• Checks phone messages.

• Forgets to send a thank-you letter (or, if warranted, a crank letter).

Gift Certificate No. 1721

----------Detach here, send to lover----------

Gift Certificate

Bearer entitled to:

• One evening of bliss

• One night of ectasy

- Personalized service (includes tune-up)
- Make improper advances
- Touch me here
- My full cooperation
- Sleep late (beside me)

*Expires 2nd day of new year.

What I Put Under the Christmas Tree

Our annual Yuletide poll of happy lovers.
"Free samples."
> – Jamal

"A highly-trained service technician."
> – Dominique

"I even gift wrapped myself."
> – Megan

"A gift basket with no strings attached."
> – Whitney

What I Found Under the Christmas Tree

Our annual Yuletide poll of joyful lovers:

"Just what I've always needed—an oak hiking staff to help me walk after having sex with my tigress wife."
> – Jack

"A Ralph Lauren rain suit. It'll keep me dry if we set off the bedroom sprinkler during sizzling sex."
> – Sue

"My partner, fast asleep. The eggnog made him think he was camping in a forest."
> – Charlotte

On the First Day of Christmas

My true love whispered to me:

"'Get back under that mistletoe, Rodney, I'm having another passion attack.'"
> – Rodney, house husband

"'Get back up the chimney, Santa, my husband's still here.'"
> – Santa, Federal Express employee

"'Ding dong merrily on high.' I thought she was suggesting a new position."
> – Claude, high school principal

"'Nice yule log, Herman.'"
                    – Herman, projectionist

Holiday Party-Fare Tip

Seven out of ten people gain at least 5 pounds during this holiday season. But why deny yourself? Instead

If you're partial to:	Increase your sex rate to:
Gingerbread.	Once a week.
Fruitcake.	Twice a week, plus a brisk two-mile walk afterward.
Chocolate caramel.	Three times a week, plus a strenuous aerobic workout.
Plum pudding.	Four times weekly, plus three 5-mile runs.

What I Did for Love

"You wouldn't believe it."
Eddie G., professional jai alai player

What I Got from Great Sex

"Some really fond memories."
                    – Prue, special person
"Higher cheekbones."
                    – Jim, designer
"My waistline back."
                    – Helga, cellist
"Two husbands, four lovers and nine children."
                    – Carmen, animal trainer

What I Found Under the Christmas Tree

"An erogenous zone that came with a money-back guarantee."
                    – Clayton
"A personalized letter from Mrs. Santa Claus."
                    – Chad
"The rest of our bed. Whew, what a night."
                    – Roxanne

From Our Lover's Glossary
Morning-After Pill. A person who, no matter how wonderful the sex was the night before, wakes up grouchy and irritable. Experts claim that such behavior may or may not be caused by:
• Getting up on the wrong side of the bed (and stepping into the kitty litter).
• An insufficiently romantic breakfast (example: creamed mushrooms over organic rye flakes.)
• An overzealous wake-up call from a partner with morning mouth.

On the Second Day of Christmas
My true love whispered to me:
"'A bit more to the left, and St. Nicholas soon will be there.'"
      – Suzie, housewife
"'We have time for one more, the children are still nestled, all snug in their beds.'"
      – Emily, potter
"'Hover above me again, dear, I want to see those sugarplums.'"
      – Julia, lighting technician
"'Here comes Santa Claus.'"
      – Felicity, crossing guard

Why Are You Inhibited During Sex?
"I'm afraid to really let go because the children might hear."
      – Celia, mezzo-soprano
"My lover leaves the lights on and we're plagued by deer."
      – Thomas, lawn-care provider
"There's no lock on my office door."
      – Helen, senior vice president
"My partner—she's always pressuring me to participate."
      – Terry, key punch operator

The Enlightened Lover
Those who do not breathe abdominally during sex have a 61% greater chance of blacking out during an out-of-body orgasm.*
*One in which the person experiencing orgasm leaves his or her body and begins to orbit any nearby astral body or a Chinese restaurant.

F.Y.I.

How often does the average person think about sex?

While:	Times per Hour
Getting married	6
Getting divorced	49
Working on the first million	$1/4$
Watching the Dow Jones plunge	$1/2$
Watching the Dow Jones soar	23
Sitting through a conference	60
Making love	8
Being made love to	35

Predicting the Future
Will a potential lover be good in bed? Some sources of information.
Good: News clippings; affidavits; a resume
Better: Ex-wives or -husbands; word-of-mouth; FBI files; eye witnesses
Best: Test drive

Believe It or Else
Unless you took the right acting classes, a faked orgasm, even if it's justified:*
1. Consumes nearly twice the energy as a real one; and
2. Does not feel as good; and
3. Can be detected by an alert male partner (he will notice that the smoke alarm above the bed failed to activate); and
4. Is not a reliable form of birth control.
*When it's the only way he'll retire to a neutral corner of the bed.

Overcoming Inertia
Reasons your lover may not move during sex.
1. It's your turn.
2. It's the Sabbath.
3. Afraid to wreck new hairdo.
4. You're on top of him.
5. Breakfast tray on stomach.
6. Leg in a cast.
7. The photographer said not to.

Romantic Health Tip

A regular diet of a) healthy food* and b) divine sex with the one you love (or like a lot) can be a key factor in:
1. The fight against premature aging and
2. Helping your skin renew itself.
*leafy vegetables, caviar, and good wine

How to Survive Between Lovers

A perfect time to finally change your life.
1. Get in shape for your next lover: join a health club.
2. Don't agonize over past mistakes (you'll probably repeat them).
3. Take an adult education course: learn a romance language.
4. Do something symbolic: burn your old mattress.
5. Rent lots of movies (to help you make it through the night).
6. Flirt outrageously (to help you make it through the day).

Tip for Lovers on a Budget

Instead of spending hard-earned money on party favors, why not use your partner as a noisemaker?

The Morning After a Great Night Before

Q. Who gets up first?
A. The lover who can stand unassisted.
Q. Who makes the bed?
A. The lover who did the least work.
Q. Who makes the coffee?
A. The lover with the biggest smile.
Q. Who makes brunch?
A. Whoever has the strength.
Q. Who gets dressed first?
A. The lover who's going out for the newspaper.

Team Undercoverage

Typical reactions by newlyweds to their first simultaneous orgasms:
"We began singing gospel music and nearly dropped our tambourines."

– Marie and Winston

"We thought it was the end of the world, until the people next door started banging on the wall."
> – Alma and Mario

"I know we reinvented dynamite. Oh, the curse of too much chemistry."
> – Heather and Glenn

"Whew!"
> – Charles and Charlene

Post-Holiday Romance Tip
"After lovemaking, instead of just lying there, gasping for breath, we make the moment more intimate by naming all the people we didn't get a Christmas card from . . . and devising appropriate punishments."
> – Jack and Colleen

Holiday Dieting Tips
Popular treats and how to work them off.

Burn off	By
1 slice of fruitcake (from this Christmas)	Singing Christmas carols (duets with your lover in the shower).
1 slice of fruitcake (from last Christmas)	Searching for your partner's erogenous zone.
1 candy cane	Nibbling your lover's ear while she's wearing headphones.
30 pieces of glazed fruit	Making love under the mistletoe.

No Date for New Year's?
Some comforting statistics:
- 47% of all people with dates wish they were with someone else.
- Despite what you may think, most people are *not* having a better time than you (only a louder time).
- 61% of all partygoers have overindulged by 10 P.M. and face the dismal prospect of having to remain upright until midnight.
- At the stroke of midnight, 37% of all couples kiss the wrong person (18% miss completely and kiss a wall).
- 39% of the "complimentary" party favors distributed by restaurants malfunction by 11:24 P.M.

Personal Worsts

"Lasting only 2 minutes and 24 seconds. I forgot to carbohydrate-load."
  — Thor, barber

"First-night jitters. My car was in a tow-away zone."
  — Cornelius, labor organizer

"In the third hour of sex, perhaps because I skipped lunch, I simply ran out of energy and had to let my partner finish by herself."
  — Genghis, butler

The Tranquil Lover

New research indicates that a weekend of marathon sexual activity (stopping permitted only to eat, sleep and check in with loved ones) can cure even the most hopeless case of sexual tension.

Underwater Etiquette

During a quiet, dimly lit, Champagne-and-caviar bubble bath for two, maintain the intimate mood by waiting until afterwards to tell your lover that the tiles need grouting.

The Speechless Lover

During sex, observe a moment of silence when:
• Your partner asks, "Where did you learn that?" (You may need time to collect your wits.)
• You think you hear a prowler.
• Your wildest sexual fantasy finally comes true (a third orgasm without the assistance of a partner).
• You're awed by your partner's stamina (2 _ hours, stopping only once to make an appointment with her hairdresser).
• You're afraid you'll say the wrong thing (like, "Ohhh, Sandor," and his name is Ollie).
• Actions speak louder than words.

Female Dysfunction

The leading causes:
• Frequent interruptions (by active toddler).
• Worried about what to wear to work in the morning.
• Inferior foreplay technique of partner (doing laps around the bed).

- Poor timing (carpool driver blowing horn).
- Would rather finish novel.
- Fear of commitment (he'll think that just because we're intimate, I'll be his date for New Year's Eve).
- Fear of failure (his).

Six New Year's Resolutions
I resolve to be:
1. Less old-fashioned (and enjoy multiple orgasms with a partner).
2. Less nosy (and not ask "Where'd you learn *that?*")
3. More impulsive (and make love in places other than the mind).
4. More innovative (no more relying only on televised sporting events to sexually arouse partner).
5. Less anxious (and ask "Was it good for you?" after instead of before sex).
6. More affectionate (and also kiss my lover goodnight instead of just the cat).

A Few Last Thoughts for the Confirmed Lover
- During two hours of lovemaking, one slice of chocolate cake will sustain you far better than three vitamin E capsules.
- Inside every good lover is a great orgasm waiting to get out.
- Never sleep with a person who has four or more cats. (But it may be okay to nap a little.)
- Keep plants in your bedroom—the extra oxygen comes in handy.
- Bedsores from too much sex can be eased with corn relish.

A Whole Year of Sex: Ten Things to Be Happy About
1. The memories.
2. You always remembered to lock the door.
3. The 36 pounds you lost.
4. Your back behaved.
5. So did the cat.
6. Your moans didn't alarm the neighbors. . . too much.
7. That wondrous afterglow.
8. It was so surprisingly affordable.
9. You're with the same (or nearly the same) lover.
10. You still have another good year (at least) in you.

Year-End Review
Our list of six during-sex no-no's certain to diminish intimacy:
1. Doing two things at once (massaging our partner's back while opening the day's mail, for instance).
2. Keeping one hand on your purse (shows a lack of trust).
3. Asking what's for dinner (and it's 8:30 A.M.)
4. Excess formality during those intimate moments (i.e., instead of your lover's pet name you use a title like "Mr.," "Mrs.," "Ma'am" or "Judge").
5. Inappropriate remarks at the exact moment your partner is climaxing:
   • "How dare you go first."
   • "Cheer up."
   • "You missed your putt."

Sin Taxes: Part III
(Highlights only.)

	Sin Tax
Constantly craving:	
Sex	$3.00
Spare ribs	5¢
Failure to curtail feelings of desire:	
Toward your spouse	5¢
Toward your neighbor's spouse	$6.00
Giving in to temptation on a:	
Weekly basis	75¢
Daily basis	$1.25

Mood Wreckers
Coming to bed with:
1. Your pager.
2. A mudpack (that's still wet).
3. Curlers.
4. A bad back.
5. An unbathed body.
6. An attitude.
7. An assistant.

Happy New Year!

Tips for the last night of the year:

- *The perfect drink:* champagne
- *The perfect food:* caviar
- *The perfect erogenous zone:* in front of your fireplace
- *The perfect party favor:* edible underwear
- *The perfect noisemaker:* your lover
- *The perfect lover:* spends the night

Your Guaranteed Sexual Forecast for Next Year

Because of a significantly improved love life, you will:

- Have fewer client lunches but more "nooners."
- Finally get your blood pressure under control.
- Still not (alas) catch up on your reading.
- Upgrade your taste in underwear.
- Maintain a less rigid work ethic (finally) and, assisted by your lover, occasionally play hooky from work.
- No longer have to count on weight machines to work all your major muscle groups.
- Abandon plans to join (or open) a monastery.

Happy New Year!

Celebrate this last night of the year with the perfect:

- *Party:* just the two of you.
- *Warm-up:* a bottle of chilled Champagne.
- *Warmer-upper:* a long soak in a hot tub.
- *Erogenous zones:* (a) the back of your neck; (b) the shell of your ear, (c) a ski lodge.
- *Party favor:* caviar.
- *Party favorite:* your lover.
- *Noisemaker:* you.
- *New Year's resolution:* to keep something in reserve—for next year.

A Reminder

This is the last day of the year. For those ultrabusy couples who, despite all good intentions, manage to have sex only once a year, this, in our opinion, is the perfect night to have it.

A Bonus from Above

It is possible that Mother Nature and Father Time gave us sex:
- As an ideal gift for last-minute shoppers.
- As an all-natural sleep supplement.
- To keep our minds off golf.
- As the team sport of choice.
- To annoy fundamentalists.
- As an alternative to expensive restaurants.
- As the perfect way, without leaving home, to usher in New Year's Eve.

Little Things Mean a Lot

Ways to pamper a lover.
- Notice his new haircut (but don't tell him if it's bad).
- Tell her she looks like she's losing weight (change the subject if she asks where).
- Praise his sexual prowess (especially nice to do if he's over 87 years of age).
- Baby her (massage her feet).
- Mother him (feed him).
- Pop the question.

MONTHLY QUALITY OF LIFE® CHECKUP

•We had sex 60 times during the first week in December:
True___False___   At least we tried___
•How did partner arouse you?
Gave the "secret signal" (began licking the nape of my neck—our
dinner guests were appalled)___
Removed his slacks___
Removed her shoulder holster___
Put down her knitting and began to flirt___
•We did the following erotic things under the mistletoe:
Shared a cigarette___
Peeked at our gifts___
Ate all the kids' brownies___
Stole a kiss___
Petted above the waist___
Petted below the waist___
Went all the way (to beat the Holiday rush)___
•This month we tried something new:
Nude Scrabble___
Did it to the rhythm of Gangsta Rap (totally exhausted us)___
Electronic banking___
Doing it twice in one night___
Doing it with both of us awake___
A foursome (we did it in front of a full-length mirror)___

Signed_____

Witnessed_____

Ten Things Women Never Say
to a Man Who Takes Viagra

- Would a popsicle stick help?
- Is that all it does?
- Guess I'll take another cold shower.
- Stop begging for another chance.
- Don't I still turn you on?
- Perhaps you need a spanking.
- Prostate acting up?
- Guess you're not the man my mother warned me about.
- We can always just cuddle.
- For this I missed my Women's Group?

One Thing Women Always Say to a
Man Who takes Too Much Viagra:

Uncle!

Viagra Substitutes

Alternatives to medication should your (a) lover be allergic or (b) HMO deny your claim on the grounds that erectile difficulties do not constitute a medical emergency.

Strategy	What the Experts Say
Spanish fly (first pressing)	Like oysters and Kit Kats, a substance reputed to be a powerful aphrodisiac. If unavailable, try feeding him Memphis pork ribs one hour before lovemaking.
Entering bedroom in a sheer black babydoll and a pair of spiked heels	Seductive power of ensemble greatly diminished if (a) you're still wearing your pager or (b)he fell asleep.
Candlelight vigil	May activate smoke alarm and ruin romantic mood.
Visualize it erect by staring at it	Highly effective if observer has bedroom eyes.
Hot oil massage	Not too hot, unless you're angry.
Support condom	Unsure of his size? Simply measure his thumb and multiply by 2.77739.
Inviting the au pair to assist	Only as a last resort but a Best Bet if she's Swedish and seeking a green card.

NOTES

NOTES

NOTES

NOTES

NOTES

NOTES

NOTES

NOTES

NOTES

NOTES